Seek to See Him

Library of
Early Christology

Larry W. Hurtado
David B. Capes
April D. DeConick
Editors

SERIES INTRODUCTION

Over the past forty years or so, there has been a renewed interest in the origins and early developments of belief in Jesus, many of these studies sometimes referred to as loosely forming a kind of "new religionsgeschichtliche Schule" (new history of religion school). This body of work both resembles and differs from the German scholarship of the original "Schule," particularly in emphasizing more the roots of early Jesus-devotion in the rich and varied Jewish traditions of the Greco-Roman era.

Available from the Library of Early Christology Series

Bousset, Wilhelm. *Kyrios Christos: A History of the Belief in Christ from the Beginnings of Christianity to Irenaeus*

Capes, David B. *Old Testament Yahweh Texts in Paul's Christology*

DeConick, April D. *Seek to See Him: Ascent and Vision Mysticism in the Gospel of Thomas*

Fossum, Jarl E. *The Name of God and the Angel of the Lord: Samaritan and Jewish Concepts of Intermediation and the Origin of Gnosticism*

Gieschen, Charles A.. *Angelomorphic Christology: Antecedents and Early Evidence*

Hengel, Martin. *Between Jesus and Paul: Studies in the Earliest History of Christianity*

Hurtado, Larry W. *Ancient Jewish Monotheism and Early Christian Jesus-Devotion: The Context and Character of Christological Faith*

Juel, Donald H. *Messianic Exegesis: Christological Interpretation of the Old Testament in Early Christianity*

Newman, Carey C. *Paul's Glory-Christology: Tradition and Rhetoric*

Newman, Carey C., James R. Davila, and Gladys S. Lewis, editors. *The Jewish Roots of Christological Monotheism: Papers from the St Andrews Conference on the Historical Origins of the Worship of Jesus*

Segal, Alan F. *The Other Judaisms of Late Antiquity: Second Edition*

Segal, Alan F. *Two Powers in Heaven: Early Rabbinic Reports about Christianity and Gnosticism*

Stuckenbruck, Loren T. *Angel Veneration and Christology: A Study in Early Judaism and in the Christology of the Apocalypse of John*

Seek to See Him

Ascent and Vision Mysticism in the Gospel of Thomas

April D. DeConick

BAYLOR UNIVERSITY PRESS

Published in 1996 by E. J. Brill. Copyright © 1996 E. J. Brill, Leiden, The Netherlands
Reprinted in 2017 by Baylor University Press, Waco, Texas

All rights reserved. No part of this publication may be reproduced, stored in a retrieval system, or transmitted in any form or by any means. electronic, mechanical, photocopying, recording, or otherwise, without the prior permission of the publisher, E. J. Brill.

Authorization to photocopy items for internal or personal use is granted by E. J. Brill provided that the appropriate fees are paid directly to The Copyright Clearance Center, 222 Rosewood Drive, Suite 910, Danvers, MA, 01923, USA. Fees are subject to change.

Cover Design Savanah N. Landerholm

Library of Congress Cataloging-in-Publication Data

DeConick, April D.
    Seek to see him: ascent and vision mysticism in the Gospel of Thomas / April D. DeConick.
    xiv, 211 p. ; 25 cm.
    Originally published: Leiden: Brill, 1996
    ISBN 9-0041-0401-1 (alk. paper)
    Includes bibliographical references and index.
    1. Mysticism—Judaism. 2. Ascension of the soul. 3. Beatific vision.
[1. Gospel of Thomas—Criticism, interpretation, etc.] I. Title. II. Series.

    BS2860.T42D43   1996
    229'.8-dc20
                                95024722

Baylor University Press ISBN: 978-1-4813-0792-5 (paper)

Printed in the United States of America on acid-free paper.

To Mom

CONTENTS

Preface xiii

PART ONE
INTRODUCTION

I. The Problem: Is Thomas Gnostic? 3
   1) The Initial Studies 3
   2) The Second Wave of Studies 11
   3) Differentiating *Thomas* from Gnosticism 16
      a) The Pre-Mundane Fall 16
      b) Theological Dualism 21
   4) Conclusion 24

II. The Solution: Thomas is Mystical 28
   1) Evidence for First-Century Jewish Mysticism 28
      a) Mysticism and Apocalypticism 28
      b) Mysticism and Jewish Sectarianism 32
         i) The Therapeutae 32
         ii) The Qumranites 33
      c) Mysticism and Philo 34
   2) Mysticism and *Thomas* 38

PART TWO
ASCENT LORE IN *THOMAS:* LOGION 50

III. The Triad of Questions in Logion 50 and Mystical Ascent 43
   1) The Catechismal Paradigm 44
   2) Community Dispute 49
   3) Interrogations of the Soul at Death 50
   4) Interrogations during Mystical Ascent 55
   5) Conclusion 62

CONTENTS

IV. The Triad of Answers in Logion 50 and Tradition History.. 64
   1) From the Light... 65
      a) Light as a Primal Entity... 65
      b) The Self-Generated Light 67
      c) The Manifestation of Light into Human Beings.. 68
      d) The Place of the Light.. 70
   2) The Offspring of the Light... 73
      a) Origin and Return... 73
      b) The Elect.. 86
   3) Movement and Rest.. 93
   4) Conclusion 95

PART THREE

VISION MYSTICISM IN *THOMAS:* LOGIA 15, 83, 59, 27, 37 AND 84

V. The Vision of God or his *Kavod*.. 99
   1) Logia 15 and 83 and the *Kavod*................................... 99
      a) Etiquette in the Divine Throne Room and Logion 15... 99
      b) The Hidden *Kavod* in Logion 83......................... 100
         i) Transformation by Fire and Drink in Logia 82, 108, and 13.................................... 105
         ii) The Embodied Light in Logion 83............. 115
         iii) Knowledge of the Self in Logia 3b, 67, 56, and 80.. 117
   2) Logion 59 and Ecstatic Vision....................................... 123
   3) Conclusion 125

VI. Preparations for the *Visio Dei* in Logia 27 and 37............... 126
   1) Logion 27 and Purification for the Vision................... 126
      a) Past Interpretations of Logion 27........................ 126
      b) Understanding the Jewish Mystical Influences on Logion 27 129
         (i) Sabbath Observation................................. 129
         (ii) Abstinence From the World and Vision .. 135
   2) Logion 37 and Shedding the Body Before Visionary Ascent.. 143
   3) Conclusion 147

CONTENTS

VII. Vision of the Images in Logion 84 148
    1) Past Interpretations of the Images 148
    2) The Mythology of Separation and Return 157
        a) Adam's Lost Image 157
        b) Return to the Image 161
            (i) Reunification 161
            (ii) Vision 164
    3) Conclusion 172

PART FOUR
CONCLUSION

VIII. The Background and Theology of *Thomas* in Summary   175
    1) *Thomas'* Background Re-envisioned 175
    2) *Thomas'* Mystical Soteriology 180

Bibliography 183
Author Index 200
Logion Index 204
Name and Subject Index 205

PREFACE

Up until this point, scholarship has been fairly nonchalant about its methodological approach to *Thomas* except in the area of source criticism under the auspices of G. Quispel and in the area of form criticism under the leadership of H. Koester. Regretably, there is not a single commentary on the *Gospel of Thomas* that represents a serious, methodologically sound study of each and every Logion as we find with the New Testament gospels and their verses. Rather, what we have seen in the past is a proliferation of commentaries listing gnostic parallels to various Logia. The difficult Logia have been avoided as if they do not warrant investigation or explanation. The consequence of this is that generally scholars have been unaware of the fact that they do not truly understand the ideology of the *Gospel of Thomas* or its background, but they have proceeded in their research as if they did.

Unfortunately, due to the present state of research on *Thomas*, full commentaries will have to wait. What is called for first of all are monographs on *themes* in the *Gospel of Thomas*. I mention the excellent monograph by M. Lelyveld on the "sayings of life" in the Gospel according to *Thomas*, in which she examines the themes of kingdom and life, as an example of the type of research on *Thomas* that is needed at the present time.[1] What Lelyveld does with the Kingdom and Life Logia is basically what I do with the ascent and vision Logia in this monograph.

My special thanks to my *Doktorvater* Jarl Fossum whose encouragement, criticisms, and insights have assisted me in the composition of this thesis and throughout my graduate career. He has helped me to bring my vision of *Thomas* to life. I have greatly benefited from his voluntary exile in the United States.

My thanks go also to several other individuals. To Gilles Quispel for his many correspondences with me regarding my work on the *Gospel of Thomas*, for his own research on this gospel without which my own work would be impoverished, for his memorial participation on my dissertation committee, and for his encouragement and advocacy in the publication of this work.

---

[1] M. Lelyveld, *Les Logia de la Vie dans L'Évangile selon Thomas: a la Recherche d'une Tradition et d'une Rédaction*, NHS 34 (Leiden, 1987).

To Helmut Koester for his dedication to scholarship on Christian gospels in general and *Thomas* in particular, for opening participation for me to join the Harvard Archaeological Study Tour of Greece and Turkey in the Spring of 1987, and for serving on my doctoral committee. His article, "GNOMAI DIAPHOROI", was the first contact that I had with any literature on the *Gospel of Thomas* when I was a beginning graduate student; it sparked an enthusiasm for *Thomas* studies which has not been quelled.

To the Editorial Board of *Vigiliae Christianae*, especially to R. van den Broek and A. F. J. Klijn who have taken great care and time to read this work in its dissertation format. They have offered me their invaluable criticisms and wisdom which have made it possible for me to transform my dissertation into a monograph for their series.

To my former professors: David Terrell who is the teacher who gave me my direction in religious studies and who, over the years, has become my true friend; to Paul Mirecki who brought the world of Coptic directly from Harvard to my doorstep at Michigan.

To Gail De Conick for overseeing the building of the author and Logion indices, and Charles Gieschen for helping me proofread the galley proofs.

To those who have assisted me in securing funds to complete the dissertation: Mary Jarrette of the Rackham Fellowships Office, K. Allin Luther and Jane Hansen of the Near Eastern Department, and my sister-friend Margorie Fisher Aronow. I wish to extend a special thanks to Margie for her generosity and financial support without which the production of this monograph would have been hindered.

To my *wonderful* family whose love, support, encouragement, wisdom, and prayers have seen me through! It is to my mother, Gail, that I owe my first glimpse of the *Gospel of Thomas* itself. Many winters ago when I was still in junior college, she purchased a copy of *The Other Gospels* by Ron Cameron and enthusiastically shared it with me. With love, I now give back to her this monograph.

PART ONE

INTRODUCTION

CHAPTER ONE

THE PROBLEM: IS THOMAS GNOSTIC?

1) *The Initial Studies:*

In the late 1950's, the initial work on the newly discovered *Gospel of Thomas* was put forward by two European scholars, H.-Ch. Puech[1] and G. Quispel.[2] Both scholars agreed that *Thomas* had an affinity with encratism, a severely ascetic lifestyle characterized by abstinence from sexual activity and marriage, dietary regulations restricting or even prohibiting the intake of meat and wine, and voluntary poverty.[3] Encratism became prevalent in Syrian Christianity, but it seems to have been an early and widespread phenomenon across the Eastern Mediterranean world as evidenced by the multitude of Christian sects which practiced encratite renunciation described by Clement of Alexandria in the

---

[1] H.-Ch. Puech, "Un logion de Jésus sur bandelette funérarie", *RHR* 147 (1955) 126-129; *idem*, "Une collection des paroles de Jésus récemment retrouvée: L'Évangile selon Thomas", *CRAIBL* (1957) 146-166; *idem*, "Une collection des paroles de Jésus récemment découverte en Égypte: L'Évangile selon Thomas", *RHR* 153 (1958) 129-133; *idem*, "Explication de *l'Évangile selon Thomas* et recherches sur les Paroles de Jésus qui y sont réunies", *Annuaire du Collège de France* 58 (1958) 233-239; 59 (1959) 255-264; 60 (1960) 181; 61 (1961) 175-181.

[2] G. Quispel, "The Gospel of Thomas and the New Testament", *VC* 11 (1957) 189-207; *idem*, "Some Remarks on the Gospel of Thomas", *NTS* 5 (1958/1959) 276-290; *idem*, "L'Évangile selon Thomas et les Clémentines", *VC* 12 (1958) 181-196; *idem*, "L'Évangile selon Thomas et le Diatesssaron", *VC* 13 (1959) 87-117; *idem*, "L'Évangile selon Thomas et le 'texte occidental' du Nouveau Testament", *VC* 14 (1960) 204-215.

[3] G. Blonde understands encratism to be both a sect and a tendency within the early church at large: "Encratisme", *Dictionnaire de Spiritualité* 4 (eds. M. Viller, F. Cavallera, and J. De Guibert; Paris, 1960) 628-642. It is clear from Clement's review of early Christian marriage practices in *Stromata* 3, however, that encratism was not a sect but rather a *lifestyle* that was adopted by many Christian groups which had a negative world-view. Clement considered this lifestyle to be a form of asceticism which was unacceptably too extreme.
G. Quispel reviews encratism and the history of scholarship about this topic in "The Study of Encratism: A Historical Survey", *La Tradizione dell'Enkrateia, Atti del Colloquio Internazionale – Milano 20-23 Aprile 1982* (ed. U. Bianchi; Rome, 1985) 35-81; for a recent treatment of asceticism and sexual renunciation in early Christianity, see P. Brown, *The Body and Society: Men, Women, and Sexual Renunciation in Early Christianity*, Lectures on the History of Religions 13 (New York, 1988).

third book of his *Stromata*⁴ as well as in the Pastoral epistles *(1 Tim 4:3; Col 2:18,20-23).*⁵ So Puech writes that the author of Thomas must have been connected with the "bizarre christianisme" which was practiced in Syria and Egypt in the second century.⁶

This observation had been made already at the turn of the century by B. Grenfell and A. Hunt regarding the nature of the Greek Papyrus Oxyrhynchus fragment 1 which has since been indentified as belonging to the *Gospel of Thomas*. They described the papyrus in the following terms: "Its chief characteristics seem to have been its Encratite and mystic tendencies."⁷

G. Quispel emerged as the most prominent advocate of this thesis,⁸ even arguing that one of the sources used by the author of the *Gospel of Thomas* was of encratite origin.⁹ His argument for the overall encratite nature of the *Gospel of Thomas* is based on several observations.

To begin with, *Thomas* is the first text to use the term *monachos* (ⲙⲟⲛⲁⲭⲟⲥ) as a noun (L. 16, 49, 75).¹⁰ As M. Harl and F.-E. Morard have shown in their studies, *monachos* in *Thomas* is the Greek translation (μοναχός) of the Syriac word *iḥidaja* or "single one" or "bachelor". *Iḥidaja* probably originated from the Hebrew יחיד a noun or adjective that can indicate a pious or holy person, even sometimes a bachelor. This was the intent of *iḥidaya* before it was used to mean "monk".¹¹ Thus according to Logion 75, only the person who is

---

⁴ F. Bolgiani, "La tradizione eresiologica sull'encratismo, II. La confutazione di Clemente di Alessandria", *AAST* 96 (1961-1962) 537-664.

⁵ See F. O. Francis, "Humility and Angelic Worship in Col 2:18", *ST* 16 (1962) 109-134.

⁶ Puech, "Une collection de Paroles" (1957) 164.

⁷ B. Grenfell and A. Hunt, ΛΟΓΙΑ ΙΗΣΟΥ : *Sayings of Our Lord* (London, 1897) 16-17.

⁸ Cf. also A. F. J. Klijn, "Das Thomasevangelium und das altsyrische Christentum", *VC* 15 (1961) 146-159; H. J. W. Drijvers, "Edessa und das jüdische Christentum", 17, 23; C. Richardson, "The Gospel of Thomas: Gnostic or Encratite?", *The Heritage of the Early Church: Essays in Honor of G. V. Florovsky*, OrChrA 195 (eds. D. Neiman and M. Schatkin; Rome, 1973) 65-76; M. Lelyveld, *Les Logia de la Vie dans L'Évangile selon Thomas*, NHS 34 (Leiden, 1987).

⁹ Quispel posits that *Thomas* is based on three sources, a hermetic sayings collection, a Jewish-Christian gospel, and an encratite source, probably the *Gos. Egy.*; refer to his articles: "New Testament", 189-207; "Clémentines", 181-196; "Some Remarks", 276-290; "Diatessaron", 87-117; "The 'Gospel of Thomas' and the 'Gospel of the Hebrews'", *NTS* 12 (1966) 371-382; "The *Gospel of Thomas* Revisited", *Colloque International sur les Textes de Nag Hammadi. Québec, 22-25 août 1978*, BCNH 1 (ed. B. Barc; Québec, 1981) 218-266.

¹⁰ See G. Quispel, "*Thomas* Revisited", 237; "Encratism", 57.

¹¹ M. Harl, "A propos des *Logia* de Jésus: le sens du mot *monachos*", *REG* 73

unattached or single can enter the bridal chamber; or as Logion 49 has it, only the single person can return to the Kingdom. Salvation is connected with one's celibate and single status.

Second, research indicates that from a literary standpoint the *Gospel of Thomas* belongs to the encratite Syrian trajectory of early Christianity associated with Edessa.[12] Thus *Thomas*' kinship with

---

(1960) 464-474; F.-E. Morard, "Monachos Moine, Historie du terme grec jusqu'au 4e siècle", *Freiburger Zeitschrift für Philosophie und Theologie* (1973) 332-411, and *idem*, "Encore quelques réflexions sur monachos," *VC* 34 (1980) 395-401.

[12] See H.-Ch. Puech, "The Gospel of Thomas", *New Testament Apocrypha* 1 (eds. E. Hennecke and W. Schneemelcher; Eng. trans. R. McL. Wilson; Philadelphia, 1963) 287; Quispel, "Encratism", 55-56; A. F. C. Klijn, "Christianity in Edessa and the Gospel of Thomas", *NT* 14 (1972) 70-77, where he is critical of B. Ehlers, "Kann das Thomasevangelium aus Edessa stammen? Ein Beitrag zur Frühgeschichte des Christentum in Edessa", *NT* 12 (1970) 284-317.

H. Koester, "GNOMAI DIAPHOROI: The Origin and Nature of Diversification in the History of Early Christianity", *Trajectories through Early Christianity* (eds. J. M. Robinson and H. Koester; Philadelphia, 1971) 114-157 [= *HTR* 58 (1965)], argues for the Syrian origin of *Thomas* while maintaining that it has a "gnosticizing proclivity" (137). But gnosticism did not arrive in Edessa until rather late with Mani; on this topic, see, G. Quispel, *Makarius, das Thomasevangelium, und das Lied von der Perle*, NTSup 15 (Leiden, 1967) 66-67, and his "Gnosis and the New Sayings of Jesus", *Gnostic Studies* 2, Nederlands Historische-Archaeologisch Instituut te Istanbul 34,2 (Leiden, 1975) 199-200, where he refutes the views of H. J. W. Drijvers, "Quq and the Quqites", *Numen* 14 (1967) 104-129, and *idem*, "Edessa und das jüdische Christentum", 4-33, who thinks that the Syrian gnostic named Quq was active around 160 CE; I argue that the Quqite's myth is better labeled proto-gnostic since creation was not the result of a demiurge in opposition to the Supreme God (Theo. bar Khonai, *Scholia* 11); see also the monographs on Syrian Christianity of J. B. Segal, *Edessa 'The Blessed City'* (Oxford, 1970); and R. Murray, *Symbols of the Church and Kingdom: A Study in Early Syriac Tradition* (Cambridge, 1975).

For asceticism in Syrian Christianity, refer to R. H. Connolly, "Aphraates and Monasticism", *JTS* 6 (1905) 529; A. Vööbus, *Celibacy, a Requirement for Admission to Baptism in the Early Syrian Church*, Papers of the Estonian Theological Society in Exile 1 (Stockholm, 1951); A. Adam, "Grundbegriffe des Mönchtums in sprachlicher Sicht", *ZKG* 65 (1953/54) 209-39; E. Beck, "Ein Beitrag zur Terminologie des ältesten syrischen Mönchtums", *Antonius Magnus Eremita*, StAns 38 (Rome, 1956) 254-267; G. Kretschmar, "Ein Beitrag zur Frage nach dem Ursprung frühchristlicher Askese", *ZThK* 61 (1964) 27-67; J. Gribomont, "Le monachisme au sein de l'Église en Syrie et en Cappadoce", *Studia Monastica* 7 (1965) 2-24; P. Nagel, *Die Motivierung der Askese in der alten Kirche und der Ursprung des Mönchtums*, TU 95 (Berlin, 1966); R. Murray, "The Exhortation to Candidates for Ascetical Vows at Baptism in the Ancient Syriac Church", *NTS* 21 (1974/75) 60-70.

For connections between Judaism and Syriac asceticism, see Murray, *Symbols of Church*, 1-38; A. Guillaumont, "Monachisme et éthique judéo-chrétienne", *Judéo-Christianisme: Recherches historiques et théologiques offertes en hommage au Cardinal Jean Danielou, RSR* (Paris, 1972) 199-218; S. D. Fraade, "Ascetical Aspects of Ancient Judaism", *Jewish Spirituality from the Bible through the Middle Ages* (ed. A. Green; New York, 1986) 283-284 n. 60.

other Syrian encratite literature has been well-documented: the *Diatessaron* of Tatian;[13] the *Odes of Solomon*;[14] the *Acts of Thomas*;[15] the *Book of Thomas the Contender*;[16] the *Liber Graduum*;[17] and Macarius' *Homilies*.[18]

Third, the *Gospel of Thomas*' theology is in agreement with that of the encratites described by Clement of Alexandria in *Stromata*

---

[13] Quispel, "Diatessaron", and his *Tatian and the Gospel of Thomas* (Leiden, 1975) 28, 54, where he suggests that the parallels between *Thomas* and Tatian were the result of Tatian's use of a fifth source that was Jewish-Christian in nature and which influenced the old Syriac Gospels too. Koester postulates that Tatian used *Thomas* as well as the four canonical gospels, "GNOMIA DIAPHORI", 142. A. F. J. Klijn feels that there is not sufficient evidence to argue that Tatian employed a fifth source, "A Survey of the Researches into the Western Text of the Gospels and Acts", *NT* 3 (1959) 14, and *idem, A Survey of the Researches into the Western Text of the Gospels and Acts: Part Two* (Leiden, 1969) 5-26. The Syriac *Diatessaron* influenced the (Syriac) text of *Thomas* according to T. Baarda, "Thomas and Tatian", *Early Transmission of the Words of Jesus: Thomas, Tatian and the Text of the New Testament* (eds. J. Helderman and S. J. Noorda; Amsterdam, 1983) 37-49; H. Drijvers also contends that *Thomas* used Tatian's *Diatessaron* for a source, "Facts and Problems in Early Syriac-Speaking Christianity", *The Second Century* 2 (1982) 170-173; F. T. Fallon and R. Cameron, "The Gospel of Thomas: A Forschungsbericht and Analysis", *ANRW* 2.25.6 (New York, 1988) 4225, correctly note that if this were the case, the Greek fragment, P. Oxy. 1, would be for all practical purposes an autograph even though Drijvers thinks that *Thomas* was originally written in Syriac.

[14] Quispel, "*Thomas* Revisited", 255-256; *idem*, "Encratism", 55.

[15] H. -Ch. Puech, *En quête de la Gnose* 2 (Paris, 1978) 44 and 76, who argues that Acts 14 and 92 have storified L. 37 and L. 22 of *Thomas*; *idem*, "The Gospel of Thomas", 278-307, where he points to dependence between *Acts of Thomas* c. 136 and *Thomas* L. 2, c. 147 and L. 22, c. 170 and L. 52; G. Quispel, "Gnosticism and the New Testament", *Gnostic Studies* 1, Nederlands Historisch-Archaeologisch Instituut te Istanbul 34,1 (Leiden, 1974) 201, who points out that the Hymn of the Pearl is probably a poetical amplification of Logion 76 of *Thomas*.

[16] J. D. Turner's research supports this: *The Book of Thomas the Contender from Codex II of the Cairo Gnostic Library from Nag Hammadi (CG II, 7): The Coptic Text with Translation, Introduction, and Commentary*, SBLDS 23 (Missoula, 1975) 233-239.

[17] This text is encratite and probably reflects an early state of Messalianism according to M. Kmosko, *Liber Graduum*, Patrologia Syriaca 1, 3 (Paris, 1926) CIX. A. Guillaumont argues that it does not reflect specific views of the Messalians but is best comprehended as an encratite text associated with Edessa, "Situation et signification du Liber Graduum dans la spiritualité Syriaque", *OrChrA* (1974) 311-322; and his "Liber Graduum", in *Dictionnaire de Spiritualité* 9, 749-754. For connections between *Thomas* and this text, see D. A. Baker, "The 'Gospel of Thomas' and the Syriac 'Liber Graduum'", *NTS* 12 (1965/66) 49-55; G. Quispel, "Gnosis and the New Sayings", 198.

[18] For a discussion of the connections between *Thomas* and Macarius, see G. Quispel, "The Syrian Thomas and the Syrian Macarius", *Gnostic Studies* 2, Nederlands Historisch-Archaeologisch Instituut te Istanbul 34,2 (Leiden, 1975) 113-121; *idem, Makarius*; and A. Baker, "Pseudo-Macarius and the Gospel of Thomas", *VC* 18 (1964) 215-225.

3.[19] Like Clement's encratites, *Thomas* defends the position that the resurrection of the dead is something that has already occurred (cp. L. 51 to *Strom.* 3.6.48; 3.12.87; 3.14.95).[20] *Thomas* understands original Sin or intercourse to have been initiated by the separation of the sexes from one into two, so salvation requires the movement from two into one, recombining male and female into the androgynous prelapsarian Man (cp. L. 11, 22, 114 to *Strom.* 3.13.92). Adam is viewed as unworthy and thus through him death came into existence (cp. L. 86 to *Strom.* 3.14.95; 3.16.100; 3.17.102). Furthermore, *Thomas* is an advocate for the poor lifestyle of a wanderer (L. 33, 36, 42, 54, 63, 64, 78, 95), plausibly in imitation of Jesus, as well as abandonment of the traditional family unit (cp. L. 16, 55, 99, 101 to *Strom.* 3.6.49; 3.14.97).[21] Thus, the "world" is associated in *Thomas* with death (L. 56) and material existence (L. 80) and must be renounced completely (L. 27, 110). This renunciation includes a life of singlehood or celibacy justified on the basis of an encratite exegesis of the Genesis story[22] (L. 4, 11, 22, 23, 37, 46, 49, 75, 114), and dietary regulations which discourage consumption of wine and meat and address the issue of proper fasting procedure (cp. L. 14, 28, 60, 104 to *Strom.* 3.6.53; 3.7.58; 3.7.60; 3.12.85).

In addition to an encratite source, Quispel posits that *Thomas* also is based on a Jewish-Christian gospel.[23] He understands Jewish-Christianity to be the faction of the Hebrews in the congregration of Jerusalem who monopolized this church after the Hellenists left Jerusalem. At later times, these people are variously called

---

[19] For instance, see G. Quispel, *Makarius*, 82-113; "*Thomas* Revisited", 254-259.

[20] *Stromata* 3.12.87 refers to a version of Luke 20:34-36. On the encratite implications of this passage, refer to U. Bianchi, "The Religio-Historical Relevance of Lk 20:34-36", *Studies in Gnosticism and Hellenistic Religions, presented to Gilles Quispel on the Occasion of his 65th Birthday*, ERPO 91 (eds. R. van den Broek and M. J. Vermaseren; Leiden, 1981) 31-37.

[21] See the recent treatment of the social history of *Thomas* in S. J. Patterson, *The Gospel of Thomas and Jesus*. He uses a social model developed by G. Theissen to illuminate Thomas Christianity; the works of Theissen include: *The Sociology of Early Palestinian Christianity* (Trans. J. Bowden; Philadelphia, 1978); *The Social Setting of Pauline Christianity* (trans. J. Schütz; Philadelphia, 1982); *Studien zur Soziologie des Urchristentums*, WUNT 19 (Tübingen, 1983).

[22] Refer to De Conick and Fossum, "Stripped Before God"; see also A. D. De Conick, "Fasting From the World: Encratite Soteriology in the Gospel of Thomas", *The Notion of "Religion", in Comparative Research. Selected Proceedings of the XVIth IAHR Congress, Rome, 3rd-8th September, 1990* (ed. U. Bianchi; Rome, 1994) 425-440.

[23] Refer to n. 9 above for references to Quispel's three-source theory. For a critique of this theory, refer to Chapter Eight.

Ebionites, Nazoraeans, and Elkesaites. But they all commonly believed that Jesus was the Messiah of the Jews and they observed the Mosaic Law to some degree.[24] Quispel is slightly reluctant to label the Jewish-Christian source, although he prefers the *Gospel of the Nazorees*.[25]

Quispel modified his two-source theory, however, taking into account the later insights of J.-P. Mahé who observed the striking similarity between the Hermetic sayings tradition and some of Thomas' Logia.[26] Thus, Quispel now argues for a third written source: a Hermetic gnomology, a collection of Greek sentences similar to the Armenian *Definitions*.[27] He attributes several Logia to this Hermetic source: 3, 7, 50, 56, 67,[28] 80, 87, 111b,[29] and 112.

Hermeticism is the ancient Graeco-Egyptian religious movement which promoted the religious belief in the divinity of humanity.[30] The initiate learns that because the human is animated by

---

[24] G. Quispel, "*Thomas* Revisited", 239.
[25] Earlier in his career, Quispel argued that the Jewish-Christian source was the *Gospel of the Hebrews*; see "Some Remarks", 289; and "'The Gospel of Thomas' and the 'Gospel of the Hebrews'", *NTS* 12 (1966) 371-382.
[26] J.-P. Mahé, "Les définitions d'Hermès Trismégiste à Asclépius", *RScRel* 50 (1976) 193-214, esp. 203; see now Mahé's recent encapsulation of these insights in his article, "La Voie d'Immortalité á la Lumière des *Hermetica* de Nag Hammadi et de Découvertes plus Récentes", *VC* 45 (1991) 347-375.
[27] Quispel, "*Thomas* Revisited", 259-260.
[28] *Ibid.*, 260-261, where Quispel renders the Coptic (ⲡⲉⲧⲥⲟⲟⲩⲛ ⲙ̄ⲡⲧⲏⲣϥ ⲉϥⲣ̄ ϭⲣⲱϩ ⲟⲩⲁⲁϥ <ϥ>ⲣ̄ ϭⲣⲱϩ ⲙ̄ⲡⲙⲁ ⲧⲏⲣϥ): "Whoever knows the All but fails (to know) himself lacks everything" against the trans. by T. Lambdin, "Whoever *believes* that the All itself is deficient is (himself) completely deficient", which Quispel states, parallels from Coptic, Armenian, and Hellenistic literature prove to be an incorrect translation. I would render it in a similar fashion to Quispel: "Whoever knows everything but is deficient in self-knowledge, he is deficient in everything".
[29] *Ibid.*, 262, where Quispel renders the Coptic (ⲡⲉⲧⲁϩⲉ ⲉⲣⲟϥ ⲟⲩⲁⲁϥ ⲡⲕⲟⲥⲙⲟⲥ ⲙ̄ⲡϣⲁ ⲙ̄ⲙⲟϥ ⲁⲛ): "Whoever has discovered his true self, is more weighty than the whole world of man (kosmos)".
[30] For a recent overview of Hermeticism, refer to G. Fowden, *The Egyptian Hermes: A Historical Approach to the Pagan Mind* (Cambridge, 1986).
A good critical edition of the entire Corpus is that made by A. D. Nock and A.-J. Festugière, *Hermès Trismégiste* 1: *Corpus Hermeticum. Traités I-XII* (Paris, 1945) and *Hermès Trismégiste* 2: *Traités XIII-XVIII. Asclépius* (Paris, 1945); the edition by W. Scott, *Hermetica* 1: *Introduction, Texts, and Translation* (Oxford, 1924; reprinted London, 1968), and *idem, Hermetica* 2: *Notes on the Corpus Hermeticum* (Oxford, 1925; reprinted London 1968) contains speculative textual reconstructions, but is useful for its notes and introduction regarding the history of textual transmission; the latest modern Eng. trans. has been made by B. P Copenhaver, *Hermetica: The Greek Corpus Hermeticum and the Latin Asclepius in a new English translation, with notes and introduction* (Cambridge, 1992), from which all Eng. references to the *Corpus Hermeticum* are taken unless otherwise

an inner divine essence, he is divine or as *Corpus Hermeticum* 1.15 states: "Mankind is twofold - in the body mortal but immortal in the essential man (ἀθάνατος διὰ τὸν οὐσιώδη ἄνθρωπον)" (cf. *C.H.* 9.5). He is to learn that God is "life and light (φῶς καὶ ζωή)", and that he is from this light and life and consequently will return to his origins (*C.H.* 1.21; 13.18-19; *Asc.* 11; cf. *Exc.* of Strob. 26.12). The initiate yearns for knowledge of God while at the same time, God longs to be known by humans (*C.H.* 1.31; 10.4; 10.15; *Asc.* 41; cf. *C.H.* 7.2). Thus the emphasis is on gaining knowledge of one's self, one's divine nature.[31]

The Hermetic initiate must lead a life characterized by piety, the natural function of the human (*C.H.* 6.5; 9.4; 10.9; 16.11; *Disc. Eig. Nin.* 56.28-30), and purity which includes abstinence from the pleasures of this world (*C.H.* 1.22; *Asc.* 11.29; *Disc. Eig. Nin.* 62.28-33). This may not mean, however, that all of the Hermetics were strict ascetics. They can also speak about the need to procreate in order to perpetuate the human race (*C.H.* 2.17; 3.3) and they praise the

---

noted; also available in Dutch is the volume by R. van den Broek and G. Quispel, *Corpus Hermeticum* (Amsterdam, 1991).

For the *Excerpts of Stobaeus*, see A.-J. Festugière, *Hermès Trismégiste* 3: *Fragments extraits de Stobée. I-XXII* (Paris, 1954); and A.D. Nock and A.-J. Festugière, *Hermès Trismégiste* 4: *Fragments extraits de Stobée. XXIII-XXIX. Fragments divers* (Paris, 1954) from which all Greek references to Stobaeus are taken; and W. Scott, *Hermetica* 3: *Notes on the Latin Asclepius and the Hermetic Excerpts of Stobaeus* (Oxford, 1926; reprinted London, 1968),

For the *Definitions*, see J.-P. Mahé, *Hermès en Haute-Égypte* 2: *Le Fragment du Discours Parfait et les Définitions Hermétiques Arméniennes*, BCNH 7 (Québec, 1982).

For the Nag Hammadi Hermetic texts, see J.-P. Mahé, *Hermès en Haute-Égypte* 1 and 2: *Les Textes Hermétiques de Nag Hammadi et Leurs Parallèles Grecs et Latins*, BCNH 3 (Québec, 1978); P. A. Dirkse, J. Brashler, and D. M. Parrott, "The Discourse on the Eighth and Ninth", *Nag Hammadi Codices V, 2-5 and VI with Papyrus Berolinensis 8592, 1 and 4*, NHS 11 (ed. D. M. Parrott; Leiden, 1979) 341-373; P. A. Dirkse and J. Brashler, "The Prayer of Thanksgiving", *Nag Hammadi Codices V, 2-5 and VI with Papyrus Berolinensis 8592, 1 and 4*, NHS 11 (ed. D. M. Parrott; Leiden, 1979) 375-387. D. M. Parrott, "The Scribal Note", *Nag Hammadi Codices V, 2-5 and VI with Papyrus Berolinensis 8592, 1 and 4*, NHS 11 (ed. D. M. Parrott; Leiden, 1979) 389-393; P. A. Dirkse and D. M. Parrott, "Asclepius 21-29", *Nag Hammadi Codices V, 2-5 and VI with Papyrus Berolinensis 8592, 1 and 4*, NHS 11 (ed. D. M. Parrott; Leiden, 1979) 395-451.

For Hermetic fragments, see J.-P. Mahé, "Fragments Hermétiques dans les Papyri Vindobonenses Graecae 29456 r⁰ et 29828 r⁰", *Mémorial André-Jean Festugière* (eds. E. Lucchesi and H. D. Saggrey; Genève, 1984) 51-64.

On Arabic Hermeticism, see A. G. Blanco, "Hermeticism. A Bibliographical Approach", *ANRW* 2.17.4 (New York, 1984) 2253-2257.

[31] Hermetic passages on self-knowledge are collected by Nock and Festugière, *Hermès Trismégiste* 1, 23 n. 47; see also, H. D. Betz, "The Delphic Maxim ΓΝΩΘΙ ΣΑΥΤΟΝ in Hermetic Interpretation", *HTR* 63 (1970) 465-484.

sexual act as a great "mystery", seemingly a reflection of God's own creative potency (*Asc.* 20-21; *Asc.* [NHC] 65.16-38).³² Other treatises, perhaps better reflecting Hermeticism proper, describe the material body as a tomb and reject sex and bodily pleasure as a curse of death (*C.H.* 1.18-19, 24; 4.5-6; 7.2; 10.7-8; 13.7).³³

In short, the goal of the initiate is to become divinized like Hermes his teacher; thus the way of Hermes is the "way of immortality (ⲑⲓⲏ ⲛ̄ⲧⲙ̄ⲛ̄ⲧⲁⲧⲙⲟⲩ)" (*Disc. Eig. Nin.* 63.10-11; cf. *C.H.* 10.7; 13.3). J.-P. Mahé has recently reconstructed the stages of this immortalization process from a large corpus of early Hermetic texts.³⁴ Immortalization, in these texts, is the result of knowledge of the self, which is the same as knowledge of God; so the Hermetics speak of becoming "God" (*C.H.* 13.3, 10, 14; cf. 1.26). Thus, in *Corpus Hermeticum* 1, when one ascends back to the divine upon death, the soul will cast off different vices at each planetary stage and eventually will be absorbed into God (1.24-26). Other Hermetica maintain that absorption into the divine can occur during the initiate's lifetime while still attached to the mortal sheath (*Disc. Eig. Nin.* 57.28-58.22; *C.H.* 10; 13; cf. 11.20; 12.1; *Asc.* 6.22).

Without doubt, Hermeticism was a religious current in Syria, the land of *Thomas*' origins, at least as early as the second century. Furthermore, now that J.-P. Mahé has shown that the Hermetic sayings in the Armenian and Greek *Definitions* predate the treatises that comprise the *Corpus Hermeticum*, it is possible that Hermeticism could have been a religious tradition dating from at least the first century CE.³⁵ According to H. Drijvers, Hermeticism is found in Syria, going back to the cult of the god Nebo who was identified with Hermes in Edessa and Harran.³⁶ Archaeological evidence as

---

³² J.-P. Mahé, "Le Sens des symboles sexuels dans quelques textes Hermétiques et gnostiques", *Les Textes de Nag Hammadi: Colloque du Centre d'Histoire des Religions, Strasbourg, 23-25 Octobre 1974*, NHS 7 (Leiden, 1975) 130-133.
Corpus Hermeticum 2 was originally part of the Asclepius tracts which, in themselves, are peculiar to the Hermetic literature because of their pan-*en*theistic nature. Stobaeus, who quotes from this tract, states that it is a dialogue between Hermes and Asclepius, not Tat. This is confirmed by MS 1180 in the Greek National Library which cites section 4 sqq. as a dialogue between Hermes and Asclepius. This probably shows Stoic influence and may be at least partially responsible for the positive evaluation of procreation. *Corpus Hermeticum* 3 shows similar Stoic influence.
³³ Mahé, "symboles sexuels", 137-142.
³⁴ Mahé, "La Voie d'Immortalité", 347-375.
³⁵ Mahé, *Hermès en Haute-Égypte* 2.
³⁶ Drijvers, "Edessa", 9, 21, and 25; *idem*, "Bardaisan of Edessa and the Hermetica", *Jaarbericht van het Vooraziatisch-Egyptisch Genootschap ex Oriente Lux*

well as Muslim records yields evidence for the existence of a group around 165 C.E. known as the Sabians in Harran, a village thirty miles from Edessa.[37] Bardaisan of Edessa (ca. 154 - d.222), as Drijvers' analysis suggests, was influenced by Hermetic thought and his ideologies have parallels in *Poimandres* 15.24-26 and *Corpus Hermeticum* 12.5-9.[38] In a discussion about the power of fate, Bardaisan mentions the "Books of the Egyptians" which Drijvers interprets to have been Hermetic writings.[39] It is probable as well that the theme of self-knowledge in the Syrian *Book of Thomas the Contender* has a relationship with Hermeticism.[40]

From this evidence, it is not implausible that the Edessian *Gospel of Thomas* was influenced by Hermeticism. I would argue, however, less for a written Hermetic gnomology which has been directly incorporated into the *Gospel of Thomas* and more for the impact of Hermetic teachings, oral and written, on the particular sayings tradition which was the foundation of Thomas' gospel.

2) *The Second Wave of Studies:*

In the early 1960's, a group of scholars emerged who began associating the *Gospel of Thomas* with Gnosticism. It seems that because the *Gospel of Thomas* was found as part of the Nag Hammadi collection, and this collection was considered gnostic in nature at that time, *Thomas* came to be associated with Gnosticism. This generalization is summarized by R. McL. Wilson in his statement that *Thomas*' "Gnostic character" and "Gnostic environment" is proven because "the document was discovered in the library of a Gnostic group...".[41] Based on this, it was generalized that *Thomas*' Logia represented a "gnosticized" version of the sayings tradition or that *Thomas* had a "Gnostic ring" and must be interpreted from that angle. This interpretation is quite strained and inconclusive since several documents in the Nag Hammadi collection do not belong to Gnosticism (i.e., *Exegesis of the Soul*, the *Teachings of*

---

21 (Leiden, 1969/70) 195-196.
[37] J. B. Segal, "Pagan Syriac Monuments in the Vilayet of Urfa", *AS* 3 (1953) 97-119; *idem*, "The Sabian Mysteries. The planet cult of ancient Harran", *Vanished Civilizations* (ed. E. Bacon; London, 1963) 201-220; *idem*, "Some Syriac Inscriptions of the 2nd and 3rd Century A.D.", *BSOAS* 14 (1954) 97-120.
[38] *Ibid.*, 198-207.
[39] *Ibid.*, 190.
[40] Turner, *Book of Thomas*, 120-122; Quispel, "*Thomas* Revisited", 261.
[41] R. McL. Wilson, *Studies in the Gospel of Thomas* (London; 1960) 15-16.

Silvanus, the *Book of Thomas the Contender*, the *Sentences of Sextus*, the *Discourse on the Eighth and Ninth*, the *Prayer of Thanksgiving*, the *Scribal Note*, *Asclepius* 21-29, Plato, *Republic* 588A-589B).

Thus there was a proliferation of positions attempting to affiliate *Thomas* with a specific known form of Gnosticism. R. Grant, D. Freedman, W. Schodel, K. Smyth, and E. Cornélis argued that *Thomas* emerged from the Naassenes.[42] Conversely, L. Cerfaux, G. Garitte, and B. Gärtner pointed to the Valentinians as the Gnostic sect to which *Thomas* belonged.[43] It was E. Haenchen who noted, however, that the *Gospel of Thomas* lacks the mythology *distinctive* of the Naassenes.[44] The same can be said in regard to the lack of mythology peculiar to Valentinianism.

Because *Thomas* does not exhibit the developed mythologies of any particular Gnostic sect, numerous scholars have devoted much ink to the cause that *Thomas* ought to be associated with Gnosticism *in general*.[45] By the time he wrote his infamous article, "The Gospel

---

[42] R. Grant, "Notes on the Gospel of Thomas", *VC* 13 (1959) 170-180; R. Grant and D. Freedman, *The Secret Sayings of Jesus* (New York, 1960); W. Schoedel, "Naassene Themes in the Coptic Gospel of Thomas", *VC* 14 (1960) 225-234; K. Smyth, "Gnosticism in 'The Gospel according to Thomas'", *HeyJ* 1 (1960) 189-198; E. Cornélis, "Quelques éléments pour une comparison entre l'Évangile de Thomas et la notice d'Hippolyte sur les Naassènes", *VC* 15 (1961) 83-104.

[43] L. Cerfaux and G. Garitte, "Les paraboles du Royaume dans L'Évangile de Thomas", *Muséon* 70 (1957) 307-327; B. Gärtner, *The Theology of the Gospel of Thomas* (trans. E. Sharpe; New York, 1961).

[44] E. Haenchen, *Die Botschaft des Thomas-Evangeliums*, Theologische Bibliothek Töpelmann 6 (Berlin, 1961).

[45] Cf. R. McL. Wilson, "The Coptic 'Gospel of Thomas'", *NTS* 5 (1958/1959) 273-276; idem, "'Thomas' and the Growth of the Gospels", *HTR* 53 (1960) 231-250; J. Bauer, "Das Thomas-Evangelium in der neuesten Forschung", *Geheime Worte Jesu: Das Thomas-Evangelium* (eds. R. Grant and D. Freedman; Frankfurt, 1960) 182-205; idem, "The Synoptic Tradition in the Gospel of Thomas", *StEv* 3, TU 88 (Berlin, 1964) 314-317; R. Roques, "'L'Évangile selon Thomas': son édition critique et son identification", *RHR* 157 (1960) 187-218; idem, "Gnosticisme et Christianisme: L'Évangile selon Thomas", *Irénikon* 33 (1960) 29-40; H. Turner and H. Montefiore, *Thomas and the Evangelists*, SBT 35 (London, 1962); P. Vielhauer, "ΑΝΑΠΑΥΣΙΣ: Zum gnostischen Hintergrund des Thomasevangeliums", *Apophoreta. Festschrift für Ernest Haenchen*, BZNW 30 (ed. W. Eltester; Berlin, 1964) 281-299; W. Schrage, *Das Verhältnis des Thomas-Evangeliums zur synoptischen Tradition und zu den koptischen Evangelienübersetzungen: Zugleich ein Beitrag zur gnostischen Synopitkerdeutung*, BZNW 29 (Berlin, 1964); T. Säve-Söderbergh, "Gnostic and Canonical Gospel Traditions (with special reference to the Gospel of Thomas)", *Le Origini dello Gnosticismo, Colloquio di Messina, 13-18 Aprile, 1966. Testi e Discussioni*, Studies in the History of Religions, *NumenSup* 12 (ed. U. Bianchi; Leiden, 1967) 552-562.

For later works: J.-É. Ménard, *L'Évangile selon Thomas*, NHS 5 (Leiden, 1975); G. MacRae, "Nag Hammadi and the New Testament", *Gnosis: Festschrift für*

of Thomas", for E. Hennecke and W. Schneemelcher, even Puech, who originally thought that *Thomas* was not gnostic, felt the pressure of the arguments of his colleagues. This caused him to publish a marginal statement on the nature of *Thomas*. He states that *Thomas* is not "exclusively or originally the work of a Gnostic".[46]

The thesis that *Thomas* is a generalized gnostic text was particularly developed by E. Haenchen who insisted that the methodological starting point for interpretation of *Thomas* was its intrinsic gnostic character. Each saying must be read as if it had a hidden gnostic agenda. In particular, this gnostic agenda focuses on a theme which is shared by all gnostic sects according to Haenchen: that within each human being there is a particle of divine light which has fallen into matter as a result of a breach in the sacred sphere.

The focus on the themes that *Thomas* shares with gnostic thought was developed further by H. Koester and has become quite popular, especially in the American school. Because Koester sees a lack of a *specific* gnostic mythology in the *Thomas* Logia but the presence of "a religious perspective" which has often been associated with Gnosticism, he concludes that *Thomas* represents a gnosticized version of an early sayings gospel which predated Quelle and promoted a "realized eschatology" instead of the traditional apocalyptic scenario.[47] Thus he writes:

> The influence of Gnostic theology is clearly present in the *Gospel of Thomas*, though it is not possible to ascribe the work to any particular school or sect...The basic religious experience is not only the recognition of one's divine identity, but more specifically the recognition of one's origin (the light) and destiny (repose). In order to return to one's origin, the disciple is to become separate from the world by "stripping off" the fleshly garment and "passing by" the present corruptible existence; then the disciple can experience the new world, the kingdom of light, peace, and life.[48]

Hans Jonas (Göttingen, 1978) 152; the most recent attempt is that of M. Fieger, *Das Thomasevangelium: Einleitung, Kommentar, und Systematik* (Münster, 1991).

[46] Puech, "The Gospel of Thomas", 305-306. See also his later works, "Doctrines ésotériques et thèmes gnostiques dans l'Évangile selon Thomas'", *Annuaire du Collège de France* 62 (1962) 195-203; 63 (1963) 199-213; 64 (1964) 209-217; 65 (1965) 247-256; 66 (1966) 259-262; 67 (1967) 253-260; 68 (1968) 285-297; 69 (1969) 269-283.

[47] Koester, "GNOMAI DIAPHOROI"; *idem*, "One Jesus and Four Primitive Gospels", *Trajectories through Early Christianity* (eds. J. Robinson and H. Koester; Philadelphia, 1971) 158-204.

[48] H. Koester, "Introduction to the Gospel of Thomas", *The Other Bible: Ancient Alternative Scriptures* (ed. W. Barnstone; San Francisco, 1984) 299-300.

The assumption that the presence of similar motifs (i.e., heavenly origins, world renunciation, and a destiny of return to the divine) alone in *Thomas* and Gnosticism predicates *Thomas*' dependence on Gnosticism is rather naive, particularly since both Gnosticism and *Thomas* share a rich and diverse Jewish heritage and probably a Hermetic one as well. Moreover, the religious theme that the person must return to his divine origins of light is also found in Orphic, Platonic, and Hermetic traditions. It is by no means an exclusive gnostic trait and thus should not be used to determine the "gnostic" character of any ancient text.

Therefore, this method of reading *Thomas* as a gnostic sayings collection is very weak and problematic since it is not based on a solid historical reconstruction of the history of religions. Several scholars, especially in recent years, have raised questions about this assumption and have held that *Thomas* is *not* gnostic, although no systematic attempt has been leveled to prove this conclusively.[49]

Unfortunately, in large part, this assumption has been aided by the results of the conference in 1966 which convened to study the "Origins of Gnosticism" at Messina, Sicily. The members of this conference attempted to define "gnosis" and "Gnosticism" and to clear up confusion over the proper employment of these terms. But the *Documento finale* only served to create more confusion. The document states that "gnosis" could be applied on a generic level, denoting "knowledge of divine secrets which is reserved for an elite", while "Gnosticism" should be limited to the historical systems of the second and third centuries which were based on the mythology of the downward movement of the divine whose periphery, Sophia or Ennoia, falls into a crisis which produces the world and a situation in which the fallen sparks of spirit must be recovered.[50]

---

[49] A. J. B. Higgins, "Non-Gnostic Sayings in the Gospel of Thomas", *NT* 4 (1960) 292-306; K. Grobel, "How Gnostic is the Gospel of Thomas?", *NTS* 8 (1962) 367-373; W. H. C. Frend, "The Gospel of Thomas: Is Rehabilitation Possible?", *JTS* 18 (1967) 13-26; Y. O. Kim, "The Gospel of Thomas and the Historical Jesus", *The Northeast Asia Journal of Theology* 2 (1969) 17-30; S. L. Davies, *The Gospel of Thomas and Christian Wisdom* (New York, 1983) 18-35; B. Layton, *The Gnostic Scriptures* (New York, 1987) xvi, 359-365; Lelyveld, *Les Logia*; K. King, "Kingdom in the Gospel of Thomas", *Forum* 3 (1987) 49.

[50] *Le Origini dello Gnosticismo. Colloquio di Messina 13-18 Aprile 1966. Testi e Discussioni*, Studies in the History of Religions, NumenSup 12 (ed. U. Bianchi; Leiden, 1967) xxvi-xxix. This definition has been criticized sharply by some scholars, especially M. Smith, book review of "The Origins of Gnosticism", *JBL* 89 (1970) 82; *idem*, "The History of the term *Gnostikos*", *The Rediscovery of*

After the conference, the question arose in regard to the *Gospel of Thomas*: Was *Thomas* "gnostic" because it spoke about secret elitist knowledge? And if so, could elements of the historical Gnosticism and its myth then be inferred? This confusion can even be seen reflected in G. Quispel's post-Messina writings. He acknowledges that according to Messina's definition of "gnosis", *Thomas* qualifies as gnostic because "these sayings contain a Gnosis for the elect, the happy few". But, he adamantly states that *Thomas* is *not* gnostic in the historical sense and does not "belong to the realm of Gnosticism" because it is lacking fundamental features of the gnostic myth.[51]

Some twenty-seven years later, S. Patterson's recent analysis in his book *The Gospel of Thomas and Jesus* demonstrates the long-term continuation of the confusion generated by Messina's definition of "gnostic" and "Gnosticism". He states that some of *Thomas*' sayings belong solely to the wisdom tradition (L. 25, 26, 31, 32, 34, 35, 41, 45, 47, 54, 86, 94, 103), while others show a "very gnosticising tendency" (L. 11, 15, 18, 60, 67, 83, 84, 88), while still others have been "'gnosticized,' or at least 'esotericized,' in an artificial, plastic way" (L. 49, 50, 68-69, 92, 101). Yet Patterson acknowledges that "Thomas lacks the characteristics of a full-blown Gnosticism".[52]

The fact that *Thomas* does not mention any doctrine *exclusive* to Gnosticism, suggests that those who are advocates for the Gnostic *Thomas* stand on weak ground. Even if we were to make our starting point the Gnostic *Thomas*, and ask the question, "Is there sufficient evidence to cast *reasonable doubt* on *Thomas*' alleged gnosticism?", we would have grounds to set aside the Gnostic label

---

Gnosticism: Proceedings of the International Conference on Gnosticism at Yale, New Haven, Conn., March 28-31, 1978 2, SHR 41.2 (ed. B. Layton; Leiden, 1981) 796-807; U. Bianchi, "A propos de quelques discussions récentes sur la terminologie, la définition et la méthode de l'étude du gnosticisme", *Proceedings of the International Colloquium on Gnosticism*, KVHAH, Filol. filos. ser. 17 (Stockholm, 1977) 16-26, is in dialogue with M. Smith; K. Rudolph, *Gnosis und Gnostizismus*, WF 262 (Darmstadt, 1975); *idem*, "'Gnosis' and 'Gnosticism' - Problems of their Definition and Their Relation to the Writings of the New Testament", *The New Testament and Gnosis: Essays in honor of Robert McLachlan Wilson* (eds. A. H. B. Logan and A. J. M. Wedderburn; Edinburgh, 1983) 21-37, where he surveys the complicated and problematic usage of this terminology both before and after Messina.

[51] Quispel, "Gnosis and the New Sayings", 205-206.
[52] Patterson, *Thomas and Jesus*, 197-198.

and move on to a more substantial question. That is, can better sense be made out of the text by interpreting it within the broader religious context of the early Christian world?

To address the first of these questions, I would like to turn directly to the text of *Thomas* and posit several striking discrepancies between the ideology we find in *Thomas* and that developed by definitive Gnostic authors.

3) *Differentiating Thomas from Gnosticism:*

a) *The Pre-Mundane Fall:*

The myth of the Fallen Sophia or Anthropos is utterly lacking in *Thomas*. In the *Gospel of Thomas*, the universal Error is not found in the Godhead, but in the human. Furthermore, the material realm and humanity are not the warped creations of an ignorant demiurge.

Thus Logion 85 insists that Adam originated from "Great Power" and "Great Wealth":

ΠΕΧΕ ΙC ΧΕ ΝΤΑ ΑΔΑΜ ϢΩΠΕ ΕΒΟΛ ϨΝΝΟΥΝΟϬ ΝΔΥΝΑΜΙC ΜΝ
ΟΥΝΟϬ ΜΜΝΤΡΜΜΑΟ ΑΥΩ ΜΠΕϤϢΩΠΕ Ε[ϤΜ]ΠϢΑ ΜΜΩΤΝ
ΝΕΥΑΧΙΟC ΓΑΡ ΠΕ [ΝΕϤΝΑΧΙ] ΤΠ[Ε] ΑΝ ΜΠΜΟΥ

> Jesus said, "Adam came into being from a great power and a great wealth, but he did not become worthy of you. For had he been worthy, [he would] not [have experienced] death."[53]

The title "Great Power" is an alternative for "Great Glory" and was not an uncommon Name of God or his hypostasis in Jewish apocalyptic and mystical texts and of the Son in Jewish-Christianity.[54] For instance, in the Jewish-Christian writing, the *Teachings of*

---

[53] B. Layton, *Nag Hammadi Codex II, 2-7 together with XII, 2 Brit. Lib. Or. 4926 (1), and P. Oxy. 1, 654, 655* 1: *Gospel According to Thomas, Gospel According to Philip, Hypostasis of the Archons, and Indexes*, NHS 20 (Leiden, 1989) 84; Eng. trans. by Lambdin, 85.

[54] For a comprehensive study of these texts and their implications for the development of angelology and Christology, see J. Fossum, *The Name of God and the Angel of the Lord*, WUNT 36 (Tübingen, 1985) 179-191; idem, "Sects and Movements", *The Samaritans* (ed. A. D. Crown; Tübingen, 1989) 368-377; idem, "Colossians 1.15-18a in the Light of Jewish Mysticism and Gnosticism", *NTS* 35 (1989) 190-193. Fossum states that outside of Samaritanism and Simonianism, the title "Great Power" was not used of God, but he has missed a passage from the *Concept of Our Great Power* where the "Great Power" (36.4-5, 15, 27) refers to the supreme transcendent God who is above all "powers", including the Old Testament God, the Demiurge, the "father of the flesh" (38.20).

Silvanus, it is said of Jesus: "A Great Power and Great Glory has made the universe known" (112.8-10; cf. 106.21ff.). The Syriac version of the *Acts of Thomas*, a source which is generally understood to contain a substantial amount of Jewish-Christian ideas, addresses Christ as the "Great Power" (c. 12). Justin Martyr refers to this tradition when he writes that among the names of the Son is "Power of God" (*1 Apol.* 33.6) and that God begat as "Beginning" a "Power from himself" that is also called "the Glory of the Lord" and sometimes "Son" (*Dial.* 61.1). The Jewish-Christian sect leader, Elchasai, appeared as the Prophet like Moses, and was designated the "Hidden Power", the final manifestation of Christ. Simon Magus also appeared as the eschatological Prophet like Moses and was called the "Great Power", a divine manifestation which superseded his prior incarnation in Jesus.

It is quite in keeping with the rest of the *Gospel of Thomas* that Adam originated from a "Great Power", the Son, and not an ignorant demiurge in opposition to God. As we will see later, in Logion 77, the creator is identified with Jesus, the *Phōs*, the heavenly Light-Man, from whom everything "came forth".[55] Undoubtedly, *Thomas* is drawing on Jewish and Jewish-Christian traditions when stating that Adam was the creation of God's hypostasis, the Great Power.

Even though Adam originated from the Great Power, however, Logion 85 states that he was not "worthy", because "had he been worthy, [he would] not [have experienced] death". Thus, Adam's Fall is the cause of death according to Logion 85.

Logion 11 alludes to the pre-condition of Adam's Fall when the human separated into two sexes: "On the day when you were one, you became two (ϩⲙ̄ ⲫⲟⲟⲩ ⲉⲧⲉⲧⲛ̄ⲟ ⲛ̄ⲟⲩⲁ ⲁⲧⲉⲧⲛ̄ⲉⲓⲣⲉ ⲙ̄ⲡⲥⲛⲁⲩ)."[56] The division of the sexes was closely associated with Adam's Sin.[57] In order to return to the pristine state, this division must be rectified. This occurs, according to *Thomas*, "when you make the two into one...when you make male and female into a

---

[55] Refer to Chapter One, Section 3b.
[56] Layton, *Nag Hammadi Codex II,2-7*, 56 and 58; Eng. trans. by Lambdin, 57 and 59.
[57] It is noteworthy that many Christian and Greek thinkers associated sexual differentiation with the fall and embodiment of the soul; on this see J. H. Waszink, *Quinti Septimi Florentis Tertulliani. De Anima. Edited with Introduction and Commentary* (Amsterdam, 1947) 420.

single one, so that the male will not be male nor the female be female" (L. 22; cf. 37).[58]

This is the cry of encratism[59] where salvation is based on returning to Adam's Pre-Fall state before the division of the sexes, and subsequently before the tasting of the forbidden fruit, sexual intercourse. This notion in *Thomas* is best paralleled by the saying from the encratite *Gospel of the Egyptians*:

> When Salome asked when what she had inquired about would be known, the Lord said, "When you have trampled on the garment of shame and when the two become one and the male with the female (is) neither male nor female" (Clem. Alex., *Strom.* 3.13.92).[60]

Moreover, *Thomas* seems to be referring to the Genesis story in Logion 114 where Jesus states that woman must become "male" in order to enter the Kingdom. Since Eve was taken from Adam's side, so she must reenter him and become "male" in order to return to the prelapsarian state of Adam before the gender division:

ⲡⲉϫⲉ ⲥⲓⲙⲱⲛ ⲡⲉⲧⲣⲟⲥ ⲛⲁⲩ ϫⲉ ⲙⲁⲣⲉ ⲙⲁⲣⲓϩⲁⲙ ⲉⲓ ⲉⲃⲟⲗ ⲛ̄ϩⲏⲧⲛ̄ ϫⲉ ⲛ̄ⲥϩⲓⲟⲙⲉ ⲙ̄ⲡϣⲁ ⲁⲛ ⲙ̄ⲡⲱⲛϩ ⲡⲉϫⲉ ⲓ̄ⲥ ϫⲉ ⲉⲓⲥϩⲏⲏⲧⲉ ⲁⲛⲟⲕ ϯⲛⲁⲥⲱⲕ ⲙ̄ⲙⲟⲥ ϫⲉⲕⲁⲁⲥ ⲉⲉⲓⲛⲁⲁⲥ ⲛ̄ϩⲟⲟⲩⲧ ϣⲓⲛⲁ ⲉⲥⲛⲁϣⲱⲡⲉ ϩⲱⲱⲥ ⲛ̄ⲟⲩⲡⲛ̄ⲁ ⲉϥⲟⲛϩ ⲉϥⲉⲓⲛⲉ ⲙ̄ⲙⲱⲧⲛ̄ ⲛ̄ϩⲟⲟⲩⲧ ϫⲉ ⲥϩⲓⲙⲉ ⲛⲓⲙ ⲉⲥⲛⲁⲁⲥ ⲛ̄ϩⲟⲟⲩⲧ ⲥⲛⲁⲃⲱⲕ ⲉϩⲟⲩⲛ ⲉⲧⲙⲛ̄ⲧⲉⲣⲟ ⲛⲙ̄ⲡⲏⲩⲉ

> Simon Peter said to them, "Let Mary leave us, for women are not worthy of life." Jesus said, "I myself shall lead her in order to make her male, so that she too may become a living spirit resembling you males. For every woman who will make herself male will enter the kingdom of heaven".[61]

At first glance, it would seem that the expressions "neither male nor female" (L. 22) and "becoming male" (L. 114) contradict each

---

[58] The restoration of the androgynous prelapsarian "Man" is the ultimate goal; this idea has its roots in Platonic thought (*Symposion* 191cd). See the following works on the subject: W. Meeks, "The Image of the Androgyne: Some Uses of a Symbol in Earliest Christianity", *HR* 13 (1974) 165-208; M. Meyer, "Making Mary Male: The Categories 'Male' and 'Female' in the Gospel of Thomas", *NTS* 31 (1985) 554-570; D. R. MacDonald, *There is No Male and Female: The Fate of a Dominical Saying in Paul and Gnosticism* (Philadelphia, 1987); De Conick and Fossum, "Stripped Before God", 123-150.

[59] On encratism, refer to Chapter 1, Section 1.

[60] O. Stählin, *Clemens Alexandrinus, Werke II*, Die griechischen christlichen Schriftsteller der ersten drei Jahrhunderte 15 (new ed. by L. Früchtel; Berlin, 1962) 238.

[61] Layton, *Nag Hammadi Codex II,2-7*, 92; Eng. trans. by Lambdin, 93.

other.[62] J. J. Buckley, building on the works of K. H. Rengstorf[63] and P. Vielhauer,[64] argues that these two expressions are pointing to different states of being. In Logion 22, a new creation is demanded where the two are merged or unified while in Logion 114 the one, the female, is to become the other, the male.[65] Buckley therefore suggests that the becoming "male" stage fowarded in Logion 114 reflects a stage prior to the final state of salvation when one becomes a "living spirit" (Logion 114) which is a unification of the male and female (Logion 22).[66]

In the same year, however, M. Meyer in his article on this Logion acknowledged that Logion 114 may be a later edition to the text but he argued that Logion 22 and 114 do not have to to be interpreted as dissonant. After reviewing the usages of the terms "maleness" and "femaleness" in texts contemporary with *Thomas*, he concluded that "femaleness" is associated with "sensuality and sexuality" and must be renounced in order to become "male" or "spiritual and heavenly" as Logion 114 purports. According to Meyer, this message is quite compatible with the rest of the gospel where the spiritual state is understood to be a state of unity and asexuality which could be described in terms of "maleness".[67]

For different reasons, I would agree with Meyer that these two sayings are not necessarily dissonant. In light of the fact that the Thomasites seem to be involved in the exegesis of the Genesis story,[68] it is plausible that they interpreted these two sayings to be references to the creation of man. According to Genesis 1:27, God created the first *Man* as male and female while, according to Genesis 2:22, woman was taken out of Adam's side. So the pristine state could be described as a condition before the gender differentiation when the first *Man* was neither gender but consisted of both male and female (Gen 1:27). This *Man* appeared in the male form as Adam with woman concealed inside of him (Gen 2:22). Thus to

---

[62] Quispel, "Encratism", 61.
[63] K. H. Rengstorf, "Urchristliches Kerygma und 'gnostische' Interpretation in einigen Sprüchen des Thomasevangeliums", *Le Origini dello Gnosticismo. Colloquio di Messina 13-18 Aprile 1966. Testi e Discussioni*, Studies in the History of Religions, *NumenSup* 12 (ed. U. Bianchi; Leiden, 1967) 565-566.
[64] Vielhauer, "ΑΝΑΠΑΥΣΙΣ", 298.
[65] J. J. Buckley, "An Interpretation of Logion 114 in *The Gospel of Thomas*", *NT* 27 (1985) 253-254.
[66] *Ibid.*, 245-272.
[67] Meyer, "Making Mary Male", 554-570.
[68] For instance, refer to De Conick and Fossum, "Stripped Before God", 123-150.

make oneself "neither male nor female" (L. 22) was the same as "becoming male" (L. 114), when one returned to the pristine state of the androgynous prelapsarian *Man*. A passage from Philo illustrates that this type of interpretation was not unique to *Thomas*. In one breath, Philo tells us that the "heavenly *man*" (emphasis mine) in Genesis 1:27 was "neither male nor female" (*Op. mundi.* 134).

In the *Gospel of Thomas*, the concupiscence of Adam is the Error which needs to be rectified, not the Error of Sophia. The reunion of the sexes into the androgynous prelapsarian *Man* was believed to meet this end.

This differs from Gnosticism where it is the unity of the Pleroma which needs to be restored since the Fall was a cosmic event that only the Christ can repair. We find a very interesting passage in the Valentinian *Gospel of Philip* to this end: "Before the Christ, certain beings came from a realm that they could not re-enter, and went to a realm that they could not yet leave. Then the Christ came: he brought out those who had entered and brought in those who had left" (68.17-21). Sophia is the cause of the cosmic rupture as the *Gospel of Philip* alludes to in 60.12-14: "Echamoth is one thing and Echmoth is another. Echamoth is Wisdom simply, but Echmoth is the Wisdom of death which is the one which knows death, which is called 'the little Wisdom'". This is a reference to the separation of the lower Sophia from the higher Sophia, a separation by which the cosmic process was set in motion and death was brought into existence.[69] This cosmic mistake of Sophia caused the world to be created in its inferior condition (75.2-10).

What about the passage subsequent to 68.17-21 which introduces the Adam myth of division? This passage reads: "In the days when Eve was [in] Adam, death did not exist. When she was separated from him, death came into existence. If he [reenters] and takes it unto himself death will not exist" (68.22-25). Is this not evidence that Gnosticism taught about the Adam myth of division?

I contend that the Adam myth of division was not originally a Gnostic tenet. It would seem that we are witnessing in the *Gospel of Philip* 68.17-21 and 68.22-25 the blending of two traditions: the classic gnostic myth of the cosmic rupture and the Adam myth of division. By incorporating the Adam myth of division into the myth of the cosmic rupture, the Valentinians have created a new

---

[69] R. McL. Wilson, *The Gospel of Philip: Translated from the Coptic text, with an Introduction and Commentary* (London, 1962) 102-103.

Gnostic myth: that the cosmic rupture was mirrored on earth in the division of the sexes. The cosmic rupture of Sophia separating from her consort (cf. *Gos. Ph.* 60.12-14; 75.2-12; Iren., *Adv. haer.* 1.2.1-1.2.2) can only be rectified by the Christ who joins together the male and the female on the cosmic level (Iren., *Adv. haer.* 1.7.1). The mirror of this is marriage on earth; marriage reflects the cosmic rejoining and is thus a "great mystery" (*Gos. Ph.* 64.32; 82.1-24).[70] The *Gospel of Philip* sums this up in 70.9-21:

> If the female had not separated from the male, she and the male would not die. That beings' separation became the source of death. The Christ came to rectify the separation that had been present since the beginning and join the two (components), and give life unto those who had died by separation and join them together. Now, a woman joins with her husband in the bridal bedroom, and those who have joined in the bridal bedroom will not separate. Thus Eve became separate from Adam because it was not in the bridal bedroom that she joined him.

It is quite possible that the Valentinian tradition has been directly influenced by the *Thomas* tradition, at least on its presentation of the Adam myth.[71] This suggests that the Valentinians may have been using *Thomas* when creating their ideology and composing their literature, freely interpreting and adapting it to fit their theological needs.

b) *Theological Dualism:*
There is no theological dualism in *Thomas*. The ignorant Demiurge does not create the world in *Thomas*. Jesus, as the *Phōs*, the Light-Man, does. Thus, in Logion 77, he says: "I am the light... from me everything came forth...(ⲁⲛⲟⲕ ⲡⲉ ⲡⲟⲩⲟⲉⲓⲛ...ⲛ̄ⲧⲁ ⲡⲧⲏⲣϥ ⲉⲓ ⲉⲃⲟⲗ ⲛ̄ϩⲏⲧ)".[72] The idea that Jesus is the *Phōs*, a Man of Light, is a reference to a Jewish exegetical tradition that seems to have interpreted the "light" of Genesis 1:3 ("God said, 'Let there be *phōs*!'

---

[70] Refer to R. M. Grant, "The Mystery of Marriage in the Gospel of Philip", *VC* 15 (1961) 129-140; E. Pagels, "Adam and Eve, Christ and the Church: A Survey of Second Century Controversies concerning Marriage", *The New Testament and Gnosis: Essays in Honour of Robert McL. Wilson* (eds. A. H. B. Logan and A. J. M. Wedderburn; Edinburgh, 1983) 146-175.

[71] B. Layton suggests that Valentinus was influenced by the Thomas School in his emphasis on self-knowledge as salvation. Layton argues that *Thomas* was circulating in Egypt during Valentinus' time and that he probably knew and used the *Gospel of Thomas* as a source for some of his notions: *Gnostic Scriptures*, xvi, 220.

[72] Layton, *Nag Hammadi Codex II,2-7*, 82-83.

And *phōs* came into being") as "man" due to a pun on the word *phōs* which can mean both "light (τό φῶς)" and "man (ὁ φώς)".[73] The Jewish-Christians involved in this exegetical tradition seem to have identified the Son with the *Phōs* of Genesis 1:3.[74] Furthermore, speculations about the possible demiurgic functions of the light figure were also part of Jewish thought.[75]

The notion that the Light is a demiurgic agent is not exclusive to Jewish tradition. This is also the case in Hermeticism which owes its teaching to Egyptian conceptions of the god Helios. The sun is said to be "an image of the Maker who is above the heavens (ἥλιος εἰκών ἐστι τοῦ ἐπουρανίου δημιουργοῦ [θεοῦ])" (*Exc.* of Stobaeus 21.2). The title "Demiurge (ὁ δημιουργὸς)" is attributed to the sun (*C.H.* 16.5; cf. *Exc.* of Stobaeus 2.A.14). Furthermore, the "Light (φῶς)" is praised as the "demiurge (δημιουργέ)" and "the God (ὁ θεός)" (*C.H.* 13.19; cf. 16.8ff.).

---

[73] On this see G. Quispel, "Ezekiel 1:26 in Jewish Mysticism and Gnosis", *VC* 34 (1980) 6; Fossum, *Name*, 280.

[74] On this see J. Fossum, "Jewish-Christian Christology and Jewish Mysticism", *VC* 37 (1983) 266-267. For instance, refer to the *Teachings of Silvanus* 112.35-37, where Christ is given the names "the Firstborn, the Wisdom, the Prototype, the First Light". This latter name indicates that the Christ was identified with the primal *Phōs* which was manifested on the first day of creation. Also, see J. Zandee, "'The Teachings of Silvanus' (NHC VII,4) and Jewish-Christianity", *Studies in Gnosticism and Hellenistic Religions presented to Gilles Quispel on the Occasion of his 65th Birthday*, EPRO 91 (eds. R. van den Broek and M. J. Vermaseren; Leiden, 1981) 566, where he notes that the *Teachings of Silvanus* 113.6-7 characterizes the Son as the "Light of the Eternal Light" which foreshadows the phrase "light from light" of the Nicaenum. This is already in the Creed of Caesarea (*Epist. Euseb.* in Socrates, *Hist. Eccl.* 1.8). Thus, it is of a Palestinian provenance.

[75] In *3 Enoch* 12-13, Metatron is a light being who is given a crown etched with the letters of light by which "all the necessities of the world and all the orders of creation were created" (13.1-2). In the *Shiur Komah* circles, the primordial luminous Man is called the *Yotser Bereshith*, the "creator of the world"; on this see G. Scholem, *Major Trends in Jewish Mysticism* (New York, 1941) 65. This must be quite an early Jewish tradition since it emerges in the Sophia speculations where Sophia who is identified with the *Phōs* of Genesis 1:3 (Frag. 5 of Aristobulus according to Eus., *Praep. ev.* 13.12.9-11) is either God's associate in creation (Prov 8:30; WisSol 8:4; 9:1-2, 9) or is a demiurge herself (WisSol 7:22; 8:1, 5-6; *2 En.* 11; *Ps. Clem. Hom.* 16.12.1; Palestinian Fragmentary Tg. *Gen.* 1.1; cf. Philo who describes Sophia as "the mother of all", *Quod det. pot. insid. soleat.* 115f.; *ibid.*, 54; *Leg. all.* 2.49; *De ebriet.* 30f.). See also the *Gos. Egy.* 3.49.10-12 and 4.61.8-11 where the demiurgic aspect of the *Phōs* again erupts. There is a tradition to the effect that the Light is responsible for the creation of the heavens (cf. *3 En.* 48A.1; *Pirke de R. Eliezer* 3; *Gen. R.* 34).

It may be that during the first centuries CE, Hermetic reflections on the demiurgic agency of Helios have congealed with the Jewish exegetical tradition about *Phōs*. The welding of these two traditions is visible in the Hermetic magical papyrus where Helios is given the title "father of the world (πατὴρ κόσμου)" (PGM 4.1169). According to E. Peterson's analysis of this passage, in this appeal to Helios, there is a connection with the creation story in Genesis.[76]

In addition to this association with the traditions that the Light is responsible for the creation of the universe, the *Gospel of Thomas* is also aware of the motif that humanity comes from the Light. Thus in Logion 50, an elect portion of humanity is said to be generated from the Light through the image of the angels.[77] These elect are known by the title, "sons of light".[78] Moreover, since Logion 50 is a fragment of esoteric ascent-wisdom, it is implicitly aware of the motif that the "sons of light" will return to the Light. This is said explicitly in Logion 11: "When you come to dwell in the Light, what will you do?".

This ideology is in sharp contrast to the gnostic teaching that an ignorant inferior Demiurge creates a fallen universe and that the light of the Supreme God becomes enmeshed in his creatures. Moreover, a cosmic redemption of these light particles is necessary. The particles return to the Supreme God, escaping the snares of the Demiurge.

It is plausible that the Gnostics drew their ideas about the light-elite originating from the Supreme God and returning to him from the same Jewish-Hermetic traditions as *Thomas*. It appears that the Gnostics created a completely different myth using some of the same building blocks that *Thomas* employed.

It must also be emphasized that *Thomas* speaks of the unity of the Godhead, not its tragic division. Jesus lays claim to the fact that he is from the Undivided (ⲡⲉⲧϣⲏϣ) (L. 61; cf. L. 72). This is in contrast to the gnostic myth where the tragic rupture caused the Godhead to be divided. In Christian Gnosticism, even Jesus experiences this division. For instance, the Valentinians proclaimed:

---

[76] E. Peterson, "Die Befreiung Adams aus der ἀνάγκη", *Frühkirche, Judentum, und Gnosis* (Freiburg, 1959) 115-116. See also, A. Dupont-Sommer, "Adam. 'Père du Monde' dans la Sagesse de Solomon (10,1.2)", *RHR* 119 (1939) 182ff.
[77] For a detailed discussion, refer to Chapter Four, Section 1c.
[78] See Chapter Four, Section 2b.

> Indeed, our angels were put forth in unity, they say, being one, because they come forth from one. Now since we were divided, for this reason Jesus was baptized, that the undivided might be divided, until he unites us with them in the Fullness, so that we, the many who have become one, may all be mingled with the One that was divided for us" (Clem. Alex., *Exc.Theo.* 36.1-2).[79]

According to this text, the Pleroma has experienced a tragic division; it is no longer the primal Unity of the beginning. Jesus is divided apparently for the soteriological purpose of showing the Valentinians the way back into the original unity of the Pleroma, when they will be united with their angels.

Thomas presents the picture of a unified Godhead of Light from which creation comes. It is Adam's Sin that turns everything upside down, bringing about sex and lust, birth and ultimately death. The material world is a negative experience for these reasons, whereas in Gnosticism there is a depreciation of the world because of the cosmic Fall, the consequent division in the Godhead and creation through the will of the ignorant Demiurge.

4) *Conclusion:*

I would argue that this evidence is sufficient to cast reasonable doubt on the "gnostic" nature of *Thomas* and justifies an investigation into other possible explanations for the *Sitz im Leben* of this gospel. Moreover, it is noteworthy that contemporary research on Gnosticism itself provides further reason to argue against continuing to label *Thomas* as gnostic. These studies have been struggling with the validity and relevance of splitting off the use of "gnosis" from the historical "Gnosticism", and have indicated that "gnosis", like "Gnosticism", must be reserved for reference to the historical systems having the mythology described in the Messina document.[80] The recent observations of S. Pétrement are especially interesting:

> It is not enough to define it [Gnosticism] by the meaning of the word *gnosis*; that is to say, Gnosticism cannot be defined simply as a doctrine emphasizing the importance of *knowledge* for salvation. For there have been a number of other doctrines of salvation by

---

[79] R. P. Casey, *The Excerpta ex Theodoto of Clement of Alexandria. Edited with Translation, Introduction and Notes*, SD 1 (Cambridge, Mass., 1934) 66-67.

[80] K. Rudolph, *Gnosis* (trans. R. McL. Wilson from 2nd ed.; San Francisco, 1983) 57; Layton, *Gnostic Scriptures*, 5-22; S. Pétrement, *A Separate God: The Christian Origins of Gnosticism* (trans. C. Harrison; New York, 1990) 8-10.

knowledge that had nothing to do with Gnosticism...Gnosticism [has been] characterized by an "anticosmic attitude", that is, by a devaluation of the world,...But this characteristic is *too general*, for it also applies to doctrines that are not Gnostic...[Gnosticism] is characterized by a certain structural system: the distinction between *two levels in the supraterrestrial world*, two levels, each of which has a representative that can be called God, though *only the representative of the upper level can be the true God*. It is this which makes Gnostic doctrines impossible to confuse with others...[81]

Although Pétrement is correct to emphasize the Gnostic structural system, the *origin* of this two level structure must be taken into consideration as well, since the distinction between two levels in the supraterrestial world is also made in Middle Platonism.[82] If Pétrement's unmodified definition were correct, then Philo, according to his opinion in *Quaestiones et Solutiones in Genesin* 4.8, would be gnostic!

Scholarship on Gnosticism seems to be moving in the direction of a plausible working definition that fits the sources available to us. Thus I would agree that Gnosticism and Gnosis should be associated only with certain religious movements beginning in the late first or early second century which were characterized by the mythology of a divine figure who either falls or is forced down into the lower world. The consequent structural system involves two levels, one the realm of the Supreme God, the other the realm of a lesser god.

I would modify this by adding that the lesser god, whose place may be taken by a collective of angels, functions as a demiurge who is in opposition to the true God. Furthermore, the creation of man by the demiurge results in an anthropological dualism where the sparks of the true God are contained within the demiurge's material creation. A classical gnostic system, in addition to teaching the decline of a divine entity, is characterized by three types of dualism: cosmological, theological, and anthropological.[83]

---

[81] Pétrement, *Separate God*, 8-10.
[82] See Fossum, *Name*, 332-336.
[83] Several movements probably should be understood as proto-Gnosticisms. This use of the term "proto-Gnosticisms" is a better way to employ it than that forwarded by the Messina document. On this, refer to Fossum, *Name*, 337 n. 216. The Simonians taught that Ennoia emanated from God and carried out her Father's will when creating the angels by whom the world was made. This system also lacks a true anthropological dualism. Satornilos' teachings do not speak of the fall within the divine. Seven angels create the world and fashion man after the appearance of a luminous image coming from the realm of absolute power. The angels try to detain it, but are not able to.

If recent scholarship on Gnosticism can be used as a barometer for *Thomas* studies, it would seem that we are compeled to reevaluate *Thomas*' heritage. *Thomas* certainly differs from the developing definition of Gnosticism since, as I noted earlier, this gospel talks of the lapse of Adam, and is ignorant of the gnostic doctrines of the pre-mundane Fall and of the subsequent theological dualism characteristic of gnostic documents.

Much of the past scholarship on *Thomas*, by making *Thomas* dependent on Gnosticism, has been blinded to the fact that Gnosticism may have drawn on Logia in the *Gospel of Thomas* in order to develop and perpetuate its own ideologies and mythologies. I would argue that the evidence points to questions in the reverse: How may the *Gospel of Thomas* have influenced the development of Gnostic traditions? Or, how may the Gnostics have used *Thomas* to forward their own ideologies?

These questions, as far as I know, have not yet been seriously addressed. Yet we know from Hippolytus' writings that the Naassenes were using the *Gospel of Thomas*. They seem to have liberally redacted it. According to Hippolytus' testimony, they transmitted a gnosticized version of Logion 4: "The one who seeks me will find me in the children from seven years of age and onwards. For there, hiding in the fourteenth aeon, I am revealed" (*Ref.*, 5.7.20).[84]

The Manichaeans, as well, were not only acquainted with the *Thomas* tradition, but seem to have their own rendition of the *Gospel of Thomas*. Thus Cyril of Jerusalem says that "the Manichaeans wrote a *Gospel According to Thomas*" (*Cat.* 4.36, cf. 6.31; cf. Peter of Sicily, *Hist. Manich.* 16; Ps.-Leontius, *De sectis* 3.2; Timotheus of Constantinople, *De recept. haeret.*, *PG* 86.1.21; *Acts of the Second Council of Nicaea* 6.5; Ps.-Photius, *Contra Manichaeos* 1.14).[85]

Cerinthus taught that the world was created by a power who was separated from God and had no knowledge of God, but this power was not in opposition to God. This is similar to Justin's "Book of Baruch" where the demiurge, Elohim, did not oppose God by creating, but did not have knowledge of God either. For further discussion, refer to Fossum, *Name*, 213ff.; idem, "Gen. 1,26 and 2,7 in Judaism, Samaritanism, and Gnosticism", *JSJ* 16 (1985) 202-239; idem, "The Magharians: A Pre-Christian Jewish Sect and Its Significance for the Study of Gnosticism and Christianity", *Henoch* 9 (1987) 303-344.

[84] Eng. trans. by H. Attridge, "Appendix: The Greek Fragments", *Nag Hammadi Codex II,2-7 together with XII,2 Brit. Lib. Or. 4926 (1), and P. Oxy. 1, 654, 655 1: Gospel According to Thomas, Gospel According to Philip, Hypostasis of the Archons, and Indexes*, NHS 20 (ed. B. Layton; Leiden, 1989) 103.

[85] *Ibid.*, 105; Puech, "The Gospel of Thomas", 278-279.

It is most probable that the Valentinians, like the Manichaeans and the Naassenes, at least were acquainted with *Thomas* and incorporated some of its traditions into their works perhaps because it contains a negative world view and stresses "knowledge" as part of its soteriological scheme.

But gnostic use does not predicate gnostic origins. We should be speaking of an influx of traditions found in *Thomas* into Gnosticism, not the influx of Gnosticism into *Thomas*. The future of research on possible connections between the *Gospel of Thomas* and Gnosticism should be moving in the direction of exploring the influences that this non-gnostic Gospel's ideology may have had on emerging second century gnostic systems.

CHAPTER TWO

THE SOLUTION: THOMAS IS MYSTICAL

In the last chapter, I posed two questions: Is there sufficient evidence to cast reasonable doubt on *Thomas*' alleged gnosticism? And, if so, can the text be better explained within the broader religious context of the early Christian world? Since the evidence points to an affirmative answer to the former question, the latter question now requires investigation.

Unlike G. Quispel, however, who was intent on creating a genealogy of written sources for *Thomas*, I would rather approach the issue by speaking of religious influences which impacted the sayings tradition behind the *Gospel of Thomas*. I propose that *in addition* to encratism, Jewish-Christianity, and Hermeticism, another major tradition impacted *Thomas*' theology, a tradition which explains the esoteric nature of *Thomas*' Logia more efficaciously than Gnosticism: early Jewish mysticism.

1) *Evidence for First-Century Jewish Mysticism:*

a) *Mysticism and Apocalypticism:*
The term "Jewish mysticism" is usually employed to describe the period of mysticism beginning with the third century Hekhalot literature and centering around "Merkavah mysticism". Merkavah mysticism refers to mystical esoteric traditions connected with Jewish vision quests of God upon his Throne-Chariot, his Merkavah, as described in Ezekiel 1 (cf. Isa 6; Dan 7). The Hekhalot texts describe both the vision of the Merkavah and the ascent to the Chariot through the seven "Hekhalot" or "Palaces". The magical practices for successfully achieving the ascent and vision are explained in detail, including fasting and purification techniques, and the recitation of the secret names of the angels, elaborate hymns, and prayers.[1] These practices are intended to aid

---

[1] For descriptions of the ascent, vision, and magical practices, see the following Hekhalot texts: Hekhalot Rabbati in P. Schäfer, *Synopse zur Hekhalot-Literatur*, Texte und Studien zum Antiken Judentum 2 (Tübingen, 1981) sections 81-306; see the classic overview by M. Smith, "Observations on Hekhalot

the mystic in his ascent so that he may successfully stand before the Throne and gaze on the "*kavod*" or "Glory", the "likeness as the appearance of a man" as Ezekiel describes him in his vision (Ezek. 1:26).

These Hekhalot traditions are generally attributed to Rabbi Akiba and Rabbi Ishmael who are said to have received them from their teachers, Rabbi Nehunyah ben Ha-Qanah and Rabbi Eliezer ben Hyrkanos of the first century CE. This chain of transmission may not be entirely pseudepigraphical, suggesting that some of the first century Rabbis were experimenting with mystical ascent.

Ascents into the heavenly world and visions of the "Glory" are one of the features in Jewish apocalyptic literature of the Second Temple and early Christian periods.[2] Even though the term "Merkavah" is not used in these texts, it has been argued that the apocalyptic and Hekhalot traditions are related in some manner. This was first the thesis of G. Scholem. He proposed that the Hekhalot materials are connected with the esoteric traditions surrounding Ezekiel 1 and discussed by the Tannaim and Amoraim.

Rabbati", *Biblical and Other Studies*, Studies and Texts 1 (ed. A. Altmann; Cambridge, Mass., 1963) 142-160; Eng. trans. of chapters 15-29 by L. Grodner in D. R. Blumenthal, *Understanding Jewish Mysticism: A Source Reader: The Merkabah Tradition and the Zoharic Tradition* 1 (New York, 1978) 56-89; for Eng. trans. of chapters 1-2, 16-26, see A. Kaplan, *Meditation and Kabbalah* (York Beach, Maine, 1982) 42-54. Maʿaseh Merkavah in Schäfer, *Synopse*, sections 544-596; Eng. trans. by N. Janowitz, *The Poetics of Ascent: Theories of Language in a Rabbinic Ascent Text* (New York, 1989). Hekhalot Zutarti in Schäfer, *Synopse*, sections 355-374 and 407-426. *3 Enoch* in H. Odeberg, *The Hebrew Book of Enoch or Third Enoch* (2nd edition with a new prolegomenon by J. C. Greenfield; New York, 1973); Also see the Eng. trans. by Alexander in *OTP* 1, 255-315.

[2] The more general concept of ascent has been the subject of several works: W. Bousset, "Die Himmelsreise der Seele", *ARW* 4 (1901) 136-169, 229-273; G. Widengren, *The Ascension of the Apostle and the Heavenly Book*, Uppsala Universitets Årsskrift 7 (Uppsala 1950); C. Colpe, "Die 'Himmelsreise der Seele' ausserhalb und innerhalb der Gnosis," *Le Origini dello Gnosticismo, Colloquio di Messina 13-18 Aprile 1966*, Studies in the History of Religions, NumenSup 12 (ed. U. Bianchi; Leiden, 1967) 429-447; Alan Segal, "Heavenly Ascent in Hellenistic Judaism, Early Christianity, and their Environment," *ANRW* 2.23.2 (Berlin and New York, 1980) 1333-1394; I. P. Culianu, "L'Ascension de l'âme' dans les mystères et hors des mystères," *La Soteriologia dei culti orientali nell'Impero romano* (eds. U. Bianchi and M. J. Vermaseren; Leiden, 1982) 276-302; idem, *Psychanodia I: A Survey of the Evidence Concerning the Ascension of the Soul and Its Relevance* (Leiden, 1983); idem, *Expériences de l'Extase* (Paris, 1984); M. Dean-Otting, *Heavenly Journeys: A Study of the Motif in Hellenistic Jewish Literature* (Frankfurt, 1984); J. D. Tabor, *Things Unutterable: Paul's Ascent to Paradise in its Greco-Roman, Judaic, and Early Christian Contexts*, Studies in Judaism (New York, 1986). M. Himmelfarb, *Ascent to Heaven in Jewish and Christian Apocalypses* (Oxford, 1993).

In turn, these mystically-oriented Rabbis had been influenced by apocalyptic writings such as *1 Enoch* and the *Apocalypse of Abraham* where descriptions of heavenly journeys and the vision of the God upon his throne are found.³ I. Gruenwald has been the major proponent and developer of this thesis.⁴

A challenge to this view has been proposed by some scholars who believe that Rabbinic traditions about Ezekiel chapter 1 do not presuppose actual endeavors to ascend but are merely exegetical and speculative developments. Moreover, the Hekhalot tradition originates in circles marginal to Rabbinic Judaism during the post-Talumdic era.⁵

The recent thorough and convincing analysis of the *ma'aseh merkabah* traditions by C. Morray-Jones has led him to support a modified version of Scholem's thesis. He concludes that the mystical traditions found in the Hekhalot materials were inherited from the Jewish apocalyptic circles. Some Tannaim developed these traditions while others were suspicious of these traditions because they were also being developed by some groups who were thought to be heretical at that time.⁶

---

³ Scholem, *Major Trends*, 40-79; *idem, Jewish Gnosticism; Origins of the Kabbalah* (Princeton, 1987) 18-24; *idem, Kabbalah* (Jerusalem and New York, 1974) 8-21.

⁴ I. Gruenwald, "Knowledge and Vision: Towards a Clarification of Two 'Gnostic' Concepts in the Light of Their Alleged Origins", *Israel Oriental Studies* 3 (1973) 63-107; *idem,* "Jewish Esoteric Literature in the Time of the Mishnah and Talmud", *Immanuel* 4 (1974) 37-46; *idem,* "Aspects of the Jewish-Gnostic Controversy", *The Rediscovery of Gnosticism: Proceedings of the International Conference on Gnosticism at Yale, New Haven, Connecticut, March 28-31, 1978* 2 (ed. B. Layton; Leiden, 1980-1981) 713-723; *idem, Apocalyptic and Merkavah Mysticism*, AGJU 14 (Leiden, 1980); *idem,* "The Problems of Anti-Gnostic Polemic in Rabbinic Literature", *Studies in Gnosticism and Hellenistic Religions* (eds. R. van den Broek and M. J. Vermaseren; Leiden, 1981) 171-189; *idem,* "Jewish Merkabah Mysticisim and Gnosticism", *Studies in Jewish Mysticism* (eds. J. Dan and F. Talmage; Cambridge, Mass., 1982) 47-55; *idem,* "Jewish Apocalypticism in the Rabbinic Period", *The Encyclopedia of Religion* 1 (ed. M. Eliade; New York, 1987) 336-342; *idem, From Apocalypticism to Gnosticism, Studies in Apocalypticism, Merkavah Mysticism, and Gnosticism* (New York and Paris, 1988).

⁵ D. J. Halperin, *The Merkabah in Rabbinic Literature* (New Haven, 1980); *idem, The Faces of the Chariot* (Tübingen, 1988); P. Schäfer, "Tradition and Redaction in Hekhalot Literature, *JSJ* 14 (1983); *idem,* "The Aim and Purpose of Early Jewish Mysticism", in his *Hekhalot-Studien,* Texte und Studien zum Antiken Judentum 19 (Tübingen, 1988); *idem,* "Merkavah Mysticism and Rabbinic Judaism", *JAOS* 104 (1984) 537-554; M. Himmelfarb, "Heavenly Ascent and the Relationship of the Apocalypses and the *Hekhalot* Literature", *HUCA* 59 (1988) 73-100.

⁶ C. Morray-Jones, *Merkabah Mysticism and Talmudic Tradition* (Ph.D.

Moreover, Morray-Jones has demonstrated that within these visionary circles of early Jewish mysticism, it was believed that exceptionally righteous or worthy humans would be transformed into the divine upon gaining a vision of God. The paradigms for such transformations were the transformations of the heros of the heavenly ascent narratives such as Moses, Ezekiel, and Enoch as well as the Jewish tradition that the righteous would be transformed in the world to come.[7]

It is my contention that indeed the Merkavah mysticism of the Hekhalot materials finds its lineage in the Jewish apocalyptic traditions especially now that a relationship between Christianity, Jewish apocalypticism, and Merkavah mysticism has been documented.[8] As suggested by these recent studies on Christianity and Jewish mysticism, it seems that during the first century, mystical notions about ascent and gazing on God or his Glory had filtered into Christianity via developing Jewish apocalyptic and mystical circles. It is probable that it was filtering into Rabbinism simultaneously. Thus, it can plausibly be argued that Merkavah mysticism is steeped with early Jewish mystical and apocalyptic notions. For this reason, the rabbinic and Hekhalot texts are valuable to the study of Christianity's interface with early Jewish mysticism.

When the term "early Jewish mysticism" is employed in this study, it is understood to mean esoteric and mystical notions about visionary ascent that were expressed in the Jewish apocalyptic literature and that were influencing various Jewish, Christian, and

---

Dissertation, University of Cambridge, 1988); *idem*, "Hekhalot Literature and Talmudic Tradition: Alexander's Three Test Cases", *JSJ* 22 (1991) 1-39; *idem*, "The Body of the Glory: *Shi'ur Qomah* and Transformational Mysticism in the Epistle to the Ephesians", forthcoming.

[7] For detailed arguments, see C. Morray-Jones, "Transformational Mysticism in the Apocalyptic-Merkabah Tradition", *JJS* 48 (1992) 13ff. Refer also to M. Lieb, *The Visionary Mode: Biblical Prophecy, Hermeneutics, and Cultural Change* (London, 1991), esp. 54, 59-60, 76, 94.

[8] C. Rowland, *The Open Heaven: A Study of Apocalyptic in Judaism and Early Christianity* (New York, 1982); Fossum, *Name; idem*, "Jewish-Christian Christology", 260-287; *idem*, "Magharians", 303-344; *idem*, "Colossians", 183-201; G. Stroumsa, "Form(s) of God: Some Notes on Metatron and Christ", *HTR* 76 (1985) 269-288; A. F. Segal, *Paul the Convert: The Apostolate and Apostasy of Saul the Pharisee* (New Haven and London, 1990) 34-71; C. Morray-Jones, "Paradise Revisited (2 Cor. 12.1-12): The Jewish Mystical Background of Paul's Apostolate", "Part 1: The Jewish Sources", *HTR* 86:2 (1993) 177-217, and "Part 2: Paul's Heavenly Ascent and its Significance", *HTR* 86:3 (1993) 265-292 ; *idem*, "The Body of the Glory".

Gnostic sects, as well as some of the Tannaim. Early Jewish mysticism is not to be equated with Merkavah mysticism. Rather it should be understood that Merkavah mysticism inherits much from early Jewish mysticism as do Christianity, Gnosticism, and various Jewish sects. Early Jewish mysticism is best defined as an esoteric tendency within Second Temple Judaism which was characterized by speculation about ascent into heaven and gaining a transforming vision of the *kavod*. This esoteric tendency can not only be seen in the vision speculations in the Jewish apocalyptic literature, but also in sectarian Judaism, and in the Philonic corpus.

b) *Mysticism and Jewish Sectarianism:*[9]
   i) The Therapeutae:

The Jewish sect of the Therapeutae serves as a striking example of a first century group involved in vision quests. According to Philo, the Therapeutae are ideal Jewish mystics who seek to ascend and gain a vision of God (*De vita. Con.* 11): "But it is well that the Therapeutae, a people always taught from the first to use their sight, should desire the vision of the Existent and soar above the sun of our senses (τὸ δὲ θεραπευτικὸν γένος βλέπειν ἀεὶ προδιδασκόμενον τῆς τοῦ ὄντος θέας ἐφιέσθω καὶ τὸν αἰσθητὸν ἥλιον ὑπερβαινέτω)".[10]

These Jewish mystics led a severely ascetic lifestyle probably in preparation for their vision quests. They voluntarily abandoned their propery, possessions, and family in favor of a solitary existence in the countryside (13, 18, 20 ff.). Because their primary concern was "self-control (ἐγκράτειαν)" (34)[11] they adhered to strict dietary and fasting regulations (34-37, 73-74) and had no concern for their outward appearance (38). Furthermore, voluntary virginity and spiritual marriage were prefered over sexual activity and

---

[9] I employ the term "sectarian" in the same manner as J. D. Cohen, *From the Maccabees to the Mishnah* (Philadelphia, 1987), who uses it to express the diversity of Judaism in the first century. See also, L. H. Schiffman, *From Text to Tradition: A History of the Second Temple and Rabbinic Judaism* (Hoboken, New Jersey, 1991) who uses "sectarian" to speak about the pluralism of Judaism in this time period. There is a recent substantial treatment of this question by J. T. Sanders, *Schismatics, Sectarians, Dissidents, Deviants: The First One Hundred Years of Jewish-Christian Relations* (Valley Forge, 1993) which arrived too late for my evaluation. Thus it seems that the use of "sectarian" to describe first-century Jewish pluralism is in the process of being discussed.

[10] F. H. Colson and G. H. Whitaker, *Philo* 9 (Cambridge, Mass., 1941 and reprints) 118-119.

[11] *Ibid.*, 132-133.

carnal marriage (68).¹² We are told that because they adhere to such an austere program, they are fit to live "in the soul alone" and are called "citizens of Heaven (οὐρανοῦ πολιτῶν)" (90).¹³ Thus they seem to have believed themselves to be transformed into angelic beings, possibly as the result of their vision quests.

ii) The Qumranites:
Recently, M. Smith published a fascinating discovery: 4Q491, a fragmentary poem from Qumran in which the author claims to have been taken up and seated in heaven, "reckoned with gods and established in the holy congregation".¹⁴ This evidence supports Smith's earlier argument that mystical ascents to heaven were characteristic of the Qumran sect.

He has based this argument in the past on the fact that the Qumranites insist that they belong to the angelic congregation (*Hymns* 6.13f.; 3.20ff.; 11.10ff.; *frag.* 2.10; *Manual of Discipline* 11.5-10). Moreover, Josephus, when referring to the Essenes, states that they "immortalize (ἀθανατίζουσι) the souls, thinking the approach of the righteous to be much fought over" (*Ant.* 18.18). Smith connects the terminology "immortalize" with the ascent experience since the *Mithras Liturgy* describes visionary ascent by employing the cognate "immortalization (ἀπαθανατισμός) (PGM 4.741, 747, 771)".¹⁵ Already Bousset, Smith notes, had remarked that Josephus' observation concerning "the approach of the righteous" which is "much fought over" probably refers to the angelic opposition encountered by the Essenes who attempted to enter the heavens; thus, the Essenes were eager to know all of the angels' names which served as passwords for the journey.¹⁶ Furthermore, similarities between the Hekhalot hymns and the liturgical texts of the Qumran sect are striking, indicating that the Qumranites were attempting to ecstatically experience communion with the angels before

---

¹² On this subject, see the excellent discussion by R. A. Horsley, "Spiritual Marriage with Sophia", *VC* 33 (1979) 40-43.
¹³ *Ibid.*, 168-169.
¹⁴ M. Smith, "Two Ascended to Heaven – Jesus and the Author of 4Q491", *Jesus and the Dead Sea Scrolls* (ed. J. H. Charlesworth; New York, 1992) 290-301. Cf. Eph 2:6 where God "raised us up with him, and made us sit with him in the heavenly places in Christ Jesus" (cp. 1:26).
¹⁵ H. D. Betz, *The Greek Magical Papyri in Translation Including the Demotic Spells* (Chicago, 1986) 52-53.
¹⁶ Bousset, "Himmelsreise", 143.

God's Throne in the heavenly Temple.[17] Taken together, Smith concludes that the evidence suggests that the Qumranites were involved in mystical ascent.[18]

If Smith is correct, and it appears that he is, then we have further evidence for a Jewish sectarian group practicing ascent who, like the Therapeutae, were also severe ascetics practicing voluntary celibacy, communal possessions, fasting, vigils, behavioral restrictions, and strict observance of the Law.[19]

It is the argument of this thesis that the esoteric mystic tendency of these sectarian groups went hand in hand with their ascetic lifestyle. In other words, it seems that these groups partook of the notion that the vision-seeker was required to purify himself through ascetic behaviors in order to achieve a successful vision.

c) *Mysticism and the Philonic Corpus:*
Philo of Alexandria's corpus has been the focus of a vast amount of scholarship.[20] The relationship of Philo to an esoteric mystical

---

[17] J. Strugnell, "The Angelic Liturgy", *VTSup* 7 (Leiden, 1960) 318-345, esp. 341 where the term "merkavah" is employed; Scholem, *Jewish Gnosticism,* 29, 128; L. Schiffman, "Merkavah Speculation at Qumran", *Mystics, Philosophers and Politicians* (eds. J. Reinharz and D. Swetschinski; Durham, North Carolina, 1982) 15-47; C. Newsom, *Songs of the Sabbath Sacrifice* (Atlanta, 1985); and *idem,* "Merkavah Exegesis in the Qumran Sabbath Shirot", *JSJ* 38 (1987) 11-30.

[18] M. Smith, *Clement of Alexandria and a Secret Gospel of Mark* (Cambridge, Mass., 1973) 239-240; and *idem,* "Ascent to the Heavens and the Beginning of Christianity", *Eranos* 50 (1981) 411-412.

[19] For various treatments on the issue of celibacy at Qumran, see A. Marx, "Les racines du célibat essénien", *RQ* 7 (1970) 323-42; A. Guillaumont, "À propos du célibat des Esséniens", *Hommages à André Dupont-Sommer* (Paris, 1971) 395-404; H. Hübner, "Zölibat in Qumran?", *NTS* 17 (1971) 153-67; J. Coppens, "Le célibat essénien", *Qumran, sa piété, sa théologie et son milieu* (ed. M. Delcor; Paris, 1978); L. H. Schiffman, *Sectarian Law in the Dead Sea Scrolls: Courts, Testimony, and the Penal Code,* BJS 33 (Chico, 1983) 13, 19, 214-215.

[20] For research through 1936, see H. L. Goodhart and E. R. Goodenough, "A Bibliography of Philo", *The Politics of Philo Judaeus* (ed. E. R. Goodenough; New Haven, 1938) 130-321; from 1937-1959, see L. H. Feldman, "Scholarship on Philo and Josephus (1937-59)", *Classical World* 54 (1960/61) 281-91, and 51 (1961/62) 36-39; more recently, refer to E. Hilgert, *Studia Philonica* 1 (1972) 57-71, 2 (1973) 55-73, 3 (1974/75) 117-125, 4 (1976/77) 79-85, 5 (1978) 113-120, 6 (1979/80) 197-200; A. V. Nazzano, *Recenti Studi Filoniani (1963-70),* (Napoli, 1973); and P. Borgen, "Philo of Alexandria. A Critical and synthetical survey of research since World War II", *ANRW* 2.21.1 (Berlin, 1984) 98-154; see now also the literature cited by D. M. Scholer in his introduction to *The Works of Philo, New Updated Edition* (trans. C. D. Yonge; Peabody, Mass., 1993) xvii-xviii. And D. T. Runia, *Philo of Alexandria: An Annotated Bibliography, 1937-1986* (Leiden, 1992).

tradition has been the subject of some of this research. As early as 1919, H. Leisegang interpreted Philo against the background of Greek mysticism and the mystery cults.[21] Separately, E. Bréhier and J. Pascher compared Philo's mysticism to that of the Egyptian cult.[22]

E. R. Goodenough is the greatest advocate of the position that Philo's mysticism was associated with the mystery cults.[23] He laid stress on the fact that Philo's mysticism did not originate with his association with the mystery cults. Rather there had emerged at this time the tendency for Hellenistic Judaism to regard itself as a mystery. Goodenough summarizes his position by explaining that the Jews before Philo "were captivated by their neighbors' religion and thought"[24] and syncreticism was common. Thus Moses was syncretized with Orpheus and Hermes-Tat, while Sophia the Jewish Wisdom figure was identified with the mother-goddess Isis. "All that now needed to be done was to develop sufficient skill in allegory and the Torah could be represented as the ἱερὸς λόγος *par excellence*, whereby Judaism was at once transformed into the greatest, the only true, Mystery".[25] According to Goodenough, this transformation had taken place by Philo's time. Salvation was a mystic experience now, where man was to overcome the world of passions, rise above the created universe and the senses, and climb the mystic ladder of the Light-Stream to the Absolute God himself.[26]

The major criticism that has been lodged against Goodenough's thesis is that his attempts to demonstrate that there existed an anti-rabbinic Judaism across the Roman world that was grounded in the rites and ideas of a mystery, have failed.[27] His work, however,

---

[21] H. Leisegang, *Der Heilige Geist* 1:1 (Berlin, 1919); idem, "Philon", *PW* 20,1 (Stuttgart, 1941) cols. 1-50.

[22] E. Bréhier, *Les idées philosophiques et religieuses de Philon d'Alexandrie* (Paris, 1908); J. Pascher, 'Η Βασιλικὴ 'Οδός, *der Königsweg zu Wiedergeburt und Vergöttung bei Philon von Alexandrien* (Paderborn, 1931).

[23] E. R. Goodenough, *By Light, By Light* (New Haven, 1935); idem, *The Politics of Philo Judaeus* (New Haven, 1938); idem, *An Introduction to Philo Judaeus* (New Haven, 1940); idem, *Jewish Symbols in the Greco-Roman Period*, 1-13 (New York, 1953-68); idem, "Philo Judaeus", *IDB* 3 (New York, 1962) 796-99.

[24] *By Light*, 7.

[25] *Ibid.*, 7.

[26] *Ibid.*, 7.

[27] Borgen, "Philo", 140; M. Smith, "Goodenough's 'Jewish Symbols' in retrospect", *JBL* 86 (1967) 53-68. Other theses have formed in criticism of Goodenough: for instance, S. Sandmel contends that "Philo's view of Judaism

has left an indelible mark on Philonic interpretation: it is most probable that Philo and a mystical tendency were linked.[28] The question now seems to be: what variety of mysticism?

There is a growing opinion among scholars that Philo's mysticism may have been influenced by an early form of Jewish mysticism. Goodenough was aware of G. Scholem's work, *Major Trends in Jewish Mysticism*, and complains that "Scholem treats these [Jewish mystical texts] with little reference to Philo",[29] but he, himself, never ventured to connect the two either. He took the stand that it would be the task of the next generation of scholars to explore Merkabah mysticism in connection with Philo's writings.[30]

Several interesting studies have been made to this end. Already K. Kohler determined that elements of Merkavah mysticism can be found in Philo.[31] Moreover, H. Chadwick has suggested that agreements between Paul and Philo may be the result of a common background in Jewish mysticism.[32] This suggestion is quite feasible now that recent research on Paul has demonstrated Paul's familarity with mystical Judaism.[33]

---

differs from that of the rabbis as philosophical mysticism based on the Bible differs from halakic legalism" and "as contrastable with normative rabbinic Judaism, Philo and his associates reflect a marginal, aberrative version of Judaism which existed at a time when there were many versions of Judaism", in *Philo's Place in Judaism: A Study of Conceptions of Abraham in Jewish Literature* (New York, 1956; aug. ed. 1971) 211; see also *idem, Philo of Alexandria: An Introduction* (New York, 1979) 140-147. H. A. Wolfson argued that Philo borrowed terms and ideas from popular religion and myth because it was common terminology, not because Philo's Judaism was, in reality, a mystery; so Philo is best understood as presenting a system of religious philosophy derived from Pharisaic Judaism, in *Philo* 1 (Cambridge, Mass., 1947) 45-46; no one takes this position today.

[28] Cf. the excellent summary of Philo's mysticism by D. Winston, "Was Philo a Mystic?", *Studies in Jewish Mysticism, Proceedings of Regional Conferences Held at the University of California, Los Angeles and McGill University in April, 1978* (eds. J. Dan and F. Talmage; Cambridge, Mass.; 1982) 15-39.

[29] *Jewish Symbols* 1, 8.

[30] According to P. Borgen's conversation with Goodenough, "God's Agent in the Fourth Gospel", *Religions in Antiquity, Essays in Memory of Erwin Ramsdell Goodenough*, Studies in the History of Religions 14 (ed. J. Neusner; Leiden, 1968) 148.

[31] K. Kohler, "Merkabah", *The Jewish Encyclopedia* 8 (ed. I. Singer; New York, 1904) 500.

[32] H. Chadwick, "St. Paul and Philo of Alexandria", *BJRL* 48 (1966) 286-307.

[33] Segal, *Paul the Convert*, 34-71; C. Morray-Jones, "Paradise Revisited".

In P. Borgen's monograph *Bread from Heaven*, he states that Merkavah mysticism and Philo share the notion of a heavenly figure, Israel, "the one who sees God".[34] Also, he states that both Philo and mystical Judaism "combine ideas of heavenly beings, concepts and vision with moral/legal ideas and precepts".[35] Borgen also observes that several features of Jewish mysticism have been Platonized or Stoicized by Philo.[36] This is supported by W. Meeks who concludes that when Philo describes Moses' shared kingship with God in *Vita Mos*. 1.155-158, he is relying on Jewish exegesis and mystical ideas about heavenly ascent and kingship; these Jewish traditions are in turn Platonized and Stoicized by Philo.[37]

Without doubt, much more investigation needs to be made on the relationship between Philo and Jewish mysticism.[38] At present, based on the research that has been done on this relationship, it is plausible to conclude that Philo's writings were indebted to this esoteric tendency within Judaism. It would seem that Philo is another representative of the presence of early Jewish mysticism in the first century. In Philo's writings, however, we discover that this early mystical tendency has congealed with at least Platonism and Stoicism, if not also possibly Hermeticism.[39]

---

[34] P. Borgen, *Bread From Heaven*, NTSup 10 (Leiden, 1965) 177; idem, "God's Agent", 137-148. M. Smith, "On the Shape of God and the Humanity of Gentiles", *Religions in Antiquity. Essays in Memory of Erwin Ramsdell Goodenough* (ed. J. Neusner; Leiden, 1968) 315-326. The angel Israel is described in other texts similarly: Origen, *In Jon.* 2.31; Justin Martyr, *Dial.* 75.2; *Orig. World* 105.20-25; for occurrences in a Coptic magical papyrus, see A. M. Kropp, *Ausgewählte koptische Zaubertexte* 1 (Bruxelles, 1930) 48.

[35] "Philo", 153.

[36] P. Borgen, "Some Jewish exegetical traditions as background for Son of Man sayings in John's Gospel (John 3:13-14 and context), *ETL* (1977) 243-58.

[37] W. A. Meeks, *The Prophet-King*, NTSup 14 (Leiden, 1967) 192-195; idem, "Moses as God and King", *Religions and Antiquity*, Studies in the History of Religions, *NumenSup* 14 (ed. J. Neusner; Leiden, 1968) 354ff.

[38] Segal, "Heavenly Ascent", 1354-1359, addresses the importance of ascent and vision in the Philonic corpus.

[39] R. Reitzenstein, *Poimandres* (Leipzig, 1906) is of the opinion that Philo was influenced by Hermeticism; J. Kroll, *Die Lehren des Hermes Trismegistos*, Beiträge zur Geschichte der Philosophie und Theologie des Mittelalters 12.2.4 (Münster, 1914), opposes Reitzenstein, arguing that Philo's Logos-doctrine was the source for Hermeticism's. C. H. Dodd, *The Interpretation of the Fourth Gospel* (Cambridge, 1968) 54-73, discusses possible thematic connections between Hermeticism and Philo. Betz notes the similarity of the interpretation of the Delphic maxim in Philo and Hermeticism, "The Delphic Maxim ...in Hermetic Interpretation", 477-482.

2) *Early Jewish Mysticism and Thomas:*

It is apparent that during the Second Temple Period, an esoteric tendency was developing and manifesting itself within different varieties of Judaism including the Philonic corpus, the sectarian communities of the Therapeutae and Qumran, apocalyptic circles, and rabbinic teachings. This early Jewish mysticism filtered into Christianity, Gnosticism, and the Hekhalot literature, teaching that, after proper preparations, one could seek to ascend into heaven in order to gain heavenly knowledge and a transforming vision of the deity.

Hermeticism also promoted a form of vision mysticism which seems to have been interfacing with this esoteric Jewish tradition since both philosophical and theurgical Hermeticism taught that the vision of God was a transforming experience. M. Smith noted this in the early sixties when he argued that the famous *Mithras Liturgy* (PGM 4.475ff.), which refers to immortalization through the process of a heavenly journey and the subsequent face-to-face encounter with the deity, Helios, has affinities with the Hekhalot materials.[40] Smith's conclusions are quite plausible especially since other studies have indicated that Jewish teachings have been absorbed in some Hermetic texts.[41]

---

[40] See Smith, "Hekhalot Rabbati", 158-160; Cf. A. F. Segal, "Hellenistic Magic: Some Questions of Definition", *Studies in Gnosticism and Hellenistic Religions, presented to Gilles Quispel on the Occasion of his 65th Birthday*, EPRO 91 (eds. R. Van den Broek and M. J. Vermaseren; Leiden, 1981) 353-355. Cf. PGM Va.1-3 refers to the visionary transformation when the magician is brought into union with the deity: "'O Helios [magical words], bring me into union with you' (add the usual). Then anoint yourself, and you will have a direct vision".

Although the bulk of the Greek magical papyri were written from the third to sixth centuries CE, the material contained therein achieved its essential form by the first century CE according to A. D. Nock, "Greek Magical Papyri", *Essays on Religion and the Ancient World* 1 (ed. Z. Stewart; Cambridge, Mass., 1972) 187. Several texts actually date from the last centuries BCE on palaeographical evidence; these papyri are referenced by D. E. Aune, "The Apocalypse of John and Graeco-Roman Revelatory Magic", *NTS* 33 (1987) 495 n. 10.

The Greek magical papyri are collected by K. Preisendanz, *Papyri Graecae Magicae. Die Griechischen Zauberpapyri*, 3 volumes (new ed. A. Henrichs; Stuttgart, 1973-74). For the majority of the Demotic magical papyri, see F. L. Griffith and H. Thompson, *The Leyden Papyrus: An Egyptian Magical Book* (London, 1904; New York, 1974). A new translation of this magical material is now available in Betz, *Greek Magical Papyri*; a collection of Coptic magical texts have been recently translated in *Ancient Christian Magic: Coptic Texts of Ritual Power* (eds. M. Meyer and R. Smith; San Francisco, 1994).

[41] H. Ludin Jansen, "Die Frage nach Tendenz und Verfasserschaft im

The *Gospel of Thomas* contains several Logia which notably focus on these same motifs: ascent into heaven and the subsequent transforming vision. The origins of this tradition in early Jewish mysticism and Hermeticism requires exploration, especially since the religious perspective of ascent back to the divine has often been used to justify the Gnostic heritage of *Thomas*. Furthermore, it is only when these origins are apprehended accurately that *Thomas* can be located more precisely in the history of religions. The implications that this has for interpreting the ideology of this gospel are paramount, to say the least, and is the ultimate goal of this monograph.

In Part Two, therefore, I will begin by exploring the motif of ascent which I will argue is assumed by Logion 50. Parallels in early Christian literature tell us that this Jesus saying was understood by the believers to be a fragment of ascent lore which teaches that it is necessary for the human to return to his divine origin, the Light, by ascending through the heavenly spheres. Logion 50 represents the verbal exchange that was thought to have occurred at one of the spheres between the angelic guards and the aspirant.

In Part Three, I will analyze the Logia in *Thomas* which are associated with the themes of vision and transformation against the background of parallel teachings in early Jewish mysticism and Hermeticism. The Logia central to this vision mysticism are: the vision of the deity or its manifestation (L. 15, 27, 37, 59, and 83); transformation into the divine (L. 13, 82, and 108); Self-knowledge (L. 3b, 56, 67, 80, 111b); and the vision of the "images" (L. 84).

The implications that this analysis into *Thomas*' background has for G. Quispel's three-source theory and the theology of the *Gospel of Thomas* will be summarized in Part Four, the conclusion. This background provides the author of *Thomas* with the foundation stones to build his scheme of Christian soteriology, a scheme in which the believer is responsible for his own salvation by seeking to see God. When he achieves this *visio Dei*, the believer is translated from the fate of death to life. He has left this world and entered God's Kingdom.

Poimandres", *Proceedings of the International Colloquium on Gnosticism, Stockholm, August 20-25, 1973*, KVHAH, Filol.-filos. ser., 17 (eds. G. Widengren and D. Hellholm; Stockholm, 1977) 157ff.; B. A. Pearson, "Jewish Elements in Corpus Hermeticum I (Poimandres)", *Studies in Gnosticism and Hellenistic Religions presented to Gilles Quispel on the Occasion of his 65th Birthday*, EPRO 91 (Leiden, 1981) 336-348.

PART TWO

ASCENT LORE IN *THOMAS:* LOGION 50

CHAPTER THREE

THE TRIAD OF QUESTIONS IN LOGION 50
AND MYSTICAL ASCENT

In the *Gospel of Thomas*, an enigmatic Logion appears which structurally consists of an early triad of questions and answers. This Jesus saying, Logion 50, reads:

ⲡⲉϫⲉ ⲓ̅ⲥ̅ ϫⲉ ⲉⲩϣⲁⲛϫⲟⲟⲥ ⲛⲏⲧⲛ̅ ϫⲉ ⲛ̅ⲧⲁⲧⲉⲧⲛ̅ϣⲱⲡⲉ ⲉⲃⲟⲗ ⲧⲱⲛ
ϫⲟⲟⲥ ⲛⲁⲩ ϫⲉ ⲛ̅ⲧⲁⲛⲉⲓ ⲉⲃⲟⲗ ϩⲙ̅ ⲡⲟⲩⲟⲉⲓⲛ ⲡⲙⲁ ⲉⲛⲧⲁ ⲡⲟⲩⲟⲉⲓⲛ
ϣⲱⲡⲉ ⲙ̅ⲙⲁⲩ ⲉⲃⲟⲗ ϩⲓⲧⲟⲟⲧϥ̅ ⲟⲩⲁⲁⲧϥ̅ ⲁϥⲱϩⲣ[ⲉ ⲉⲣⲁⲧϥ] ⲁⲩⲱ
ⲁϥⲟⲩⲱⲛϩ ⲉ[ⲃ]ⲟⲗ ϩⲛ̅ ⲧⲟⲩϩⲓⲕⲱⲛ ⲉⲩϣⲁϫⲟⲟⲥ ⲛⲏⲧⲛ̅ ϫⲉ ⲛ̅ⲧⲱⲧⲛ̅ ⲡⲉ
ϫⲟⲟⲥ ϫⲉ ⲁⲛⲟⲛ ⲛⲉϥϣⲏⲣⲉ ⲁⲩⲱ ⲁⲛⲟⲛ ⲛ̅ⲥⲱⲧⲡ̅ ⲙ̅ⲡⲉⲓⲱⲧ ⲉⲧⲟⲛϩ
ⲉⲩϣⲁⲛϫⲛⲉ ⲧⲏⲩⲧⲛ̅ ϫⲉ ⲟⲩ ⲡⲉ ⲡⲙⲁⲉⲓⲛ ⲙ̅ⲡⲉⲧⲛ̅ⲉⲓⲱⲧ ⲉⲧϩⲛ̅ ⲧⲏⲩⲧⲛ̅
ϫⲟⲟⲥ ⲉⲣⲟⲟⲩ ϫⲉ ⲟⲩⲕⲓⲙ ⲡⲉ ⲙⲛ̅ ⲟⲩⲁⲛⲁⲡⲁⲩⲥⲓⲥ

> Jesus said:
> "If they say to you,
> 'Where did you come from?',
> say to them,
> 'We came from the light',
>
> (the place where the light came into being on its
> own accord and established [itself] and became
> manifest through their image).
>
> If they say to you, 'Is it you?',
> say
> 'We are its children,
> and we are the elect of the Living Father.'
>
> If they ask you,
> 'What is the sign of your Father in you?',
> say to them,
> 'It is movement and repose.'"[1]

Because the *Gospel of Thomas* is a collection of sayings, the context of Logion 50 has not been preserved. Scholars have conjectured about this context, proposing hypotheses ranging from Hellenistic

---

[1] B. Layton, *Nag Hammadi Codex II, 2-7 together with XII, 2 Brit. Lib. Or. 4926 (1), and P. Oxy. 1, 654,, 655 1: Gospel According to Thomas, Gospel According to Philip, Hypostasis of the Archons, and Indexes*, NHS 20 (Leiden, 1989) 72; Eng. trans. by Lambdin, 73; punctuation my own.

catechetical literature to a historical community dispute. Moreover, not surprisingly, it has been noted in some commentaries written on the *Gospel of Thomas* that Logion 50 has affinities with a number of passages in Gnostic writings (Iren., *Adv. Haer.* 1.21.5; Epiph., *Pan.* 36.3.2-6, 26.13.2-3; *1 Apoc. Jas.* 33.11-34.1; *Gos. Mary* 15-17;[2] *Apoc. Paul* 22.24-23.26).[3] Thus these scholars have assumed that, even though Logion 50 does not explicitly mention post-mortem ascent, it must allude to the gnostic belief that when the believer dies and his soul ascends back to the Pleroma, he can anticipate being questioned by the archons. This argument is strengthened, they add, by the fact that the preceding Logion (49) speaks about returning to the Kingdom.

Unless the dispute over the context of Logion 50 can be resolved, the purpose and meaning of this saying for *Thomas* will remain an enigma. Thus an exploration into the *Sitz im Leben* of Logion 50 is in order especially since no one has noted yet that this Logion also has striking affinities with fragments of pre-mortem ascent lore from the Jewish mystical tradition and passages from texts influenced by this tradition. Moreover, it should be recognized that Logion 49, although clearly advocating ascent to the Kingdom, can be read as a reference to mystical ascent as well as post-mortem ascent.

1) *The Catechismal Paradigm:*

According to F. Fallon and R. Cameron, the questions in Logion 50 may reflect in part the Hellenistic catechismal technique of the philosophers. They have stated that "one might relate it (Logion 50) to the catechetical type of instruction literature widespread in

---

[2] E. Haenchen drew attention to a gnostic *Tendenz* in Logion 50 in his *Die Botschaft des Thomas-Evangeliums*, Theologische Bibliothek Töpelmann 6 (Berlin, 1961) 39-41, 44. J.-E. Ménard, *L'Évangile selon Thomas*, NHS 5 (Leiden, 1875) 153, includes *Pistis Sophia* 186,18-189,4 along with the texts listed above. R. Kasser, *L'Évangile selon Thomas: Présentation et commentaire théologique*, Bibliotèque Théologique (Neuchâtel, 1961) 78-79, refers also to the Gnostic texts *Pistis Sophia* 186,18-189,4 and the *Gospel of Mary* 15-17.

I do not include *Pistis Sophia* in the following discussion because, not only is it a very late gnostic text making it impossible for Logion 50 to be dependent on this text, but 186,18-189,4 does not contain questions or answers of any sort and can not be considered a parallel to Logion 50.

[3] W. R. Murdock and G. W. MacRae, "The Apocalypse of Paul", *Nag Hammadi Codices V,2-5 and VI with Papyrus Berolinensis 8502, 1 and 4*, NHS 11 (ed. D. M. Parrott; Leiden, 1979) 49.

antiquity".[4] They make no attempt, however, to prove or even discuss this statement. Apparently, they are refering to the mode of teaching among the philosophers which was based on the creation of dialogues by posing rhetorical questions which could then be followed by a discourse of doctrine.

A. Norden, in his monumental work *Agnostos Theos*, has collected passages from the philosophers which can be associated with the question of one's true identity.[5] Of particular importance to the exegesis of the questions in Logion 50 is a passage from Seneca.[6] In *Epistle* 82.6, Seneca teaches that the soul can be released from the bond of "Fate (*fortuna*)" because "she can seize none except him that clings to her". But this release from the clutches of Fate is only made possible "through knowledge of the self and of the world of nature (*quod sola praestabit sui naturaeque cognitio*)". Thus:

> *Sciat, quo iturus sit, unde ortus, quod illi bonum, quod malum sit, quid petat, quid evitet,...*
>
> The soul should know whither it is going and whence it came, what is good for it and what is evil, what it seeks and what it avoids,...[7]

In this passage, we find the Hellenistic philosophical tenet that it is necessary to be released from the captivity of Fate who has seized and thus controls one's destiny. The only way to do this, according to Seneca, is to have knowledge of the truth of the origin and destiny of one's soul.

The Hermetic literature, probably influenced by Hellenistic philosophy, contains abundant references to the catechismal format of questions and answers. But, in this literature the mortal is the one who asks the questions of the god rather than as we find in Logion 50 where the one who is questioned is clearly the mortal. These enquiries include topics ranging from the nature of incorporeality (*C.H.* 2.12), god (*C.H.* 2.12), and deification (*C.H.* 10.7), to the way to gain life (*C.H.* 1.21) and to know the Father (*C.H.* 14.4).

---

[4] F. T. Fallon and R. Cameron, "The Gospel of Thomas: A Forschungsbericht and Analysis", *ANRW* 2.25.6 (New York, 1988) 4209.

[5] E. Norden, *Agnostos Theos: Untersuchungen zur Formengeschichte Religiöser Rede* (Berlin, 1913) 95-109.

[6] *Ibid.*, 103.

[7] R. M. Gummere, *Seneca, Ad Lucilium Epistulae Morales* 2, LCL (Cambridge, Mass., 1920 and reprints) 242-243.

Since knowledge of one's divinity guaranteed one's deification according to Hermeticism, these questions and answers were vital.

It seems that enquiries into one's origin and nature were not uncommon in the Hellenistic world and were even encouraged since it was believed that this knowledge either insured success in overcoming Fate, as Seneca relates, or in becoming divine as the Hermetic literature dictates.

Furthermore, it seems that these types of questions filtered into Jewish tradition. Philonic discourse contains an impressive passage in *De Cherubim* 114 which attempts to answer the vital questions of origins and destiny:

> πόθεν δὲ ἦλθεν ἡ ψυχή, ποῖ δὲ χωρήσει, πόσον δὲ χρόνον ἡμῖν ὁμοδίαιτος ἔσται; τίς δέ ἐστι τὴν οὐσίαν ἔχομεν εἰπεῖν; πότε δὲ καὶ ἐκτησάμεθα αὐτήν; πρὸ γενέσεως; ἀλλ' οὐχ ὑπήρχομεν. μετὰ τὸν θάνατον;

> Whence came the soul, whither will it go, how long will it be our mate and comrade? Can we tell its essential nature? When did we get it? Before birth? But then there was no "ourselves". What of it after death?[8]

These questions are followed with his Hermetic-like teaching that the soul is God's possession and that "it is the master's custom, when he will, to take back his own" (*ibid.*, 118).

Concern over these questions surfaces in the Rabbinic tradition as well. In the Mishnah *Aboth* 3.1, the first century rabbi 'Aqabiah ben Mahalaleel says:

> Consider three things and thou wilt not come into the hands of transgression. Know whence thou comest; and whither thou art going; and before whom thou art about to give account and reckoning. Know whence thou comest: from a fetid drop, and whither thou art going: to worm and maggot..."

According to this text, knowing the proper answer to these questions insures that you do not fall into "the hands of transgression". So it seems, here again, we see that knowing one's origins and destiny has a redemptive purpose.

Ben 'Azai comments on 'Aqabiah ben Mahalaleel in *Derekh Eres Rabba* 3. His interpretation of the origin and destiny of man is equally dismal:

---

[8] F. H. Colson and G. H. Whitaker, *Philo* 2, *LCL* 227 (Cambridge, Mass., 1927 and reprints) 76-77.

Whence did he come? From a place of darkness; and whither is he going? To a place of darkness and gloom. Whence did he come? From an impure place; and whither is he going? To defile other people,...⁹

Contrary to this view is the one preserved in a medieval Rabbinic commentary. The soul is asked, "Whence comest thou?" and responds, "Hewn from the Throne of Glory". The soul is asked, "Whither art thou going?" and responds, "Returning to God whence the soul was taken..."¹⁰ Even though this text is comparably recent, it is probably preserving a primitive answer to these questions since both views seem to be conflated in *Aboth de-R. Nathan* 2.32:

> Rabbi Simeon ben Ele'azar said: "Whence did he come? From a place of fire, and he returns to a place of fire. And whence did he come? From a place of compression, and he returns to a place of compression [that is, the grave]..."¹¹

S. Lieberman argues that the notion that man comes from God's fire and will return to it is an "old orthodox saying referring to the soul", but because the Gnostics appropriated this tradition, the rabbis reacted against it, generally building up the tradition of man's lowly nature instead of his exalted one.¹² There is much more fluidity between Judaism and Gnosticism than Lieberman's argument allows. Thus his argument cannot establish the primitive nature of this saying. It is significant, however, that the notion that humanity's origin is the light or fire to which humanity will return is shared by many ancient traditions including Hermeticism, Gnosticism, Judaism, and Christianity.¹³ Thus it does seem to be a quite primitive and widespread belief.

Questions about one's origins seem to be behind passages in at least two Valentinian texts. We find in the *Gospel of Truth* the following aphorism: "He who possesses Gnosis knows whence he is come and where he is going" (22.13-14). Or the often-quoted passage from the *Excerpts of Theodotus* 78.2 where liberation is described as:

---

⁹ M. Higger, *Massekhtot Derkh Erez* (1935) 155.
¹⁰ מנחה חדשה a,1,28a; quoted in S. Lieberman, "How Much Greek in Jewish Palestine?", *Biblical and Other Studies*, Studies and Texts 1 (ed. A. Altmann; Cambridge, Mass., 1963) 136.
¹¹ S. Schechter, מסכת אבות דרבי נתן בשתי נוסאות, Versions A and B (Vienna, 1887, reprinted New York, 1945) 35a.
¹² Lieberman, "How Much Greek", 137.
¹³ For a discussion of this, refer to Chapter Four, Section 2a.

ἡ γνῶσις, τίνες ἦμεν, τί γεγόναμεν. ποῦ ἦμεν, ἢ ποῦ ἐνεβλήθημεν. ποῦ σπεύδομεν, πόθεν λυτρούμεθα. τί γέννησις, τί ἀναγέννησις.

the knowledge of who we were, and what we have become, where we were or where we were placed, whither we hasten, from what we are redeemed, what birth is and what rebirth.[14]

Non-gnostic Christian texts also exhibit answers to the questions of one's origin. For instance, in the *Teachings of Silvanus*[15] 4.92.10f., we read:

But before everything else, know your origin. Know yourself, from what substance you are and from what race and from what tribe.

Additionally, the redemptive quality of this knowledge is brought out in the Greek *Acts of Thomas* chapter 15 (cp. c. 34) where the Bridegroom states that he has been shown "how to seek myself and know who I was, and who and in what manner I now am, that I may again become that which I was".[16] Thus, knowledge of one's origins brings about a return to the original primordial state.[17]

---

[14] R. P. Casey, *The Excerpta ex Theodoto of Clement of Alexandria*, SD (London, 1934) 88-89.

G. Widengren, *The Gnostic Attitude* (trans. B. A. Pearson; Santa Barbara, 1973) 12-14, has suggested an Iranian background for these questions and answers found in *Exc. ex Theod.* 78.2; cf. his article, "Der iranische Hintergrund der Gnosis", *ZRGG* 2 (1952), 103-104. He refers to *Pandnamak* section 3.5, but this is a late Pahlavi text. Widengren suggests that the Iranian origin is to be found in a much earlier passage, *Yasna* 43.7-8. Widengren does not quote the text itself. This text, however, is not a solid parallel to Logion 50, since its context is not the ascent of the soul to the otherwordly realm; rather this is a unique revelation granted to the prophet Zarathustra. *Yasna* 43.7-8 reads: "When he came to me as Good Mind and asked me: 'Who art thou, whose art thou? Shall I appoint by a sign the days when inquiry shall be made about thy living possessions and thyself?' I made answer to him: 'I am Zarathustra, first, a true enemy to the wicked with all my might, but a powerful support for the righteous, so that I may attain the future blessings of the absolute Dominion by praising and singing then, O Wise One!'" (J. Duchesne-Guillemin, *The Hymns of Zarathustra. Being a Translation of the Gathas together with Introduction and Commentary* [London, 1952] 135).

[15] Regarding the Jewish-Christian background to this text, see the excellent study by J. Zandee, "'The Teachings of Silvanus' (NHC VII, 4) and Jewish Christianity", *Studies in Gnosticism and Hellenistic Religions, Presented to Gilles Quispel on the Occasion of his 65th Birthday*, EPRO 91 (eds. R. van den Broek and M. J. Vermaseren; Leiden; 1981) 498ff.

[16] A. F. J. Klijn, *The Acts of Thomas. Introduction-Text- Commentary*, NTSup 5 (Leiden, 1962) 198.

[17] This idea is present in other texts including the *Acts of Andrew* c. 6 (L.B. II I, p. 40, 25-26), *Apostolic Constitutions* 7.33.4, 6.39.2, Gregory of Nyssa, *de prof. Christ.* (PG 46,c.243), Origen, *comm. Cant.* 2.143.2.

The questions in Logion 50 are similar to a universal philosophical catechismal tradition among the Hellenistic schools and Hermeticism where rhetorical questions served as foils for discourse. We discover that the question of one's origin was particularly important because this knowledge was believed to have a redemptive quality. These types of questions and ideas seem to have filtered into Judaism, early Christian and later gnostic literature.

Yet, even if Logion 50 is indebted to this philosophical tradition, something unique has occurred in this saying. These philosophical questions are not posed rhetorically for catechismal purposes. They are serious test questions intended to discover the true identity of the one being questioned. It seems that the Greek philosophical tradition is not enough to explain the origins of the questions in Logion 50.

2) *Community Dispute:*

Apparently, M. Lelyveld recognized the fact that these questions were not simply rhetorical foils for the discourse of doctrine. She posed the theory that these were serious questions which developed out of the historical separation of the Christian community from the Jewish one. The interrogators are the Jews, while those being instructed on how to respond to the interrogators represent the Christian community.[18]

Although this hypothesis is a fascinating interpretation of Logion 50, it does not resolve some very significant points. First of all, it is next to impossible to find references, in early Christian literature, to opponents posing these types of questions to the Christians. Lelyveld strains to find such corresponding questions elsewhere when she refers to Mark 6:2. But clearly here the questions are aimed at Jesus and his authority, not the early Christians themselves. Furthermore, the questions are quite different from Logion 50:

    1) "Where did this man get all this?"
    2) "What is the wisdom given to him?"

Moreover, these questions are followed, not by a third question, but by an exclamation attempting to explain *why* the Jews are even

---

[18] M. Lelyveld, *Les Logia de la Vie dans L'Évangile selon Thomas: A la Recherche d'une Tradition et d'une Rédaction*, NHS 34 (Leiden, 1987) 99-112.

questioning Jesus at all: "What mighty works are wrought by his hands!".

Second, these questions do not sound like the real questions that the Jews would have asked the Christians during those strained times. There would have been no need to have asked the Christians where they came from. Even more perplexing is the postulation that a group of Jews would have asked the Christians, "Is it you?", or "What is the sign?".

The question that needs to be seriously considered in this case is: What is the *Sitz im Leben* in which these questions make the *most* sense? To answer this question, I will argue that we need to explore two themes: interrogations of the soul at death and interrogation during mystical ascent.

3) *Interrogations of the Soul at Death:*

The ancient Egyptian belief that the soul can expect to be interrogated when it attempts to pass through the seven "Arits" or forts may form part of the background to Logion 50, especially by way of the questions. According to the Egyptian *Book of the Dead*, at each "Arit" there were stationed three gods: a doorkeeper, a watchmen, and a herald who interview the arriving soul (c. CXLIV, CXLVI, CXLVII).[19]

This type of interrogation is displayed vividly in chapter CXXV where the soul attempts to pass through the Hall of Maati. It is said of the gods there: "They say unto me, 'Who art thou?'" and they ask, "'What is thy name'?" (CXXV.21).[20] Moreover, the gods insist that the soul recite their names before they will open the gates to him (CXXV.27-37).[21] Only then is the soul allowed passage to come before the god Osiris. Thus Thoth gives the commandment to the soul: "Advance now, [thy name] shall be announced to him" (CXXV.44).[22]

The purpose of the interrogation is to access the identity of the

---

[19] E. A. Wallis Budge, *The Book of the Dead: The Papyrus of Ani, Scribe and Treasurer of the Temples of Egypt, About B.C. 1450* 1 (New York and London, 1913 and reprints) 137, 268-274.

[20] E. A. Wallis Budge, *The Book of the Dead: The Papyrus of Ani, Scribe and Treasurer of the Temples of Egypt, About B.C. 1450* 2 (New York and London, 1913 and reprints) 589-590.

[21] *Ibid.*, 591-594.

[22] *Ibid.*, 595.

soul so that he may be properly introduced to Osiris. Moreover, by naming the gods, the soul demonstrates that he possesses the proper knowledge of the realm and therefore belongs there (CXXV.27). After he has demonstrated this, the soul's purity is questioned as well: the unclean soul will not be brought before the great god (CXXV.39-40). Thus the intent of the interrogation is threefold: to establish the actual identity of the soul; to see that the soul has the knowledge which will confirm that he belongs in this realm; and to demonstrate that the soul is in the state of purification necessary to stand before Osiris.

The Orphic grave plates attest to the tradition of soul interrogation as well. According to W. Guthrie, "the dead man is given those portions of his sacred literature which will instruct him how to behave when he finds himself on the road to the lower world. They tell him the way he is to go and the words he is to say".[23]

The plate of particular interest to the present discussion is plate 8 from Southern Italy and dates from the fourth or third century BCE. This plate relates that the soul is required to say to the "guardians" who are beside the "Lake of Memory" in the "House of Hades": "I am a child of Earth and starry Heaven; But my race is of Heaven (alone)".[24] In three parallel texts from the second century BCE found in Eleuthernai in Crete, the same formula is found, only now the questions of the guardians are preserved. The plates read: "Who art thou?...Whence art thou? - I am the son of Earth and starry Heaven".[25] Another text from Thessaly is comparable: "Who are you? Where are you from? I am a child of Earth and of starry Heaven, but my race is of Heaven (alone)".[26]

The early Christians seem to be aware of these ideas as can be detected in the second-century gnostic text, the *First Apocalypse of James* 33.2-34.20.[27] In this text, Jesus teaches James the proper responses to the angelic guards or "toll collectors (ⲧⲉⲗⲱⲛⲏⲥ)"

---

[23] W. Guthrie, *Orpheus and Greek Religion: A Study of the Orphic Movement* (New York, 1966) 172.
[24] *Ibid.*, 173.
[25] *Ibid.*, 173.
[26] Eng. trans. by M. W. Meyer, *The Ancient Mysteries: A Sourcebook. Sacred Texts of the Mystery Religions of the Ancient Mediterranean World* (San Francisco, 1987) 101, is based on the published edition by J. Breslin, *A Greek Prayer* (Malibu, n.d.); see also, G. Murray, "Critical Appendix on the Orphic Tablets", *Prolegomena to the Study of Greek Religion* (ed. J. Harrison; New York, 1959, 3rd ed.) 659-73.
[27] *Ibid.*, 67.

(33.8). These responses are to be used by James during his ascent following his martyrdom. Jesus explains that the guards "will arm themselves" (33.4) and that three of them "will seize you" (33.5). Then, the interrogation begins.

> When you come into their power, one of them who is their guard will say to you, "Who are you or where are you from?" You are to say to him, "I am a son, and I am from the Father." He will say to you, "What sort of son are you, and to what father do you belong?" You are to say to him, "I am from the Pre-existent Father, and a son in the Pre-existence One." [When he says] to you, [...], you are to [say to him,...] in the [...] that I might [...]. "[...of] alien things?" You are to say to him, "They are not entirely alien, but they are from Achamoth, who is the female. And these she produced as she brought down the race from the Pre-existent One. So then they are not alien, but they are ours. They are indeed ours because she who is mistress of them is from the Pre-existent One. At the same time they are alien because the Pre-existent One did not have intercourse with her, when she produced them." When he also says to you, "Where will you go?," you are to say to him, "To the place from which I have come, there shall I return." And if you say these things, you will escape their attacks.[28]

Some of the questions and responses taught by Jesus in this apocalypse are similar to those preserved in Logion 50 of *Thomas*. It is quite possible that this apocalypse is dependent here on Logion 50 or the sayings tradition behind it, reflecting a very primitive Jesus tradition in which Jesus imparts ascent wisdom to his disciples in the form of a triad of questions and responses. This triad of questions and responses addresses the issue of the origin of the mystic and his connections with the divine sphere.

This primitive triad has been expanded by the author of the *1 Apocalypse of James* to include a section of gnostic theology which addresses the issue of the divinity of the gnostic in relationship to Achamoth and the Pre-existent One (33.24-34.15). Structurally and thematically this section seems to be independent of the primitive triad of questions and responses. It is best understood as a late gnostic interpolation into an early Jesus tradition as found in Logion 50.

Comparable to Logion 50's version, "Where did you come from? (ⲚⲦⲀⲦⲈⲦⲚ̄ϢⲰⲠⲈ ⲈⲂⲞⲖ ⲦⲰⲚ)", the first triad of questions preserved in

---

[28] William R. Schoedel, "(First) Apocalypse of James", *Nag Hammadi Codices V, 2-5 and VI with Papyrus Berolinensis 8502, 1 and 4*, NHS 11 (ed. D. M. Parrott; Leiden, 1979) 85-89.

the *1 Apocalypse of James* focuses on the issue of identity. Thus Jesus explains that the chief guard will ask James, "Who are you or from where are you (ⲛ̅ⲧⲕ̅ ⲛⲓⲙ ⲏ ⲛ̅ⲧⲕ̅ ⲟⲩⲉⲃⲟⲗⲧⲱⲛ)?" (33.15). The author seems to be clarifying the original question "From where are you?" for his audience by introducing this question with another: "Who are you?" Thus, the author understands that one's identity is based on one's origins.

The second question posed by the guard is a more specific inquiry into James' connections with the heavenly realm: "What sort of son are you, and to what father do you belong (ⲛ̅ⲧⲕ̅ (ⲡⲁ)ⲁϣ ⲛ̅ϣⲏⲣⲉ ⲁⲩⲱ ⲛ̅ⲧⲕ̅ ⲡⲁⲛⲓⲙ ⲛ̅ⲉⲓⲱⲧ)?" (33.19-20). This question is reminiscent of the second question in Logion 50 which asks, "Is it you (ⲛ̅ⲧⲱⲧⲛ̅)?", especially when Logion 50's response is taken into consideration as well: "We are its sons and we are the elect of the living Father (ⲁⲛⲟⲛ ⲛⲉϥϣⲏⲣⲉ ⲁⲩⲱ ⲁⲛⲟⲛ ⲛ̅ⲥⲱⲧⲡ̅ ⲙ̅ⲡⲉⲓⲱⲧ ⲉⲧⲟⲛϩ)." It is plausible that the author of the *1 Apocalypse of James* is dependent upon Logion 50 or its source since the author is probably attempting to clarify the vague question from Logion 50, "Is it you?", by using material from this Logion's response to create a more direct question: "What sort of son are you, and to what father do you belong?" The author then creates the response to this question to forward his own gnostic theology. Thus Jesus teaches James to say that he is "from the Pre-existent Father (ⲟⲩⲉⲃⲟⲗ ϩⲙ̅ ⲡⲓⲱⲧ ⲉⲧⲣ̅ ϣⲟⲣⲡ̅ (ⲛ̅ϣⲟⲟⲡ))" (33.21-22) and is "a son in the Pre-existent One (ⲟⲩϣⲏⲣⲉ ⲉϥϩⲙ̅ ⲡⲉⲧ(ⲣ̅)ϣⲟⲣⲡ̅ ⲛ̅ϣⲟⲟⲡ)" (33.23-24).

The final question of the triad addresses James' ultimate ascent goal: "Where will you go (ⲉⲕⲛⲁⲃⲱⲕ ⲉⲧⲱⲛ)?" (34.16). James is told to respond in this manner: "To the place from which I have come there shall I return (ⲉⲡⲙⲁ ⲉⲧⲁⲓⲉⲓ ⲉⲃⲟⲗ ⲙ̅ⲙⲁⲩ ⲉⲓⲛⲁⲃⲱⲕ ⲟⲛ ⲉⲙⲁⲩ)" (34.17-18). Even though this question/response clause does not refer to a "sign" as Logion 50's version does, this clause seems to display knowledge of the preceding Logion 49 which states that the disciples are from the Kingdom and therefore will return to it:

ⲡⲉϫⲉ ⲓ̅ⲥ̅ ϫⲉ ϩⲉⲛⲙⲁⲕⲁⲣⲓⲟⲥ ⲛⲉ ⲛ̅ⲙⲟⲛⲁⲭⲟⲥ ⲁⲩⲱ ⲉⲧⲥⲟⲧⲡ ϫⲉ ⲧⲉⲧⲛⲁϩⲉ ⲁⲧⲙⲛ̅ⲧⲉⲣⲟ ϫⲉ ⲛ̅ⲧⲱⲧⲛ̅ ϩⲛ̅ⲉⲃⲟⲗ ⲛ̅ϩⲏⲧⲥ̅ ⲡⲁⲗⲓⲛ ⲉⲧⲉⲧⲛⲁⲃⲱⲕ ⲉⲙⲁⲩ

Jesus said, "Blessed are the solitary and elect, for you will find the Kingdom. For you are from it, and to it you will return.[29]

---

[29] Layton, *Nag Hammadi Codex II, 2-7*, 72; Eng. trans. by Lambdin, 73.

It is conceivable that the author of the *1 Apocalypse of James* was working from the same saying as that found in the *Gospel of Thomas* in the creation of this ascent triad. Instead of preserving this sayings tradition verbatim, he attempted to clarify the question/response clauses for his gnostic audience. Thus the vague "Is it you?" becomes "What sort of son are you, and to what father do you belong?", and the riddle-like "What is the sign of your father which is in you?" is changed to a more direct question, "Where will you go?", appended with a response built from Logion 49. Furthermore, we can see clearly that the author of the *1 Apocalypse of James* has "gnosticized" Logion 50 by introducing Gnostic theology and language about Achamoth and the Pre-existent One.

Both Irenaeus in his discussion of the Marcosians (*Adv. haer.* 1.21.5) and Epiphanius in his description of the Heracleonites (*Haer.* 36.3.1-2) provide parallels to the *1 Apocalypse of James* 33.21-34.18. The context provided by both heresiologists for this passage is that of the gnostic death rite. Thus, Jesus is no longer the spokesperson of the ascent-wisdom. In the rendition of Irenaeus and Epiphanius, it is the gnostics themselves who teach the necessary wisdom so that the deceased can successfully pass the examination of the guards and ascend above the worldly powers. The heresiologists no longer preserve the three primitive questions as found in the *1 Apocalypse of James* and Logion 50. They simply retain the responses.

> And they instruct them, on their reaching the principalities and powers, to make use of these words: "I am a son from the Father - the Father who had a pre-existence, and a son in Him who is pre-existent. I have come to behold all things, both those which belong to myself and others, but to Achamoth, who is female in nature, and made these things for herself. For I derive being from Him who is pre-existent, and I come again to my own place whence I went forth" (Iren., *Adv. haer.* 1.21.5).[30]

The first response, "I am a son from the Father - the Father who is pre-existent, and a son in Him who is pre-existent", reflects the *1 Apocalypse of James* 33.21-22 rather than Logion 50's simple answer, "We are its children, the elect of the Living Father". The mention

---

[30] For a convenient summary of the work in the context of the patristic traditions, see J. Quasten, *Patrology* 1 (Westminster; 1950) 288-313. For the text, see *Irénée de Lyon, Contre les Hérésies* II, SC 264 (eds. A. Rousseau and L. Doutreleau; Paris, 1979).

of Achamoth and the final clause "and I come again to my own place whence I went forth" provide further parallels to the *1 Apocalypse of James*. This suggests that the gnostics responsible for the passage preserved by Irenaeus and Epiphanius were aquainted with the version of this tradition in the *1 Apocalypse of James* rather than Logion 50.

Epiphanius in *Panarion* 26.13.2-3 records that in a gospel attributed to Philip, Jesus teaches ascent-wisdom. In this text, the soul is to declare that it has gained knowledge of itself and has not procreated with the archon; rather it has "pulled up his roots" and knows its divine origins. This passage, although witnessing to the theme that the soul will be required to answer questions when ascending, provides no true form or literary parallel to Logion 50.

Clearly, the Greek tradition as well as the Egyptian preserved the belief that the soul would be interrogated upon its journey to its place of rest at death. This notion seems to have influenced the gnostic understanding of the context of the parallels to Logion 50. Although these parallels to Logion 50 are striking, it must be emphasized that the references to the post-mortem context are secondary late additions to the Jesus saying itself. In the *Apocalypse of James*, the Jesus saying has been interpolated into the context of James' marytrdom, and in the patristic passages, it is the apologists who tell us that the context for this tradition was the gnostic death rite.

Thus we can not assume that Logion 50 in the *Gospel of Thomas* must reflect a post-mortem ascent as well. This is even more prominent when one realizes that, as I will discuss later, [31] elsewhere *Thomas* alludes to the journey to God as a mystical endeavor that occurs during the believer's lifetime (L. 59). Thus I argue that we must consider the possibility that Logion 50 is associated with the Jewish mystical tradition, specifically the teaching that the mystic will be interrogated during his pre-mortem ascent through the heavenly realms.

4) *Interrogations during Mystical Ascent:*

A large portion of the Jewish apocalyptic and Hekhalot literature is devoted to describing the ascent of several biblical heroes into the divine realm. These texts and characters include:

---

[31] See Chapter Five, Section 2.

1. Abraham (*Apocalypse of Abraham; Testament of Abraham*)
2. Adam (*Life of Adam and Eve* 25-28; *Apocalypse of Moses* 37-39)
3. Baruch (*3 Baruch*)
4. Enoch (*1 Enoch; 2 Enoch; 3 Enoch*)
5. Isaiah (*Ascension of Isaiah*)
6. Levi (*Testament of Levi* 2.6-5.3)
7. Isaac (*Testament of Isaac*)
8. Moses (*Assumption of Moses*)

As the hero seeks entrance to the heavenly realm, he often encounters angels who are hostile to his ascent. This infamous theme is probably associated with the tradition that the angels will question the aspirant since their hostility seems to extend from their insistence that humans in general are unworthy to be in the divine sphere.[32] This is quite vivid in *3 Enoch* where the angels object to the ascent of the human Enoch. Thus they pose several rhetorical questions before God: "What right has this one to ascend to the height of heights? Is he not descended from those who perished in the waters of the Flood? What right has he to be in heaven?" (4.7). As soon as Enoch reaches the "heavenly heights", the angels whine, posing their objections to God: "What is this smell of one born of a woman?[33] Why does a white drop ascend on high and serve among those who cleave the flames?" (5.2). The argument presented by the angels here is based on the terrestrial origin of Enoch: he was created out of the combination of a white drop of semen and a woman; thus he has no right to be in the fiery realms of heaven.

This hostility is referred to in the earlier *Apocalypse of Abraham*[34] where Abraham is told by Azazel that if he ascends to heaven, the angels will destroy him (13.6). In *Bavli Hagigah* 15b, the angels

---

[32] D. J. Halperin hypothesizes that behind the theme of angelic hostility lies the Lucifer myth (Isaiah 14.12-15) where, just as Lucifer was viewed as an "invader", so the one ascending is viewed as an "invader": "Ascension or Invasion: Implications of the Heavenly Journey in Ancient Judaism," *Religion* 18 (1988) 47-67.

[33] The expression, "one born of woman", is found in Job 14.1 and 15.14 where it is used to describe humanity's degraded condition; of the several cases where this phrase occurs, many are in the context of ascent; see Ginzberg, *The Legends of the Jews* 6: *Notes to Volume III and IV: From Moses into he Wilderness to Esther* (Philadelphia, 1928 and reprints) 57.

[34] This text is dated 70 CE to the mid-second century CE according to R. Rubinkiewicz in his introduction to this text in *OTP* 1, 683.

wanted to kill or drive away Rabbi Akiba from experiencing God's Glory. When Moses ascends to Heaven in order to receive the Torah, tradition tells us that he is afraid that the angels will burn him with their fiery breath (*Bavli Shabbat* 88b-89a) or that they will kill him (*Shemot Rabba* 42.4; cf. *Pesikta Rabbati* 96b-98a[35]). Again we find the refrain that because of Moses' humanity, he does not belong in heaven (*Bavli Shabbat* 88b-89a; *Gedullat Mosheh* 273).[36] In the *Hekhalot Fragments*[37] (lines 28-38), the danger facing the mystic is compared to the danger facing a man who is lost in a forest and who arrives at a place filled with beasts which lounge at him, threatening to rip him to pieces. It is most probable that the beasts represent the angels guarding the palace gates.

Thus severe dangers await the aspirant in the heavenly realms. The angels required him to pass elaborate tests and provide them with a secret incantation, password names, or recite an elaborate hymn (*Apoc. Abr.* 17-18; *Hekh. Rabb.* 1.1, 2.5-5.3, 16.4-25.6; *Hekh. Zutt.*, 413-415; *Bavli Hag.* 14b; *Ma'aseh Merk.* para. 9, 11, and 15). In fact, comparable to the question in Logion 50, "What is the sign?", in *Hekhalot Rabbati*, the angel Dumi'el stops the mystic at the sixth gate and demands a sign from him: "Show the seal".[38] It should be noted, however, that Dumi'el, asks for a physical sign rather than a verbal one. These were known as "seals" and were magical pictures which insured safe passage through the realms of heaven.[39]

Hermeticism may be influencing the tradition that secret passwords and incantations are required to thwart the angels'

---

[35] For the development of the term *mal'akei habbalah*, "angel of destruction", which occurs in this text, see I. Gruenwald, "Knowledge and Vision: Towards a Clarification of Their Alleged Origins", *Israel Oriental Studies* 3 (1973) 97 n. 36. See further, P. Schafer, *Rivalitat zwischen Engeln und Menschen* (Berlin, 1975) 128 ff.

[36] S. A. Wertheimer, *Batei-Midrašot* (Jerusalem, 1950) 273. For a complete discussion of these texts, see J. P. Schultz, "Angelic Opposition to the Ascension of Moses and the Revelation of the Law", *JQR* 61 (1971) 282-307.

[37] The *Hekhalot* Fragments are published by I. Gruenwald, "New Passages from *Hekhalot* Literature", *Tarbiz* 38 (1969) 354-372, and *Tarbiz* 39 (1970) 216-217; a summary of these fragments is contained in I. Gruenwald, *Apocalyptic and Merkavah Mysticism*, AGJU 14 (Leiden, 1980) 188-190.

[38] Gruenwald, *Apocalyptic and Merkavah Mysticism*, 166. Morton Smith offers a summary and discussion of this text: "Observations on Hekhalot Rabbati", *Biblical and Other Studies* (ed. Alexander Altmann; Cambridge, Mass., 1963) 142-160.

[39] Refer to G. Scholem, *Jewish Gnosticism, Merkavah Mysticism and Talmudic Tradition* (New York, 1960) 69ff.; K. Rudolph, *Gnosis* (trans. R. McL. Wilson; San Francisco, 1983) 172-174.

hostility. In the *Mithras Liturgy*,⁴⁰ when the mystic sees the gods staring and rushing at him, he is supposed to say: "Silence! Silence! Silence! Symbol of the living, incorruptible god! Guard me, Silence, NECHTHEIIR THANMELOU!". Then the mystic is supposed to make a hissing and popping noise⁴¹ and say these words: "PROPROPHEGGE MORIOS PROPHYR PROPHEGGE NEMETHIRE ARPSENTEN PITETMI MEOY ENARTH PHYRKECHO PSYRIDARIO TYRE PHILBA" (*PGM* 4.556-565).⁴² Each of the gods that he meets must be greeted with his appropriate Greek name (4.675-692).⁴³ In addition to immortal names, magical words are to be invoked (4.604-616).⁴⁴

It is plausible that Logion 50 is a primitive fragment associated with these traditions. Logion 50 teaches that when you ascend, you should anticipate opposition from the angelic guards who will demand to know your origin and a sign for verification that your claims are accurate. Their concern seems to be to determine whether or not you really belong in heaven. This tradition is structurally the same as the ascent motif found in Hekhalot texts although this latter tradition teaches that secret passwords, names, and hymns must be chanted and magical seals must be shown during the ascent in order to thwart the hostility of the angels.

The Jewish tradition is also aware of the tradition of angelic interrogation during mystic ascent. This can be seen in a passage from the *History of the Rechabites*.⁴⁵ When Zosimus successfully ascends to the shore of the Paradisiac island, he encounters one of the Blessed Ones, an Earthly Angel. This Earthly Angel is seated, posted as a guard whose duty it is to greet the arriving righteous and thwart the unworthy. The guard questions Zosimus about his

---

⁴⁰ Smith, "Observations", 158-159, sees the connections between the Hekhalot materials and the *Mithras Liturgy*.

⁴¹ For the meaning of the hissing and popping noises in magic, see R. Lasch, "Das Pfeifen und Schnalzen und seine Beziehung zu Dämonenglauben und Zauberei", *ARW* 18 (1915) 589-593; A. Dieterich, *Eine Mithrasliturgie* (Berlin, 1923) 40-43, 228-229.

⁴² H. D. Betz, *The Greek Magical Papyri in Translation Including the Demotic Spells* (Chicago, 1986) 49.

⁴³ *Ibid.*, 51.

⁴⁴ *Ibid.*, 50.

⁴⁵ This text is part of the Jewish portion of the *History of the Rechabites* and is dated to the second century CE according to Charlesworth in his introduction to this text, *OTP* 2, 444-445.

origin before he allows Zosimus access to the island: "Have you come from the world of vanity?" (5.1-2).

In the majority of the ascent stories in Jewish apocalyptic and mystical literature, however, the hero does not enter the sacred zone alone. Rather, he is escorted through the heavenly spheres by a prominent angelic figure. Thus:

1. Abraham by Iaoel (*Apocalypse of Abraham*) and by Michael (*Testament of Abraham*)
2. Adam by Michael (*Life of Adam and Eve* 25-28; *Apocalypse of Moses* 37-39)
3. Baruch by Phanael (*3 Baruch*)
4. Enoch by Uriel, Raguel, Michael, and Raphael (*1 Enoch*) by Samoila and Raguila (*2 Enoch*); Ishmael by Metatron (*3 Enoch*)
5. Isaiah by a "glorious angel" (*Ascension of Isaiah*)
6. Levi by an angel (*Testament of Levi* 2.6-5.3)
7. Isaac by Michael (*Testament of Isaac*)

Because the biblical hero is in the presence of an angelic escort, the hero is often allowed to pass unmolested through the heavenly gates (*Test. Abr.* 11, 12.4; *3 Bar* 11.1-6; *1 Enoch*; *2 Enoch* 3, 7, 8, 11, 18, 19, 20, 22; *Asc. Isa.* 7.13, 7.18, 7.24, 7.28, 7.32, 8.1, 8.16; *Test. Levi* 5.1-2).[46]

Therefore, it is *not* very frequent in this literature that we discover the angelic guards actually questioning the hero himself. But this theme is not completely absent either. For instance, this theme seems to be behind the Jewish mystical text in *3 Enoch* 2.[47] When Rabbi Ishmael reaches the Throne, the angelic guards pose a series of questions to Ishmael's escort, Metatron. These questions focus on Ishmael's worthiness to be in the divine realm: "Youth, why have you allowed one born of woman to come in and behold the chariot? From what nation is he? From what tribe? What is his character?" (2.2). These questions are comparable to

---

[46] Johann Maier observes that it is significant to the ascent experience as to whether or not the person has been invited by God to heaven; those who have been invited are not really endangered (apocalyptic literature) while those who choose to embark on the journey themselves will experience danger (Hekhalot texts): "Das Gefährdungsmotiv bei der Himmelsreise in der jüdischen Apokalyptik und 'Gnosis'," *Kairos* 5 (1963) 22-24, 28-30.

[47] Dated by P. S. Alexander to the time period between 450 CE to 850 CE in "The Historical Setting of the Hebrew Book of Enoch," *JJS* 28 (1977) 165.

those in Logion 50: "Where did you come from?", "Is it you?", and "What is the sign?". Obviously the questions in *3 Enoch* 2.2, as in Logion 50, are intended to reveal information about the origin of the mystic. In the case of *3 Enoch* 2.2, Ishmael's origin is questioned in order to determine whether or not he is worthy of entering the holiest realm of heaven.

Even though this text is rather late, the tradition that the angels question the aspirant is quite primitive and can be seen underneath Isaiah's remarks in the *Ascension of Isaiah* 10.28-29:[48] "no one questioned me because of the angel who led me". Supposedly, the one who is ascending will be questioned by the heavenly angels. Isaiah, however, is not questioned because he has an angel as an escort.[49]

Mystical ascent may be the proper context for a passage found in the second or third century Christian text contained in the Berlin Codex, the *Gospel of Mary*,[50] where Jesus the "Savior" is depicted as the teacher of ascent wisdom to Mary Magdalene. Starting on folio fifteen, the soul is said to be in dialogue with the powers which guard the heavenly realms. When the soul encounters Ignorance, the third Power, the question of the soul's destination is raised: "Where are you going? (ⲉⲣⲉⲃⲏⲕ ⲉⲧⲱⲛ) (15.14)". The fourth Power asks the soul: "Whence do you come?"(ⲉⲣⲉⲛⲏⲩ ⲍⲓⲛ ⲧⲱⲛ) (16.14) and "Where are you going? (ⲉⲣⲉⲃⲏⲕ ⲉⲧⲱⲛ)" (16.15). The focus of

---

[48] Isaiah's vision is dated to the second century CE or earlier according to M. A. Knibb in his introduction to this text in *OTP* 2, 150.

[49] It is interesting that even though Isaiah is escorted, when he is led into the seventh heaven, the angel in charge of the "praise of the sixth heaven" calls out the following question in protest: "How far is he who dwells in the flesh to go up?". This question, however, is not addressed to Isaiah.

[50] This text is dated to the second century CE according to Anne Pasquier, *L'Evangile selon Marie*, BCNH 10 (Quebec, 1983) 4; for discussions of this text, refer to W. C. Till, "Die Berliner gnostische Handschrift", *Europäischer Wissenschafts-Dienst* 4 (1944) 19-21; idem, *Die gnostischen Schriften des Koptischen Papyrus Berolinensis 8502*, TU 60 (Berlin, 1955; second edition, H. M. Schenke; Berlin, 1972); W. C. Till and G. P. Carratelli, "Εὐαγγέλιον κατα Μαρίαμ", *La parola de passato* 1 (1946) 260-265; R. McL. Wilson, "The New Testament in the Gnostic Gospel of Mary", *NTS* 3 (1956/57) 236-243; G. Quispel, "Das Hebräerevangelium im gnostischen Evangelium nach Maria", *VC* 11 (1957) 139-144; R. McL. Wilson and G. W. MacRae, "The Gospel according to Mary", *Nag Hammadi Codices V,2-5 and VI with Papyrus Berolinensis 8502, 1 and 4*, NHS 11 (ed. D. M. Parrott; Leiden, 1979) 453-471, (third century dating found on p. 454; all Coptic references are to this edition); and A. Pasquier, "L'eschatologie dans l'Évangile selon Marie: étude des notions de nature et d'image", *Colloque International sur les Textes de Nag Hammadi, Québec, 22-25 août 1978*, BCNH 1 (ed. B. Barc; Québec, 1981) 390-404.

these questions, as in *Thomas*, hinges on one's origins and thus one's right to return to the heavenly realms.

The responses in *Mary*, however, are completely different from those of Logion 50. It seems that the framework of ascent and interrogation are similar as well as the types of questions. But the parallelism between *Mary* and the Logion 50 tradition ceases here.

The Coptic Gnostic *Apocalypse of Paul* found among the Nag Hammadi writings shares in the mystical ascent traditions thus far described. It is a later development of Paul's pre-mortem ascent as refered to in 2 Corinthians 12:2-4. The author describes his vision of Paul's encounter with the angelic guard of the seventh heaven:

> The old man spoke, saying to [me], "Where are you going, Paul, O blessed one and the one who was set apart from his mother's womb?"...And I replied, saying to the old man, "I am going to the place from which I came." And the old man responded to me, "Where are you from?" But I replied, saying, "I am going down to the world of the dead in order to lead captive the captivity that was led captive in the captivity of Babylon." The old man replied to me, saying, "How will you be able to get away from me?..." [The] Spirit spoke, saying, "Give him [the] sign that you have, and [he will] open for you." And then I gave [him] the sign (22.24-23.26).[51]

Here the guard poses a series of questions to Paul, a series of questions probably reflecting knowledge of the same early triad as we find in *Thomas*. In the *Apocalypse of Paul*, this triad has been expanded and reworked narratologically.

The first question posed by the angelic guard to Paul concerns Paul's destination, "Where are you going, Paul (ⲉⲕⲛⲁⲃⲱⲕ ⲉⲧⲱⲛ ⲡⲁⲩⲗⲟⲥ)?" (23.2). Paul responds, "I am going to the place from which I came (ⲉⲓⲛⲁⲃⲱⲕ ⲉⲡⲧⲟⲡⲟⲥ ⲛ̄ⲧⲁⲓⲉⲓ ⲉⲃⲟⲗ ⲛ̄ϩⲏⲧϥ̄)" (23.9-10). This is similar to the ideas presented in Logion 49 where the disciple is told that he is from the Kingdom and will return to this place again (ⲛ̄ⲧⲱⲧⲛ̄ ϩⲛ̄ⲉⲃⲟⲗ ⲛ̄ϩⲏⲧⲥ̄ ⲡⲁⲗⲓⲛ ⲉⲧⲉⲧⲛⲁⲃⲱⲕ ⲉⲙⲁⲩ). The author of the *Apocalypse of Paul* may have created the question of destination and Paul's answer from the ideas set forth in Logion 49.

The angel then inquires, similar to the first question in Logion 50 (ⲛ̄ⲧⲁⲧⲉⲧⲛ̄ϣⲱⲡⲉ ⲉⲃⲟⲗ ⲧⲱⲛ), into Paul's origins: "Where are you from (ⲉⲕⲧⲱⲛ ⲡⲉ)?" (23.11). Paul responds in a riddle-like fashion designed to elevate Paul's wisdom above that of the angels.

---

[51] Murdock and MacRae, "The Apocalypse of Paul", 58-61. All Coptic references are taken from this edition.

The author of this apocalypse demonstrates knowledge of the final question in Logion 50's triad as well. He, like the author of the passage previously discussed in the *1 Apocalypse of James*, seems to be uncertain about the implications of this final clause, but, instead of eliminating it and substituting a different subject as the author of the *1 Apocalypse of James* did, this author attempts to clarify narratologically the final clause in Logion 50, "What is the sign (ⲟⲩ ⲡⲉ ⲡⲙⲁⲉⲓⲛ)?". Thus the angel asks Paul, "How will you be able to get away from me?". Paul's spiritual escort suggests, "Give him [the] sign that you have (ϯ ⲛⲁϥ ⲙ̄ [ⲡⲓ]ⲥⲏⲙⲁⲓⲟⲛ ⲉⲧⲛ̄ⲧⲟⲟⲧⲕ̄), and [he will] open for you" (23.23-24). Paul gives the angel "the sign", and the seventh gate is opened for Paul's safe passage.

Like the remark of Dumi'el in *Hekhalot Rabbati*, "Show the seal", this passage seems to understand the sign to be a physical sign rather than a verbal one (cp. Orphites according to Orig., *c. Cels.* 6.30, 7.40; *Apoc. Paul* 22.24-23.26; *Pis. Sophia*; 1 and 2 *Books of Jeu*; *Untitled Gnostic Treatise* [Bruce MS. 96]).[52] The *Apocalypse of Paul* shares in this understanding of signs and seems to interpret accordingly the tradition associated with Logion 50 where the "sign" is depicted as the proper verbal response. Thus Paul "gives" a sign to the angel.

5) *Conclusion:*

It can not be denied that the questions in Logion 50 have parallels in the Hellenistic catechismal tradition. But this is not enough to explain the way in which they are employed in Logion 50. Egyptian and Orphic traditions followed by some gnostic traditions preserve questions of one's origin and nature in the context of soul interrogation at death. These parallels are striking but they do not account for the fact that Logion 50 does not explicitly provide the context of death as the parallels do, nor the fact that other Logia in the *Gospel of Thomas* advocate a mystical ascent before death (cf. L. 59).

For this idea, we must turn to the Jewish mystical sources where we discover the motif that the mystic could expect the angelic

---

[52] On signs, see G. Scholem, *Major Trends in Jewish Mysticism* (New York, 1941) 50; idem, *Jewish Gnosticism*, 32-33; idem, "Über eine Formel in den Koptisch-gnostischen Schriften und ihren jüdischen Ursprung", *ZNW* 30 (1931) 170-176.

guards to be hostile and question his right and worthiness to be in heaven. Moreover, he could anticipate life-or-death tests to be administered by the angels. He had to memorize passwords and hymns in order to appease the guards of heaven and insure his safe passage.

Undoubtedly, Logion 50 reflects the notion that the soul will be asked questions when it ascends. This notion has been informed by early Jewish mysticism which also knew of the tradition that the unescorted mystic would be questioned by the angels. Logion 50 must represent a tradition, however, not yet aware of or affected by magical names and passwords as are the later *Mithras Liturgy*, gnostic texts, and Hekhalot materials.

In addition to concluding that L. 50 is an early Jesus tradition about ascent, it has been demonstrated that some later Gnostic texts display knowledge of this Jesus tradition. The authors of these later texts are redacting this sayings tradition for their own purposes, whether it be to provide a gnostic viewpoint about post-mortem ascent as in the *1 Apocalypse of James* or to create a smooth narrative about pre-mortem ascent as in the *Apocalypse of Paul*. In each case, it is the *Thomas* rendition that is the earliest and the least theologically manipulated.

This investigation suggests that the tradition responsible for Logion 50, and in some cases perhaps the *Gospel of Thomas* itself, was known and reinterpreted by the Gnostics for their own purposes. Gnostic use, however, does not demonstrate Gnostic origins or intent. Rather, it appears that only at a later date was Gnostic theology read into the non-gnostic Logion 50 by eclectic gnostic authors and teachers.

CHAPTER FOUR

THE TRIAD OF ANSWERS IN LOGION 50
AND TRADITION HISTORY

It was determined in the last chapter that Logion 50 makes *most* sense when it is understood as a fragment of early Christian ascent lore. It refered to the belief that it is necessary for the human to return to his divine origin, the Light, by ascending through the heavenly spheres. It is plausible that this notion was informed by early Jewish mysticism which taught that the heavenly realms are populated by angels whose purpose it is to guard the divine realm and to keep impure or unworthy aspirants from entering the sacred zone of heaven. Thus, at the entrance to each sphere, at least one, if not several, angelic guards are stationed whose duty it is to thwart the ascent of the mystic by testing the aspirant.

In Logion 50, the verbal exchange between angels and mystic at one of these levels is preserved. Jesus is providing his followers with three proper responses to three "test" questions posed by the angelic guards. If these responses are used during an ascent, the mystic is guaranteed an unresisted journey through the heaven.

M. Meyer, in his recent work, has summed up prior interpretations by scholars of these responses: the themes present in these responses have been used as evidence for the presence of a gnostic ideology in *Thomas*. Even though Meyer himself exercises caution in classifying *Thomas* as a Gnostic product, he writes the following about Logion 50: "Among these more mystical and gnosticizing sayings in Thomas is saying 50...Several features of this saying (answers to the powers, origin in the light, motion and rest) are typical of gnostic passages in other documents..."[1] F. Fallon and R. Cameron speak similarly regarding Logion 50: it reflects "at least implicitly, Gnostic speculative tendencies", even though "Gnostic mythology is not narrated in the Gos. Thom.".[2]

I have already pointed out the flaws in this type of derivative reasoning which seems to be weakly informed from the perspective

---

[1] M. Meyer, *The Gospel of Thomas: The Hidden Sayings of Jesus* (San Francisco, 1992) 12.
[2] Fallon and Cameron, "Gospel of Thomas", 4231.

of the history of religions. Thus I will precede by analyzing the themes in the responses against a broader contemporary religious context in order to aid in the task of determining the ideological milieu of *Thomas*.

1) *From the Light:*

Jesus argues in Logion 50 that his followers are to be allowed safe access to the heavens because their true origin is from the Light. This simple response has been redacted at some point in the history of the transmission of this saying in order to explain the light origin in more detail. Thus the Light is defined as "the place where the Light came into existence through its own agency" and "established itself", and that the Light "became manifest through their image". This expansion serves to explain to the reader that the Light is a primal self-generated entity. Moreover, the Light is pre-existent and is manifested during creation.

a) *Light as a Primal Entity:*
Several Jewish texts allude to the pre-existence of the "Light". *4 Ezra* 6.39 exegetes Genesis 1.3 as follows: "Then you [God] commanded that a ray of light be brought forth from your treasuries..." (cp. *2 Bar.* 59.11). The Light, according to this text, was not "created" by God's command, "Let there be light", but rather was manifested from his light treasury which apparently existed before creation.[3] Similarly, a Jewish liturgical text embedded in the seventh Apostolic Constitution proclaims that God brought "the light out of Thy treasures".[4]

Philonic interpretation also teaches of the existence of Light before creation. Philo, in *Quod Deus sit Immutabilis* 58, distinguishes between the "created light (φῶς γενητόν)" and a light that existed before creation. Philo explains that God did not need eyes "which have no power of perception without the light which meets our

---

[3] C. Rowland, *The Open Heaven: A Study of Apocalyptic in Judaism and Early Christianity* (London, 1982) 148; O. H. Steck, "Die Aufnahme von Genesis 1 in Jubilaen 2 und Esra 6," *JSJ* 8 (1977) 176; H. Conzelmann, "φῶς, etc.", *TDNT* 9 (1974) 324.

[4] Fragment 7, *Constitutiones* 8, xii, 9; translated by E. R. Goodenough, *By Light, Light* (New Haven, 1935) 321; edited and published by W. Bousset, "Eine judische Gebetssammlung im siebenten Buch der Apostolischen Konstitutionen," *Wilhelm Bousset, Religionsgeschichtliche Studien*, NTSup 50 (ed. A. F. Verheule; Leiden, 1979) 231-286.

sense. But that light is created, whereas God saw before creation, being Himself His own light".⁵ Notably in *De Cherubim* 97, Philo also claims that God can see the unseen because "He Himself is His own light". He expounds on this statement, explaining that "the eye of the Absolutely Existent needs no other light to effect perception, but He Himself is the archetypal essence of which myriads of rays are the effluence (ἀρχέτυπος αὐγὴ μυρίας ἀκτῖνας ἐκβάλλει)".⁶ Thus, according to Philo, God is the embodiment of the archetype of light, an archetype which apparently existed before creation.

In *De Opificio Mundi* 55, Philo refers to this primal light as the original "intellectual light (τοῦ νοητοῦ φωτὸς)".⁷ When Philo discusses the primal light in chapter 35 of the same text, he uses γίνομαι, to come into being, not γεννάω, to be born or created. Thus: "light came into being (φῶς ἐγένετο)".⁸ Philo seems to be referring to a teaching about the origin of an uncreated light, a light that existed with/as God prior to creation. At creation, this light came into being: it was manifested in creation. Philo explains: "Now that invisible light perceptible only by mind has come into being as an image of the Divine Logos (τὸ δὲ ἀόρατον καὶ νοητὸν φῶς ἐκεῖνο θείου λόγου γέγονεν εἰκὼν)" (*De Opif. Mundi* 31).⁹ The light, therefore, comes into being and is manifested in creation as the image of the Logos.

The description of creation in *2 Enoch* 24-25 lends evidence to a comparable tradition. In *2 Enoch* A 24.4, God explains that "before any visible things had come into existence, and the light had not yet opened up, I, in the midst of the light, moved around in the invisible things...". According to this text, the light is pre-existent; God is encompassed in this primal light. Then God commands that one of "the invisible things" become manifest visibly (J 25.1). Adoil, a man-like figure, descends with a great light in his stomach.¹⁰ Upon his disintegration, the light is released and God

---

⁵ F. H. Colson and G. H. Whitaker, *Philo* 3, LCL 247 (Cambridge, Mass., 1930 and reprints) 38-39.

⁶ F. H. Colson and G. H. Whitaker, *Philo* 2, LCL 227 (Cambridge, Mass., 1927 and reprints) 66-67.

⁷ F. H. Colson and G. H. Whitaker, *Philo* 1, LCL 226 (Cambridge, Mass., 1929 and reprints) 42-43.

⁸ *Ibid.*, 26-27.

⁹ *Ibid.*, 24-25.

¹⁰ For a summary of interpretations of the etymology of the name Adoil, refer to J. Fossum, *The Name of God and the Angel of the Lord*, WUNT 36

states that again He was in the midst of the great light (25.1-3). This great light is said to have "revealed" (version J) or "carried" (version A) "all the creation" in it (25.3) and "the foundation of the higher elements" (25.4) or the stars and constellations.

It is significant that the pre-existent Light is also known in Hermeticism where God is Light. Thus, in *Corpus Hermeticum* 1.6, Poimandres states: "I am the light you saw, mind, your god". This Light existed before creation (1.6) and is the "archetypal form, the preprinciple that exists before a beginning without end" (1.8).

b) *The Self-Generated Light:*
In addition to the primal Light, Logion 50 states that the Light originated "from its own agency". This is not a Jewish concept. Rather, it is rooted in the Hermetic construct of the "self-begotten" God.

In Hermeticism, the Father is generally understood to be "unbegotten". He is, for instance, described in *Corpus Hermeticum* 8.2 as eternal because he "exists through himself (αὐτὸς ἑαυτοῦ ἀίδιος)". The title attributed to him here is "unbegotten (ἀγέννητος)" (cf. *C.H.* 14.2). Moreover, it is clearly explained that the "Father did not come to be by another's agency (ὁ [πατὴρ] ὑπὸ ἑτέρου οὐκ ἐγένετο)"; rather "it was by his own agency (ὑφ' ἑαυτοῦ)".

Since the unbegotten Father originates from his own agency, we sometimes find that the Father is also called "self-begotten (αὐτογόνε)" (*Excerpts* of Stobaeus 23.58). Thus, fragments of Hermetica relate that God is without parents because he has been generated by none but himself (Lactantius, *Div. inst.* 1.6.4; *Epit.* 4.4). He is said to be "his own father (αὐτοπάτορα) and "his own mother (αὐτομήτορα)" (Lactantius, *Div. inst.* 4.8.5).

The Discourse on the Eighth and Ninth also mentions the "self-begotten one". But, in this case, he is the second hypostasis in a divine triad which consists of the unbegotten God, the self-begotten God, and the begotten God (ⲡⲁⲩⲧⲟⲅⲉⲛⲏⲧⲟⲥ [57.15-16]; ⲡⲁⲩⲧⲟⲅⲉⲛⲛⲏ‹ⲥ› [63.22]). J.-P. Mahé suggests that this should be connected to the

---

(Tübingen, 1985) 288-289; these interpretations include יד אל: "The Hand of God" (R. H. Charles, *The Apocrypha and Pseudepigrapha of the Old Testament* 2 [Oxford, 1913 and reprints] 455, n. *ad* 25.1 [long recension]); עד, "eternity", with the suffix -el (A. Vaillant, *Le livre des secrets d'Hénoch*, TIES 4 [Paris, second ed. 1976] xi); and *Adonai-el* (G. Quispel, "Hermeticism and the New Testament, especially Paul", *Religion: Gnostizismus und Verwandtes*, ANRW 2.22 [forthcoming]).

ancient tradition that the title "Trimegistos", "of three-fold greatness", means that the unified Godhead of the ineffable One consists of threefold powers of majesty.[11]

This Hermetic tradition illuminates God's description in the philosophical religious text, *Eugnostos the Blessed* (NHC III). According to this tractate, God is "immortal and eternal, having no birth (ⲟⲩⲁⲑⲁⲛⲁⲧⲟⲥ ⲡⲉ ⲟⲩϣⲁ ⲁⲛⲏ ϩⲉ ⲡⲉ ⲉⲙⲛ̄ⲧⲉϥ ϫⲡⲟ)" (71.18-20).[12] He is described as the "unbegotten (ⲟⲩⲁⲅⲉⲛⲛⲏⲧⲟⲥ)" (71.22)[13] who "sees himself within himself, like a mirror (ⲉϥⲛⲁⲩ ⲉⲣⲟϥ ⲙ̄ⲙⲓⲛ ⲙ̄ⲙⲟϥ ⲛ̄ϩⲣⲁⲓ ⲛ̄ϩⲏⲧϥ̄ ⲛ̄ⲑⲉ ⲛ̄ⲟⲩ ⲉⲓⲁⲗ)" (75.4-5)[14] and thus the "Self-Father (ⲛ̄ⲁⲩⲧⲟⲡⲁⲧⲱⲣ)" is in the likeness of the Fore-Father (75.6).[15] Thus he is called the "Self-Begetter (ⲡⲁⲩⲧⲟⲅⲉⲛⲉⲧⲱⲣ)" (75.7).[16] The Self-Begetter is described further in 76.15-19: "The First (ⲡⲉϩⲟⲩⲉⲓⲧ) who appeared before the universe in infinity is Self-grown (ⲟⲩⲁⲩⲧⲟⲫⲩⲏⲥ), Self-constructed Father (ⲛ̄ⲁⲩⲧⲟⲕⲧⲓⲥⲧⲟⲥ), and is full of shining, ineffable light (ⲉϥϫⲏⲕ ⲉⲃⲟⲗ ϩⲙ̄ ⲡⲟⲩⲟⲉⲓⲛ ⲉⲧⲣ̄ⲟⲩⲟⲉⲓⲛ)".[17] Thus we find here the motif of the self-generated God of Light!

c) *The Manifestation of Light into Human Beings:*

Logion 50 contains the perplexing statement that the Light became manifest "through their image (ϩⲛ̄ ⲧⲟⲩϩⲓⲕⲱⲛ)". How is this to be explained?

First, the antecedent of "their" must be understood. The phrase, "the place where the light came into being on its own accord and established [itself] and became manifest through their image", is a later explanation appended to the saying's original answer, "We came from the light". This signifies that "their" must refer to the interrogators themselves. In this case, the interrogators are the angels. The Light therefore manifests itself through the images of the angels into human beings.

It is not a motif unique to *Thomas* that man was created in the

---

[11] J.-P. Mahé, "La Voie d'Immortalité á la lumière des Hermetica de Nag Hammadi et de Découvertes plus Récentes", *VC* 45 (1991) 360.

[12] D. M. Parrott, *Nag Hammadi Codices III,3-4 and V,1 with Papyrus Berolinensis 8502,3 and Oxyrhynchus Papyrus 1081, Eugnostos and the Sophia of Jesus Christ*, NHS 27 (Leiden, 1991) 52.

[13] *Ibid.*, 52.
[14] *Ibid.*, 72.
[15] *Ibid.*, 72.
[16] *Ibid.*, 72.
[17] *Ibid.*, 80 and 82.

image of the angels.[18] There is a Rabbinic tradition to this effect. According to *Exodus Rabba* 30.16, "man was created in the form of the angels". This must be the meaning behind *Numbers Rabba* 16.24, where the statement that humans are like the immortal angels is prooftexted by Genesis 3:22 *and* Genesis 1:27:

> *I said: Ye are godlike beings, and all of you sons of the Most High* (Ps 82:6), like the ministering angels, who are immortal...*Behold, the man was as one of us* (Gen 3:22). Similarly, *And God created man in His own image* (Gen 1.27)...[19]

In the Samaritan Targum on Genesis 9:6, "for God made man in his own image", it is stated: "Have I not created man in the image of the angels?". This is probably a reference to the plural "*elohim*" in Genesis 1:26 where God commands, "Let *us* make man in *our* image" as well as a possible association with Genesis 3:22 where man has become "like one of us". It seems that Logion 50 is also to be associated with Genesis 1:26 since it states that the Light was manifested through a collective image.

The theology of Valentinus' pupil, Marcus, must also be discussed since here we find a heavenly figure manifested through "forms" or "angels". It was recognized in the 1920s by M. Gaster, that Marcus' theology is intimately related to the Jewish mystical literature and represented an early second century form of *Shiur Komah* speculation since Marcus' theology is based on speculation on the divine Name and its pronounciation as well as descriptions of God's mystical form.[20]

---

[18] Refer to J. Fossum, "Gen. 1,26 and 2,7 in Judaism, Samaritanism, and Gnosticism", *JSJ* 16 (1985) 202-239, esp. 214-215 and n.39. Other discussions of Genesis 1:26 include E. Sjöberg, "אדם בן und בר אנש im Hebräischen und Aramäischen", *Acta Orientalia* 21 (1950-1951) 57-65 and 91-107; R. McL. Wilson, "The Early History of the Exegesis of Gen. 1.26", TU 63 (1957).

[19] The Targum *Onkelos* Gen 1:27b, 5:1, and 9:6, seems to be teaching that man was created in the image of the angels since "Elohim" is not paraphrased, as is usually the case in *Onkelos*. Thus "Elohim" here is probably designating the angels. Man was created with four attributes of the angels according to *Genesis Rabba* 8.11; these attributes of the ministering angels include standing upright, speech, understanding, and sight. Moreover, we are told that the angels were "created in the image and likeness [of God]". Likewise the Holy One said, "Behold, I will create him [man] in [my] image and likeness, [so that he will partake] of the [character of the] celestial beings". Cf. *Mekhilta Bashallah* 7.73ff.

[20] M. Gaster, "Das Shiur Komah", *Studies and Texts in Folklore, Magic, Medieval Romance, Hebrew Apocrypha and Samaritan Archaeology* 2 (New York, 1971) 1343-1348; on this, see also G. Scholem, *On the Mystical Shape of the Godhead: Basic Concepts in the Kabbalah* (Foreword J. Dan; trans. J. Neugroschel;

Vital to the present discussion is Marcus' description of the genesis of human beings. According to Marcus:

> When, in the beginning, the fatherless father, who is neither grasped by the mind nor has a substance and who is neither man nor woman, wanted to express His ineffable being and make His invisible being visible, He opened his mouth and produced a word that resembled Him. In coming to him, it showed him that it was thereby becoming manifest as the shape of the invisible (Iren., *Adv. Haer.* 1.14.1; Epiph., *Pan.* 34.4.3).

Thus, God who is "neither man nor woman" made himself visible through sounding out particular letters of the alphabet. Furthermore, this primal human being, the Anthropos, is called the "body of truth" and is said to be made up of the "letters" or "forms" of the alphabet. These forms are the "angels" who are "continually beholding the Father's face" (Iren., *Adv. Haer.* 1.14.1; Epiph., *Pan.* 34.4.7). When this primal being pronounced "a word which resembled him", the divine Name of God, the invisible became manifest. The primal human being manifested sounds which were the forms of the angels. Thus humans were said to be emitted "in their image" (Iren., *Adv. Haer.* 1.13.6; Epiph., *Pan.* 34.3.7)![21]

d) *The Place of the Light:*
The notion in Logion 50 that the Light is from a particular "place (τοπος)" may also be reflecting Hermetic thought. According to Hermetic teaching, there exists an ungenerated "place (*locus*= τόπος)" in which the universe now is contained. Prior to creation, however, this place existed as an antecedent condition of the

---

ed. and revised according to 1976 Hebrew edition J. Chipman; New York, 1991) 25-28; G. Stroumsa, "Form(s) of God: Some Notes on Metatron and Christ", *HTR* 76 (1983) 280-281.

[21] The tradition that the Light was manifested through a singular image must be mentioned. In *Corpus Hermeticum* 1, God is Light (1.6; 1.12) who gives birth to a Man, the Anthropos, who had "the father's image" (1.12). Later, this light-image embraces the material world and takes on the human form (1.14). This is comparable to some Philonic passages in *De Opificio Mundi* previously mentioned. According to Philo, Light was pre-existent (35; 55). At creation, this primal Light manifested itself as "an image of the Divine Logos" (31). Moreover, man was created according to the divine image of this Logos (*Op. mund.* 25, 69, 139; *Leg. All.* 3.96; *Quis. rer.* 230-231; *Quaest. Gen.* 2.62; cf. *Fug.* 68-71). This tradition is also reflected in Satornil's myth where the first human being was a creation of the angels in response to the appearance of a luminous image. Thus they said to one another, "Let us create a human being after the image and after the likeness" (Iren., *Adv. Haer.* 1.24.1).

creation of the universe (Latin *Asclepius* 15). This "place" is "incorporeal" (*C.H.* 2.4). The *Excerpts* of Stobaei 24.8 relate that the souls "come from one place (ἐξ ἑνὸς οὖσαι χωρίου), that place where the Maker fashioned them". Interestingly they are described as "neither male nor female". Furthermore, at death, the soul returns to "its own proper place (ἐπὶ τὴν ἰδίαν χώραν)" (*Ibid.* 25.5). The heavens are divided into two spaces (*Ibid.* 25.9): the upper region is for the gods and stars; the space between the moon and the earth is the place for the souls. *Excerpt* 24.7 sums it up: "For the souls have certain places whence they came (αὗται τόπους ἔχουσιν ὅθεν ὡρμῶσι)". It is apparent that Hermeticism promoted the belief that the soul originated from a particular "place" and it would return to that place at death.

Thus, the *Gospel of Thomas* is probably reflecting these Hermetic ideas in Logion 50 where the human is said to originate from the "place" where the Light came into being. According to other passages in *Thomas*, it is clear that this "place" is a locale associated with the "life" and the divine world. In Logion 4, this place is called the "place of life (ⲡⲧⲟⲡⲟⲥ ⲙ̄ⲡⲱⲛϩ)": "The old man in days will not hesitate to ask a small child seven days old about the *place of life*, and he will live".

Jesus, according to Logion 24, now dwells in this place. The disciples ask Jesus to show them "the *place* (ⲡⲧⲟⲡⲟⲥ) where you are, for we must seek it". This "place", however, is not a place that one is going to return to at death, as Hermeticism teaches. Rather, it is a place that the disciples are apparently commanded to "seek" because they demand of Jesus in this Logion to show them the place where he is, since they must seek it. This suggests that Jesus, being the Light (L.77), has returned to this place through his ascent. Now, it is necessary for his followers to attempt the same by means of mystical ascent.

The tradition of practicing ascent to Jesus' heavenly "place" was apparently well-known in some Christian circles[22] because the *Apocryphon of James*, which does not seem to be gnostic, records that Jesus told his disciples: "I shall go to the place from which I have come. If you desire to come with me, come" (2.23 ff.). When Jesus finally ascends to the right hand of the Father (cf. Mark 14:62), Peter and James ascend with him for a short time,

---

[22] Cf. *1 Clem.* 5.4, 7; *Barn.* 19.1; *2 Clem.* 1.2; *Odes Sol.* 4.1-2; Tobit 3:6.

being called back to earth by the voices of the other disciples (14.21 ff.).

In Mandeism, it is explicitly stated that "the true and faithful Nazoreans will ascend and see the place of life" (*Ginza* p. 323, lines 13ff.). This is also found in the *Book of John* 236, line 26: the savior's disciples "ascend to the place of light". In the *Book of John* 244, the dwelling place for the righteous is the "place of light" while in the Mandean *Liturgy* 138, the savior leads the righteous to "the great place of light and the brilliant dwelling" (cf. *Lit.* 135; 226).

The *Dialogue of the Savior*, which seems to be based on a sayings source closely related to the older sayings tradition which appears in the *Gospel of Thomas*,[23] is in conversation with this type of mystical soteriological paradigm. The dialogue between Jesus and his disciples attempts to answer the question, "if a person has ascended, had a vision, and been deified, why does he still die?" (cf. 3, 65-68, 84-85). Thus Matthew wants to "see" the "place of life" where there is no "wickedness" but is the place of "pure [light]" (27). Jesus tells him that he will not be able to see this place as long as he is wearing the "flesh" (28; cp. L. 37). Jesus emphasizes that since Matthew is "from [that] place" then he will return to that place (34; cf. 38). Thus, the *Dialogue* states that even though the vision of the "Eternal Existent" is the "great vision", the deification can not be actualized until after one has died and discarded the body (31; cf. 52, 65-68, 84-85). It seems that the *Dialogue* promotes visionary ascent (36-44) with the qualification that the immortalization can not be complete until after death.[24]

The Gospel of John seems to contain a polemic against the mystical soteriological scheme such as we find in *Thomas*.[25] In 7.33-34, Jesus proclaims that he will be going to God and "you will seek me and you will not find me; where I am you cannot come". Jesus' proclamations are repeated by John: "I go away, and you will seek me and die in your sin; where I am going, you cannot come" (8.21); "Little children, yet a little while I am with you. You will seek me; and as I said to the Jews so now I say to you, 'Where

---

[23] H. Koester and E. Pagels, "Introduction", *Nag Hammadi Codex III,5. The Dialogue of the Savior*, NHS 26 (ed. S. Emmel; Leiden, 1984) 2-8.

[24] For a full discussion, refer to A. D. De Conick, "The *Dialogue of the Savior* and the Mystical Sayings of Jesus", *VC* 49 (1995).

[25] For a more thorough discussion of this theme, refer to my forthcoming article, "'Blessed are those who have not seen' (John 20:29): Johannine Polemic Against Ascent and Vision Mysticism".

I am going you cannot come'" (13.33); and "Simon Peter said to him, 'Lord, where are you going?' Jesus answered, 'Where I am going you cannot follow me now; but you shall follow afterward'" (13.36).

John is arguing against the type of insistence found in *Thomas* that one must actively seek to ascend to the place where Jesus is. Thus, John creates the construct that Jesus will go and "prepare a place (τόπον) for you" then "I will come again and will take you to myself, that where I am you may be also" (14.3). John may be attacking the ascent tradition found in the *Gospel of Thomas* when he has Thomas then confess: "Lord, we do not know where you are going; how can we know the way?" (14.5). Thus, for the Johannine community, *Thomas*' theology of mystical ascent is inoperative. John builds a case against *Thomas*' assertion that the followers must seek the place where Jesus now is, by transmitting that Jesus stated that it was impossible to follow him into heaven. John taught that Jesus will ascend, and when the place is made ready, he will return and retrieve his faithful to this prepared place.

2) *The Offspring of the Light:*

a) *Origin and Return:*
The second clause of Logion 50 further defines the relationship between the Thomasites and the Light. They are not only "from the Light" but they are "sons (ⲛⲉϥϣⲏⲣⲉ)" of the Light. Throughout the *Gospel of Thomas*, a strict dichotomy is established between the Light and the Darkness to the extent that there is developed here a very sectarian world view: the Thomasites are from the Light (L. 50), filled with the Light (L. 24, L. 60; cf. L.33), and will return to the Light (L. 11; or Kingdom/Heaven, L. 18, L. 19, L. 46, L. 49, L. 114); those who do not belong to this elect community, belong to the Light's antithesis, the Darkness (L. 24, L. 60; cf. L. 68). Furthermore, when the Thomasites return to the Light, they expect to gain a vision of the Light of the Father (L. 83).[26]

As R. Bultmann has shown in his excellent article on the history of light symbolism in antiquity, the dualistic worldview, where Light and Darkness are in opposition to each other, is well-developed in Hellenistic Greek philosophy and the Hellenistic

---

[26] Refer to Chapter Five, Section 1b, for further discussion.

mystery-religions.[27] Specifically, Light is synonymous with "life" and "spirit" and is associated with the Godhead and the heavens. Darkness, however, is equivalent with death and earthly existence. Furthermore, the true home of man's soul is the heavens and the Light to which he returns at death (cf. Sen., *Ep.* 102.22-23; *Cons. ad Helv.* 8.5-6; Plut., *de genio Socr.* 590bff.). Bultmann correctly argues that this dualism has been influenced by ancient Chaldaean theology which taught: "It behooves thee to hasten to the Light, and to the beams of the Father; From whence was sent to thee a soul clothed with much Mind" (*Chald. Or.*, 201-204).[28]

The Jewish traditions on this subject arguably were heirs to this Greco-Roman milieu. Furthermore, the dualistic and sectarian worldview present in the *Gospel of Thomas* seems to be grounded in the early Jewish tradition that a segment of humanity came from the Light. This special group of humans sometimes called themselves, "sons of light". Moreover, they expected to return to the Light either at death, during the eschatological finale, or through mystical transcendence.

Such themes are present in a striking passage in *1 Enoch* 108.11-14. Certain spirits are said to have been generated or "born of light", while others were "born in darkness" (v. 11). Those who belong to the light along with those from the dark who were faithful to God and loved his Name will be brought "into the bright light" (v. 12), apparently at the Eschaton. They will be "resplendent" (v. 13) for the ages. Furthermore they will see those who were "born in darkness" and who remained unrighteous, being taken "into darkness" (v. 14).

According to this text, a special segment of humanity is born from the Light, while the rest of humanity is generated from the darkness; each segment will return to its source at the eschatological finale. It is possible, however, to have been born in darkness and to escape one's dark destiny by becoming a righteous God-loving person. If one is righteous, one will then be transformed or "changed" (v. 11) and will partake of the future light. Thus it is stated: "But now you shall shine like the lights of heaven, and you

---

[27] R. Bultmann, "Zur Geschichte der Lichtsymbolik im Altertum", *Exegetica. Aufsätze zur Erforschung des Neuen Testaments* (ed. E. Dinkler; Tübingen, 1967) 323-355, esp. 342-355.

[28] T. Stanley, *The Chaldaean Oracles as Set Down by Julianus* (New Jersey, n.d.) 17.

shall be seen" (104.2-3). The righteous people, according to *1 Enoch* 58.2-6, expect to be in "the light of the sun" at the Eschaton; the elect will be engulfed in "the light of eternal life". Finally, "they shall seek light and find righteousness with the Lord of the Spirits...there shall be a light that has no end and they shall not have to count days (anymore)...".[29]

The Qumran community claimed special allegiance to the Light, calling themselves "sons of light".[30] This designation is connected to the motif that their origin was the Light.[31]

In *QS* 3.19-21, 24-25, we find a passage in which the "generations of truth" are born from "a spring of light". These people are the "sons of righteousness" and they are led by the "prince of lights". Furthermore, they walk in "the ways of light". Thus God and his "angel of truth" help the "sons of light". In opposition to the "sons of light" are the "generations of injustice" who spring forth from the "well of darkness". The "angel of darkness" controls them so that they walk in the "ways of darkness".[32]

A rigid and dualistic outlook is promoted by the Qumran sect:

---

[29] *2 Baruch* 51.3 contains a comparable view of the End when the righteous will be transformed: "the shape of their face will be changed into the light of their beauty". Futhermore, according to this passage, the righteous will become like "the angels and be equal to the stars" (cp. Dan. 12.3; *2 Enoch* 66.7; *4 Ezra* 7.97), their light changing into "the splendor of glory".

[30] See *1QS* 1.9, 2.16, 3.13, 3.24, 3.25; *1QM* 1.3, 1.9, 1.11, 1.13, 1.16; *4QCat^9* 12+ 1.7, 1.11; *4QFl* 1+ 1.19; *4Q510* 1 1.7.

[31] H. Lichtenberger, *Studien zum Menschenbild in Texten der Qumrangemeinde*, SUNT 15 (Göttingen, 1980) 130 n. 31, notes that the usage of the title "sons of light" by the Qumranites is fundamentally connected with their origin, essence, and future; he associates 1 *QS* 3.17ff. with Gen. 1:3-5; thus, he says, the Qumranites understand this designation in a different way from the manner in which it is used in other texts where it means that certain people are living in accordance with the Light (i.e., *Test. Job 43.6*; Lk 16:8; Jn 12:26; 1 Thess 5:5; Eph 5:8; Ign., *Phild.* 2.1; *Apoc. Jas.* 25.17; *Keph.* 37.19, 58.1ff., 163.30ff., 191.21; *Ginza* R 10.11; L 451.6). Lichtenberger includes *1 Enoch* 108.11 in this list too. But, as I have argued above, this passage is comparable to 1 *QS* 3.17ff. since it speaks of a group of people who are born from the Light.

[32] See Sir 33.7-15 where God creates both good men and evil men; also Sir 42.24 where God creates everything in opposite pairs; *Test. Asher* 1.3-6.6; *Barn.* speaks of the Way of Light v. the Way of Darkness (18-21); *Didache* 1-6 speaks of the Way of Life v. the Way of Death. This is based on biblical tradition which states that God set two ways before man: Deut 11:26ff., 30:15ff.; Ps 1, 119:1; Prov 2:13ff.; cf. 1:15; 4:14. There are two spirits in whose ways men walk: 1 *QS* 3.18-19, 25-4.26; cf. *Test. Judah* 20.1; Hermas, *Mand.* 5.1.2ff.; 2.5. In *Ps. Clem. Hom.* 20.2-3, the two "kings" (one over the present world, and one over the next) correspond to two "ways". God is behind it all. In *Barn.* 18.1, the angels of God and angels of Satan are set over two distinct ways.

they are the elect community, having come from the spring of Light. So important was the Light to this community that it has been argued that they worshipped the God of Israel in the image of Helios.[33] Over and against this elect body, is the community of darkness. Because the Qumran sect belongs to the Light, they expect aid and victory from God and have special status in the world, considering themselves to be like the angels. Those in the darkness can only anticipate defeat and destruction.

Thus God has predestined the fate of each man, whether he would belong to the "sons of light", the elect community, or whether he would be a doomed member of the community of darkness (cf. *1QS* 4.22bff., 4.26, 9.14-15). Their lives on earth as well as their future destiny depended upon God's allotment. Only the "sons of light", the "elect ones" are the ones who have heeded the ways of the Teacher of Righteousness and belong to the chosen remnant of the nation of Israel (cf. *CD* 3.20bff.). Only they can expect to be victorious in the great War at the Eschaton (*1QM* 1.1ff.).[34]

Embedded within the first century text, *Pseudo-Philo*,[35] is another relevant passage which witnesses to the existence of the theme that man's origin and destiny is the Light.[36] In chapter 28, Kenaz[37] relates a cosmogonic vision in which he sees "flames that do not burn" in the midst of nothingness (28.7). From this flame, a spark arises and creates a floor or foundation (28.8). Then the upper foundation is created from a spring leaping forth from the original flame (28.8). This seems to refer to the creation of heaven as the upper foundation and earth as the lower floor, since in 60.2 we read

---

[33] M. Smith, "Helios in Palestine", *Eretz Israel* 16 (1982) 199-214.

[34] Refer to E. Merrill, *Qumran and Predestination: A Theological Study of the Thanksgiving Hymns*, STDJ 8 (Leiden, 1975).

[35] A first century date is attached to this text according to D. J. Harrington in his introduction to this text in Charlesworth, *OTP* 2, 299; Harrington's translation is used here; see also, M. R. James, *The Biblical Antiquities of Philo*, in *Translations of Early Documents 1: Palestinian Jewish Texts* (London 1917), 165f.; *Pseudo-Philon: Les Antiquités Bibliques* 1, SC 229 (ed. D. J. Harrington and J. Cazeaux; Paris, 1976); refer to Rowland, *Open Heaven* 473, n. 23.

[36] The importance of light imagery in *Pseudo-Philo* was noted by M. Philonenka, "Essénisme et Gnose chez le Pseudo-Philon: Le symbolisme de la lumière dans le *Liber Antiquitatum Biblicarum*", *Le Origini dello Gnosticismo. Colloquio di Messina 13-18 Aprile 1966*, Studies in the History of Religions, NumenSup 12 (ed. U. Bianchi; Leiden, 1967) 401-410. Philonenka, however, does not deal with Kenaz's vision.

[37] Cf. Judges 3:9-11 where Kenaz is the father of Othniel.

that the "upper part" is called "heaven" while the "lower", earth.[38]

Significantly, Kenaz's vision continues: "Now between the upper foundation and the lower there came forth from the light of that invisible place,[39] as it were, the images of men (*de lumine invisibilis loci advenerunt quasi imagines hominum*)".[40] After a period of several thousand years during which the images dwelled as "men" there, a change occurred as a consequence of Adam's sin. Thus the text continues, stating that "those who went forth from the light of the invisible place, they will be those who will have the name 'man'.[41] And when he will sin against me and the time will be fulfilled, the spark will be put out and the spring will stop, and so they will be transformed" (28.9).

It seems that we have a reference here to the creation of "images" of men out of the Light prior to the existence of human men. It appears that on account of Adam's sin, these "men" were severed from the Light.[42] They were transformed into material beings.[43] Furthermore, Kenaz relates that he anticipates the "repose of the just (*requies iustorum*)" after death to be a state comparable to these luminous beginnings (28.10).[44] Thus he encourages us to "die to the corruptible world" (28.10).

Philo seems to be aware of the tradition that the origin and ultimate destiny of man is the Light since fragments of this tradition are found in his writings. In an obscure text in *Quaestiones et Solutiones in Genesin* 3.18 we read: "And the third (point) is that he who has progressed even to the very end is near to what is called by some the forgotten and unknown light". The obscurity of this

---

[38] Rowland, *Open Heaven*, 153-155, argues that the two foundations represent two firmaments of heaven, the men are fallen angels who await the final judgement for their punishment, the sin is that of the angels. This is a very creative interpretation but even as Rowland concedes, it does not explain the reference to Adam in the text. Moreover, when *Pseudo-Philo* 60.2 is used as a parallel description of the same cosmological event, it is only logical to conclude that the vision be interpreted as argued in this paper.

[39] The "place" of the Light here is comparable to the "place" where the Light came into being in Logion 50. On the theme of the "place" in the *Gospel of Thomas*, see Chapter Five, Section 1d.

[40] *Pseudo-Philon* (ed. Harrington and Cazeaux) 228 lines 65-66.

[41] Variant reading: "they will be those who dwell, and the name of that man...". See Charlesworth, *OTP* 2, 342 n. 28f.

[42] For a discussion of Adam's separation from the Light, see Chapter 7, Section 2a.

[43] This anthropogony is similar to that of *Thomas*; refer to Chapter Seven, Section 2a, for a detailed discussion.

[44] *Pseudo-Philon* (eds. Harrington and Cazeaux) 228 lines 78-79.

text caused Aucher to punctuate and render it differently: "*qui est adhuc proficiscens, ad ipsam summitatem invitandus, prope est ad lumen, quod apud aliquos dicitur oblivioni traditum ac incognitum*".[45] It is explained in the Arm. glossator in these words: "He who is alienated from sin has made a beginning of virtue; of this some say that such a man is near the unknown light, which he formerly knew, but strayed from through sin, and now has come back to".[46]

Even though Philo's emphasis is on the alienation of man from the Light because of sin, underlying this is the motif that man will return to the Light to which he once belonged. Thus, when Philo speaks of Aaron's death, he explains: "When Aaron dies, that is, when he is made perfect, he goes up into Hor, which is 'Light' (Num 20:25)" (*Leg. all.* 3.45).

It may be that Philo associates this idea with his doctrine of the soul which will return to its divine origin at death. Thus he speaks of death as the soul's "separation and detachment from the body and its return to the place whence it came: and it came, as was shown in the story of creation, from God" (*De Abr.* 258; cf. *Quaest. in Gen.* 3.11, 3.45; *De Cher.* 114-118; *Sacr. Abel et Cain* 2.5; *Sacr.* 2.5).

Rabbinic traditions seem to be aware of the motif that a portion of humanity originates from the Light. This is arguably behind a passage in *Genesis Rabbah*. The righteous are understood to be the "lights" of Genesis 1:16 who "rule over that which has been created to give light in the day and over that which has been created to give light in the night" (6.14).

In *Leviticus Rabba* 18.3, Rabbi Yohanan explicates Exodus 24.1. In so doing, he refers to the dualistic mythology of darkness and light. He argues that the Angel of Death commands the darkness. But the light dwells in the people of Israel; because of this they are free from the Angel of Death. As Rabbi Yehuda stated, they have the title "the children of God, of Light".

The notion that humanity is from the light and therefore will return to the light may be alluded to in a terse saying attributed to Rabbi Simeon ben Eleʻazar[47] in *Aboth de-R. Nathan* 2.32. When

---

[45] R. Marcus, *Philo Supplement* 1, LCL 380 (Cambridge, Mass., 1953 and reprints) 203, n. j.

[46] *Ibid.*, p. 203, n. j.

[47] A rabbi who flourished in the second century CE; see Lieberman, "How Much Greek?", 137 n. 17.

addressing humanity's origins, he says: "Whence did he come? From a place of fire, and he returns to a place of fire."[48]

It appears that several Jewish traditions were aware of a particular anthropogony which held that at least some men spring from the Light and were sometimes described as "sons of light". They were a special generation and were in opposition to those who were born from the darkness. The "sons of light" would return eventually to their luminous beginnings. This anthropogony, undoubtedly, has influenced the *Gospel of Thomas* in general and Logion 50 specifically.

Related to this is the Hermetic motif that each person will return to the place from which they came. *Asclepius* 11 relates that "god may restore us, pure and holy, to the nature of our higher part, to the divine". The unholy, however, have another lot: "For the unfaithful it goes differently: return to heaven is denied them..." *Excerpt* 26.12 sums up this philosophy: at death "all things go back again to the place whence they have come down". Thus if humans are from the Father who consists of "light and life", then when man learns that "you are from light and life" then "you shall advance to life once again" (*C.H.* 1.21). Similiarly, God is praised as "life and light" in *Corpus Hermeticum* 13.18-19, and to him "the universe returns".

Likewise, the *Gospel of Thomas* not only emphasizes a specific return to the Light such as we find implicit in Logion 50 and explicit in Logion 11 where Jesus poses the question, "When you come to dwell in the Light, what will you do?", but *Thomas* also is aware of this more general Hermetic teaching about returning to one's origins. This motif, however, has clearly been filtered through Jewish thought. This is displayed quite simply in Logion 49. Here, in one breath, Jesus speaks of being from the Kingdom and returning to it: "Blessed are the solitary and elect, for you will find the Kingdom. For you are from it, and to it you will return." It is quite obvious that two sayings are strung together here. The first is a simple beatitude about those who find the Kingdom. The second is a Hermetic teaching about returning to one's origins. The first saying interprets the second. By being thusly juxtaposed, a general Hermetic teaching takes on a Jewish flavor: the return will be to a specific place, the Kingdom.

---

[48] Schechter, אבות דרבי נתן, 35a.

Or Logion 18 which speaks of discovering "the beginning" in order to know "the end". Jesus teaches: "Blessed is he who will take his place in the beginning; he will know the end and will not experience death". This sounds very much like it is based on Hermetic philosophy about returning to one's origins.

Logion 18, however, is further interpreted by the succeeding Logion 19b where we find Hermetic wisdom (L. 18) reinterpreted in Jewish mythological language (L. 19). Returning to the beginning is reentering Paradise. The soteriological scheme implicit in Logion 19b teaches that it is necessary to return to the Pre-Fall condition of Adam by ascending to Paradise and mystically encountering the five trees of Paradise there. In so doing, one overcomes death.

ογṄτητṄ ⲅⲁⲣ ⲙ̄ⲙⲁγ Ṅⲧογ Ṅϣⲏⲛ ϩ̄ⲙ̄ ⲡⲁⲣⲁⲇⲓⲥⲟⲥ ⲉⲥⲉⲕⲓⲙ ⲁⲛ Ṅϣⲱⲙ ⲙ̄ⲡⲣⲱ ⲁγⲱ ⲙⲁⲣⲉ ⲛⲟγϭⲱⲃⲉ ϩⲉ ⲉⲃⲟⲗ ⲡⲉⲧⲛⲁⲥⲟγⲱⲛⲟγ ϥⲛⲁϫⲓ ϯⲡⲉ ⲁⲛ ⲙ̄ⲙⲟγ

For there are five trees for you in Paradise which are unmoving summer and winter and whose leaves do not fall. Whoever will know them will not experience death.[49]

Past interpretations of this text have centered around the five trees as representative of the five noetic senses which may correspond on the spiritual level to the five bodily senses.[50] Most recently, M. Williams has argued that the immovability of the five trees is due to their transcendent nature as well as their association with the unchangable Mind or noetic faculties.[51] Moreover, these five immutable noetic senses provide access to the realm which transcends the changable material realm.[52]

This is only a partial understanding of Logion 19b since this interpretation does not take into account the probable context for the encounter with the trees of Paradise: the disciples must have ascended to Paradise in order to encounter the trees awaiting them in the Garden.

---

[49] Layton, *Nag Hammadi Codex II,2-7*, 60; Eng. trans. mine.
[50] J. Doresse, *The Secret Books of the Egyptian Gnostics* (Rochester, Vermont, 1958 and 1986) 345; R. M. Grant and D. N. Freedman, *The Secret Sayings of Jesus* (New York, 1960) 139; Ménard, *L'Évangile*, 107; M. Williams, *The Immovable Race: A Gnostic Designation and the Theme of Stability in Late Antiquity*, NHS 29 (Leiden, 1985) 18-22.
[51] Williams, *Immovable Race*, 20. For my interpretation of the "unmoving" five trees, refer to Chapter Four, Section 2b.
[52] *Ibid.*, 22.

The notion of ascending in order to encounter the five trees and overcome death is intimately connected with the Hermetic perspective that a specific number of vices form the material man, while a like number of virtues form the spiritual man.[53] According to Reitzenstein, two basic numerological systems arose. One system arose from the twelve divisions of the zodiac and appears most clearly in Manichaeism where there are twelve children of the primal deity, the light-aeons who form god himself. They are powers or virtues. Man is transformed into divinity when he puts on the twelve deifying garments.[54]

Corpus Hermeticum 13 also refers to these ideas. In this chapter, in order for Tat to experience his spiritual Self which is described as "rebirth", he is told by Hermes that he must cleanse himself of the twelve vices of matter: ignorance, grief, incontinence, lust, injustice, greed, deceit, envy, treachery, anger, recklessness, and malice (13.7). According to Hermes, these twelve vices use the body to torture the "inward person" (13.7). The only way for rebirth to occur, is to withdraw from these twelve vices and come to the ten powers or levels of god which expel the vices: knowledge of god, knowledge of joy, continence, perserverance, justice, liberality, truth, good, light, and life (13.8). Thus "the arrival of the decad sets in order a birth of mind that expels the twelve; we have been divinized by this birth" (13.10).

The second numerological system was based on the series of five and can be traced to the five plantary spheres (excluding the sun and moon) and the list of elements (breeze, wind, earth, water, and fire).[55] Again, Manichaeism not only preserves elements of this system, but interprets much of its own ideologies into this system.[56] The world of light has five compartments: intelligence,

---

[53] On this see especially R. Reitzenstein, "Appendix XIII: Virtues and Vices as Members", *Hellenistic Mystery-Religions: Their Basic Ideas and Significance*, Pittsburgh Theological Monograph Series 15 (trans. J. E. Steely; Pittsburg, 1978) 47-51, 209-212, and 338-351; G. Mussies, "Catalogues of Sins and Virtues Personified (NHC II,5)", *Studies in Gnosticism and Hellenistic Religions presented to Gilles Quispel on the Occasion of his 65th Birthday*, EPRO 91 (eds. R. van den Broek and M. J. Vermaseren; Leiden, 1981) 315-335. For lists of vices in Jewish-Christianity and Judaism, refer to Zandee, "Silvanus", 502-503.

[54] See F. Cumont, *Recherches sur le Manichéisme* 1: *La Cosmogonie manichéenne* (Brussels, 1908) 35.

[55] On these lists, see Reitzenstein, *Hellenistic Mystery-Religions*, 279ff.

[56] For a complete discussion, see I. Culianu, *The Tree of Gnosis: Gnostic Mythology from Early Christianity to Modern Nihilism* (trans. H. S. Wiesner and I. Culianu; San Francisco, 1992) 161-188.

reason, thought, reflection, and will (*Acts of Archelaus* 10.1 p. 15,10-11.24; Epiph. *Pan.* 66.6-7 and 25-31; cf. *Fihrist* 9.1). The Kingdom of Darkness, or Matter, has five members or compartments of evil: smoke, fire, wind, water, darkness (Aug. *De mor. Man.* 2.9.14; cf. *Fihrist 9.1*). Each of these five compartments has its own Archon, metal, taste, and religious error.[57] The mythology continues along these pentadantic lines, including references to five trees which, in the Manichaean myth, were "the negative influences of the five evil planets, of the twelve evil signs of the Zodiac, and of all troops of heavenly Archons".[58]

This numerological system seems to also be behind the ascent teaching in *Corpus Hermeticum* 1 which contains a list of seven bad influences. The reference to seven no doubt refers to a reflection of the original five planets plus the sun and the moon. *Poimandres* teaches that when ascending, the material body surrenders these bad influences at each of the seven successive cosmic levels and, in so doing, it is transformed into god. Thus the human being "rushes up through the cosmic framework" and surrenders at each of the zones one of the vices until he is "stripped of the effects of the cosmic framework" and "enters into god" (*C.H.* 1.24-26).

This pentadantic system is quite primitive as evidenced in Colossians 3:5-15 where the Christian is commanded to "put to death (νεκρώσατε)" the earthly parts of the human (τὰ μέλη τὰ ἐπὶ τῆς γῆς) (3:5).[59] What follows are two lists of five vices which make up this "earthly" self: fornication, impurity, passion, evil desire, and covetousness (3:5); anger, wrath, malice, slander, and foul speech (3:8). A "new nature" must be "put on" which is a renewal of God's Image (ἐνδυσάμενοι τὸν νέον τὸν ἀνακαινούμενον εἰς ἐπίγνωσιν κατ' εἰκόνα τοῦ κτίσαντος αὐτόν) (3:10). This "new nature" is

---

[57] Culianu, *Tree*, 175.

[58] Culianu, *Tree*, 168, 175-176. For references to the five trees in Manichaeism, see C. R. C. Alberry, *A Manichaean Psalm-Book Part II. Manichaean Manuscripts in the Chester Beatty Collection 2* (Stuttgart, 1938) 161.15ff.; H. J. Polotsky and A. Böhlig, *Kephalaia 1, Manichaische Handschriften der Staatlichen Museen Berlin, Bd. 1* (Stuttgart, 1940) 30.20ff., 48.15, 121.7f.; V. Arnold-Döben, *Die Bildersprache des Manichäismus*, Arbeitsmaterialien zur Religionsgeschichte 3 (Köln, 1978) 7-44; W. B. Henning, *Sogdica*, James G. Forlong Fund 21 (London, 1940) 3; É. Chavannes and P. Pelliot, *Un traité manichéen retrouvé en Chine* (Paris, 1912) 65-67.

[59] P. W. van der Horst, "Observations on a Pauline Expression", *NTS* 19 (1973) 181-187, discusses the Pauline expression, "putting off the old man", in light of Skeptic philosophy.

described as consisting of two sets of five virtues: compassion, kindness, lowliness, meekness, patience (3:12); forbearance, forgiveness, love, peace, thankfulness (3:13-15).

I propose that the notion that one must go to Paradise and become acquainted with the five trees in the Garden in order to overcome death is associated with the Hermetic traditions that when one ascends, one discards the vices which constitute the material man and one is to replace these vices with the virtues of the spiritual man. This is the rebirth of the real Self. In Logion 19b, the five trees refer to five virtues or powers to which the aspirant surrenders after he discards the material man. In so doing, he achieves divinity and immortality.

This Hermetic concept is expressed in the language of Jewish mythology. The ascent is to Paradise where one is returning to the primordial state of the Garden before death arrived. The virtues are the ever-leafed trees planted in Paradise.[60]

This soteriological scheme of ascent implicit in Logion 19b is explicit in the Syrian *Odes of Solomon*. In *Ode* 11, we are told about a mystic who, upon ascending to Paradise, dons a garment of light. Then the Odist says:

> And he took me to his Paradise, wherein is the wealth of the Lord's pleasure.
>
> I contemplated blooming and fruit-bearing trees, and self-grown was their crown.
>
> Their branches were flourishing and their fruits were shining; their roots (were) from an immortal land.
>
> And a river of gladness was irrigating them, and the region round about them in the land of eternal life (*Ode* 11.16-16c).

The trees are then interpreted in a following stanza to refer to the righteous or virtuous people who have been "planted" in God's immortal land and who have taken their place in "Paradise" (*Ode* 11.18). Thus they "grow in the growth of the trees" and are therefore "blessed" and "have passed from darkness into light" (*Ode* 11.19). Even though this text does not interpret the trees as "virtues", this *Ode* does allegorize the trees as the righteous people and sets

---

[60] There was a Jewish teaching that the Messiah would "open the gates of Paradise" and "grant to the saints to eat of the Tree of Life" (*T.Levi* 18.10-11).

forth the contemplation of these trees within the framework of ascent to Paradise and a vision of several trees.

Another Christian text, *Physiologus* 34.18-20, knows of the tradition that the virtues could be associated with the concept of the Tree of Life. In this passage, however, there is only one Tree, so the author understands the fruits of the Tree of Life in Paradise to be the four virtues: joy (χαρά), peace (εἰρήνη), self-control (ἐγκράτεια), and long-suffering (μακροθυμία).

Thus adaptation of the Hermetic theme of the virtues into Jewish mythology is not unique to *Thomas*. In fact, it is already evident in Philo. According to Philo's allegory, the Trees of Paradise are virtues that God planted for the nourishment of the soul and for the acquistion of immortality. Thus he interprets the commandment in Genesis 2:16, "From every tree that is in the garden thou shalt eat feedingly thereon", to mean that the soul must gain benefit "not from a single tree or from a single virtue but from all the virtues" (*Leg. All.* 1.97). The purpose of eating these fruits is to nourish the soul "by the acquistion of things noble, and the practice of things rightful" (1.98).

In *De Confusione Linguarum* 61, Philo states simply that Paradise "was not a garden of the plants of the soul, but of heavenly virtues". Moreover, from the Tree of Life arises immortality; it has been "planted in the midst of the Garden, even Goodness with the particular virtues" (*De mig. Abr.* 36-37). So it seems that the Tree of Life is Goodness planted in companionship with the other trees or virtues.

Specifically what are these virtues? According to *De Plantatione* 36, the Trees in the Garden are listed as follows: Life, Immortality, Knowledge, Apprehension, and Understanding of the Conception of good and evil (ζωῆς, ἀθανασίας, εἰδήσεως, καταλήψεως, συνέσεως, καλοῦ καὶ πονηροῦ φαντασίας).[61] Not surprisingly the number of Trees listed are five. This "garden of virtues" brings "the soul to perfect happiness" and "immortality". Contrary to this is the "path according to evil" which can only end "in death". This path of evil probably represents the vices which are in opposition to the virtues.[62]

---

[61] *Philo* 3, 230-231; I understand the final genitive clause "καλοῦ καὶ πονηροῦ φαντασίας" as qualifying "συνέσεως".

[62] The Philonic corpus contains remnants of these ideas as well, expressing the need for the elimination of certain vices of the sensible self in order

In *Quaestiones et Solutiones in Genesin* 1.6, Philo mentions that Paradise is "full of all kinds of trees". The Creator planted "His ideas" "like trees". These trees symbolize "Wisdom" and "Knowledge" of the divine and human and their causes. The Tree of Life specifically represents "the knowledge, not only of things on the earth, but also of the eldest and highest Cause of all things". Furthermore, when one is able "to obtain a clear impression (σαφεῖαν φαντασίαν)" of the trees and their meanings, "he will be fortunate and blessed and truly immortal".

Philo applies this metaphor to the Adam story. Adam, the first man, was appointed to be "ruler of all trees" (*De agric.* 8). When he was in the Garden prior to the Fall, one of his duties was to cultivate the trees. Thus: "when he was cultivating wisdom in Paradise, he took care of the cultivation of wisdom as if of trees" (*Quaest. Gen.* 1.56). Moreover, Adam nourished himself on "immortal and beneficial fruits" of the trees "through which he became immortal" (*Ibid.* 1.56). Following the Fall, however, Adam no longer nourished himself on these virtues; now he was overcome by the vices, practicing the "works of ignorance" which polluted his body and blinded his mind. Thus man now starves, wasting away and suffering the miseries of death (*Ibid.* 1.56; cf. *De agric.* 8-19).

Significant as well to this discussion is the description in Philo of the nature of the Trees of Paradise. He explains: "But not ineptly is the word 'beautiful' used, for it would be natural that plants should be ever flourishing and evergreen, as belong to Paradise, without suffering the extremity of being leafless" (*Quaest. Gen.* 1.9).

Without doubt, Logion 19b is associated with this curious blend that we have found in Philo of Hermetic traditions about astrology and ascent and Jewish mythology about Paradise. This hermeticized Jewish mythology can be summarized as follows: the trees

---

to be able to surrender to holiness (*i.e.*, *De Vita Mosis* 2.288; *De Virtutibus* 164). When discussing anthropological notions, Philo turns to Genesis 3:19 and weaves Hermetic notions about the vices of the earthly man and virtues of the heavenly man into the biblical narrative. According to Philo, the human consists of both earth and heaven. But the first human became corrupted and "gave himself wholly over to the earth, the denser and heavier element" (*Quaest. Gen.* 1.51). If the first human, however, "had been desirous of virtue, which makes the soul immortal, he would certainly have obtained heaven as his lot" (*Ibid.* 1.51). Thus Philo concludes on a moralistic note that earth is "the beginning and end of the evil and vile man" while heaven "of the virtuous man" (*Ibid.* 1.51).

in the Garden are the virtues which the soul was nourished on prior to Adam's Fall and which gave immortality to the consumer. The consequence of Sin and the expulsion from Paradise was that the human took on an earthy denser form which was associated with the opposite of these virtues, that is, the vices. This is an "evil" path which can only end in death. How can a person be redeemed from this situation? He must shed the vices and return to the Pre-Fall state of Adam by ascending to Paradise and becoming the cultivator of the five trees of virtue there. He must pick and eat the fruits of these leafy trees, and in so doing immortality is his gift. Or as Logion 19b renders it: "For there are five trees for you in Paradise which are unmoved summer and winter and whose leaves do not fall. Whoever becomes acquainted with them will not experience death".

b) *The Elect:*

The concept of an elect or chosen people who belong to God is a well-documented Jewish tradition which has been traced back to Deuteronomy 7:6: "For you are a people holy to the Lord your God; the Lord your God has chosen (בחר) you to be a people for his own possession, out of all the peoples that are on the face of the earth".[63]

Behind this motif of election is the idea that the nation is the "people of Yahweh", that this election is their national history. Thus the motif of election was employed to designate Israel as the people of God. Furthermore, the chosen people were addressed in a special way as adopted "sons" of God (Exod 4:22f.; Jer 31:9, 20; Deut 14:1, 32:5, 19; Isa 43:6, 45:11; Hos 2:1; cf. Deut 32:6, 18; Jer 3:4). As "sons" of God, they were God's chosen and protected people whose duty is was to be obedient to him.

The elect were viewed later on as distinct from sinners (Isa 65:9, 15). Thus in some strains of apocalypticism, the elect are synonomous with the righteous or holy ones (*1 En* 38.2-5, 41.2, 48.1, 61.13, 70.3). The sinners and wicked ones are in opposition to them (*1 En* 5.7, 41.2, 50.1f.). Therefore, the concept is restricted in some groups to represent an elite faithful remnant of the Jews (cf.

---

[63] See H. H. Rowley, *The Biblical Doctrine of Election* (London, 1950); T. C. Vriezen, *Die Erwählung Israels nach dem Alten Testament*, ATANT 24 (Zurich, 1953); *idem, An Outline of Old Testament Theology* (Newton, Mass., 1958).

Jub. 1.29; *Sib.* 3.69; *Wis.* 3.9; *4 Ezra* 2.38, 16.74f.; *1 En* 51.1f., 62.8; *2 Bar* 30.2, 75.5f.; *Apoc. Abr.* 29.17).

This is the understanding of the Qumranites who believed that only the initiates of their community belonged to God's "new covenant" and were reckoned among God's "elect".[64] In *CD* 3.20bff., only the "sons of Zadok" are the elect ones of Israel, the chosen ones who have remained pure while the rest of the children of Israel have gone astray:

> The priests are the converts of Israel who went out from the land of Judah, and <the Levites are> those who joined them, and the sons of Zadok are the chosen ones of Israel, the renowned men who shall appear at the end of days" (*CD* 4.2b-4).

As the chosen ones, they already are united with the community of the heavenly angels. Thus in *1QS* 11.7-9, we read:

> [God] has caused [His chosen ones] to inherit
>   the lot of the Holy Ones,
> He has joined their assembly
>   to the Sons of Heaven,
> to be a council of the Community,
>   a foundation of the Building of Holiness,
>   an eternal Plantation throughout all ages
>   to come.

Furthermore, the elect lot of each Qumranite had been predestined by God. We are told in *1QS* 3.13ff. that before the Qumranites existed, God had established their whole design. As the chosen "sons of light" or "sons of heaven", they were in contrast to the wicked ones who walked in the ways of darkness and whom God did not chose (cf. *1QS* 4.22bff.; 4.26; 9.14-15).

The Mandeans, descendents of a baptismal sect from Palestine,[65] equated the "sons of light" with the angels with whom they claimed association (*Lit.* 18).[66] Moreover, people predestined to eternal life were also called "sons of life".[67] Thus, it is not surprising

---

[64] See G. Vermes, *The Dead Sea Scrolls. Qumran in Perspective* (Philadelphia, revised ed. 1977) 169-175. In addition to the texts discussed below, refer also to *1QH* 2.13b; *1QpHab* 5.4, 9.12a; *1QpPsa* 1-10, 2.5a; *1QS* 8.6b, 9.14c, where the title "chosen ones" refers to the Qumranites.

[65] See K. Rudolph, "Der Mandäismus in der neuen Gnosisforschung", *Gnosis* (eds. B. Aland et al.; Göttingen, 1978) 244-277.

[66] M. Lidzbarski, *Mandäische Liturgien*, Abhandlungen der Königlichen Gesellschaft der Wissenschaften zu Göttingen 17 (Berlin, 1921) 18.

[67] See W. Brandt, *Mandäische Schriften* (Göttingen, 1893) 13.

that the term "elect" is applied to both believers (*Lit.* 75, 106-107;[68] *Joh.* 102, 221[69]) and angels (*Joh.* 69[70]).

In his attempt to explain why the "chosen people", the Jews, were rejecting Jesus Christ, Paul reaches for the remnant motif. In Romans 11:1ff., he explains that historically the nation of Israel has always consisted of two parts: those people who have been disobedient and unfaithful and a remnant which has remained obedient and faithful (11:2b-4). Thus even during Paul's time, this remnant remains and represents those who are turning to Jesus (11:5,7; cf. 9:6-13). Furthermore, "they were not yet born and had done nothing either good or bad" but God ordained this present situation where the Jews were not turning to Christ in order that God's "purpose of election (ἐκλογὴν) might continue" (9:11). Thus Paul connects election with predestination and the foreknowledge of God (cf. Rom 8:29-30, 11:2; 2 Thess 2:13; Gal 1:13-16; cp. 2 Tim 1:9 and 1 Pet 1:2).

Thus the idea that the "elect" are predestined seems to be not uncommon in early Christianity. The *Odes of Solomon* also testify to this tradition. In *Ode* 8.13 we read that God "recognized them" and "imprinted a seal on their faces" even "before they existed". Thus: "I willed and fashioned mind and heart; and they are my own. And upon my right hand I have set my elect ones" (8.18).

This is the background for the use of "elect" in Logion 50. The concept of election is being employed in a restricted sense. It is applied only to the Thomasites who are the elect of the Father and who are distinct from any outsiders belonging to the darkness. The parallelism between the two clauses "sons of light" and "elect of the living father" suggests that the Thomasites understood their special relationship with God to be "elect" in the sense of sonship. It is notable that the concept of the elect no longer includes the ideas of being adopted by God or being a righteous faithful person as it did in Judaism. The Thomasites are elect due to their claim that they originate from the Light.

Thus, the Thomasites did not see themselves as a *remnant* of God's people. According to *Thomas*, it is their divine genesis alone which makes them a special elite among humans, an elite whose return to the Light is assured. They were God's elect because they

---

[68] Lidzbarski, *Liturgien*, 75, 106-107.
[69] M. Lidzbarski, *Das Johannesbuch der Mandäer* (Berlin, 1915) 102, 221.
[70] *Ibid.*, 69.

were God's own children, born from his light, or as Logion 3 phrases it, they were "sons of the living Father".

Furthermore, the notion of election has been intimately associated in *Thomas* with the term ⲙⲟⲛⲁⲭⲟⲥ which describes the celibate encratite.[71] Thus in Logion 49, we find that the elect (ⲉⲧⲥⲟⲧⲡ) are the celibates (ⲙⲟⲛⲁⲭⲟⲥ): "Blessed are the solitary and elect, for you will find the kingdom. For you are from it, and to it you will return".[72]

It is said in Logion 23, that the elect shall be chosen "one out of a thousand, and two out of ten thousand, and they shall stand as a single one (ⲟⲩⲁ ⲉⲃⲟⲗ ϩⲛ ϣⲟ ⲁⲩⲱ ⲥⲛⲁⲩ ⲉⲃⲟⲗ ϩⲛ ⲧⲃⲁ ⲁⲩⲱ ⲥⲉⲛⲁⲱϩⲉ ⲉⲣⲁⲧⲟⲩ ⲉⲩⲟ ⲟⲩⲁ ⲟⲩⲱⲧ)".[73] Thus the chosen ones are given the descriptive title: "standing encratites".[74]

In Logion 16, it is said that the elect will "stand" (ⲥⲉⲛⲁⲱϩⲉ ⲉⲣⲁⲧϥ) against their birth relatives:

ⲟⲩⲛ ϯⲟⲩ ⲅⲁⲣ ⲛⲁϣⲱⲡⲉ ϩⲛ ⲟⲩⲏⲉⲓ ⲟⲩⲛ ϣⲟⲙⲧ ⲛⲁϣⲱⲡⲉ ⲉϫⲛ ⲥⲛⲁⲩ ⲁⲩⲱ ⲥⲛⲁⲩ ⲉϫⲛ ϣⲟⲙⲧ ⲡⲉⲓⲱⲧ ⲉϫⲙ ⲡϣⲏⲣⲉ ⲁⲩⲱ ⲡϣⲏⲣⲉ ⲉϫⲙ ⲡⲉⲓⲱⲧ ⲁⲩⲱ ⲥⲉⲛⲁⲱϩⲉ ⲉⲣⲁⲧⲟⲩ ⲉⲩⲟ ⲙ̄ⲙⲟⲛⲁⲭⲟⲥ

For there will be five in a house: three will be against two, and two against three, the father against the son, and the son against the father. And they will stand solitary.[75]

According to *Thomas*, divorcing one's biological family in order to become part of a new radical ethos, a new spiritual family, is necessary in order to be worthy of Jesus and become his disciple (L. 55, 99, 101).[76] The severing of ties with one's family is a central feature of early Christianity in general (cf. Lk 14:26//Mt 10:37).[77]

---

[71] Refer to Chapter One, Section 1.
[72] Layton, *Nag Hammadi Codex II,2-7*, 72; Eng. trans. by Lambdin, 73.
[73] *Ibid.*, 64-65.
[74] A. F. J. Klijn, "The 'Single One' in the Gospel of Thomas", 271-272, argues convincingly that ⲙⲟⲛⲁⲭⲟⲥ in Logia 16, 49, and 75, is synonymous in connotation with ⲟⲩⲁ ⲟⲩⲱⲧ in Logia 4, 22, and 23, and with ⲟⲩⲁ in Logia 11, 22, and 106; S. Patterson disagrees but offers no alternative argument, *The Gospel of Thomas and Jesus* (Sonoma, 1993) 152 n. 124.
[75] Layton, *Nag Hammadi Codex II,2-7*, 60; Eng. trans. by Lambdin, 61.
[76] On the radical redefinition of family in *Thomas*, see Patterson, *Gospel of Thomas and Jesus*, 134-135, 199-202.
[77] On this theme, refer to G. Theissen, *The Sociology of Early Palestinian Christianity* (trans. J. Bowden; Philadelphia, 1978) 11-12; *idem*, "Itinerant Radicalism: The Tradition of Jesus Sayings from the Perspective of the Sociology of Literature, *Radical Religion* 2 (trans A. Wire; 1976) 84-93. See also, G. Quispel, "The Study of Encratism: A Historical Survey", *La Tradizione dell'Enkrateia. Atti del Colloquio Internazionale - Milano 20-23 Aprile 1982* (ed. U.

What is unique in this Logion is that this radical concept is associated with the behavior of "standing solitary". Thus by becoming an encratite, a celibate single, one rejects the normal family life. Now that one participates in this new encratite lifestyle, one is said to have achieved a new state of being: the state of "standing" as an encratite.

But precisely what does it mean to "stand" as an encratite? Could this be a reference to angelic status since angels are not only celibate, but in Jewish apocalyptic texts, "standing" is associated with angelic behavior? Thus the angels and archangels in Jewish apocalyptic texts are described as those who "stand" before God (*1 En* 39.12f., 40.1, 47.3, 68.2; *2 En* 21.1; *Test. Abr.* 7-8; cf. *1 En* 49.2). When a person ascended and was transformed, he took his place with the angels "standing" around God's throne. Thus Isaiah saw the righteous in heaven: "They were like the angels who stand there in great glory" (*Asc. Isa.* 9.9-10). This suggests that the one who was transformed would participate in the cultic service before God's throne. Connected to this is the idea that as a "Standing One", a person gained immortality. Thus, in *2 Enoch* 22.10, Enoch becomes an angel and is commanded in 22.6 to "stand" before the face of God unto eternity.

It is in the Samaritan and Simonian traditions that the imperishability of the "standing" condition is emphasized.[78] The title "Standing Ones" is used to identify the angels.[79] Associated with this is immortality. Thus we read in a Samaritan hymn: "He [God] is standing forever; He exists unto eternity. Standing Ones [angels] and mortals are under His rule".[80] When Moses ascended to receive the Torah, "he joined with the angels", as Deuteronomy says "Stand by Me now" (*Memar Marqa* 4.12).[81]

Bianchi; Rome, 1985) 78-79.

[78] Fossum, *Name*, 119ff.; Williams, *Immovable Race*, has not made note of this distinction but interprets the notion of stability *only* according to the philosophical tradition which understood it to mean immutability; for a discussion, see the review of *Immovable Race* by G. Quispel, *VC* 40 (1986) 411-412.

[79] Fossum, *Name* 55ff., 120ff., and 139ff.

[80] A. E. Cowley, *The Samaritan Liturgy* (Oxford, 1909) 27.18.

[81] Cf. Marqa calls Moses a "Standing One": "Mighty is the great prophet, who clad himself in the Name of the Godhead and received the five books. And he was standing between the two assemblies, between the Standing Ones and the mortals" (Cowley, *Samaritan Liturgy*, 54.31f.). See Fossum, *Name*, 124, for a complete discussion of this passage.

Because God and his angels are imperishable according to Samaritan traditions, when a mortal like Moses is transformed into a "Standing One", this means that he not only has been elevated to the position of an angelic being, but is partaking of God's everlasting nature as well.[82]

Could it be the case that the "elect", the "standing encratites", in the *Gospel of Thomas*, were thought to be imperishable like the angels? The affirmative is supported according to Logion 18. Here the true disciple who "stands in the beginning", is blessed and *will not die*:

ΟΥΜΑΚΑΡΙΟC ΠΕΤΝΑ[[Ϩ]]ΩϨΕ ΕΡΑΤϤ ϨΝ ΤΑΡΧΗ ΑΥΩ ϤΝΑCΟΥΩΝ ΘϨΑΗ ΑΥΩ ϤΝΑϪΙ ϯΠΕ ΑΝ ΜΜΟΥ

Blessed is he who will stand in the beginning; he will know the end and will not experience death.[83]

As previously argued, the "beginning" here refers to Paradise since this Logion parallels Logion 19b where the believer must ascend to Paradise and become a new person by acquiring the virtues planted in the Garden; by so doing, he gains life. Furthermore, these five trees in Logion 19 are described as "unmoving (ΕCΕΚΙΜ ΑΝ)". This must mean that these heavenly trees or virtues are representative of God's "standing" nature. When one returns to Paradise and takes on the virtues, one is partaking of the imperishable nature of God.[84] Thus the text states: "Whoever knows them [the five trees] will not experience death". This is comparable to Logion 18: when one "stands" in the beginning, one has returned to Paradise as a righteous one and has achieved an angelic-like status; when one "stands" before God, one is partaking of imperishability and "will not experience death".

It is possible that the phrase "he will know the end" reflects the welding of a Hermetic idea with a Jesus saying which may have consisted of the two parallel clauses: "Blessed is he who will stand in the beginning; he will not experience death". The phrase "he will know the end" of Logion 18 may have been inserted in order to provide a better parallel with the next Logion which speaks

---

[82] This differs from Philo's use of "standing" to denote immutability; *ibid.*, 119ff.
[83] Layton, *Nag Hammadi Codex II, 2-7*, 60; Eng. trans. mine.
[84] In contradiction to the view of M. Williams who stresses the immutability of the five trees. Refer to Chapter Four, Section 2a.

of "knowing" the five trees in Paradise so that one does not experience death (L. 19).

Whatever is the case, this new state of being has been connected to the condition of the prelapsarian Adam who lived at the beginning, in Paradise. The encratites associated with *Thomas* believed that they were imitating Adam before he sinned by leading celibate single lives. As clones of the Sinless Adam, they had returned to the beginning before death existed: they were "standing" in Paradise as immortals before God. Thus to "stand" as an encratite implied that by rejecting sex, one now lived in the Paradisiac state of the Pre-Fall Adam before Sin and Death. Death no longer held sway over the "standing encratite" because the encratite was imperishable.

It is notable that this condition set them on par with the celibate angels who stand before God. This brings to mind the fact that the Thomasites believed that the resurrection had already occurred (L. 51). The encratite tradition held that marriage was not part of this angelic post-resurrection state (Lk 20:34-36; Clem. Alex., *Strom.* 3.12.87; cf. 3.6.48).[85] Thus the Thomasites probably understood their "standing encratite" status to be a condition of the people of the resurrection who were already "equal to the angels" and "sons of God" (cf. L. 3; L. 50).

The association of the descriptive titles "sons of light", "sons of God", and "standing encratites" or celibates who have achieved angelic status, with the Elect people is not unique to *Thomas*. As we saw earlier, election of particular humans and their subsequent acquistion of angelic status were also connected with the "sons of light" in the Qumran community of celibates. As was pointed out above, Mandean literature calls the believers as well as the angels "sons of light". Moreover, the term "elect" is applied to both the believers and angels. As we saw earlier, the *Odes of Solomon* 8.13 and 8.15 apply the term "elect" to those people whom God foreknew and whom he has now set aside on his right hand. This probably indicates that they have angelic status. In *Ode* 4.8, the phrase "elect archangels" is in parallelism to God's heavenly "hosts". This cummulative evidence from the Qumran writings,

---

[85] Refer to U. Bianchi, "The Religio-Historical Relevance of Lk 20:34-36", *Studies in Gnosticism and Hellenistic Religions, presented to Gilles Quispel on the Occasion of his 65th Birthday*, EPRO 91 (eds. R. van den Broek and M. J. Vermaseren; Leiden, 1981) 31-37.

the Mandean literature, the *Odes of Solomon*, and *Thomas* points to a common Jewish milieu where the predestined believers, the elect, were equated with the angels.

3) *Movement and Rest:*

As mentioned earlier, it is not unusual in Jewish mystical teaching for the angelic guards to demand a sign or password from the person attempting a mystical ascent. According to the *Gospel of Thomas*, the "sign" verifying that the aspirant is indeed the person he claims to be and belongs in the sacred zone is the verbal phrase: "It is movement and rest".

Not surprisingly, in the past, scholars have associated this last phrase of Logion 50 with Gnosticism, since the gnostics in general understood "rest (ἀνάπαυσις)" to describe the final redemptive state.[86] Scholars, however, seem to have had a difficult time explaining not only "movement" as a gnostic concept but also its coupling with "rest".[87] I would argue that this coupling of "movement" with "rest" is the result of a reinterpretation of the Hermetic concept of God the Immovable who has set the world in motion.

In *Corpus Hermeticum* 5.5, the person who is ascending sees the "Immovable set in motion (τὸν ἀκίνητον διακινούμενον)". This movement is explained to be the cosmic order:

---

[86] Haenchen, *Botschaft*, 73; B. Gärtner, *The Theology of the Gospel According to Thomas* (trans. E. Sharpe; New York, 1961) 265-267; Kasser, *L'Évangile*, 79; P. Vielhauer, "ΑΝΑΠΑΥΣΙΣ Zum gnostischen Hintergrund des Thomasevangeliums", *Apaphoreta. Festschrift für Ernst Haenchen*, BZNW 30 (ed. W. Eltester; Berlin, 1964) 294-296; Ménard, *L'Évangile*, 154; Grant and Freedman, *Secret Sayings*, 160-161. Patterson, *Gospel of Thomas and Jesus*, 133-134, seems confused about the use of the term "rest", suggesting that sometimes *Thomas* uses "rest" in a gnostic sense (L. 50, 60), while other times not (L. 51, 86, 90). Also refer to the exhaustive study on Rest in the *Gospel of Truth*, J. Helderman, *Die Anapausis im Evangelium Veritatis*, NHS 18 (Leiden, 1984).

[87] Haenchen, *Botschaft*, 73, understands movement to refer to constant seeking and finding; Kasser, *L'Évangile*, 73, speaks of a First Cause; Vielhauer, "ΑΝΑΠΑΥΣΙΣ", 295-296, refers to a passage from Codex Brucianus, but even he concedes that rest and movement here are not formal parallels to Logion 50: "the light that cometh from their [Powers'] eyes to them it is repose. The movement of their hands is their swift flight..." (c. 39); for ed., see C. A. Baynes, *A Coptic Gnostic Treatise contained in the Codex Brucianus [Bruce MS. 96. Bod. Lib. Oxford]. A Translation from the Coptic: Transcript and Commentary* (Cambridge, 1933) 124.

Grant and Freedman, *Secret Sayings*, 161, do try and solve the coupling of movement and rest by referring to the Naassenes' "unmoved mover" (Hipp., *Ref.*, 5.7.25); but as we will see, this is probably borrowed from Hermeticism.

Would that you could grow wings and fly up into the air, lifted between earth and heaven to see the solid earth, the fluid sea, the streaming rivers, the pliant air, the piercing fire, the coursing stars, and heaven speeding on its axis about the same points. Oh, this is a most happy sight to see, my child, to have a vision of all these in a single instant, to see the motionless set in motion and the invisible made visible through the things that it makes. This is the order of the cosmos, and this is the cosmos of order.

Corpus Hermeticum 2.6 explains that God is the Mover of the created order, that is, the created order moves in his rest. Thus: "everything moved is moved not in something moved but in something at rest (πᾶν δὲ τὸ κινούμενον οὐκ ἐν κινουμένῳ κινεῖται ἀλλ' ἐν ἑστῶτι). And the Mover is also at rest (καὶ τὸ κινοῦν δὲ ἕστηκεν) unable to be moved conjointly". The text continues in 2.8 by stating that the "motion of the cosmos and every living thing made of matter" is "moved in immobility and by immobility (ἐν στάσει καὶ ὑπὸ στάσεως κινεῖται)". Thus, all movement occurs within his non-motion. Even though, God is immovable, he sets the cosmos in motion.

Therefore, Book 6.1 teaches that God is "good" and that the "good must be the substance of all motion and generation (κινήσεως καὶ γενέσεως) (for nothing is abandoned by it), but this substance has an energy about it that stays at rest (στατικὴν), that has no lack and no excess, that is perfectly complete, a source of supply, present in the beginning of all things".[88] So the universe is in movement while incorporeal Mind is at rest in itself. Asclepius explains to Trismegistus that the nature of "the place in which the universe is moved" is "incorporeal" (*C.H.* 2.12). It is "Mind" which is "a whole wholly enclosing itself, free of all body, unerring, unaffected, untouched, at rest in itself (αὐτὸς ἐν ἑαυτῷ ἑστώς), capable of containing all things and preserving all that exists..." (*Ibid.*, 2.12).

According to the Latin *Asclepius* 32, "the beginnings of everything" are "god and eternity". The created world is "mobile (*mobilis*)" but it also has "a steadfastness free of motion (*inmobilem firmitatem*)". Consciousness, since it "resembles divinity", is "immobile

---

[88] This teaching differs from Philo's usage of the terms "movement" and "rest". In his opinion, God is at rest while the cosmos is in motion (*De Post. Caini* 23). This view displays Philo's Platonic concern about God's transcendence. The wise man partakes of God's stability or rest (ἠρεμίας), turning away from the movement of the created world (*ibid.*, 23, 27-28).

in itself (*inmobilis ipse*)" and "moves itself in its own stability (*in stabilitate se commouet sua*). It is "resting with God (*consistens cum deo*)". *Corpus Hermeticum* 10.11 sums up this line of reasoning: "The immobility (στάσις) of mind intitates the motion (κίνησιν) of matter".

This understanding of the universe has influenced Logion 50. What characterizes the worthy person ascending, according to Logion 50, is that he is not only part of the cosmic order of movement but also participates in God's immobility, the state of rest. The verifying "sign" that he belongs to God's elect is that he knows that even though he belongs to the created order, he also belongs to God. He participates in the nature of the Unmoved Mover. He contains the motion of the macrocosmos within himself while at the same time partaking of God's rest. Thus Logion 50 speaks of the "sign of your father (ⲡⲙⲁⲉⲓⲛ ⲙ̄ⲡⲉⲧⲛ̄ⲉⲓⲱⲧ) which is *in* you (ⲉⲧϩⲛ̄ ⲧⲏⲩⲧⲛ̄)".

Not surprisingly, the succeeding Logion 51 has adapted the Hermetic concept of rest to the Jewish dialogue regarding the resurrection of the dead. In this Logion, the disciples pose the question to Jesus: "When will the rest of the dead (ⲧⲁⲛⲁⲡⲁⲩⲥⲓⲥ ⲛ̄ⲛⲉⲧⲙⲟⲟⲩⲧ) take place, and when will the new world come?" Jesus responds, "What you look for has come, but you do not know it". Apparently, the disciples have misunderstood that they are already experiencing God's rest. They are already living in the state of the resurrection because they now are partaking of God's nature.

4) *Conclusion:*

The answers provided in Logion 50 are a curious blend of Hermetic and Jewish traditions. Concepts such as the Hermetic self-generated God have congealed with Jewish and Hermetic beliefs in the pre-existence of Light. The notion that the Light is manifested into the creation of humans through "their" image must be a reference to Genesis 1:26 and to the Jewish teaching that man was created in the image of the angels.

The Thomasites believed that they were the offspring of the Light and the elect of the Father: Judaism and Hermeticism both knew of the anthropogony that man's origin was the Light and that his destiny would demand his return. From Judaism, the

Thomasites inherited their self-designation as God's elect although they have recontextualized it to refer to the fact that they are elect not due to adoption but *because* they are God's own children, "sons of light". As the elect, they are the "standing encratites", those who have rejected the traditional family in favor of a single celibate lifestyle. This lifestyle is comparable to that of the angels who are standing in heaven before God.

The coupling of movement and rest has been influenced by Hermeticism's Unmoved Mover. Thus, the sign that the Thomasite belongs in heaven is the knowledge that he participates in the movement of the cosmos and rest of God. This participation in God's nature is a present experience rather than a future eschatological hope.

PART THREE

VISION MYSTICISM IN *THOMAS:*
LOGIA 15, 83, 59, 27, 37 AND 84

CHAPTER FIVE

THE VISION OF GOD OR HIS *KAVOD*

In Part Two, we discovered that Logion 50 is a fragment of ancient ascent lore which has affinities with Jewish mystical accounts of encounters with heaven's guardian angels during ascent to God. The mystical quest in the Jewish tradition, however, was not only for the purpose of touring the sacred realms. The quest ultimately culminated in the great vision of the enthroned deity.

Thus, accounts of Jewish mystical visionary experiences often include descriptions of the approach to God's throne. Several characteristics of these experiences prevail. First, God or his manifestation is seated on his throne-chariot surrounded by his heavenly court. When the mystic enters this heavenly room and sees the enthroned deity, he falls to the ground and worships him. Second, the manifestation of God, the *kavod* or Glory, is described in anthropomorphic terms as a man-like figure whose body or image emits light or fire. Third, encountering this light or drinking from the fountains in heaven is a transformative experience to the worthy mystic. Fourth, this mystical adventure is something which must be performed *before* death. Several Logia in the *Gospel of Thomas* which allude to these four Jewish mystical themes shall be examined in detail in this chapter.

1) *Logia 15 and 83 and the Kavod:*

a) *Etiquette in the Divine Throne Room and Logion 15:*
The vision of the Father in Logion 15 is described using courtly terminology which reflects knowledge of the Jewish mystical descriptions of God's divine throne room where God or his manifestation is seated on the Merkavah while the angels of his court surround him and worship him in song.[1]

ⲡⲉϫⲉ ⲓ̅ⲥ̅ ϫⲉ ϩⲟⲧⲁⲛ ⲉⲧⲉⲧⲛ̄ϣⲁⲛⲛⲁⲩ ⲉⲡⲉⲧⲉ ⲙ̄ⲡⲟⲩ ϫⲡⲟϥ ⲉⲃⲟⲗ ϩⲛ̄
ⲧⲥϩⲓⲙⲉ ⲡⲉϩⲧ ⲑⲏⲩⲧⲛ̄ ⲉϫⲙ̄ ⲡⲉⲧⲛ̄ϩⲟ ⲛ̄ⲧⲉⲧⲛ̄ⲟⲩⲱϣⲧ ⲛⲁϥ ⲡⲉⲧⲙ̄ⲙⲁⲩ
ⲡⲉ ⲡⲉⲧⲛ̄ⲉⲓⲱⲧ

---

[1] For a comprehensive look at the content of visions of God in Jewish Apocalyptic literature, refer to C. Rowland, "The Visions of God in Apocalyptic Literature", *JSJ* 10 (1979) 137-154.

100   CHAPTER FIVE

> Jesus said, "When you see the one who was not born of woman, prostrate yourselves on your faces and worship him. That one is your Father."[2]

It is not unusual for the mystic who enters the throne room to prostrate himself before the divine King and enter into his worship. For instance, in *1 Enoch* 14.24, when the mystic comes before the enthroned God who is surrounded by his heavenly court of angels, he falls prostrate on the ground before him. Similarly, *2 Enoch* 22.4 records that when Enoch sees God's face of light, he falls down flat on his face and worships him.

The Father is further described as "not born of woman". This expression has affinities with the Jewish phrase "one born of woman" which is found in Job 14:1 and 15:14. Here it describes the degraded condition of humanity. Moses' ascent was objected to by the angels because he was "born of woman" and was thus not worthy to be in heaven (cf. *Sukkah* 52.a; *Ma'ayan ha-Hokmah* 60-61; *Pesik. R.* 20,98a, 25,128a). According to *Megillah* 13b, this phrase is connected with mortality. Thus the mortal condition is due to the fact that the person was born from the womb of a woman. Moreover, according to *3 Enoch* 5.2, the phrase is associated with sexual generation. Thus the angels used this phrase to object to Enoch's ascent into heaven because he was created from a drop of semen entering the womb of a woman.

It would seem that the phrase "not born of woman" applied to God suggests that unlike humans who are generated by procreation, God is self-generated. This coincides with the ideology of Logion 50 where the Light is said to be self-generated.[3] Thus it seems that the Father and the Light have been assimilated in *Thomas*' tradition.

b) *The Hidden Kavod in Logion 83:*

This is further supported by Logion 83 which tells of "the image of the light of the Father":

ⲡⲉϫⲉ ⲓ̅ⲥ̅ ϫⲉ ⲛϩⲓⲕⲱⲛ ⲥⲉⲟⲩⲟⲛϩ ⲉⲃⲟⲗ ⲙ̅ⲡⲣⲱⲙⲉ ⲁⲩⲱ ⲡⲟⲩⲟⲉⲓⲛ
ⲉⲧⲛ̅ϩⲏⲧⲟⲩ ϥϩⲏⲡ ϩⲛ̅ ⲑⲓⲕⲱⲛ ⲙ̅ⲡⲟⲩⲟⲉⲓⲛ ⲙ̅ⲡⲉⲓⲱⲧ ϥⲛⲁϭⲱⲗⲡ ⲉⲃⲟⲗ
ⲁⲩⲱ ⲧⲉϥϩⲓⲕⲱⲛ ϩⲏⲡ ⲉⲃⲟⲗ ϩⲓⲧⲛ̅ ⲡⲉϥⲟⲩⲟⲉⲓⲛ

---

[2] B. Layton, *Nag Hammadi Codex II,2-7, together with XIII,2, Brit. Lib. Or. 4926(1), and P. Oxy. 1, 654, 655 1: Gospel According to Thomas, Gospel According to Philip, Hypostasis of the Archons, and Indexes* (Leiden, 1989) 60.; Eng, trans. by Lambdin, 61.

[3] Refer to Chapter Four, Section 1b.

Jesus said, "The images are manifest to man, but the light in them remains concealed in the image of the light of the Father. It [the light] will become manifest, but his [the Father's] image will remain concealed by his light.[4]

This Logion has been labeled an "extremely difficult logion".[5] The following analysis is an attempt to make some sense of this Logion by stressing its Jewish mystical foundation and its association with Syrian theology.

First, it appears that the most sensible antecedent to ϥ (he/it) in the Coptic verbal construction ϥⲛⲁϭⲱⲗⲡ (he/it will become manifest) is ⲡⲟⲩⲟⲉⲓⲛ ⲙ̄ⲡⲉⲓⲱⲧ (the light of the father). This is a different rendering from past translations which seem to understand the antecedent to be ⲡⲉⲓⲱⲧ (the father).[6] The text is senseless if Father is taken as the antecedent because if God *can* be seen, how is it that his image *cannot* be seen? Moreover, there is a primitive Jewish tradition that teaches that one could not directly see God himself. This tradition goes back to the Exodus story where Moses is told that no one can see God face to face (Exod 33:20).

Because of this belief, there developed the theology of God's Glory or his *kavod* which concealed God while at the same time revealing him. In the Priestly source of the Pentateuch, the Glory is a light phenomenon associated with the pillar of cloud and fire which surrounded Yahweh as he led the Israelites through the desert or when his presence was at the Tabernacle (cf. Exod 16:10b; 24:16-17, 43-44; 40:34-35, 38; Num 17:7; 1 Kings 8:10-11; Lev 9:23-24; 1 Sam 3:3, 4:21). Later, a bodily form in the appearance of a human being was attributed to the Glory (i.e. Exod 33:18-34:8).[7]

This is quite developed in Ezekiel. The prophet recounts that he saw in a heavenly vision, a "likeness as the appearance of a man (דמות כמראה אדם)" seated upon the Throne-Chariot (1:26). He describes the enthroned deity as follows in 1:27:

> And upward from what had the appearance of his loins I saw as it were gleaming bronze, like the appearance of fire enclosed round

---

[4] Layton, *Nag Hammadi Codex II,2-7*, 84; trans. my own.
[5] G. Quispel, "Genius and Spirit", *Essays on the Nag Hammadi Texts in Honour of Pahor Labib*, NHS 56 (ed. M. Krause; Leiden, 1975) 159.
[6] See A. Guillaumont, H. -Ch. Puech, G. Quispel, W. Till, and Yassah 'Abd al Masih, *The Gospel According to Thomas* (San Francisco, 1959), 45; Lambdin, in Layton, *Nag Hammadi Codex II,2-7*, 85; M. Meyer, *The Gospel of Thomas: The Hidden Sayings of Jesus* (San Francisco, 1992) 57.
[7] J. Fossum, "Glory כבוד δόξα", *Dictionary of Deities and Demons in the Bible* (ed. K. van der Toorn *et. al.*; Leiden, 1995).

about; and downward from what had the appearance of his loins I saw as it were the appearance of fire, and there was brightness round about him.

Ezekiel states that this radiant light deity, this Man-like form, is the "Glory (*kavod*) of Yahweh" (1:28; cf. 8:2; 9:3-4; 10:4; 11:22-23; 43:1-5; 44:1-2; 47:1).[8] The term "image" or "likeness" was synonymous with "form", "body", and "glory".[9] So, the Glory, God's "body" or "image", was believed to be surrounded by radiant light, and when the mystic looked at God, he saw this light-man seated on the Throne.

Therefore, in the mystical tradition, we find that God's *kavod* can be beheld by prepared mystics.[10] Otherwise, it is "hidden" from view. A passage in the *Shiur Qomah* explains: "His דמות is hidden from everyone, but no one's דמות is hidden from Him".[11] This idea can also be seen in a legend recounted by Rabbi Banaah in the Babylonian Talmud, *Baba Batra* 58a. When Rabbi Banaah wanted to see the graves of the patriarchs, he was allowed to do this in the case of the human Abraham because Abraham is the "likeness of my image (בדמות דיוקני)". He was forbidden in the case of Adam because Adam is "my image itself (בדיוקני עצמה)". Thus he is told: "Thou hast seen the likeness of my image, my image itself thou mayest not see". Here Adam has been construed as the *kavod* itself which remains hidden from view.

Connected to this is the attribution of the name "Hidden" to the *kavod* in some circles. This is most evident in the Elchasite sect. The prophet, Elchasai, is called "Hidden Power, since ἤλ means

---

[8] *Ibid.*

[9] J. Fossum, "Jewish-Christian Christology and Jewish Mysticism", VC 37 (1983) 263; *idem, The Name of God and the Angel of the Lord*, WUNT 36 (Tübingen, 1985) 283-284. A useful survey of the linguistic data is found in S. Kim, *The Origins of Paul's Gospel*, WUNT 4 (Tübingen, 1981) 195-205.

[10] Regarding the rabbinic ambiguity about whether or not one can see God, refer to I. Gruenwald, *Apocalyptic and Merkavah Mysticism*, AGJU 14 (Leiden, 1980) esp. 93-97, who proposes on page 94 that the negative opinion on seeing God in this literature, rules out "the possibility of a direct visual encounter with God"; I. Chernus, "Visions of God in Merkabah Mysticism", *JSJ* 13 (1982) 123-146, who outlines all of the passages in mystical literature where visions of God are mentioned and concludes that the majority of mystics "did think it possible for certain individuals, both human and celestial, to see God", 141; in his article, however, Chernus makes a sharp distinction between seeing God and seeing the *kavod*, not understanding that in Jewish thought God was the *kavod* and the *kavod* was God.

[11] M. S. Cohen, *The Shi'ur Qomah: Texts and Recensions*, Texte und Studien zum Antiken Judentum 9 (Tübingen, 1985) 113.

'power' and ξαι 'hidden'" (Hipp., *Ref.* 19.2.2).¹² The Semitic חיל כסי is behind Elchasai's name. In the Syriac translation of the *Pseudo-Clementines*, *haylâ kasyâ* refers to the God who is incomprehensible.¹³

Moreover, the Elkesaites, we are told, "suppose that the Christ is a figure similar to men, invisible to men, with a length of 96 miles, that is, 24 schoenoi, and a breadth of 6 schoenoi, 24 miles, and with a thickness of other dimensions" (Epiph., *Ref.* 30.17.6). Here the body of the "invisible" Christ is being described, just as the later *Shuir Komah* mystics describe the measures of God's body. For example, Rabbi Akiba remarks in the *Lesser Hekhalot* regarding the anthropomorphosis of the *Shuir Komah* as the "hidden glory": "He is like us, as it were, but greater than everything, and that is His glory which is hidden from us".¹⁴ Rabbi Ishmael is told by his angelic interpreter: "I am going to tell you what is the measure of the Holy One, blessed be He, that is hidden from all the creatures" (*Sefer Raziel*, 37a).

Thus the *kavod* could be spoken of in terms of its "hiddenness" which could be revealed to the mystics. This may be the intent of a passage from *Hekhalot Zutrati* 45b:¹⁵ "God who is beyond the sight of His creatures and hidden to the angels who serve Him, has revealed Himself to R. Akiba in the vision of the Merkabah".

It is interesting, in light of this discussion, that God's image in *Thomas* is said to be hidden (L. 83), and yet Jesus proclaims that "there is nothing hidden which will not become manifest" (L. 5; cf. 6b). Since the Thomasites were mystics they would have probably understood this Jesus saying (cf. Mk 4:22; Mt 10:26; Lk 8:17, 12:2) to refer to God's hidden *kavod* which would become manifest to them during their ascent experience. It is quite possible that Logion 83 of *Thomas* is one of our earliest attestations to this notion that God's image or *kavod* can be hidden. Note that here, God's image is concealed by the light radiating around God. This must be grounded in the early idea that God's form was enshrouded with light.

---

[12] A. F. J. Klijn and G. J. Reinink, *Patristic Evidence for the Jewish-Christian Sects*, NTSup 36 (Leiden, 1973) 156.

[13] *Rec.* 2.50.2; 2.51.6; Fossum, "Jewish-Christian Christology", 273.

[14] G. Scholem, *Major Trends in Jewish Mysticism* (New York, 1941) 66; for the Hebrew text of the *Lesser Hekhalot* see now P. Schäfer, *Synopse zur Hekhalot-Literatur*, Texte und Studien zum Antiken Judentum 2 (Tübingen, 1981) 148, section 352.

[15] Scholem, *Major Trends*, 364 n. 80.

This theology is very primitive and can be traced back to *1 Enoch* 14.20ff., where the seer Enoch describes his vision of the "Great Glory". He states that the Glory was robed in a gown "which was shining more brightly than the sun". Furthermore: "None of the angels was able to come in and see the face of the Excellent and the Glorious One; and no one of the flesh can see him". According to Enoch, this is because "the flaming fire was round about him, and a great fire stood before him". Thus it seems that Enoch attests to the tradition that God's form remains hidden behind his light. The visionary can only gain access to a vision of the deity through the deity's light.

Enoch's vision in *2 Enoch* 22 is comparable. There Michael brings Enoch "in front of the face of the Lord" and Enoch says that he "saw the appearance of the face of the Lord" (22.1).[16] What he describes, however, indicates that he did not see God's face directly but through a light screen. Thus the face that Enoch beheld was "like iron made burning hot in a fire [and] brought out, and it emits sparks and is incandescent".

Philo attests to this tradition as well. In the *De mutatione nominum* 7, he describes Moses' vision of God after Moses has ascended to heaven in Exodus 33. According to Philo, Moses "entered into the darkness" which means into "existence invisible and incorporeal". While in this heavenly sphere, Moses "searched everywhere and into everything in his desire to see (ἰδεῖν) clearly and plainly Him, the object of our much yearning, Who alone is good".[17] Yet Philo insists that God Himself "by His very nature cannot be seen (ὁρᾶσθαι)" (*ibid.* 9).[18] The reason that God cannot be seen is explained by Philo in *De fuga et inventione* 165: "the man that wishes to set his gaze upon the Supreme Essence, before he sees (ἰδεῖν) Him will be blinded by the rays that beam forth all around Him".[19] Consequently, Philo concludes that God said to Moses, "What is behind Me thou shalt see, but My face thou shalt by no means see (Exod. 33.23)".[20] Obviously, Philo is transmitting here

---

[16] R. H. Charles, *The Apocrypha and Pseudepigrapha of the Old Testament in English* 2 (Oxford, 1913 and reprints) 442.
[17] F. H. Colson and G. H. Whitaker, *Philo* 5, LCL 275 (Cambridge, Mass., 1934 and reprints) 144-145.
[18] *Ibid.*, 146-147.
[19] *Ibid.*, 100-101.
[20] In a late twelfth-century text by the Jewish mystic Judah ben Barzillai al-Bargeloni, we find these traditions developed to the extent that now the

the Jewish tradition that God's essence is encompassed by his light. Moreover, seeing God's face directly would place the mystic in mortal danger: the vision would consume him by fire.

The Qumran documents contain a passage of interest. In *1QH* 7, the hymnist writes in praise of God: "Thou hast revealed Thyself to me in Thy Power as perfect light". The "Power" is an alternative name of God's Glory.[21] The hymnist is therefore indicating that God's essence can not be perceived directly. Rather God reveals himself, his "Power" or his "*kavod*", through a manifestation of light.

Logion 83 is partaking of these mystical notions. In Logion 83, the *kavod* or image of God is concealed by its own light. The "Hidden" *kavod* is only revealed to the worthy mystic who approaches the throne and falls prostrate on his face, worshipping God.

i) Transformation by Fire and Drink in Logia 82, 108, and 13: When encountering God in a heavenly ascent experience, the mystic expected that the Hidden *kavod* would be revealed through its light. In the Jewish mystical tradition, encountering the light of God was a transforming experience. Thus, Jewish tradition taught that the righteous will be transformed into beings of light or fire resembling or superior to the angels.[22] This idea is evident in *Pesikta Rabbati* 11.7 (end):

---

mystic can only see the "back" of the light (cf. Exod 33): "And that great light is called the Glory of our God...For any 'seeing' that is spoken of regarding an angel or a prophet, concerning this created light...refers to the Holy One blessed be He showing then the end [or "back"] of the light to whom He wishes, but no man can see the beginning of the primordial light and the content of his glory and the image of his brilliance" (*Kommentar zum Buch Jezira* [ed. Halberstam; 1885] 16-18; quoted in G. Scholem, *On the Mystical Shape of the Godhead: Basic Concepts in the Kabbalah* [forward J. Dan; trans. J. Neugroschel; ed. and revised according to 1976 Hebrew ed. J. Chipman; New York, 1991] 155).

[21] Fossum, *Name*, 179ff.

[22] See C. Morray-Jones, "Transformational Mysticism in the Apocalyptic-Merkavah Tradition", *JJS* 48 (1992) 13ff.; cf. *Pesikta Rabbati* 35.2, *JT Shabb*. 6.9 (8d), *BT Sanh*. 93a; cp. *2 Enoch* 22.7-10 where Enoch becomes "like one of the glorious ones, and there was no observable difference" so that he can "stand in front of my [God's] face forever"; and also *Ascension of Isaiah* 9 where the transformation into an angelic being is described in terms of the exchange of garments: it is probable that the motif of donning an angelic-garment is a less terrifying manner in which to describe the event of the fiery transformation of the flesh.

> In this world, Israel cleave unto the Holy One, blessed be He, as it is said: "But ye that did cleave unto the LORD" (Deuteronomy 4:4). But in the time to come they become like (Him). Just as the Holy One, blessed be He, is fire consuming fire, according to what is written: "For the LORD is consuming fire" (Deuteronomy 4:24), so shall they be consuming fire, according to what is written: "...and the light of Israel shall be for a fire and his Holy One for a flame" (Isaiah 10:17).[23]

By being transformed, the righteous are being conformed to the *kavod* or God's light manifestation.

The traditions about the hero Moses suggest that in order to be in the presence of God and the heavenly hosts, it is necessary that one's flesh be turned into fire. In the *Midrash Gedullah Mosheh* section 2,[24] Metatron raises the objection before God: "Moses is unable to withstand the angels, for the angels are princes of fire, while he is flesh and blood". So God commands Metatron to "change his flesh into torches of fire". Consequently, Metatron changed Moses' flesh "to torches of fire, and his eyes to Merkabah-wheels, and his strength to that of Gabriel, and his tongue to flame".

Apparently this Mosaic tradition is quite primitive since Philo's commentary on Exodus indicates that even as early as the first century, it was believed that Moses underwent a transformation into light when he mounted Sinai. Philo relates that first, Moses took with him Aaron, Nadab, and Abihu. But these men could not stand the rays emitted from God because, Philo explains, there are only a few individuals who like salamanders can live in fire, the inner region of God (*Quaest. Ex.* 2.27-28; *cf. Mig.* 166). It is Moses who goes up beyond heaven into God (*Quaest. Exod.* 2.40). There Moses becomes Mind, uniting with God, his own *logos* becoming luminous (*Ibid.* 2.44).

Similarly traditions about the paradigm-mystic Enoch suggest that a fiery transformation is connected with ascent motifs. Thus when Enoch ascends to the throne in *3 Enoch* 15, he states:

---

[23] M. Friedmann, *Pesikta Rabbati* 1 (Vienna 1880, second ed. Tel Aviv, 1963) 46b, and trans. Braude (New Haven and London, 1968) 215; the idea that the righteous will be changed to fire is found at *Num. R.* 2.13; *Pesik. R.* 35.2; *Midrash Tehillim* 1.20; *3 En* 48C; *Alphabet of R. Aqiba*, S. A. Wertheimer, *Batei-Midrašot* 2 (Jerusalem, 1953) 352.

[24] Ed. by S. A. Wertheimer, *Batei-Midrašot* 1 (Jerusalem, 1950) 277; this motif is also present in *Midrash Tehillim* 90.1, and *Deut. R.* 11.4.

At once my flesh turned to flame, my sinews to blazing fire, my bones to juniper coals, my eyelashes to lightening flashes, my eyeballs to fiery torches, the hairs of my head to hot flames, all my limbs to wings of burning fire, and the substance of my body to blazing fire.

In a striking passage from *Hekhalot Rabbati* 3.4, it is stated that no creature's eyes can behold the Garment of God including the angels':

For he who beholds it - yea, he who glances and sees it - his eyeballs are ignited and whirled around: his eyeballs cast forth fire and spew forth fiery torches, and they set him ablaze and burn him up - for fire issues forth from the man who beholds and sets him ablaze and burns him up.

Whether this passage is describing the dangers confronting the mystic[25] or the mystical transfiguration taking place within him,[26] is not as essential to this discussion as the acknowledgment that when the visionary sees God's garment, he can expect that his body will be transformed into fire and if he is unworthy, this will be a fatal experience.[27]

This motif is not exclusive to Jewish traditions. According to *Corpus Hermeticum* 10, the visionary experience transforms one into an immortal being. This vision is so dazzling that one is almost blinded by the sight. So in 10.4, Tat says to Hermes, "You have filled us with a vision, father, which is good and very beautiful, and my mind's eye is almost [blinded] in such a vision". Hermes explains that this vision brings with it immortality. Furthermore he quells Tat's fear that this vision will cause harm to the mystic. He explains that those who are prepared for the vision will find that it will probe them more sharply with its splendor than the fiery rays of the sun, but will do no damage:

Yes, but the vision of the good is not like the ray of the sun which, because it is fiery, dazzles the eyes with light and makes them

---

[25] Chernus, "Visions", 128-130.
[26] G. Scholem, *Jewish Gnosticism, Merkabah Mysticism, and Talmudic Tradition* (New York, 1965) 60.
[27] Morray-Jones, "Transformational Mysticism," 25; cf. M. Lieb, *The Visionary Mode: Biblical Prophecy, Hermeneutics, and Cultural Change* (London, 1991) 95-96 who notes the rabbinic tradition of the *ḥashmal* (living creatures speaking fire) that surrounds the Enthroned Figure: according to this tradition, the rabbis taught that "there was once a child who was reading at his teacher's house the Book of Ezekiel, and he apprehended what *ḥashmal* was, whereupon a fire went forth from *ḥashmal* and consumed him".

shut. On the contrary, it illuminates to the extent that one capable of receiving the influence of intellectual splendor can receive it. It probes more sharply, but it does no harm, and it is full of all immortality (ἀθανασίας) (10.4).

In *Corpus Hermeticum* 10.5-6, Hermes continues, teaching Tat that "we are still too weak now for this sight", but the person who is capable of seeing the Good and thus knowing it "can understand nothing else". Hermes describes the consequent transformation:

> He stays still, all bodily sense and motion forgotten. Having illuminated all his mind, this beauty kindles his whole soul and by means of body draws it upward, and beauty changes his whole person into essence. For when soul has looked on <the> beauty of the good, my child, it cannot be deified (ἀποθεωθῆναι) while in a human body.[28]

Thus, in Hermeticism, we find a transformational mysticism associated with the visionary experience. The vision is described using the language of light: the sight of the Good will cause no harm to the prepared mystic but it will probe him more sharply than the sun's dazzling and fiery rays. This vision deified the mystic. It is not unlikely that the esoteric Jewish tradition of transformational fire mysticism is associated with the Hermetic notions regarding ascent and the transforming vision.

It is within this context that Logion 82 in the *Gospel of Thomas* is best understood.[29] Here Jesus states:

> ΠΕΤϨΗΝ ΕΡΟΕΙ ΕϤϨΗΝ ΕΤCΑΤΕ ΑΥⲰ ΠΕΤΟΥΗΥ ⲘⲘΟΕΙ ϤΟΥΗΥ ⲚⲦⲘⲚⲦΕΡΟ.
>
> He who is near me is near the fire, and he who is far from me is far from the kingdom.[30]

---

[28] Cp. Stobaeus who describes the deifying aspect of "the vision of the beautiful and the good" in his *Excerpts* 6.18, stating that a knowledgeable person can "behold Him with his own eyes, and beholding become blessed (θεασάμενος μακάριος γενέσθαι)". This transformation can not occur, however, when the person is "in the body". Thus one must "exercise the soul beforehand here, in order that when it goes there, where it is permitted to see God, it may not miss the way".

[29] Luke 12:49 preserves another saying of Jesus containing fire imagery: "I came to cast fire upon the earth; and would that it were already kindled". Notice that the fire in this saying is understood to be cast upon the earth as an apocalyptic purging while in the *Thomas* Logion, the fire is associated with one's proximity to Jesus and the Kingdom.

[30] Layton, *Nag Hammadi Codex II,2-7*, 84.; trans. by Lambdin, 85.

The parallelism of the two stitches indicates that the proximity to the "fire" or the "Kingdom" is one and the same thing. Moreover, Jesus claims to be there as well. Consequently, this Logion can be interpreted as follows: the person who is near to Jesus has ascended to the place of the light or fire, where Jesus now is, the heavenly Kingdom; the person who is not near to Jesus, has not yet ascended there.

This interpretation is even more intriguing when the succeeding Logion 83 is taken into consideration: the Logion regarding viewing the "image of the light of the Father". When Logion 82 and Logion 83 are taken together, there is no doubt that the fire is connected with the light of God's image. Jesus is thus understood to be in the Kingdom or in the presence of God's light or fire. And it is necessary for Jesus' followers to ascend to this place in order to be with him.

Although Logion 82 does not mention the transforming power of the fire directly, it is most probable that the early Thomasites were familar with the fire transformation motif from their Jewish and Hermetic heritage. Once in the presence of Jesus and the fire of God, they could expect to be transformed into an angelic-like figure, resembling the light of God himself.

Logion 108 confirms that *Thomas* was familiar with transformational mysticism. In this Logion, Jesus says:

ΠΕΤΑϹⲰ ΕΒΟⲖ ϨⲚ ΤΑΤΑΠΡΟ ϤΝΑϢⲰΠΕ ⲚΤΑϨΕ ΑⲚΟΚ ϨⲰ
ϮⲚΑϢⲰΠΕ ΕΝΤΟϤ ΠΕ ΑⲨⲰ ΝΕΘΗΠ ΝΑ ΟⲨⲰⲚϨ ΕΡΟϤ

He who will drink from my mouth will become like me. I myself shall become he, and the things that are hidden will be revealed to him.[31]

The metaphor of drink[32] in Jewish literature was connected with the phenomenon of ascent: the revelation of hidden wisdom during the ascent is described in the metaphorical terms of drink.[33] In *1 Enoch* 48.1-2, Enoch sees in heaven "the fountain of

---

[31] Layton, *Nag Hammadi Codex II,2-7*, 90.; trans. by Lambdin, 91.

[32] On the subject of divine and wineless intoxication, refer to H. Lewy, *Sobria Ebrietas*, BZNW 9 (1929) 1-175.

[33] Drink and transformation are connected in some texts which do *not* mention ascent. I.e., Jn 4.10-15, where Jesus is the living water which brings eternal life. R. Bultmann gives the complete background to the phrase "living water": *The Gospel of John. A Commentary* (trans., G. R. Beasley-Murray, R. W. N. Hoare, and J. K. Riches; Philadelphia, 1971) 182ff., 303-305. Those who receive milk from the Father's breast become perfect and belong to those

righteousness" and "around it were many fountains of wisdom, and all the thirsty drank, and were filled with wisdom". After drinking from these fountains, "their dwelling places become with the holy, righteous, and elect ones". Thus those who ascend into this realm are given the secrets of heaven and a divine home by drinking from the fountains of wisdom. The hidden wisdom is revealed and "is poured out like water" (*1 En* 49.1).[34] According to *4 Ezra* 1.47, Ezra is commanded to keep hidden the contents of seventy books, "for in them is the spring of understanding, the fountain of wisdom, and the stream of knowledge".

Some traditions allege that when Moses received the Torah on Mount Sinai, in addition he also received "the root of wisdom, and the riches of understanding and the fount of knowledge" (*2 Baruch* 59.7). According to Samaritanism, Moses drank from seven "glorious" fountains where he ascended (*Memar Marqa* 2.1).[35]

This tradition of ascent and drink is also evident in Gnosticism: in Justin's *Book of Baruch*, Elohim and all the righteous drink of the water in heaven after their ascent (Hipp., *Ref.* 5.27.2-3).

It seems that the ascent imagery of drink and the acquistion of secret knowledge is bound up intimately with fire and transformational language as well. A most remarkable example of this is contained in one of Ezra's visions in *4 Ezra* 14.38-41:

> ...a voice called me saying: "Ezra, open your mouth and drink what I give you to drink." Then I opened my mouth, and behold, a full cup was offered to me; it was full of something like water, but its color was like fire. And I took it and drank; and when I had drunk it, my heart poured forth understanding, and wisdom increased in my breast, for my spirit retained its memory; and my mouth was opened, and was no longer closed.

Ezra is given a cup of fire-water to drink. Upon drinking it, he acquires knowledge which formerly was hidden from him. The language used to describe his experience reflects his transformation: his heart and spirit are changed; his mouth is opened. The

---

of the right hand (*Ode Sol.* 19.1-5). These are the elect (*Ode Sol.* 8.13, 15). 1 Pet 2.2 states that spiritual milk nourishes salvation. In John 7:37-39, Jesus' saying, "if any one thirst, let him come to me and drink", is interpreted by the Johannine author to be the reception of the Spirit.

[34] See further, K. Rudolph, *Die Mandäer* 2, FRLANT 75 (Göttingen, 1961) 384ff., 398f.; G. W. H. Lampe, *The Seal of the Spirit* (London, 1951) 111 n. 2.

[35] J. Macdonald, *Memar Marqah. The Teaching of Marqah* 2, BZAW 84 (Berlin, 1963) 81.

language of drink has congealed with the language of fire transformation. Could the language of drink be an alternative way to describe the mystical experience of fire transformation?[36]

For instance, Philo uses the language of drink to describe the condition of fire transformation. In *Legum Allegoriae* 1.82-84, Philo explains that by praising God the person "is exempt from body and matter"; in other words, praise "takes a man out of himself" and allows the mind to go out "from itself" and offer itself "up to God". Consequently, after ascending, this person "is permeated by fire..., and is drunk with sober drunkenness".

Ode 11 of the Syrian *Odes of Solomon* lends support to the view that "being drunk" and encountering "fire" are equivalent metaphors describing the mystical transformation into the divine. In this Ode, the hymnist tells of an ascent experience where "speaking waters touched my lips from the spring of the Lord generously. And so I drank and became intoxicated, from the living water that does not die" (11.6-7). This person continues to speak of his experience, detaching himself from the world and being permeated by the light of God: "And I abandoned the folly cast upon the earth, and stripped it off and cast it from me. And the Lord renewed me with his garment and possessed me by his light" (11.10-11). Furthermore, the hymnist alludes to his vision as he is taken to Paradise: "And the Lord (is) like the sun upon the face of the land" (11.13). Thus Ode 11 uses both the metaphors of drink and light permeation to describe the mystical transformation which is associated with vision quests.[37]

It may be that this is also the best context in which to interpret Logion 13, since the concepts of drink and fire appear here too:

ⲡⲉϫⲉ ⲓ̅ⲥ̅ ⲛ̄ⲛⲉϥⲙⲁⲑⲏⲧⲏⲥ ϫⲉ ⲧⲛ̄ⲧⲱⲛⲧ ⲛ̄ⲧⲉⲧⲛ̄ϫⲟⲟⲥ ⲛⲁⲉⲓ ϫⲉ ⲉⲉⲓⲛⲉ
ⲛ̄ⲛⲓⲙ ⲡⲉϫⲁϥⲛⲁϥ ⲛ̄ϭⲓⲥⲓⲙⲱⲛ ⲡⲉⲧⲣⲟⲥ ϫⲉ ⲉⲕⲉⲓⲛⲉ ⲛ̄ⲟⲩⲁⲅⲅⲉⲗⲟⲥ
ⲛ̄ⲇⲓⲕⲁⲓⲟⲥ ⲡⲉϫⲁϥ ⲛⲁϥ ⲛ̄ϭⲓ ⲙⲁⲑⲑⲁⲓⲟⲥ ϫⲉ ⲉⲕⲉⲓⲛⲉ ⲛ̄ⲟⲩⲣⲱⲙⲉ

---

[36] According to I. Gruenwald, "Knowledge and Vision: Towards a Clarification of Two 'Gnostic' Concepts in the Light of Their Alleged Origins", *Israel Oriental Studies* 3 (1973) 72 n. 37, "Water-imagery goes almost hand in hand with the light-imagery". He notes that this is the case in Qumran, *Odes of Solomon*, and Mandaic religion.

[37] Note too that early Christianity speaks of being "filled with the spirit" using both of these metaphors: the tongues of fire from heaven come down and rest upon the people in Acts 2:2-3 at Pentecost; Paul associates being filled with the spirit with drinking a spiritual drink (1 Cor. 10:2-4, 12:13; cf. Eph. 5:18). Refer to Lewy, *Sobria Ebrietas*, 55-56, on the subject of divine intoxication and being full of the Spirit.

ⲛ̄ⲫⲓⲗⲟⲥⲟⲫⲟⲥ ⲛ̄ⲣⲙ̄ⲛ̄ϩⲏⲧ ⲡⲉϫⲁϥ ⲛⲁϥ ⲛ̄ϭⲓ ⲑⲱⲙⲁⲥ ϫⲉ ⲡⲥⲁϩ
ϩⲟⲗⲱⲥ ⲧⲁⲧⲁⲡⲣⲟ ⲛⲁϣ⟨ϣ⟩ⲁⲡϥ ⲁⲛ ⲉⲧⲣⲁϫⲟⲟⲥ ϫⲉ ⲉⲕⲉⲓⲛⲉ ⲛ̄ⲛⲓⲙ
ⲡⲉϫⲉ ⲓⲏ̄ⲥ̄ ϫⲉ ⲁⲛⲟⲕ ⲡⲉⲕⲥⲁϩ ⲁⲛ ⲉⲡⲉⲓ ⲁⲕⲥⲱ ⲁⲕϯϩⲉ ⲉⲃⲟⲗ ϩⲛ̄
ⲧⲡⲏⲅⲏ ⲉⲧⲃⲣ̄ⲃⲣⲉ ⲧⲁⲉⲓ ⲁⲛⲟⲕ ⲛ̄ⲧⲁⲉⲓϣⲓⲧⲥ̄ ⲁⲩⲱ ⲁϥϫⲓⲧϥ̄
ⲁϥⲁⲛⲁⲭⲱⲣⲉⲓ ⲁϥϫⲱ ⲛⲁϥ ⲛ̄ϣⲟⲙⲧ ⲛ̄ϣⲁϫⲉ ⲛ̄ⲧⲁⲣⲉ ⲑⲱⲙⲁⲥ ⲇⲉ ⲉⲓ
ϣⲁⲛⲉϥ ϣⲃⲉⲉⲣ ⲁⲩϫⲛⲟⲩϥ ϫⲉ ⲛ̄ⲧⲁ ⲓ̄ⲥ̄ ϫⲟⲟⲥ ϫⲉ ⲟⲩ ⲛⲁⲕ ⲡⲉϫⲁϥ
ⲛⲁⲩ ⲛ̄ϭⲓ ⲑⲱⲙⲁⲥ ϫⲉⲉⲓϣⲁⲛ ϫⲱ ⲛⲏⲧⲛ̄ ⲟⲩⲁ ϩⲛ̄ ⲛ̄ϣⲁϫⲉ
ⲛ̄ⲧⲁϥϫⲟⲟⲩ ⲛⲁⲉⲓ ⲧⲉⲧⲛⲁϥⲓ ⲱⲛⲉ ⲛ̄ⲧⲉⲧⲛ̄ⲛⲟⲩϫⲉ ⲉⲣⲟⲉⲓ ⲁⲩⲱ ⲛ̄ⲧⲉ
ⲟⲩⲕⲱϩⲧ ⲉⲓ ⲉⲃⲟⲗ ϩⲛ̄ ⲛ̄ⲱⲛⲉ ⲛ̄ⲥⲣⲱⲕϩ ⲙ̄ⲙⲱⲧⲛ̄

> Jesus said to his disciples, "Compare me to someone and tell me whom I am like." Simon Peter said to him, "You are like a righteous angel." Matthew said, "You are like a wise philosopher." Thomas said, "Teacher, my mouth is utterly incapable of saying whom you are like." Jesus said, "I am not your teacher. Because you have drunk, you have become intoxicated from the bubbling spring which I have measured out." And he took him and withdrew and told him three words. When Thomas returned to his companions, they asked him, "What did Jesus say to you?" Thomas said to them, "If I tell you one of the words which he told me, you will pick up stones and throw them at me; a fire will come out of the stones and burn you up."[38]

According to this Logion, when Jesus asks his disciples, "Compare me to someone and tell me whom I am like?", Thomas delivers the correct response: "Teacher, my mouth is utterly incapable of saying whom you are like". This answer demonstrates to Jesus that Thomas has gained a full understanding of Jesus' identity. Thus Jesus tells Thomas that he no longer is his teacher.[39] Furthermore: "Because you have drunk, you have become intoxicated from the bubbling spring that I measured out". Thomas is filled with Jesus' water.

Clues to Jesus' identity are found in the continuation of Logion 13. Jesus takes Thomas aside and tells him three words. When Thomas returns to the company of the disciples, they inquire into this secret transmission. Thomas responds: "If I tell you one of the words he spoke to me, you will pick up rocks and stone me, and fire will come from the rocks and consume you".

Since stoning is the penalty for blasphemy in Judaism (Lev 24:16; *Sahn.* 7.5), Jesus in Logion 13 has identified himself with God's secret divine Name consisting of three words, אהיה אשר אהיה

---

[38] Layton, *Nag Hammadi Codex II,2-7*, 58; trans. my own.
[39] According to S. Patterson, *The Gospel of Thomas and Jesus* (Somona, 1993), 206, this statement indicates that Thomas has been elevated to an equal status with Jesus.

THE VISION OF GOD OR HIS *KAVOD*   113

(Exod 3:14).⁴⁰ It is thus understandable that Thomas says that his mouth is incapable of identifying Jesus (ϩολως ταταπρο ναϣϣαπϥ αν ετραχοος χε εκεινε ⲛ̄ⲛⲓⲙ). This can only be a reference to the Jewish tradition of the unutterable and unpronouncable Name of God, the *Shem hammephorash*.⁴¹

This situation is akin to the tale in John 10:30ff. When Jesus states, "I and the Father are one" (10:30), the Jews pick up rocks to stone Jesus (10:31). They tell Jesus that "we stone you for blasphemy; because you, being a man, make yourself God" (10:34). Thus Jesus in the Gospel of John is expressing his unity with God the Father by laying claim to the possession of the divine Name (cf. 17:11).⁴² Stoning is the consequence of such claims.⁴³

What then does Thomas understand that the other disciples do not? That Jesus is Yahweh, the Name of God, and thus is God's manifestation or *kavod*. Furthermore, Jesus proclaims that Thomas has undergone a mystical transformation. As in Logion 108, he has drunk the divine drink and so has been deified.

---

⁴⁰ B. Gärtner, *The Theology of the Gospel According to Thomas* (trans. E. Sharpe; New York, 1961) 123, correctly argued that the "three words" belong to the speculation about Jesus' unspeakable Name (cf. *Acts Thom* c. 136) and that this motif emanated from Jewish speculation about the Name of God, "I am that I am"; H. -Ch. Puech, "Une collection de paroles de Jésus récemment retrouvée: l'Évangile selon Thomas", *CRAIBL* (1957) 156, suggested that the three-fold Name, "Father, Son, and Holy Spirit", is the "three words"; R. M. Grant and D. N. Freedman, *The Secret Sayings of Jesus* (New York, 1960) 133-134, believed that it is the three words according to the Naassenes (Hipp., *Ref.* 5.8.5); H. -M. Schenke, "The Function and Background of the Beloved Disciple in the Gospel of John," *Nag Hammadi, Gnosticism, and Early Christianity* (eds. C. W. Hedrick and R. Hodgson, Jr. (Peabody, 1986) 124, offers a wild conjecture seemingly unconcerned about the fact that the text insists that the spoken words are blasphemous: "It does not require much to imagine that one of these three 'words' could have been something like: 'You will remain until I come (σὺ μένεις ἕως ἔρχομαι) or 'you will not experience death until I come (σὺ οὐ μὴ γεύσῃ θανάτου ἕως ἔρχομαι)'."

⁴¹ H. Bietenhard, "ὄνομα, etc.", *TDNT* 5 (1967) 268-269.

⁴² The background to this theme in the Gospel of John is the development in Judaism of the forms of the Name, אני הוא and אני והוא. Since the personal Name of God יהוה was withdrawn from public use, the pronunciation of God's actual Name, the שם המפורש was considered to have extreme power. Circumlocutions of this Name eventually also came to be considered powerful. Thus אני הוא is treated as the Name of God in Jewish sources as well as the slightly altered form, אני והוא, "I and He", which denoted the solidarity of Israel and God. Thus, the divine Name hinted at in John 10:30 is probably the latter. John, however, substitutes Jesus for Israel. For a complete discussion, see C. H. Dodd, *The Interpretation of the Fourth Gospel* (Cambridge, 1968) 93-96.

⁴³ Refer to Fossum, *Name*, 126 n. 151.

So what is the meaning of the statement regarding fire coming forth from the rocks and consuming the disciples? Only when this statement is viewed in the context of fire transformation is it sensible. As noted earlier, there are dangers involved when one seeks to encounter the divine but is not properly prepared or worthy. One of these dangers is not living through the fire transformation. Here the transformation occurs as the result of encountering the divine unutterable Name. This encounter seems to function in the same way as the *visio Dei*.[44] Thomas' knowledge of Jesus' identity and his encounter with the divine Name made him worthy to be transformed. But the other disciples' ignorance makes them unworthy. Thus if they were to encounter the divine Name, they would be consumed and die rather than be transformed by God's fire.

The *Acts of Thomas* (Greek) 47 seems to be aware of Logion 13 or the tradition embedded in it. Significantly, it describes Thomas' transformation in terms of fire rather than drink. According to this text, Thomas says, "thou art he that hast shown unto us many mysteries; thou didst call me apart from all my fellows and spakest unto me three words wherewith I am *inflamed*, and am not able to speak them unto others". The *Acts of Thomas* seems to be relying on Logion 13 in the composition of this passage. This suggests that the author is aware of the metaphorical tradition of transformation which equates being permeated by fire with being drunk since he states that Thomas was "inflamed" rather than, as Logion 13 records, "drunk".

Thus it would seem that the *Gospel of Thomas* is aware of mystical transformation and prefers to use the metaphor of drink over that of fire, although Logia 13 and 82 seem to be aware of the latter. It can be argued that the Thomasites believed that once they had ascended to heaven and were with Jesus, they would become drunk with him or permeated by him and thus would be transformed into Jesus himself, just as Logion 108 indicates. There would be no observable difference between Jesus and themselves. And, since Jesus calls himself "the light" in Logion 77,[45] it is

---

[44] It is not surprising that in Hekhalot mysticism, the mystic can encounter God's Name. In the *Hekhalot Zutarti* (Schäfer, *Synopse*, sections 350-352), Isaiah sees God's Name embodied in his Glory. Cf. C. Morray-Jones, "The Glorious Beloved: 'The Shi'ur Qomah' and Merkabah Mysticism in Some Rabbinic and Early Christian Sources" (paper delivered for 1993 Annual SBL in "Rabbinic and Patristic Exegesis Group").

[45] Refer to Chapter One, Section 3b.

plausible that the Thomasites expected to be transfigured into beings of light during their heavenly encounter with Jesus.

ii) The Embodied Light in Logion 83:
In the earlier discussion of Logion 83, it was shown that the mystic expected to encounter the "Hidden" *kavod*, the Body of God which was concealed within its light. This divine condition however, is contrasted with the human situation, where the human's image or body is visible while the light within the human body is hidden in the light enveloping God's body or *kavod*. Thus the saying reads: "The images are manifest to man, but the light in them remains concealed in the image of the light of the Father". The divine image, the light or spiritual body is said to be within the human image, the material body. This is to be associated with the teaching purported in Logion 24 that "there is light within a person from the light (ⲟⲩⲛ̄ ⲟⲩⲟⲉⲓⲛ ϣⲟⲟⲡ ⲙ̄ⲫⲟⲩⲛ ⲛ̄ⲛⲟⲩⲣⲙ̄ⲟⲩⲟⲉⲓⲛ)".[46]

In *Thomas*, this inner light seems to be connected to the soul which has taken up residence in the body. Jesus differentiates between the soul and the body, exclaiming in Logion 29: "I am amazed at how this Great Wealth (ⲧⲉⲉⲓⲛⲟϭ ⲙ̄ⲙⲛ̄ⲧⲣⲙ̄ⲙⲁⲟ) has come to dwell in this poverty"[47] (cf. L. 87 and 112). The phrase "Great Wealth" seems to be a technical term in the *Gospel of Thomas* which is equivalent to "Great Power" since, in Logion 85, Adam is said to have come from "Great Power and Great Wealth (ⲛⲟⲩⲛⲟϭ ⲛ̄ⲇⲩⲛⲁⲙⲓⲥ ⲙⲛ̄ ⲟⲩⲛⲟϭ ⲙ̄ⲙⲛ̄ⲧⲣⲙ̄ⲙⲁⲟ)".[48] The parallelism in Logion 85 suggests that "Great Wealth", according to *Thomas*, is equivalent to "Great Power".

The title "Great Power" or "Power" is one of the many names of the intermediary figure, God's agent, in Jewish and Christian circles.[49] For instance, in Justin Martyr, the "Power of God" is also the "Spirit" (*1 Apol.* 33.6). The *Teachings of Silvanus* enumerates these names identifying the "Power" with "Christ" and "Light" (106.21-28). Furthermore, as we saw in Chapter One, Section 3a, the title "Great Power" is an alternative for "Great Glory". Thus it is understandable that, in the philosophical tract *Eugnostos the Blessed*, the heavenly "Adam of Light" who is God's "image" is

---

[46] Layton, *Nag Hammadi Codex II,2-7*, 64; Eng. trans. mine.
[47] *Ibid.*, 66; Eng. trans. mine.
[48] *Ibid.*, 84; Eng. trans. by Lambdin, 85.
[49] Fossum, "Jewish-Christian Christology", 271-273.

characterized as the "Great Power" (75.5-6; 76.19-24; 81.12). Or in *Silvanus* that "a Great Power and a Great Glory has made the universe known" (112.8-10). Thus when Logion 24 states that the "Great Wealth" has come to dwell in the body, it is the same as saying that the "Great Power", the "Great Glory", the "Spirit", or the "Light" has put on the human image.

There is a Hermetic tradition to this effect. The Hermeticist Zosimos taught that the inner man Adam was called "*Phōs*" which means "Man (φώς), which is Light (φῶς)".[50] The *Phōs* put on the external fleshly Adam which was wrought from the elements of Heimarmene or Fate. Because the human body carries within it this *Phōs*, "men are called φῶτας".

Similarly, in *Poimandres*, the heavenly Light-Man, the Anthropos, inhabits the body (*C.H.* 1.14). Thus the human being is twofold, immortal in the "essential man (τὸν οὐσιώδη ἄνθρωπον)", but subject to Fate in his mortal body (*C.H.* 1.15). The *Phōs* in Zosimos and the Anthropos in *Poimandres* are present as the higher element, the "soul and spirit" (*C.H.* 1.17).

Jewish-Christianity is involved in this discussion. The Jewish-Christians argue that Christ, the Great Power, put on the first man (*Acts Thom.* 10, Syriac). Furthermore, Christ is the first man and "a general soul" (Symmachians in Marius Victorinus, *ep. ad Gal.* 1.15).[51] According to the *Pseudo-Clementines Recognitions* 1.28.4, God made man whose "internal Form (*interna species*)" is "older" than the creation of the human body.[52] This internal Form must be the Form or Body of God. This motif is probably responsible for the Ebionite and Elchasite teachings that Christ, as the True Prophet, clothed himself not only with the body of Adam, but also with the subsequent bodies of the patriarchs and Jesus.[53]

Clearly Logia 83, 24, and 29 belong to this milieu by teaching that the higher element, the Body of God, the Light, or the soul

---

[50] C. G. Jung who provides a trans. of Zosimos made in collaboration with M.-L. von Franz in his *Psychology and Alchemy*, The Collected Works of C. G. Jung 12 (trans. R. F. C. Hull; London, 1968) 363; for Greek text, refer to M. Berthelot, *Collection des Anciens Alchimistes Grecs* 3 (Paris, 1888) xlix, 4-12; R. Reitzenstein, *Poimandres* (Leipzig, 1906) 103ff. provides Greek text and commentary; for amended Greek text and commentary, see W. Scott, *Hermetica* 4: *Testimonia with introduction, addenda, and indices* (Oxford, 1936; reprinted London, 1968) 104-153.

[51] Klijn and Reinink, *Patristic Evidence*, 232.

[52] On this see, Fossum, "Jewish-Christian Christology", 267-268.

[53] *Ibid.*, 267-271.

came to dwell within the human body. How did this situation occur? Although the *Gospel of Thomas* does not contain a Logion which explicitly addresses this question, there is a clue in the text of Logion 85. According to this Logion, Adam came from "Great Wealth" and "Great Power", but because he showed himself unworthy, he experienced death. Without doubt, this is a reference to Adam's Sin and Fall. It is probable that the readers of the *Gospel of Thomas* would have equated this event with the Fall and embodiment of the soul, when Adam was given "garments of skins" to wear, since salvation, according to Logion 37, involved the stripping of this bodily garment.[54] This actually is an encratite teaching as we know from Clement of Alexandria's report on the encratite teacher, Julius Cassianus. He stated that the consequence of the Sin or Desire is "birth" and "death", and resulted in the Fall of the soul into the body or "garments of skins" (*Strom.* 3.13.91-93). This must be how the "Great Wealth" or "Light" came to dwell within the poverty of the human body (L. 29) and became concealed there (L. 83).

iii) Knowledge of the Self in Logia 3b, 67, 56, and 80:
As might be expected, salvation must involve contact with this divine inner element. This is quite explicit in Logion 70a, where Jesus says: "If you bring forth what is within you (ⲡⲏ ϩⲛ̄ ⲑⲏⲧⲛ̄), what you have will save you".[55] This can only be a reference to the higher element, the "Light" or the soul which has been concealed within the poverty which is the human body.

But what does it mean to bring forth this element? Logion 3b illuminates this situation:

ϩⲟⲧⲁⲛ ⲉⲧⲉⲧⲛ̄ϣⲁⲛⲥⲟⲩⲱⲛ ⲑⲏⲧⲛ̄ ⲧⲟⲧⲉ ⲥⲉⲛⲁⲥⲟⲩⲱ(ⲛ) ⲧⲏⲛⲉ ⲁⲩⲱ ⲧⲉⲧⲛⲁⲉⲓⲙⲉ ϫⲉ ⲛ̄ⲧⲱⲧⲛ̄ ⲡⲉ ⲛ̄ϣⲏⲣⲉ ⲙ̄ⲡⲉⲓⲱⲧ ⲉⲧⲟⲛϩ ⲉϣⲱⲡⲉ ⲇⲉ ⲧⲉⲧⲛⲁⲥⲟⲩⲱⲛ ⲑⲏⲧⲛ̄ ⲁⲛ ⲉⲉⲓⲉ ⲧⲉⲧⲛ̄ϣⲟⲟⲡ ϩⲛ̄ ⲟⲩⲙⲛ̄ⲧϩⲏⲕⲉ ⲁⲩⲱ ⲛ̄ⲧⲱⲧⲛ̄ ⲡⲉ ⲧⲙⲛ̄ⲧϩⲏⲕⲉ

When you come to know yourselves, then you will become known, and you will realize that it is you who are the sons of the living Father. But if you will not know yourselves, you dwell in poverty and it is you who are that poverty.[56]

---

[54] For a complete discussion, refer to A. De Conick and J. Fossum, "Stripped Before God: A New Interpretation of Logion 37 in the Gospel of Thomas", *VC* 45 (1991) 124-132; cf. below, Chapter Six, Section 2.
[55] Layton, *Nag Hammadi Codex II,2-7*, 80; Eng. trans. by Meyer, 53.
[56] *Ibid.*, 54; Eng. trans. by Lambdin, 55.

According to this text, the divine dwelling within, the true Self, will continue to dwell in the poverty of the body unless one acquires knowledge about this true Self. Thus when one recognizes that one is a "son of the Living Father" who is dwelling in a material body, one will not continue to live in this impoverished condition.

Comparable to Logion 3b is Logion 111. Here the Jesus saying, "The heavens and earth will roll up in your presence, and whoever is living from (the source of) the Living One will not see death" (ⲙ̄ⲡⲏⲩⲉ ⲛⲁϭⲱⲗ ⲁⲩⲱ ⲡⲕⲁϩ ⲙ̄ⲡⲉⲧⲛ̄ⲙ̄ⲧⲟ ⲉⲃⲟⲗ ⲁⲩⲱ ⲡⲉⲧⲟⲛϩ ⲉⲃⲟⲗ ϩⲛ̄ ⲡⲉⲧⲟⲛϩ ϥⲛⲁⲛⲁⲩ ⲁⲛ ⲉⲙⲟⲩ)",[57] is explicated by another Jesus saying which the author introduces with the gloss, "Does not Jesus say". This gloss indicates that the author understands the latter saying to be an explanation of the former. According to the latter saying, "Whoever finds himself is superior to the world (ⲡⲉⲧⲁϩⲉ ⲉⲣⲟϥ ⲟⲩⲁⲁϥ ⲡⲕⲟⲥⲙⲟⲥ ⲙ̄ⲡϣⲁ ⲙ̄ⲙⲟϥ ⲁⲛ)".[58] So "finding oneself" was understood by the author to mirror the phrase "living from (the source of) the Living One". Thus, it is plausible that the phrase, "living from (the source of) the Living One", means that one has contacted the divine inner element, the true Self, and is living accordingly as a "son of the Living Father" (cf. L. 3b). One has found the source of life within oneself. One has recognized one's divine nature and now has the knowledge that this nature has made one superior to the material world. Death will not be experienced.

The vitalness of this Self-knowledge is summed up in Logion 67. According to this saying, one can know everything and still be deficient if one does not have Self-knowledge:

> ⲡⲉϫⲉ ⲓ̄ⲥ̄ ϫⲉ ⲡⲉⲧⲥⲟⲟⲩⲛ ⲙ̄ⲡⲧⲏⲣϥ ⲉϥⲣ̄ ϭⲣⲱϩ ⲟⲩⲁⲁϥ ϥⲣ̄ ϭⲣⲱϩ ⲙ̄ⲡⲙⲁ ⲧⲏⲣϥ
>
> Jesus said, "Whoever knows everything but is deficient in self-knowledge, he is deficient in everything".[59]

It seems that Self-knowledge in *Thomas* has two sides. It is revelatory and redemptive since only by "knowing" one's spiritual Self, which is the "Light" or the soul will one be known by

---

[57] Layton, *Nag Hammadi II,2-7*, 92; Eng. trans. mine.
[58] *Ibid.*, 92; Eng. trans. by Lambdin, 93.
[59] Trans. my own. Refer to Chapter One, Section 1 for different renderings of the Coptic.

God (L. 3b) and not see death (L. 111). But, this knowledge also includes the recognition that the world and the material body are only corpses:

ⲡⲉⲧⲁϩⲥⲟⲩⲱⲛ ⲡⲕⲟⲥⲙⲟⲥ ⲁϥϩⲉ ⲉⲩⲡⲧⲱⲙⲁ ⲁⲩⲱ ⲡⲉⲛⲧⲁϩϩⲉ ⲁⲡⲧⲱⲙⲁ ⲡⲕⲟⲥⲙⲟⲥ ⲙⲡϣⲁ ⲙⲙⲟϥ ⲁⲛ

Whoever has come to understand the world has found (only) a corpse, and whoever has found a corpse is superior to the world (L. 56).[60]

ⲡⲉⲛⲧⲁϩⲥⲟⲩⲱⲛ ⲡⲕⲟⲥⲙⲟⲥ ⲁϥϩⲉ ⲉⲡⲥⲱⲙⲁ ⲡⲉⲛⲧⲁϩϩⲉ ⲇⲉ ⲉⲡⲥⲱⲙⲁ ⲡⲕⲟⲥⲙⲟⲥ ⲙⲡϣⲁ ⲙⲙⲟϥ ⲁⲛ

He who has recognized the world has found the body, but he who has found the body is superior to the world (L. 80).[61]

Thomas' understanding of Self-knowledge is indebted to Hermeticism. J. Mahé, for instance, has identified a Hermetic saying which seems to have influenced *Thomas*. He points to a sentence found in *Definitions of Hermes Trismegistos to Asklepios* which reads: "Who knows himself, knows (the) All".[62] Thus, in Hermeticism, the famous Delphic maxim, "know yourself", is an appeal to recognize one's essentially divine Self.[63]

In *Corpus Hermeticum* 1, we discover several sayings with this nuance:

Let him <who> is Mind recognize himself as immortal, that desire is the cause of death, and let him recognize all that exists (ἀναγνωρισάτω ⟨ὁ⟩ ἔννους ἑαυτὸν ὄντα ἀθάνατον, καὶ τὸν αἴτιον τοῦ θανάτου ἔρωτα, καὶ πάντα τὰ ὄντα) (1.18).[64]

The one who recognized himself (ὁ ἀναγνωρίσας ἑαυτὸν) attained the chosen good, but the one who loved the body that came from error of desire goes on in darkness, errant, suffering sensibly the effects of death (1.19).

He who has understood himself advances toward god (ὁ νοήσας ἑαυτὸν εἰς αὐτὸν χωρεῖ) (1.21).

---

[60] Layton, *Nag Hammadi Codex II,2-7*, 74; eng. trans. by Lambdin, 75.
[61] *Ibid.*, 82; Eng. trans. by Lambdin, 83.
[62] J. -P. Mahé, "Les définitions d'Hermès Trismégiste à Asclépius", *RSR* 50 (1976) 193-214, esp. 203.
[63] See H. D. Betz, "The Delphic Maxim ΓΝΩΘΙ ΣΑΥΤΟΝ in Hermetic Interpretation", *HTR* 63 (1970) 471, where he surveys the growth of this theme through the Greek philosophers and into Hermeticism.
[64] Trans. my own.

Let the person who is Mind recognize himself (ὁ ἔννους ἄνθρωπος ἀναγνωρισάτω ἑαυτόν) (1.21).[65]

The themes of deification and immortalization are associated with Self-knowledge according to these passages. Self-understanding includes the knowledge that one is "*Nous*" or "Mind" the highest god (1.6), and this recognition advances one toward god.

Furthermore, the aspirant cannot be led to the "portals of knowledge" until he first rips off "the tunic that you wear, the garment of ignorance, the foundation of vice, the bonds of corruption, the dark cage, the living death, the sentient corpse, the portable tomb, the resident thief..." (*C.H.* 7.2). Because the person chooses to wear this "odious tunic", he is dragged down and is unable to "look up and see the fair vision of truth and the good that lies within" and he is incapable of recognizing the wicked plot of the sense organs which are blocked up with matter and pleasure (7.3).

In another tract, *Corpus Hermeticum* 10.8, we are told that "the vice of the soul is ignorance". The ignorant soul is blind and "discerns none of the things that are nor their nature nor the good", it is "shaken by the bodily passions" and becomes "wretched", a "slave to vile and monstrous bodies, bearing the body like a burden, not ruling but being ruled".

How can one change this condition? Through knowledge. Thus "the virtue of the soul...is knowledge (γνῶσις); for one who knows is good and reverent and already divine (θεῖος)" (*C.H.* 10.9). One must "leave the senses of the body idle" so "the birth of divinity will begin (ἔσται ἡ γένεσις τῆς θεότητος)" (*C.H.* 13.7).

Betz argues that Philo's interpretations of the Delphic maxim are so similar to those found in the Hermetic writings that they must at least share a common philosophical tradition.[66] In *De fuga* 46, he admonishes his reader to "learn well the country of the senses; know thyself, and the parts of which thou dost consist, what each is, and for what it was made, and how it is meant to work". Self-knowledge is summed up by Philo as understanding the function of the body and the "Mind that is in thee".

Or as *De migratione Abrahami* 7-8 explains, to "know yourself" is the same as Moses' command in Exodus 34:12, "πρόσεχε σεαυτῷ": "evermore be coming to know thyself, as Moses teaches thee in

---

[65] Trans. my own.
[66] Betz suggested this already in his study, "The Delphic Maxim...in Hermetic Interpretation", 477ff.

many places, saying 'Give heed to thyself'". One is a stranger in the land of the body and so one needs to aquire the knowledge of the Self in order to rule as King, escaping the "prison-house", the body, and departing sense perception.

Subsequently, in chapter 137, the Delphic maxim is cited again and it is interpreted to mean: "say clearly who you are, in body, in soul, in sense-perception, in reason and speech, in each single one, even the most minute, of the subdivisions of your being". Philo warns that "until you have scrutinized and come to know yourselves", it is senseless to even study Nature. Only after Self-investigation can the Mind reach "the summit" and pay tribute to God there (139). Philo summarizes this view in chapter 13 where he suggests that Self-knowledge is possible because the Mind "knows itself" and converses with the "things of mind", driving out that part of the soul which is inclined to the "province of sense-perception".

Philo puts this doctrine into the mouth of Moses in chapters 184-195. Moses attacks those aspirants who seek to ascend and discover the mysteries of the universe before they have gained Self-knowledge. He commands them to "come down therefore from heaven" and "explore yourselves only and your own nature" (185). Only after the aspirant gains this knowledge is he capable of ascending in order to achieve immortality and so is commanded to "bestir yourselves and seek for your departure hence, for it is a call not to death but to immortality" (189). This departure requires the withdrawal from the "perceptions and other bodily faculties" (190) since the senses are a hindrance to the visionary experience (191). It is in this way that the mind will "arrive at the Father of piety and holiness" (194) and will reach the goal, crowning "the accurate self-knowledge it has gained with the knowledge of God Himself" (195).

Apparently, for Philo, Self-knowledge is knowledge of one's spiritual Self. This knowledge, however, brings with it knowledge of the worthlessness of the sensible self, the material body. Realization of this means that one must now drive out the self of the senses. Thus we discover several passages which teach that the body is a "corpse" and that this must be recognized:

> For he is well aware that the body, our "leathern" bulk ("leathern" is the meaning of "Er"), is wicked and a plotter against the soul, and is even a corpse and a dead thing (*Leg. All.* 3.69).

> But the philosopher being enamoured of the noble thing that lives in himself, cares for the soul, and pays no regard to that which is really a corpse, the body..." (*Ibid.* 3.72).
>
> When, then, O soul, wilt thou in fullest measure realize thyself to be a corpse-bearer? (*Ibid.* 3.74).
>
> And since earth is a place of wretchedness, even that heavenly man is a mixture consisting of soul and body; and from his birth until his end he is nothing else than a corpse-bearer (*Quaest. Gen.* 1.93; cf. 2.12).
>
> The wise man does not seek a grave, for the body is the grave of the soul, in which it is buried as if in a grave..." (*Ibid.* 4.75).
>
> "It is not wide of mark to say that the soul of the wise man, having a body that is inanimate and heavy, like a bronze statue, is always carrying a corpse" (*Ibid.* 4.77; cf. *De agric.* 25)

According to Philo, knowledge of the divine Self is tied closely with knowledge of the nothingness of the material self. It is in this sense that he probably meant the following: "he who has thoroughly comprehended himself, thoroughly despairs of himself, having as a step to this ascertained the nothingness in all respects of created being. And the man who has despaired of himself, is beginning to know Him that IS" (*De somn.* 1.60).

Thus it seems that the acquistion of Self-knowledge according to Hermetic writings and the writings of Philo which may have been influenced by Hermeticism has two sides: understanding the divinity of the Self and recognizing the worthlessness of the material body. This Self-knowledge is life-giving, bringing with it transformation into the divine as well as the destruction of death.

Without doubt, Self-knowledge as it is described in *Thomas* is associated with Hermeticism, where knowledge calls for an understanding of one's own divinity as well as the nothingness of the material body. It appears, however, that this Hermetic tradition was welded with Jewish mythological language prior to the composition of *Thomas*.

The Greek Oxyrhynchos version of Logion 3b transmits a significant variant which demonstrates this welding of Hermetic philosophy about Self-knowledge with the Jewish mythological terminology of the Kingdom. Fitzmyer has reconstructed the Greek as follows:

[ὃς ἂν ἑαυτὸν] ᾿γνῷ, ταύτην εὑρή[σει]

[Whoever] knows [himself] will fin[d] it (the Kingdom).[67]

The redemptive act of Self-knowledge is stressed in this saying: knowledge of one's divine Self, that is one's identity as a child of God, is required in order to access the Kingdom and thus gain salvation. The message of the redemptive quality of Self-knowledge which Hermeticism emphasizes appears in Logion 3b (Greek) in a Jewish garb: in order to enter God's Kingdom, one must know oneself, that one is divine, belonging to the elect congregation of "sons of the Living Father", and that one's material body and existence in this world is impoverished and needs to be renounced. Thus one has successfully contacted the divine dwelling within, the true Self, by acquiring Self-knowledge. Then one has discovered the Kingdom and encountered God.

2) *Logion 59 and Ecstatic Vision:*

The final Logion to be mentioned in the context of achieving a vision of the deity is Logion 59:

ΠΕϪΕ ΙC ϪΕ ϬⲰϢⲦ ⲚⲤⲀ ΠΕΤΟⲚϨ ϨⲰⲤ ΕΤΕΤⲚ̄ΟⲚϨ ϨⲒⲚⲀ ϪΕ ⲚΕΤⲘ̄ⲘΟⲨ ⲀⲨⲰ Ⲛ̄ⲦΕⲦⲚ̄ϢⲒⲚΕ ΕⲚⲀⲨ ΕⲢΟϤ ⲀⲨⲰ ⲦΕⲦⲚⲀϢϬⲘ̄ ϬΟⲘ ⲀⲚ ΕⲚⲀⲨ

Jesus said, "Look for the Living One while you are alive, lest you die and then seek to see him and you will be unable to see (him)."[68]

This Logion makes it very clear that the vision quest is something one must do during one's lifetime, not after death: it is an ecstatic experience rather than an eschatological one.[69] Jesus commands his followers to "look for (ϬⲰϢⲦ Ⲛ̄ⲤⲀ)" the "living" God while they are still alive.

The attribution "living" has its origin in Jewish traditions where it refers to God as a divine being (cf. Josh 3:10; Hos 1:10; Ps 84:2).[70]

---

[67] J. A. Fitzmyer, "The Oxyrhynchos Logoi and the Coptic Gospel of Thomas", *Essays on the Semitic Background of the New Testament* (London, 1971) 375.

[68] Layton, *Nag Hammadi Codex II,2-7*, 74; Eng. trans. mine.

[69] W. Bousset distinguishes two types of soul journeys: eschatological (after the body's death), and ecstatic (during the life of the performer) which anticipates the eschatological. Refer to his "Die Himmelsreise der Seele", *ARW* 4 (1901) 136-169.

[70] On all the occurrences of this title in Greek versions of the Old Testament and Pseudepigrapha, refer to W. Bousset, *Die Religion des Judentums im späthellenistischen Zeitalter*, Handbuch zum Neuen Testament 21 (3rd ed. H. Gressmann; Tübingen, 1926) 311 n. 4.

The Christians are heir to this tradition. Thus in Revelation 1:18 the "Living One" is a divine name of the Christ. In the *Dialogue of the Savior* 44, the phrase "living God" is employed (cf. 46 which is to probably be reconstructed "[the] living [God]"). Jesus, in the *Acts of Thomas*, is called "Living (One) who (art) from the Living (One)" (c. 60) and in chapter 136, he is said to be the "Son of the living God".

This understanding is reflected in the *Gospel of Thomas* as well where "living" is employed as a title for God. This is quite clear both in Logion 37, where the disciples are told that they will see the "Son of the Living One", and in Logion 3 where the "living Father" is found. The same phrase is used in Logion 50: God is called the "living Father". This must also be the meaning behind the introductory phrase to *Thomas* where Jesus is portrayed as a divine being because he too has the title "living".

In *Thomas*, Jesus warns that if they wait to "seek to see" the Living God after they die, they will not be able to have the desired vision. Logically, it follows from this that they will not achieve their salvation but will experience death instead. Thus, in Logion 59, Jesus is commanding his followers to be mystics: to seek a vision of God during their lifetimes as the way to overcome death and gain life or immortality.

The Syrian mystic Macarius develops this theme substantially. According to his writings, it is necessary to "gaze continually" on Christ. Then the Christ "out of his Spirit, out of the substance of the light itself, ineffable light" paints "a heavenly image" and presents it as the spouse for the believer's soul (*Hom.* 30.4). Only when this image has been "stamped on" the soul, can the person enter the Kingdom; if the soul does not bear the image, then it is rejected (*Hom.* 30.5). One, therefore, must gaze on the Christ, approach the Lord, and beg to receive the Spirit "while here on earth". For if anyone "...while on this earth does not seek and has not received life for his soul, namely, the divine light of the Spirit, when he departs from his body, he is already separated into the places of darkness on the leftside". He ends up "in hell" (*Hom.* 30.6).[71]

It is notable that this type of vision quest during the lifetime of the seeker parallels Jewish mystical tradition rather than the gnostic systems in general. The Jewish mystics sought visions

---

[71] G. A. Maloney, *Pseudo-Macarius. The Fifty Spiritual Homilies and the Great Letter*, The Classics of Western Spirituality (New Jersey, 1992) 191-192.

during their lifetimes, while the gnostics believed in post-mortem ascent when they would shed the body and return to the Pleroma.[72]

3) *Conclusion:*

It is clear from the discussion of these vision Logia in *Thomas* that the Thomasites attempted to secure visions of the Father or his light-emitting *kavod*. They did not, however, expect to see God directly. The "Hidden" *kavod* would be revealed to them through the light emanating from it. This visionary experience was a transformative one, deifying them. Furthermore, this transformation was described metaphorically in the terms of encountering God's "fire" or becoming drunk with a divine "drink" after having ascended to heaven.

The *Gospel of Thomas* insists that this ascent is an ecstatic experience rather than an eschatological one. Those who are *not* mystics will not have life eternal.

Furthermore, the human condition was contrasted with the divine. Unlike God whose image or body is concealed by his light, the human image or body is visible while the divine light is hidden within it. This light, soul, or "Great Wealth" seems to have been embodied as a consequence of Adam's Sin. This divine dwelling within, the true Self, must be brought forth and contacted. Acquiring knowledge that one's true Self is divine, opens to the person the doors of the Kingdom and full participation in divinity.

---

[72] See Gruenwald, "Knowledge and Vision", 92.

CHAPTER SIX

PREPARATIONS FOR THE VISIO DEI IN LOGIA 27 AND 37[1]

The *visio Dei* promised to be a transformative experience fraught with grave danger. If the mystic was unworthy or impure, he would be consumed by the light or fire emanating from God's Body or Glory. In the *Gospel of Thomas*, Logia 27 and 37 outline the preparations that the mystic must perform in order to be worthy to "see" God.

1) *Logion 27 and Purification for the Visio Dei:*

> ἐὰν μὴ νηστεύσηται τὸν κόσμον οὐ μὴ εὕρηται τὴν βασιλείαν τοῦ θεοῦ καὶ ἐὰν μὴ σαββατίσητε τὸ σάββατον οὐκ ὄψεσθε τὸν πατέρα[2]
>
> ετε⟨τῆ⟩ τⲙ̄ⲣⲛⲏⲥⲧⲉⲩⲉ ⲉⲡⲕⲟⲥⲙⲟⲥ ⲧⲉⲧⲛⲁϩⲉ ⲁⲛ ⲉⲧⲙⲛ̄ⲧⲉⲣⲟ ⲉⲧⲉⲧⲛ̄ⲧⲙ̄ⲉⲓⲣⲉ ⲙ̄ⲡⲥⲁⲙⲃⲁⲧⲟⲛ ⲛ̄ⲥⲁⲃⲃⲁⲧⲟⲛ ⲛ̄ⲧⲉⲧⲛⲁⲛⲁⲩ ⲁⲛ ⲉⲡⲉⲓⲱⲧ
>
> If you do not fast from the world, you will not find the Kingdom. If you do not observe the Sabbath as Sabbath, you will not see the Father.[3]

a) *Past Interpretations of Logion 27:*

In 1897, B. Grenfell and A. Hunt published their Greek version of what would later become known as Logion 27 of the *Gospel of Thomas*.[4] Their reconstruction of the text allowed for the accusative τὸν κόσμον to follow the verb νηστεύειν. They noted that the meaning "fast to the world" is very "harsh".[5] Apparently, they had this particular saying in mind when they drew the conclusion regard

---

[1] The following discussion on Logion 27 is an expansion of my article, "Fasting from the World: Encratite Soteriology in the *Gospel of Thomas*", *The Notion of "Religion" in Comparative Research, Selected Proceedings of the XVIth IAHR Congress, Rome, 3rd-8th September, 1990* (ed. U. Bianchi; Rome, 1994) 425-440.

[2] Layton, *Nag Hammadi Codex II,2-7*, 118, where H. Attridge has reconstructed the greek fragment; see also the prior work of B. Grenfell and A. Hunt, ΛΟΓΙΑ ΙΗΣΟΥ: *Sayings of Our Lord from an Early Greek Papyrus*, (London, 1897) 10.

[3] Layton, *Nag Hammadi Codex II,2-7*, 64.; Eng. trans. my own.

[4] Grenfell and Hunt, *Sayings of Our Lord*, 10-11.

[5] *Ibid.*, 10.

ing Papyrus Oxyrhynchus 1 that "its chief characteristics seem to have been its Encratite and mystic tendencies".[6]

When the Coptic text was discovered, it was shown that, indeed, Grenfell and Hunt were correct to have understood the accusative to be an accusative of respect since the Coptic has the preposition ϵ-, "to", before ⲕⲟⲥⲙⲟⲥ.[7] Thus the translations: "to fast to the world", "to fast as regards the world", "to fast from the world", or "to fast the world".

A. Guillaumont and A. Baker separately have shown that the Syriac preposition *l* may be responsible for both the accusative and dative translations since *l* may signify either a direct or indirect object.[8] This is seen on three occasions in the Syriac *Liber Graduum* where the phrase "fasting to the world (*smwhy l'lm'*)" is used (373.18-19; 373.23-24; 828.13).[9]

Futhermore, Baker notes that in the Syriac tradition, this very phrase reflects an ascetic attitude. In *Liber Graduum* 824.19-20, the perfect disciple is to "recede from all evils" which is consequently called "fasting to the world" (828.13) or "fasting from the world and its delights" (89.24-25). He states that the meaning is the same as that preserved in the encratite *Acts of Paul and Thecla*, "blessed are those who have renounced the world (μακάριοι οἱ ἀποταξάμενοι τῷ κόσμῳ)",[10] or *Thomas* Logion 110 where Jesus gives the commandment "renounce the world (ⲙⲁⲣⲉϥⲁⲣⲛⲁ ⲙ̄ⲡⲕⲟⲥⲙⲟⲥ)".[11]

Baker argues that Clement of Alexandria, when transmitting the saying preserved in *Stromata* 3.15.99, "Blessed are they who are fasting from the world (μακάριος οὗτοί εἰσιν οἱ τοῦ κόσμου νηστεύοντες)", used the genitive construction to attempt to translate the phrase "withdrawal from the world" just as the genitive is later employed in this way by Basil (*P.G.* 33.375C) and Macarius (*P.G.*, 37.716A and 809B) to express world abstinence (ἀναχωρήσας τοῦ κόσμου).

The most recent interpretation of Logion 27, made by T.

---

[6] *Ibid.*, 16-17.
[7] J.A. Fitzmyer, "The Oxyrhynchus Logoi", 391.
[8] A. Guillaumont, "Νηστεύειν τόν κόσμον (P. Oxy. 1, verso, I,5-6)", *BIFAO* 61 (1962) 15-23; A. Baker, "'Fasting to the World'", *JBL* 84 (1965) 291-294.
[9] M. Kmosko, *Liber Graduum*, Patrologia Syriaca 1,3 (Paris, 1926).
[10] R. A. Lipsius and M. Bonnet, *Acta Apostolorum Apocrypha* 1 (Leipzig, 1891) 238.
[11] Layton, *Nag Hammadi Codex II,2-7*, 92; Lambdin, Eng. trans. in same volume, 93.

128   CHAPTER SIX

Baarda,[12] attempts to extrapolate this Logion from its encratite context and place it within a gnostic milieu. In his article, he examines Logion 27 in light of gnostic texts and phrases, attempting to reconstruct the intent of the author of *Thomas* whom he assumes to be a gnostic. He acknowledges that "the saying or the two elements of the saying belonged to a very archaic Jewish-Christian tradition which may have preserved items of the preaching of Jesus, in which both the practice of fasting and the observation of the Sabbath were said to be conditions for the life of the believer".[13] But because Baarda starts with "the presumption that the present collection of sayings known as the Gospel of Thomas is a Gnostic florilegium",[14] he insists that the author of *Thomas* intended the Logion to reflect gnostic ideology instead.

Baarda concludes that Logion 27 uses the word "Sabbath" as a parallel to the "World". This fits with the gnostic belief that the "Sabbath" is either the Demiurge or the created cosmos of the Demiurge. Thus fasting and sabbatizing denote the gnostic depreciation of this world since the Kingdom is where the true origin and destiny of the gnostic exists.

Obviously, Baarda's argument is based entirely on his assumption that the *Gospel of Thomas* is a gnostic Gospel. Because *Thomas* is a gnostic Gospel, it must be illuminated by Gnostic parallels. A gnostic understanding is then extrapolated, and so this confirms *Thomas* as a gnostic Gospel with a gnostic author and a hidden gnostic meaning.

The *Gospel of Thomas*, however, is demonstratively *not* gnostic. Research indicates that the actual milieu for this gospel is the ascetic Syrian trajectory of primitive Christianity. Moreover, *Thomas* relies on Hermetic and primitive Jewish mystical traditions. Thus there is no reason to assume that a gnostic patina overlays the "archaic Jewish-Christian tradition" that Baarda argues Logion 27 once belonged too.[15] A valid analysis of Logion 27 must recognize it as a Jewish-Christian Logion which is associated with the early Jewish mystical trajectory.

---

[12] T. Baarda, "'If you do not Sabbatize the Sabbath...'. The Sabbath as God or World in Gnostic Understanding (Ev. Thom., Log. 27)", *Knowledge of God in the Graeco-Roman World*, EPRO 112 (eds. R. van den Broek, T. Baarda, and J. Mansfeld; Leiden, 1988) 178-201.
[13] *Ibid.*, 180.
[14] *Ibid.*, 200.
[15] Baarda, "Sabbatize the Sabbath", 245.

b) *Understanding the Jewish Mystical Influences on Logion 27:*
   (i) Sabbath Observation:

Unlike Baarda's Gnostic eisegesis of Logion 27, I suggest that Logion 27 is more appropriately exegeted as an early Christian Logion with Jewish origins that reflects the encratite Syrian milieu of *Thomas*.

As Grenfell and Hunt first observed about this Logion, it consists of two parallel clauses which are intended to balance each other.[16] Thus we can visibly present this Logion as follows:

> if you do not fast from the world=
> if you do not observe the Sabbath as Sabbath
>
> you will not find the Kingdom=
> you will not see the Father

"Finding the Kingdom" and "seeing the Father" mirror each other. The visionary experience itself can be expressed in Kingdom terminology: gaining a vision of the Father is discovering the Kingdom.

Two actions are prerequistes to this vision: that one "fast as regards the world" and that one "observe the Sabbath as a Sabbath". The phrase to "observe the Sabbath as a Sabbath" obviously is a strong admonition to keep the Jewish Sabbath law. The same expression is employed in this regard in Lev. 23:32 (σαββατιεῖτε τὰ σάββατα) and 2 Chron. 36:21 (τὰ σάββατα σαββατίσαι),[17] so *Thomas* may be seen to be a witness to a Septuagintism. If so, there can be no doubt that the phrase stems from Jewish-Christians who lived in a place where the language of the LXX had a strong influence. The Gentile Christians did not observe the Sabbath.

Logion 12 indicates that the Thomasites were tied closely to the law-abiding "Hebrews" of the primitive Jerusalem organization of which James was the leader (cf. *Ps.-Clem. Rec.* 1.43; Euseb., *Hist. Eccl.* 2.1.3, 2.23.4; Epiph., *Pan.* 78.8):

---

[16] Grenfell and Hunt, *Sayings of Our Lord*, 10-11.
[17] P. Brown, "The Sabbath and the Week in Thomas 27", *NT* 34 (1992) 193, proposes that 27b should be translated: "if you keep not the (entire) week as Sabbath". He bases his argument on the employment of caββatoy in Mark 16:9 where it translates "on the first day of the week (πρώτῃ σαββάτου)". It must be noted, however, that Mark 16:9 is not a good parallel to Logion 27b which uses ñcaββaton in conjunction with the verbal construction ετετñtπειρε πcaμβaton. This construction parallels Lev 23:32 and 2 Chron 36:21 exactly where the meaning clearly indicates observation of the Sabbath day.

The disciples said to Jesus, "We know that you will depart from us. Who is to be our leader?" Jesus said to them, "Wherever you are, you are to go to James the righteous, because of whom (ⲉⲧⲃⲏⲧϥ) heaven and earth came into being."[18]

Although this text certainly supports the thesis that the Thomasites held James in high esteem, it is interesting that he is connected to the founding of the world. Ultimately, this may be a reference to Proverbs 10:25b which refers to the righteous man as the "foundation of the world". The implication is that the righteous man is a creative agent. Thus *Genesis Rabba* 8.5 and *Midrash Ruth* 2.3 state that the righteous assisted God with creation, sitting in counsel with him before the world was created. Furthermore, with reference to 1 Chronicles 4:23 and Genesis 2:7, these righteous are interpreted to be "makers" or "formers" of man.[19] There is present in Jewish sources the notion that the world was created for the sake of Abraham (*Gen. R.* 14.6; cp. *Gen. R.* 43.7), Moses (*Gen. R.* 1.4), Israel (*Sifre Deut.* 47; *4 Ezra* 6.55-9), and righteous men in general (*2 Baruch* 15.7-8). Furthermore, a minimum number of righteous men exist in the world in order to sustain it and behold the face of God every day (*y. 'Abod. Zar.* 2.1 [40c]; *b. Sukk.* 45b; *b. Sanh.* 97b; *b. Hul.* 92a; *Gen. R.* 35.2, 49.3; *Midrash Tehillim* 5.5; cf. *b. Ber.* 17b). C. Morray-Jones argues that this evidence suggests that the idea was current in the Jewish visionary-mystical circles that righteous men or exceptionally worthy humans were able to look on God and achieve a transformation analogous to that ascribed to the heroes of the ascent-narratives and to the righteous in the future world.[20] Later Jewish mystical traditions substantially develop the theme of the *tsaddik*.[21] It would seem that Logion 12 of *Thomas* is one of the earliest known references to this idea.

Moreover, observing at least a portion of the Jewish Law was not just the experience of Jewish-Christian sects such as the Ebionites (Eus., *Hist. Eccl.* 3.27.5; Epiph., *Pan.* 30.2.2), the Nazoraeans (Epiph., *Pan.* 29.7.5), and the Elchasites (Epiph., *Pan.* 29.3.5; Hipp., *Ref.* 9.16.3). The amount of polemic alone in early Christian literature against Sabbath observation is enormous and suggests that from the inception of Christianity, Sabbath observation played an important

---

[18] Eng. trans. mine.
[19] Refer to J. Fossum, "Gen 1,26 and 2,7 in Judaism, Samaritanism, and Gnosticism", *JSJ* 16 (1985) 215ff.
[20] Morray-Jones, "Transformational Mysticism", 19-20.
[21] Scholem, *Mystical Shape*, 88-139.

even though controversial role.²² Still during the time of Epiphanius, worship was held on Saturday in several churches (*De fide* 24.7). Socrates states that the Egyptians in the environs of Alexandria and Thebais were especially known to have assembled on the Sabbath (*HE* 5.22; cf. Sozomen, *HE* 7.19.8). And according to the Council of Laodicea (*Can.* 16), "the Gospels and other parts of scripture shall be read aloud" on the Sabbath (cf. Cassian, *Inst. Coenob.* 2.6 and 3.2).

The *Apostolic Constitutions* contain two significant passages which point to both Sabbath and Sunday observation. In 2.59.3, we find the following: "Especially on the sabbath day and on the day when the Lord is risen hasten to church eager for knowledge in order to devote (your) praise to God who made the universe through Jesus...". The Sabbath was a celebration of creation, while Sunday served to remember Jesus' resurrection: "Celebrate the sabbath and the Lord's day as festival days, for the former is a memorial of creation, the latter a memorial of the resurrection" (7.23.3; cf. 2.36.2; 7.36.1; Ps.-Ignatius, *Magn.* 9.1).

G. Quispel thinks that Logion 27 comes from the Jewish-Christian source behind *Thomas*.²³ It must be noted, however, that Logion 27 is also encratite. If Quispel is correct, it means that some of the Jewish-Christians were encratites. This is not implausible since James is described by Eusebius as adhering to ascetic practices including not consuming wine or meat (*Eccl. Hist.* 2.23.4-7) and may have promoted the ideal of virginity since Epiphanius is aware of James' association with "the virgins" (Epiph., *Pan.* 30.2.6). He writes that the Ebionites used to "pride themselves on their virginity because of James, the brother of the Lord. <Thus> they even address their writings to elders and virgins".²⁴ It would appear that the relationship between encratism and Jewish-Christianity (the remnant of the Hebrews from Jerusalem) needs much more work.²⁵

---

²² For a complete discussion of this, see W. Rordorf, *Sunday. The History of the Day of Rest and Worship in the Earliest Centuries of the Christian Church* (trans. A. A. K. Graham; London, 1968) 118-153.

²³ G. Quispel, "The *Gospel of Thomas* Revisited", *Colloque International sur les Textes de Nag Hammadi, Québec, 22-25 août 1978*, BCHN 1 (ed. B. Barc; Québec, 1981) 243, 247.

²⁴ P. R. Amidon, *The Panarion of St. Epiphanius, Bishop of Salamis. Selected Passages* (New York and Oxford, 1990) 94.

²⁵ Regarding the connection between encratism and Judaism, and Aramaic Christianity, see the works of G. Quispel who argues that encratism was

It is interesting that *Jubilees* 50:8 alludes to a Jewish tradition that proper Sabbath observation meant that one was celibate on the Sabbath: "Every man who will profane this day, who will lie with his wife,...let him die". Futhermore, *Jubilees* connects the Sabbath with the Kingdom, declaring that the Sabbath is "a day of the holy Kingdom for all Israel" (50:9).

G. Anderson has suggested that the foundation for this practice can be traced to the similarities between the creation of the Sabbath in Genesis 2.1-3 and the creation of the tabernacle (Exod 39:32, 43; 40:9, 33b-34). Since sexual activity was forbidden in the Temple, it was also prohibited on the Sabbath.[26]

The *Hasîdîm*[27] were even stricter on this point, advocating not

---

a phenomenon which was developed by Alexandrian Christianity: "The Study of Encratism. A Historical Survey", *La Tradizione dell'Enkrateia, Atti del Colloquio Internazionale Milano 20-23 Aprile 1982* (ed. U. Bianchi; Rome, 1985) 55-63; and his "L'Evangile selon Thomas et Les Origines de l'Ascese Chretienne", *Gnostic Studies* 2, Nederlands Historisch-Archaeologisch Instituut te Istanbul 34,2 (Leiden, 1975) 98-112. See as well the writings of E. Peterson who thought that encratism was early and had a Palestinian origin: "Einige Beobachtungen zu den Aufängen der christlichen Askese", *Frühkirche, Judentum, und Gnosis* (Freiburg, 1959) 209-220; *idem*, "Einige Bemerkungen zum Hamburger Papyrusfragment der 'Acta Pauli'", *ibid.*, 183-208; *idem*, "Die 'Taufe' im Acherusischen See", *ibid.*, 310-332. Refer also to the works of A. Vööbus, *Celibacy, A Requirement for Admission to Baptism in the Early Syrian Church*, Papers of the Estonian Theological Society in Exile 1 (Stockholm, 1951); *idem, History of Asceticism in the Syrian Orient. A Contribution to the History and Culture in the Near East: Early Monasticism in Mesopotamia and Syria* 2, CSCO 197/17 (Louvain, 1960).

[26] G. Anderson, "Celibacy or Consummation in the Garden? Reflections on Early Jewish and Christian Interpretations of the Garden of Eden", *HTR* 82 (1989) 129-130. Other scholars have noted the similarities between the creation of the Sabbath and the tabernacle: J. Blenkinsopp, *Prophecy and Canon: A Contribution to the Study of Jewish Origins* (Notre Dame, 1977) 59-69; M. Weinfeld, "Sabbath, Temple and the Enthronement of the Lord", *Mélanges bibliques et orientaux en l'honneur de M. Henri Cazelles*, AOAT 212 (eds. A. Caquot and M. Delcor; Neukirchen-Vluyn, 1981) 501-512; J. D. Levenson, *Sinai and Zion: An Entry into the Jewish Bible* (San Francisco, 1985) 142-145.

[27] The *Hasîdîm* is usually translated "saints", "faithful ones", or "pious ones" and is associated with a group of pious Jews who were noted for their loyalty to the Torah and who resisted the Seleucid rule in Judah (1 Macc 2:42; 7:14; 2 Macc 14:6). On these passages, see P. Davies, "Hasidim in the Maccabean Period", *JJS* 28 (1977) 128; J. J. Collins, *The Apocalyptic Vision of the Book of Daniel*, HSM 16 (Missoula, 1977) 201-205. On the origins of this group, refer to R. T. Beckwith, "The Prehistory and the Relationship of the Pharisees, Sadducees, and Essenes: A Tenative Reconstruction", *RevQ* 11 (1982) 3-46, esp. 17-22 and 41-42; J. T. Milik, *Ten Years of Discovery in the Wilderness of Judea*, SBT 26 (London, 1959) 80; M. Hengel, *Judaism and Hellenism* 1 (Philadelphia, 1974) 224-228; M. Black, *The Scrolls and Christian Origins*, BJS 48 (Chico, 1961) 16. In Talmudic literature, this group seems to be used as an example rather than a

only celibacy on the Sabbath, but also that one had to remain continent from the preceding Wednesday. The reason for this was so that the woman would not be ritually impure by reason of any residue of semen.[28] A *baraita* cited in *b. Nid.* 38ab states that sexual intercourse was prohibited after Wednesday by the early *hasîdîm*. The Amoraim argue that the reason for this behavior is based on calculations of the gestation period of a woman. If one had intercourse after Wednesday, the birth could occur on a Sabbath day:

> Samuel, differing from R. Judah: "He follows the view of the pious men of old; for it was taught: The pious men of old performed their marital duty on a Wednesday only, in order that their wives should not be led to a desecration of the Sabbath. 'On Wednesday', but not later? - Read: From Wednesday onwards. Mar Zutra stated: What was the reason of the pious men of old? - Because it is written, *And the Lord gave her conception* [*herayon*], and the numerical value of *herayon* is two hundred and seventy-one."

This *baraita*, according to L. Finkelstein, may reflect an early ascetic branch of Judaism that was sexually abstinent for three days prior to the Sabbath so as to be in a clean state for the holy day. Exodus 19.10, 15 seems to be the source of the three day calculation:

> And the Lord said to Moses, "Go to the people and consecrate them today and tomorrow, and let them wash their garments"...And he [Moses] said to the people, "Be ready by the third day; do not go near a woman".

Because this view was not favored by the Rabbis, it was reinterpreted in this *baraita*.[29]

The Samaritans generally avoided sexual intercourse on the Sabbath because they argued that it causes Levitical impurity (Lev 15:18).[30] The Samaritan sect leader Sakta also held this injunction. It is possible that his prohibition of sexual activity on the Sabbath, however, is connected to ascent preparations since it can be argued

---

divergent legal tradition (*m. Ber.* 5.1; *t. B. Qam.* 2.6; *b. Nid.* 38ab; *b. Ned.* 10a; *B. Menah.* 40b-41a; refer to S. Safrai, "The Pharisees and the Hasidim", *Sidic* 10 (1977) 12-16; *idem*, "The Pious (*Hasidim*) and the Men of Deeds", *Zion* 50 (1985) 133-154.

[28] S. Safrai, *The Jewish People in the First Century: Historical Geography, Political History, Social, Cultural, and Religious Life and Institutions* 2 (eds. S. Safrai and M. Stern; Philadelphia, 1976) 205.

[29] L. Finkelstein, *MGWJ* 76 (1932) 529-530.

[30] S. Lowy, "Some Aspects of Normative and Sectarian Interpretation of Scriptures", *ALUOS* 6 (Leiden, 1969) 112f., 144 ns. 118ff.

that Sakta professed a realized eschatology where the resurrection could be fully experienced in this life.[31]

Collectively, this datum suggests that some early Jews were advocating that proper Sabbath observation meant that one be celibate at least on the Sabbath day. It is quite possible, based on *Thomas*' celibate ideal, that Logion 27 is alluding to this practice. This interpretation is especially favorable since in Logion 27, like in *Jubilees*, the practice of abstinence on the Sabbath is connected with participation in the Kingdom. It is plausible that *Thomas* is not only requiring that the Sabbath be observed on the Sabbath but also that it be observed properly by being in a purified celibate state.

This is even more likely when one considers that the association between Sabbath observation and celibacy was very familar to the encratites described by Clement of Alexandria (*Strom.* 3.15.98) who justified their celibacy by quoting Isaiah 56:3ff.:

> "Let not the eunuch say, I am dry wood. To eunuchs the Lord says this, If you keep my sabbaths and do all that I command you, I will give to you a place better than sons and daughters".

In encratite tradition, celibacy seems to be connected with Sabbath observation based on exegesis of Isaiah. Thus it can be argued that *Thomas* is reflecting a tradition that proper Sabbath observation included sexual abstinence.

This interpretation is even more enticing when one takes into consideration the fact that some Jews believed that the new world at the End would be a Sabbath when Paradise would be restored.[32] This tradition was incorporated into Christian eschatological hopes. In some circles this hope was already realized. Thus according to Hebrews 3:7-4:11, the Israelites will not be allowed to enter God's rest because of their disobedience. God is granting his people a second chance of entering his rest. This day has dawned: it is "today" (4:7), the era of Christ. And now the Christians can enjoy this final Sabbath which God has prepared for them. The Christians are admonished: "Let us therefore strive to enter that rest, that no one fall by the same sort of disobedience" (4:11). The eschatological Sabbath hope of the Jews was a present reality for these Christians.

---

[31] Refer to J. Fossum, "Sects and Movements", *The Samaritans* (ed. A. D. Crown; Tübingen, 1989) 351-352.
[32] Rordorf, *Sunday*, 49 ns. 1-3, and 88-89.

I suggest that the Thomasites may have upheld the belief that proper Sabbath observation included celibacy because the Sabbath signified entering into this new world, the world of Paradise before sex and death existed. The Sabbath was a weekly celebration for them of their return to Paradise and the sinless condition of the First Man.

(ii) Abstinence From the World and Vision:
The phrase to "fast as regards the world" is a metaphor meaning abstinence from involvement in the world. It is most appropriately understood as promoting the overall encratite lifestyle encouraged throughout *Thomas*, as I argued in Chapter One. The phrase, "fast from the world", describes the adopted lifestyle of the followers of *Thomas*. They were abstaining from the world and were renouncing it completely by becoming poor wandering celibates with restricted diets.

According to Logion 27, this abstinence is a prerequiste for the vision experience.[33] In other words, the purpose of the encratite lifestyle promoted in the *Gospel of Thomas* is to serve as a preparation for the vision quest. In order to be a successful visionary, one has to be living in the purified Pre-Fall state.

It is in this context that the Logion complex 49-50 is probably best exegeted:

> Blessed are the solitary and elect, for you will find the Kingdom. For you are from it, and to it you will return.
>
> If they say to you, "Where did you come from?", say to them, "We came from the light, the place where the light came into being on its own accord and established [itself] and [where the light] became manifest through their image". If they say to you, "Is it you?", say, "We are its children, and we are the elect of the living Father". If they ask you, "What is the sign of your Father in you?", say to them, "It is movement and repose".

---

[33] F. O. Francis, "Humility and Angelic Worship in Col 2:18", *ST* 16 (1962) 109-134, has noted the connection between ascent and asceticism and suggests that this ascetic-mystic piety is the proper milieu for Col 2:18: "Let no one disqualify you, insisting on self-abasement and worship of angels, taking his stand on visions...". Thus this Jewish mystical tradition has been carried over into Christianity here and also in Hermas, *Vis.* 3, 10 and 6; Tert., *On Fasting* 6, 7, and 9. Also, in the *Test. Job*, Job provides girdles of virginity for each of his daughters (46:7ff.). It is stated that these girdles are valued for life in heaven (47:3) and when each daughter puts on her girdle, she begins speaking in angelic tongues (c. 49-50).

Even though a vision of the Father is not mentioned explicitly in this complex, we do find the common denominator of encratism combined with ascent. Thus Logion 49 states that only the elect "*monachos*" or bachelors will return to the Kingdom.[34] According to S. Patterson's sociological interpretation of *Thomas*, "*monachos*" in Logion 49 refers to "those who have taken up the life of the wandering radical"[35] which includes sexual asceticism.[36] Logion 49 contains the directives for a successful ascent in Logion 50 which immediately follows. It seems, on the basis of the vision Logia presently being discussed, that Logia 49-50 also witness to the encratite preparations necessary to return to the Kingdom, probably for visionary purposes.

In Judaism, it is not at all unusual that ascent experiences are preceded by some sort of physical preparations including fasting and other forms of asceticism in order to purify the visionary sufficiently for his dangerous journey into the divine.

Daniel 10:3 records that in order to prepare for his vision, Daniel "ate no delicacies", abstained from meat and wine, and did not anoint himself for three weeks. This diet resembles that inferred by *Thomas*: no meat and no wine. *4 Ezra* also knows of this tradition: the prophet goes through a series of fasts for the duration of three weeks (5.13, 5.2, 6.31, 6.35). There is even the tale that he held to a special diet for seven days, eating only "the flowers of the field" (12.50) in order to prepare himself for one of his visions. Elsewhere in *4 Ezra* this flower diet is further qualified: Ezra is supposed to eat only "the flowers of the field, and taste no meat and drink no wine; but eat only flowers" (9.24-25). This is similar to the report in the *Ascension of Isaiah* 2.9-11 that Isaiah, Micah, Ananias, Joel, Habakkuk, and Josab "who believed in the ascension into

---

[34] On this, refer to Chapter One, Section 1.
[35] Patterson, *Thomas and Jesus*, 200.
[36] *Ibid.*, 153, where he argues that "*monachos*" in *Thomas* carries with it the connotation of sexual asceticism"; he bases this statement on M. Meyer's observations in his article, "Making Mary Male: The Categories 'Male' and 'Female' in the Gospel of Thomas", *NTS* 31 (1985) 557-558. Patterson seems unaware, however, of the Harl's and Morard's major contributions to the study of the word "*monachos*", chiefly that "*monachos*" refers to an unmarried and thus sexually inactive individual; these works include: M. Harl, "A propos des *Logia* de Jésus: le sens du mot *monachos*", *REG* 73 (1960) 464-474"; F.-E. Morard, "Monachos Moine, Historie du terme grec jusqu'au 4ᵉ siècle", *Freiburger Zeitschrift für Philosophie und Theologie* (1973) 332-411; idem, "Encore quelques réflexions sur monachos", *VC* 34 (1980) 395-401.

heaven" ate "wild herbs (which) they gathered from the mountains" and cooked. They lived on this herbal diet for two years.

In *2 Baruch*, the fasting preparation tradition is also present (5.7, 9.2, 12.5, 21.1, 47.2), generally lasting for seven days. Abraham is instructed in the *Apocalypse of Abraham* 9.7-8 as follows: "for forty days abstain from every kind of food cooked by fire, and from drinking of wine, and from anointing (yourself) with oil". Clearly primitive Jewish tradition taught that prophetic and visionary experiences must be preceded by some sort of fasting usually involving abstinence from meat and wine.

What about the Therapeutae? According to Philo's report, they were "a people always taught from the first to use their sight" and they "desire the vision of the Existent and soar above the sun of our senses" (*Vit. Cont.* 11). These Jewish mystics led a very ascetic lifestyle, most probably as a way to prepare for their vision quests. They "abandon their property to their sons or daughters or to other kinsfolk" (13) thus abandoning both possessions and family (18). Then they wander out into the countryside and take up with other like themselves in the area (20ff.). For six days of the week each mystic lives in solitude while on the seventh day they come together in a general assembly (30).

Philo relates that "self-control (ἐγκράτειαν)" is of paramount importance to them (34).[37] Thus they fast during daylight hours sometimes forgetting to eat for six days in a row (34-35). Philo compares their abstinence to "the grasshoppers who are said to live on air" (35). Even on their festive seventh day, they only consume "common bread with salt for a relish flavoured further by the daintier with hyssop, and their drink is spring water" (37). Philo makes a point that the table "is kept pure from the flesh of animals" (73) and that they abstain from wine for their entire lifetime (74). They are not concerned about what they wear, clothing themselves in shaggy skin coats in the winter and linen shirts in the summer (38).

Voluntary virginity is a cherished virtue among the Therapeutae (68) and it seems that spiritual marriage is preferred over carnal marriage. Thus Philo writes: "Eager to have her [Sophia] for their lifemate they have spurned the pleasures of the body and desire no mortal offspring but those immortal children which only the soul

---

[37] F. H. Colson and G. H. Whitaker, *Philo* 9, LCL 363 (Cambridge, Mass., 1941 and reprints) 132-133.

that is dear to God can bring to the birth unaided because the Father has sown in her spiritual rays enabling her to behold (θεωρεῖν) the verities of wisdom" (68).[38] Even their beds are made of planks of wood in order to aid in refraining from "the love-lures of pleasure" (69). Their austere lifestyle allows them to live "in the soul alone" and thus they are both "citizens of Heaven and the world" (90).

The lifestyle promoted by the Therapeutae mirrors that of *Thomas'* encratism: celibacy, abstinence from meat and wine, voluntary poverty, and abandonment of the traditional family unit. This type of lifestyle, for both communities, is the way in which one purifies and prepares oneself for one's vision quest thus allowing one to be admitted to the company of angels, the citizens of heaven.

The Qumran community is comparable. Evidence seems to indicate that the Qumranites are a Jewish group practicing ascent who, like the Therapeutae, were also severe ascetics and celibates.[39] This, in itself, may illuminate the austere lifestyle of the Qumranites which included voluntary celibacy, communal possessions, fasting, vigils, behavioral restrictions, and strict observance of the Law.

This type of discipline seems to be aimed at purification. It has been argued that the desire to achieve this state of purity was derived from the temporary requirement of sexual "holiness" for the dedicated *gibbôr hayil* during times of war[40] or from the Qumranites' wish to live as the prophets and experience radical transformation.[41]

It is plausible, however, that the ascetic behaviors were also aimed at purification for the purpose of mystic ascent into heaven and joining with the company of the angels. This seems to be the case in *Hymn* 3.20f., where the Qumranite is said to be "cleansed" by God of "a perverse spirit of great sin" so that he may "stand with the host of the Holy Ones" and "may enter into community with

---

[38] *Ibid.*, 154-155.
[39] Refer to Chapter Two, Section 1b for a discussion of Qumran's view of ascent.
[40] M. Black, "The Tradition of Hasidaean-Essene Asceticism: Its Origins and Influence", *Aspects du Judéo-Christianisme* (Paris, 1965) 19-33; *idem, Scrolls,* 27-32.
[41] B. Thiering, "The Biblical Source of Qumran Asceticism", *JBL* 93 (1974) 429-444.

the congregation of the Sons of Heaven". *Hymn* 11.9ff. states that the Qumranite has been "purified" and "made holy" for the sake of God's "Glory" so that "he may be one [with] the children of Thy truth and partake of the lot of Thy Holy Ones" and that "he may stand before Thee with the everlasting host and with [Thy] spirits [of holiness]". In 4Q491, the Qumranite who has taken his place among the angels, tells us that "none [find fault with me]".[42] Apparently, the Qumran sect is transmitting a Jewish mystical tendency here: purification through ascetic practices and proper Torah observation is necessary to enter heaven and join the company of the angels before God's throne.

Philo's own thoughts on this subject are equally illuminating. When interpreting Jeremiah 3.4, "Didst thou not call upon Me as thy house, thy father and thy husband of thy virginity?", he states that God is a house, "the incorporeal dwelling-place of incorporeal ideas" (*Cher.* 49). Philo then poses the rhetorical question: "Why then, soul of man, when thou shouldest live the virgin life in the house of God and cling to knowledge, dost thou stand aloof from them and embrace outward sense, which unmans and defiles thee?" (52). It seems that Philo suggests here that to enter and reside in God's house, one must be a celibate, rejecting participation in sexual pleasure and thereby returning to a virgin state. Thus he says: "When God begins to consort with the soul, He makes what before was a woman into a virgin again, for He takes away the degenerate and emasculate passions which unmanned it and plants instead the native growth of unpolluted virtues" (50).

The idea is furthered in Philo's exegesis of the Noah story. Philo equates the human body with the Ark (*Quaest. in Gn.* 2.19) and states that Genesis 7.23 "Noah remained alone and those who were with him in the ark" means that Noah remained in the Ark, the body, "which is pure of all passions and spiritual diseases..." (2.25). Thus Philo claims that those who were in the Ark abstained "from sexual intercourse with their wives" (2.49) apparently because Noah and his family were purifying the Ark, their bodies: "When the soul is about to wash off and cleanse its sins," Philo explains, "[it should] (not join) any of the female sex..." (2.49).

When Noah finally "opened the covering of the Ark" (Gen.

---

[42] Trans. by M. Smith, "Two Ascended to Heaven - Jesus and the Author of 4Q491", *Jesus and the Dead Sea Scrolls* (ed. J. H. Charlesworth; New York, 1992) 296.

8.13), the mind lept upward and "cut off all forms of (sensual) pleasure" so that it was able to experience "naked and incorporeal natures" (2.46). Noah, in this purified celibate condition is equated with the Pre-Fall Adam, the real image of God. Therefore Philo concludes that Noah was "the beginning of a second genesis of man, of equal honor with him who was first made in (His) image" (2.56).

From this allegory, it seems that Philo is transmitting a tradition that in order to ascend out of the body and into the incorporeal realm, one must first overcome all the passions, including sexual desire, by becoming a celibate. Noah, in so doing, regained the image of God. Since the biblical heros are viewed by Philo as paradigms for contemporary humans, it is possible that Philo is suggesting that once one becomes a celibate visionary like Noah, he has regained God's image.

These same ideas are spelled out in Philo's allegory on the Exodus from Egypt. Israel, the "mind fond of seeing" must be led out of Egypt if it is going to achieve a vision (*Mut.* 207-209). Therefore, the Passover, according to Philo, symbolizes the abandonment of a life of passions and beginning the journey to God (*Heres.* 192; *Sac.* 63; *Mig.* 25). It is Moses' duty to lead Israel so that "they shall see the place which indeed is the Logos, where stands the undeviating and unchanging God...For it well befits those who have become comrades of Wisdom to desire to see the Existent One; but if they cannot do so, at least to see His image, the most sacred Logos..." (*Conf.* 95-97).

Furthermore, when Moses led them across the Red Sea and the Egyptian army was destroyed, the body itself was destroyed: it was the death of the lower mind and its sensuous manifestations (*Ebr.* 111; *Conf.* 70; *Leg. All.* 2.102, 3.172; *Agr.* 78-83). The forty year exile in the desert was for the purpose of kneading "the savage and untamed passion by the aid of Logos the Softener, softening it as though it were food" (*Mig.*154f.).

Philo's insistence that it is necessary to reject the body and all of its passions is summed up neatly in *Leg. All.* 3.15-27 where Jacob's flight from Laban is interpreted. When Jacob flees Laban, he is overcoming the objects of sense, the world of matter: "he crosses the river of objects of sense, that swamps and drowns the soul under the flood of the passions" (3.18). Then he sets his sights for the mountain of Gilead. Having thus renounced the sense world,

Jacob's soul can now receive God's manifestation and is worthy to be given God's secret mysteries (3.27).

Rabbinic literature attests to a striking tradition about Moses' preparations before he ascended the mountain to receive the Torah (cf. Exod 24). *B. Yoma* 4a preserves a quotation from Rabbi Nathan in which he states that six days had to pass before Moses could receive the Torah.[43] This was "so that he would be cleansed of all foods and drinks in his bowels, and thus become like the angels".[44] It seems that this tradition indicates that when one ascends and enters the company of the angels, one must be prepared for the transformation into an angel or angelic-like being; this apparently included no longer needing food or drink as sustenance.

The Merkavah and Hekhalot literature lay out the necessary physical preparations for a vision. Special diets and fasts are employed. For instance, in *Merkavah Shelemah* 5a (cf. *Hekhalot Rabbati* 30.1) all vegetables are forbidden during the time of preparation: "He [the mystic] should not taste any vegetables".[45] *Ma'aseh Merkavah* para. 11 requires that the mystic "will sit forty (days) in fast, will eat his bread with salt and should not eat any kind of filth".[46] The bread that the mystic is allowed to eat must be baked by his own hand (*Hekhalot Rabbati* 30.1; *Merkavah Shelemah* 4b) and bread baked by women must be avoided: "He should not eat bread baked by a woman, nor should he drink water touched by a woman; but he should knead with his own hands, and grind himself, and bake for himself one bread every day and eat".[47]

According to *Hekhalot Rabbati* 20.1, the ascetic preparations last for twelve days during which time the vision-seeker must live in absolute seclusion; it is only when these twelve days of solitary confinement are completed that "he may engage in every activity he wishes in connection with the study of the Law: whether it is

---

[43] Noteworthy is the tradition that before Jesus took Peter, James, and John up the mountain in order to witness the transfiguration, they waited for "six days" (Mark 9:2).

[44] Other Rabbinic sources know of the tradition that angels do not have to eat (*b. Hag.* 16a; cf. *b. Yoma* 75b).

[45] Schäfer, *Synopse*, 8-11, sections 13-17. Eng. trans. in Gruenwald, *Apocalyptic and Merkavah Mysticism*, 101 n. 12.

[46] Schäfer, *Synopse*, section 560. Eng. trans. in N. Janowitz, *The Poetics of Ascent: Theories of Language in a Rabbinic Ascent Text* (New York, 1989) 43.

[47] Schäfer, *Synopse*, 126-129, section 288; Eng. trans in I. Gruenwald, *Apocalyptic and Merkavah Mysticism*, 101 n. 14.

Scripture, the Mishnah or the Talmud, and even beholding the Merkavah. For he now lives in purity and asceticism".[48]

In addition to these ascetic behaviors, there is a Hekhalot tradition that it is also a requirement that the vision-seeker observe Torah. Thus *Hekhalot Rabbati* 13.2 reads:

> What is the technique of the Merkavah mystic like? It is like having a ladder in one's house and being able to go up and down at will. This may be done by anyone who is pure of idolatry, sexual offenses, bloodshed, slander, vain oaths, profanation of the Name, impertinence, and unjustified enmity, and who keeps every positive and negative commandment.[49]

In the same text, there is a description of Rabbi Nehunyah ben Ha-Qanah's ascent (16.4-25.1). When he reaches the sixth gate, the angelic guard Dumi'el states that only the one who has thoroughly studied the written and oral law or has been observant of all the law will be allowed to ascend into the seventh palace.

G. Scholem also notes that Torah observation is connected to the vision quest. When discussing the halakhic character of Hekhalot mysticism, Scholem refers to *Hekhalot Rabbati* where the procedure used to bring Rabbi Nehuniah ben Ha-Qanah from a state of vision ecstasy to a state of normal consciousness is described.

> Immediately I [Rabbi Ishmael] took a piece of very fine woolen cloth and gave it to Rabbi Akiba, and Rabbi Akiba gave it to a woman who immersed herself and yet had not become pure, and let her immerse herself [a second time]...They went and did so, and laid the cloth before Rabbi Ishmael. He inserted into it a bough of myrtle full of oil that had been soaked in pure balsam and they placed it upon the knees of Rabbi Nehuniah ben Ha-Qanah; and immediately they dismissed him before the throne of glory where he had been sitting and beholding...[50]

Scholem adeptly concludes: "What is important here is not the set of fictitious circumstances attending this procedure, but, rather, the cumulative effect of all these provisions, demonstrating that even

---

[48] Schäfer, *Synopse*, 98-99, section 225. Gruenwald, *Apocalyptic and Merkavah Mysticism*, 172, provides the Eng. trans.

[49] Schäfer, *Synopse*, 76-77, section 172. Eng. trans. in Gruenwald, *Apocalyptic and Merkavah Mysticism*, 160-161.

[50] Hebrew text in G. Scholem, *Jewish Gnosticism*, 11 n. 4; English provided on same page, attributed to M. Smith. On this passage, see L. H. Schiffman, "The Recall of Rabbi Nehuniah ben Ha-Qanah from Ecstasy in the *Hekhalot Rabbati*", *Association for Jewish Studies Review* 1 (1976) 269-281, and Gruenwald's interpretation, *Apocalyptic and Merkavah Mysticism*, 164 and ns. 50 and 51.

the slightest possible suspicion of impurity, defined according to strictest rabbinic law, is enough to have the ecstatic dismissed from before the throne".[51]

This again suggests that the success of the vision was bound up with one's purity. For the Jewish mystics, the method of purification involved ascetic and dietary practices, and sometimes even Torah observation. This is the background to Logion 27: in order to prepare for a vision, the vision-seeker had to purify himself. This purification included Sabbath observation in addition to encratite practices. In other words, Logion 27 prescribes that encratism or renunciation of the world through celibacy, and the observation of certain dietary regulations was the way the vision-seeker made himself worthy to have a successful vision quest. Additionally, observation of certain Torah regulations is required. These notions are well-grounded in Jewish tradition and suggest that the mysticisim promoted by the *Gospel of Thomas* was inherited from Judaism.[52]

2) *Logion 37 and Shedding the Body Before Visionary Ascent:*

ΠΕΧΕ ΝΕϥΜΑΘΗΤΗC ΧΕ ΑϢ Ν̄ϨΟΟΥ ΕΚΝΑΟΥΩΝϨ ΕΒΟΛ ΝΑΝ ΑΥΩ ΑϢ Ν̄ϨΟΟΥ ΕΝΑΝΑΥ ΕΡΟΚ

ΠΕΧΕ ΙC ΧΕ ϨΟΤΑΝ ΕΤΕΤΝ̄ϢΑΚΕΚ ΤΗΥΤΝ̄ ΕϨΗΥ Μ̄ΠΕΤΝ̄ϢΙΠΕ ΑΥΩ Ν̄ΤΕΤΝ̄ϤΙ Ν̄ΝΕΤΝ̄ϢΤΗΝ Ν̄ΤΕΤΝ̄ΚΑΑΥ ϨΑ ΠΕCΗΤ Ν̄ΝΕΤΝ̄ΟΥΕΡΗΤΕ Ν̄ΘΕ Ν̄ΝΙΚΟΥΕΙ Ν̄ϢΗΡΕ ϢΗΜ Ν̄ΤΕΤΝ̄ΧΟΠΧΠ̄ Μ̄ΜΟΟΥ

ΤΟΤΕ [ΤΕΤ]ΝΑΝΑΥ ΕΠϢΗΡΕ Μ̄ΠΕΤΟΝϨ ΑΥΩ ΤΕΤΝΑΡ̄ ϨΟΤΕ ΑΝ

---

[51] Scholem, *Jewish Gnosticism*, 11-12.
[52] This discussion brings new light to Matthew's beatitude, "Blessed are the pure in heart" (οἱ καθαροὶ τῇ καρδίᾳ), for they shall see God" (Mt. 5:8). It is quite possible that Matthew is preserving a Jesus tradition similar to Logion 27: in order to gain a vision of the deity, it is necessary to purify oneself. Matthew's rendition, however, seems to be representing a spiritualized eschatological redaction of the more primitive mystical saying captured in Logion 27. Matthew tones down the physical asceticism in favor of a more spiritualized understanding just as he has done with the beatitude "Blessed are the poor in spirit" (Mt 5:3; cp. the more archaic Logion 54, "Blessed are the poor"). Cf. *Ps. Clem. Hom.* 17.7 where this saying is found in the context of visionary ascent: God's form is "beautiful" and only the "pure in heart" can see him!; the *Hekhalot Zutrati* 322-324 and 331-332 speaks of seeing the King in his beauty; cf. 1 Jn 3:2b-3 which alludes to this Jesus tradition as well as the transformational aspects of the vision: "we know that when he appears we shall be like him, for we shall see him as he is. And everyone who thus hopes in him purifies himself as he is pure"; Rev 22:4; *Acts of Paul and Thecla* 5.12-13; *Exc. ex Theod.* 10.6-11.2.

> His disciples said, "When will you become revealed to us and when shall we see you?"
>
> Jesus said, "When you disrobe without being ashamed
>
> and take up your garments and place them under your feet like little children and tread on them,
>
> then [you will see] the Son of the Living One, and you will not be afraid."[53]

Recently there appeared in *Vigiliae Christianae* an article entitled, "Stripped Before God: A New Interpretation of Logion 37 in the Gospel of Thomas",[54] in which I, in collaboration with J. Fossum, conclude that this Logion, far from speaking about baptism as J. Z. Smith has argued in the past,[55] employs encratite teaching in order to explicate its ascent soteriology.[56] It was suggested that Logion 37 structurally consists of three motifs:

(1) stripping off the garments without shame
(2) treading upon them like children
(3) gaining the capacity to see the deity without fear

It was argued that motif (1) is rooted in speculation concerning Genesis 3:21. According to this passage, as a consequence of Adam and Eve's sin, God made them "garments of skins, and clothed them." These skin garments, according to the Jewish and Christian literature we reviewed, are identical to the human body of flesh and need to be shed. This literature also points to the fact that the removal of the material body was a motif intimately connected

---

[53] Layton, *Nag Hammadi Codex II,2-7*, 68; Eng. trans.by Lambdin, 69. P.Oxy. 655 preserves the first part of the Greek version of this Logion; J. Fitzymer attempts to reconstruct the fragmentary Greek from the Coptic in "The Oxyrhynchus *Logoi* and the Coptic Gospel According to Thomas", *Essays on the Semitic Background of the New Testament* (London, 1971) 408-410.

[54] A. De Conick and J. Fossum, "Stripped Before God: A New Interpretation of Logion 37 in the Gospel of Thomas," *VC* 45 (1991) 123-150.

[55] J. Z. Smith, "The Garments of Shame," *HR* 5 (1966) 217-238.

[56] An article by P. A. Mirecki, "Coptic Manichaean Psalm 278 and Gospel of Thomas 37", *Manichaica Selecta. Studies presented to Professor Julien Ries on the occasion of his seventieth birthday*, Manichaean Studies 1 (eds. A. van Tongerloo and S. Giverson; Lovanii, 1991) 243-262, appeared in the same year as the article that I co-authored with Fossum, "Stripped Before God". We were not aware of each other's articles. Thus, although Mirecki's analysis of the Manichaean psalm is careful and precise, he accepts Smith's conclusions as "definitive" on Logion 37 (255) and incorrectly assumes a baptismal context for Logion 37.

with ascent experiences (*Odes Sol.* 11.10-12, 21.3-4 and 6-7, 25.8; *Leg. all.* 2.55-56, 3.46-47; *De somn.* 1.36, 1.43; *De post. Caini* 136-137; *De gig.* 54; *Dial. Sav.* 84-85).[57] The qualification that one must be "shameless" in this stripping, alludes to Genesis 2:25 which states that the primordial condition of Adam was a condition in which Adam and Eve were naked and not ashamed. Only after the Fall were their eyes opened and they knew that they were naked (Gen. 3:7). Motif (1) should be understood as follows: when a person strips off the human body of flesh, he is regaining Adam's Pre-Fall state and returning to the primordial experience of shamelessness.

The analysis of Motif (2) suggests that the action of treading is a metaphor for renunciation (Jos., *Ant.* 2.9.7; *On Anoint.* 40,11-17; *Hyp. Arch.* 97,2-10; *Man. Psalm-Book* CCLXXVIII, lines 26-27).[58] *Thomas* seems to employ the garment metaphor in much the same manner as the encratite leader Cassianus in his interpretation of a saying found in the *Gospel of the Egyptians* (*Strom.* 3.13.92). The saying reads:

> When Salome asked when what she had inquired about would be known, the Lord said, "When you have trampled on the garment of shame and when the two become one and the male with the female (is) neither male nor female."[59]

Cassianus explains that since sexual intercourse is the original sin, sexual tendencies must be renounced. Thus the person must trample on the garment of shame by becoming asexual. Rather than using gender language as the *Gospel of the Egyptians*, *Thomas* expresses the notion of asexuality by employing the imagery of "little children".[60] The image *paidion* is used by Ireneaus (*Adv. haer.* 3.22.4; *Demo.* 12), Theophilius of Antioch (*Ad Auto.* 2.25), and

---

[57] Several Christian texts refer to the removal of the material body at the resurrection; refer to De Conick and Fossum, "Stripped Before God," 130-131 for a discussion of these texts.

[58] To this discussion, I add that there is the notion that "trampling" on the object also refers to "mastery" over the object. This is the case in *T. Levi* 18.12, *T. Sim.* 6.6, and *T. Zeb.* 9.8 (cf. Lk 10:19). This notion seems to be present in *On Anoint.* 40,11-17 and *Hpy. Arch.* 97,2-10 too.

[59] O. Stählin, *Clemens Alexandrinus, Werke II*, Die griechischen christlichen Schriftsteller der ersten drei Jahrhunderte 15, new edition by L. Früchtel (Berlin, 1962) 238.

[60] *Thomas* employs the image of little children in Logia 21 and 22 too where this image represents the asexual encratite ideal. E. Peterson has collocated these two Logia with Christian texts where Adam is said to be a *paidion* or a *nepios*, "Acta Pauli", 195.

Clement of Alexandria (*Prot.* 11.111.1) to describe Adam in Paradise before the Fall. Only when he succumbs to lust is Adam no longer a child but a man. According to Motif (2), the person who renounces the body is the person who has become a little child. He has renounced sex and thereby has become a celibate. In so doing he has returned to the Pre-Fall state of Adam who was the child innocent of concupiscence.[61]

This renunciation of sexuality is connected in Motif (3) with gaining the ability to have a vision of the deity, to "see" God without fear. As already noted in the preceding discussion, vision quests of God or his divine manifestation were the feats of the Jewish apocalypticists and mystics ascending to heaven. Apocalyptic and mystical texts as early as *1 Enoch* 14.67 are demonstrative of this.

Philonic literature expresses this idea as well.[62] Furthermore, it is quite common in Jewish literature for the notion of stripping off the material body to be connected with the ascent and vision (especially *2 Enoch* 22 and *Asc. Isa.* 7 and 9). That the mystical vision is to be experienced without fear alludes to Genesis 3:10 when Adam is "afraid" of his nakedness after the Fall and hides himself from the sight of God. Thus to return to fearlessness in God's presence indicates that the person has returned to the primordial Adamic condition, that is before Adam had a garment of skin but was naked and unafraid to see God and converse with him. Moreover, since Jewish literature contends that having a vision of the deity transforms the mystic into an angelic-like being,[63] it can be argued that the Thomasites sought to see God in order to be transformed into the divine.

To conclude this brief synopsis, Logion 37 describes the soteriological scheme in the *Gospel of Thomas* as follows: it is necessary to renounce the body and become a celibate by mimicking Adam when he was still a child innocent of sex. In so doing, the person

---

[61] H. Kee, "'Becoming a Child' in the Gospel of Thomas," *JBL* 82 (1963) 307-314, is not aware of the tradition that Adam was an innocent child before the Fall, although he links the idea of being a child and being a single one (L. 22), which A. F. J. Klijn, "The 'Single One' in the Gospel of Thomas," *JBL* 81 (1962) 271-278, derives from Jewish speculation concerning the Pre-Fall Adam where "singleness" included asexuality.

[62] Refer to a discussion of specific texts in De Conick and Fossum, "Stripped Before God," 135-136.

[63] See Morray-Jones, "Transformational Mysticism", 1-31.

achieves a new state, a Paradisiac state which allows him to ascend into heaven and gaze at God without fear and unencumbered by the shame of Adam's sin.[64]

3) *Conclusion:*

The transformational metamorphosis which resulted from the *visio Dei* was thought to be a dangerous experience since the impure or unworthy aspirant would be consumed by God's fire rather than transformed by it. Thus the Thomasites advocated adherence to at least a portion of the Jewish Law, and a strict code of encratite behavior including sexual abstinence and dietary regulations. This world abstinence was a requirement for a successful visionary experience. Thus, encratism is intimately linked in *Thomas*' Logia with the *visio Dei* and its transformative soteriology. The model for this clearly stems from early Jewish mysticism which also advocated adherence to the Law, a strict code of behavior, and diet for a prescribed time period prior to the ascent.

---

[64] To this discussion, I would like to add a reference to 1 John 3.2b-3 which alludes to a Jesus tradition comparable to Logion 37. This text reads: "we know that when he appears we shall be like him, for we shall see him as he is. And every one who thus hopes in him purifies himself as he is pure".

CHAPTER SEVEN

VISION OF THE IMAGES IN LOGION 84

Experiences of the encounter with the Transcendent are described using two different languages: a psychologic language which describes this encounter as an internal personal experience, and a mythical language which describes this encounter as a journey into the divine realm in order to experience the Trancendent there. In the *Gospel of Thomas*, we find both languages operating.

As we already saw in Chapter Five, Sections 1bii and iii, *Thomas* employs psychologic language in order to describe the encounter with the divine element within. Thus according to Logia 83, 24, and 29, the Transcendent has taken up residence within the human body. Furthermore, this divinity must be encountered through Self-knowledge (L. 3b, 111, 67, 56, and 80) and is described in the terms of bringing forth one's internal divinity (L. 70a). This encounter with the divine is redemptive (L. 3b, 111; cf. 67).

As we will see in this Chapter, the same encounter with the Transcendent is described in Logion 84 only in the garb of religious mythology rather than psychology. This Logion reads as follows:

> ⲚϨⲞⲞⲨ ⲈⲦⲈⲦⲚ̄ⲚⲀⲨ ⲈⲠⲈⲦⲚ̄ⲈⲒⲚⲈ ϢⲀⲢⲈⲦⲚ̄ⲢⲀϢⲈ ϨⲞⲦⲀⲚ ⲆⲈ ⲈⲦⲈⲦⲚ̄ϢⲀⲚⲚⲀⲨ ⲀⲚⲈⲦⲚ̄ϨⲒⲔⲰⲚ Ⲛ̄ⲦⲀϨϢⲰⲠⲈ ϨⲒ ⲦⲈⲦⲚⲈϨⲎ ⲞⲨⲦⲈ ⲘⲀⲨⲘⲞⲨ ⲞⲨⲦⲈ ⲘⲀⲨⲞⲨⲰⲚϨ ⲈⲂⲞⲖ ⲦⲈⲦⲚⲀϤⲒ ϨⲀ ⲞⲨⲎⲢ
>
> When you see your likeness, you rejoice. But when you see your images which came into being before you, and which neither die nor become manifest, how much you will have to bear![1]

1) *Past Interpretations of the Images:*

H. -Ch. Puech wrote a brief essay on the esoteric doctrines and gnostic themes in the *Gospel of Thomas* in which he discusses Logion 84. Puech correctly identifies the dichotomy between the human likeness (ⲈⲒⲚⲈ) and the heavenly image (ⲈⲒⲔⲰⲚ) in Logion 84 and connects the heavenly image with the concept of the

---

[1] Layton, *Nag Hammadi Codex II, 2-7*, 84; Eng. trans. by Lambdin, 85.

divine Self or guardian angel which needs to be encountered and rejoined. The fundamental model that he employs for comparative purposes is the Valentinian scheme of the angels with whom one must be reunited in the End.[2] His observations are in need of some discussion since his view of the gnostic background of Logion 84 has continued to be argued by others.[3]

Thomas' use of "images" in Logion 84 where one's earthly "likeness" must encounter one's heavenly double or "image", differs substantially from the mythology of the "images" in Valentinianism. First, in Valentinianism, the "image" is associated with the human being (cf. *Ex Theo* c. 15) and must eventually rejoin its "angel". So it is said in the *Gospel of Philip* 58.10-14: "You who have joined the perfect light with the holy spirit, unite the angels with us also, as being the images". In 65.1-26, it is stated that the image and the angel must join together so that unclean spirits are not able to pollute the person. Thus in Valentinianism, the term *"image"* is *not* applied to the angel or heavenly counterpart as it is in *Thomas.*

This leads us to the second major difference between the "images" in Logion 84 and the "images" in Valentinianism. According to the *Gospel of Philip*, the angel with whom you are to be reunited is your sexual opposite. In 65.8-11, it is explained that no one can escape the sexual advances of the unclean spirits unless one has taken on the appropriate "male power" or "female power" which are respectively "the bridegroom and the bride". Thus "if the image and the angel are united with one another", the original androgyny is restored, and the unclean spirit can no longer violate the person (65.24-26).

In the case of the *Excerpta ex Theodoto*, the angels are the "male" aspect of the original androgynous Man of Genesis 1:27, while the "superior seed" represents the female aspect. This seed was removed from Adam and became Eve. Those of the female "superior seed" must "become men (ἀπανδρωθέντα)" by uniting with the male angel. In this way, the original androgyny of the primal Man is restored since Eve has reentered Adam (c. 21). Thus: "we are raised up 'equal to angels', and restored to unity with the males,

---

[2] H. -Ch. Puech, "Historie des Religions. Académie des Inscriptions et Belles-Lettres", *Annuaire du Collège de France* 62 (1962) 199-213.

[3] Cf. Gärtner, *Theology*, 204-206; J. Ménard, *L'Évangile selon Thomas*, NHS 5 (Leiden, 1975) 186; J. S. Kloppenborg, M. W. Meyer, S. J. Patterson, M. G. Steinhauser, *Q Thomas Reader* (Sonoma, 1990) 98-99.

member for member" (c. 22; cf. c. 79-80). Therefore, our angels are our "bridegrooms" (c. 64). Similarly, Irenaeus relates that "the spiritual seed, again, being divested of their animal souls, and becoming intelligent spirits, shall in an irresistible and invisible manner enter into the Pleroma, and be bestowed as brides on those angels who wait upon the Savior" (*Adv. haer.* 1.7.1).

The *Gospel of Philip* and the *Excerpta ex Theodoto* may be representing differences in dogma between various Valentinian schools on this point. Irregardless of this, it is clear that underlying both views was the belief that the union would take place between the "images" and the "angels" and that it would be a union of sexual opposites. This is in contradistinction to the motif of the "images" in Logion 84 where the "images" are personal heavenly doubles, divine representations of each person, rather than the person's sexual opposite.

What is the background for the notion that each person has his own individual heavenly image or double? G. Quispel has argued that this idea is tied to the Greco-Roman concept of the *daimon* or *genius*: each person was believed to have a *daimon* or *genius* which was a guardian spirit or angel who could be described as the exact counterpart to the person to whom he belonged.[4] Thus Plutarch

---

[4] G. Quispel, "Das Ewige Ebenbild des Menschen. Zur Begegnung mit dem Selbst in der Gnosis", *Gnostic Studies* 1, Nederlands Historisch-Archaeologisch Instituut te Istanbul 34,1 (Leiden, 1974) 140-157; idem, "Genius and Spirit", 155-169; idem, *Makarius, das Thomasevangelium, und von der Perle*, NTSup 15 (Leiden, 1967) 39-64; idem, "Makarius und das Lied von der Perle", *Le Origini dello Gnosticismo, Colloquio di Messina 13-18 Aprile 1966*, Studies in the History of Religions, NumenSup 12 (ed. U. Bianchi; Leiden, 1967) 625-644.

The *daimon* according to Plato, was assigned to the person at birth, accompanied him through his life, and guided his soul to Hades (*Phaedr.* 107); Pindar emphasizes their protective role (*Ol.* 8.16; 13.101; *Pyth.* 1.167; cp. Aeschyl., *Sept.* 639); they are companions to the gods too, carrying prayers to the gods from humans, and gifts to humans from the gods (Plat., *Sympos.* 202; Appul., *de Deo Socrat.* 7); *daimons* were also known to be departed souls (Lucian, *De Mort. Pereg.* 36; Dorville, *ad Chariton* 1.4); the *daimon* of Plotinus was summoned on one occasion and was visibly manifest (Porphyry, *Vita Plot.* 10).

There is an old Greek idea that there were *two* personal *daimones*, one good and one evil. See P. Boyance, "Les Deux Démons Personnels dans l'Antiquité Grecque et Latine", *RP* 59 (1935) 189-202, who traces it back to Empedocles. Cf. J. Dillon, *The Middle Platonists*, CLL (London, 1977) 219ff., and 317ff., for Ammonius and Plutarch.

The *genii* are powers which generate life and protect and accompany the person. At birth, each person obtained a *genius*. According to Horace (*Epist.* 2.2.187), the *genius* will manifest itself sometimes as a good, other times as an

writes about a certain Elysius who has a vision of a young man who resembles his dead son Euthynous (*Consolatio ad Apollonium* 109b-d). When Elysius asked who he was, the young man replied, "I am the *daimon* (δαίμων) of your son".[5]

The connection between one's "image" and one's *daimon* can be traced back to the Pythagoreans, according to Quispel. He notes the story of Lysis' *daimon* in Plutarch's *De Genio Socratis* 583b and 585ef. The Pythagoreans had a rite which was performed at their burials and which gave the deceased "full possession of the blessed end". This rite seems to have involved a vision of the "image (εἴδωλον)" of the person. Apparently, Lysis had died in a foreign land and his corpse had not undergone the proper rites. So when his image was summoned, there was no appearance because "his soul, already judged, had been joined by lot to another *daimon* (δαίμονι) and released for another birth".[6]

Quispel argues that the Jews picked up this idea from the Greeks and combined it with their own lore about God's image and lore about the angels. Rabbi Joshua ben Levi who lived around 250 CE is ascribed with an exegesis of Psalm 55:19 in such a fashion. A

---

evil *genius*. Servius (*ad Aen.* 6.743) says that a person at birth gets two *genii*, one leading us to good, the other to evil (cf. Val. Max. 1.7 section 7; Plut., *Brut.* 36).

It has been argued by J. H. Moulton that the notion of the Zoroastrian *fravashi* has influenced Jewish angelology about one's "double": see, "'It is his angel'", *JTS* 3 (1902) 514-527; it should be noted, however, that the *fravashis* has parallels with the *daimon* and *genuis* since there were *fravashis* of communities and homes as well as individuals. It seems that the *fravashi* was usually connected with the pious but was subject to any moral degeneration of the individual. Thus the *fravashi* is an Iranian concept which bridges the Greco-Roman *daimon-genius* and the Iranian *daena*.

For possible connections with the Persian *daena*, see C. Colpe, "Daena, Lichtjungfrau, zweite Gestalt: Verbindungen und Unterschiede zwischen zarathustrischer und manichäischer Selbst-Anschauung", *Studies in Gnosticism and Hellenistic Religions, presented to Gilles Quispel on the Occasion of his 65th Birthday*, EPRO 91 (eds. R. van den Broek and M. J. Vermaseren; Leiden, 1981) 58-77; Colpe argues that the concept of the heavenly Self in Valentinianism and Manichaeism originates from Greece and Israel and only at a later date has this coalesced with the *daena*. On the concept of the *daena* as the spiritual self, see A. von Gall, *Basileia tou theou* (Heidelberg, 1926) 99-102, 111-115; M. Mole, "Le Pont Cinvat et l'Initiation dans le Mazdeisme", *Revue de l'Historie des Religions* 157 (1960) 155-185. The *daena* is quite different from the "image" motif since the *daena* is female and becomes more beautiful with the good deeds of the person.

[5] F. C. Babbitt, *Plutarch's Moralia* 2, LCL 222 (Cambridge, Mass., 1928 and reprints) 146-149.
[6] *Ibid.*, 436-437.

tradition transmitted in *Deuteronomy Rabba* 4.4 and *Midrash Tehillim* 55.3 (146b) gives the following interpretation of Psalm 55:19, "He has redeemed my soul in peace":

> The image (אִיקוֹנְיָא [=εἰκόνιον]) walks before the person, and the [heavenly] heralds proclaim before him, saying: "Make way for the image of God!"[7]

Thus in the Midrash on Psalm 55 section 3 (146b), he states that the "image (אִיקוֹנְיָא = εἰκόνιον)" proceeds the man and calls out to the demons who encircle him, "Make way for the image of God". Likewise, *Deuteronomy Rabba* 4.4 states that the image (אִיקוֹנְיָא = εἰκόνιον) protects the soul from bad demons, in the form of his guardian angel who walks before the person into the world. Because the person is protected by his image or angel, the demons flee.

A passage from *Genesis Rabba* 78.3 (50a) supports the idea that the angel was thought to be the image of the man. According to this text, Rabbi Hania ben Hanina (*c.* 260 CE) says that the Elohim who fought with Jacob (Gen 32:29) was Esau's guardian angel, for Jacob says to Esau: "...to see your face is like seeing the face of Elohim..." (Gen 33:10).[8]

This is not a unique passage in Jewish literature. There is a tradition, for instance, that an angel appears in Moses' shape (דמות) and those who sought to capture him were under the impression that the angel was Moses (*Deut. R.* 2.26-27; *pBerakh* 9, 13a, 37; *Midr HL* 7.5). The Midrash on *Qoheleth* (87.4) tells of an angel who descended in the shape (דמות) of Solomon and even sat upon his

---

[7] The variant in the *Midrash Tehillim* 17:8, "Images from among the angels walk..." The Venice edition (1545) does not contain the word אִיקוֹנְיָא. Thus, W. Bacher, *Die Agada der palästinensischen Amoräer* 1 (Strassburg, 1892) 134, thinks that it is corrupt. S. Krauss, *Griechische und lateinische Lehnwörter im Talmud, Midrash und Targum* 2 (Berlin, 1899) 41 and 532, suggests קוניא = κοινωνία, "association", "communion", "fellowship". The translator of *Deuteronomy Rabba* in the Soncino edition, J. Rabbinowitz, *Midrash Rabbah* 7 (London and New York, 1939, reprint 1983) 92 n. 5, retained the word "image", but inferred, "hence a *procession* in which images are carried".

Since אִיקוֹנִין is plural of אִיקוֹן, the text may cause confusion. Note, however, that אִיקוֹנְיָא can be singular <εἰκόνιον as well as plural of אִיקוֹן. Consult I. Levy, *Neuhebräisches und chaldäisches Wörterbuch über die Talmudim und Midraschim* 1, p. 70, 394f.; S. Krauss, *Griechische und lateinische Lehnwörter im Talmud, Midrash und Targum* 1, p. 40f., 202f.; M. Jastrow, *A Dictionary of the Targumim, the Talmud, Babli and Yerushalmi, and the Midrashic Literature* 1 (New York, 1950) 60.

[8] See Str.-B. 2, 707, who cite this text in order to explain the preceding passage.

throne! The angels in both of these cases may be seen as the heavenly counterparts of Moses and Solomon.[9] There is also a passage from the *Legend of the Ten Martyrs* in which God speaks to Metatron, telling him that he is the heavenly counterpart of Rabbi Ishmael on earth:

> I have a servant on earth, as you are my servant on high. His glory is like your glory, and his appearance (מראה) is like your appearance.[10]

The notion that each person has an image which was identified with one's guardian angel, was probably already part of Jewish tradition much earlier than Rabbi Joshua ben Levi's time since primitive Jewish-Christian tradition also refers to this idea.[11] For instance, in Acts 12, there is preserved the story about Peter's imprisonment and miraculous escape. When he ventures to the house of Mary the mother of John Mark, the maid Rhoda recognizes Peter's voice and runs to announce his arrival. The others tell her that she is crazy. When she persists that her announcement is true, they provide the explanation: "It is his angel!" (12:15). It can be surmised from this story that primitive Jewish-Christian tradition held that each individual had a guardian angel or *iqonin*, an image of himself, which resembles the person in outer appearance and even voice.

Quispel notes that Matthew 18:10 provides evidence for this tradition too: "See that you do not despise one of these little ones; for

---

[9] In the *Testament of Isaac* 2.3-4, the guardian angel of Isaac looks like his father, Abraham. Also relevant is the tradition about Jacob's "image" or *"eikon"* which is engraved upon the throne of God (*Gen. R.* 18.18; *b. Hullin* 91b). Jacob may be representing the collective people of Israel since he is the heavenly counterpart of Israel and since God embraces Jacob's *eikon* when he is worshipped by the people (*Hekhalot Rabbati* 9.4; e.g. *2 Baruch* 15:7-8). For a synopsis of the versions of this in the Palestinian targum to Gen 28:12, see C. Rowland, "John 1.51, Jewish Apocalyptic and Targumic Tradition", *NTS* 30 (1984) 498-507. J. Fossum argues in his forthcoming article, "John 1.51, Targumic Tradition, and Jewish Mysticism", that the tradition that Jacob's image was *engraved* upon the throne is secondary; originally, Jacob's "image" = form was *seated* upon the throne. Thus, the man-like figure upon the throne was Jacob's guardian angel!

[10] A. Jellinek, *Bet ha-Midrasch* 6 (Jerusalem, second edition, 1938) 21. I owe credit to Jarl Fossum for sharing this text with me.

[11] Quispel does not explain why the word *eikon* was used by the Jews to describe the guardian angel rather than the Greek loan word *daimon*. Perhaps because the word *daimon* had negative connotations for the Jews, the descriptive term *eikon* was implemented instead.

I tell you that in heaven their angels always behold the face of my Father who is in heaven." Here is the notion that each child has a guardian angel who dwells in heaven before God's throne. Even though this saying of Jesus does not explicitly state that the angels are heavenly doubles to their earthly counterparts, this is implicit in the tradition. This is evident in the fifth century Syrian text, *Testamentum Domini*, where the following statement is found regarding the guardian angel: "For of every soul the image (*salma*) or type is standing before the face of God even before the foundation of the world".[12]

Furthermore, Quispel explores traces of the notion of the heavenly double in forms of early Christianity which reflect connections with the primitive Jewish-Christian movement: in notions of the "twin" in the Syrian Thomas traditions, in the Manichaean doctrine of twinship and Mani's guardian angel, in Hermas' vision of the angel of repentance as well as of the true prophet, in the motif of the guardian angel in Origen,[13] in the Valentinian doctrine of the *mysterium conjunctionis* or *syzygy*, and in the story in *Pistis Sophia* chapter 61 where Jesus' brother, the Spirit, is his counterpart. It would seem that the idea of a heavenly double was a major constituent of primitive Jewish-Christian dogma inherited from Jewish teachings.

Thus, it is not surprising that Jewish Kabbalah texts abound with references to this heavenly double, the צלם or image of God which, according to G. Scholem, refers to the "unique, individual spiritual shape of each human being" or the "self" in this literature.[14] Scholem suggests that this idea in Kabbalism is associated with fragments of pseudepigraphic Hermetic literature contained in the magical papyri where evocations of the spiritual being or "perfected nature" of the person are found.[15] He quotes, for instance, the

---

[12] I. E. Rahmani II, *Testamentum Domini nostri Jesu Christi* (Moguntiae, 1899) 97.

[13] For a recent treatment of this, refer to J. W. Trigg, "The Angel of Great Counsel: Christ and the Angelic Hierarchy in Origen's Theology", *JTS* 42 (1991) 35-51. According to Origen, each person has a guardian spirit. For the unbaptized, this spirit is a demon which is replaced by an angel at baptism. When the person becomes more spiritually adept, the Lord himself, the Angel of the Great Counsel, takes the place of the guardian angel.

[14] Scholem, *Mystical Shape*, 251-273, quote on 251.

[15] Scholem is indebted to the studies of H. Corbin on interpretations of the "perfected nature" in such major twelfth- century philosophers as Abul Barakat and esoterics like Suhrawardi of Aleppo. Corbin defines the "per-

Arabic manual *Ghayat al-hakim* where Hermes reports that a beautiful shape appeared to him. When he asked the shape, "Who are you?", the shape answered, "I am your perfected nature".[16] Hermes relates that the perfected nature is "the pneuma of the philosopher, connected with his star and guiding him..."[17]

Scholem also associates the "perfected nature" with the "perfected body", the "ethereal or astral body", in the *Mithras Liturgy*. This "body" is the celestial garment, the primal celestial image, which is kept in heaven and comes out to meet and envelop the soul when it returns to the upper world.[18]

Noteworthy is E. Peterson's association of the "perfected body" mentioned in the *Mithras Liturgy* with "form (μορφή)" in another magical prayer, PGM 4.1167ff:

> You, the only one and blessed one among the aions, and father of the world, I call upon with cosmic prayers. Draw near to me, you who breathed animation into the whole world, you who have put the fire on the ocean of heaven and separated the earth from the water. Hearken Form (μορφή) and Spirit, and earth and sea, to the words of the wise one of the divine necessity, and attend to my prayer like seeds of fire.

Here the "Form" and "Spirit" are mentioned prior to the earth and sea probably because they were created before the earth and sea.[19] Furthermore, the "Form" is the μορφή which Adam originally had possessed in Paradise.[20] This heavenly "Form" must be preexistent or have been created on the first or second day of creation

---

fected nature" as both the divine intellect and the guardian angel of the individual. Refer to Corbin's fascinating studies, "Le Récit d'Initiation et l'Hermetisme en Iran", *Eranos* 17 (1949/50) 158-187; idem, *Avicenne et le Récit Visionnaire* I (Paris 1954).

[16] Scholem, *Mystical Shape*, 255.
[17] *Ibid.*, 256.
[18] A. Dietrich, *Eine Mithras Liturgie* (Leipzig, 1923) 4; R. Reitzenstein, *Hellenistic Mystery-Religions: Their Basic Ideas and Significance*, Pittsburgh Theological Monograph Series 15 (trans. J. E. Steely; Pittsburg, 1978) 200; R. Reitzenstein, "Griechische Lehren", *Studien zum antiken Synkretismus aus Iran und Griechenland*, Studien der Bibliothek Warburg 7 (Leipzig, 1926) 76 esp. n. 2, 112-114.

The "astral body" is examined by G. R. S. Mead, "The Spirit Body: An Excursion into Alexandrian Psycho-Physiology", *The Quest* (1910) 472-488; idem, *The Doctrine of the Subtle Body in Western Tradition* (London 1919); E. R. Dodds, his appendix "The Astral Body in Neoplatonism" in his edition of Proclus, *The Elements of Theology* (Oxford 1933) 313-321.

[19] E. Peterson, "Die Befreiung Adams aus der 'Ἀνάγκη'", *Frühkirche, Judentum und Gnosis* (Rome, Freiburg, Vienna, 1959) 113.
[20] *Ibid.*, 113; cp. 119 n. 41.

prior to the creation of the earth and the sea.²¹ This text supports Scholem's thesis that the magical papyri are part of the background for the idea of man's heavenly images.

Scholem, however, does not see the background to the heavenly double to be solely Hermetic lore in the magical texts. He also refers to the idea found in early Judaism that there is a heavenly garment waiting for the arrival of the person in heaven.²² Thus it appears from Scholem's research that the heavenly double in Kabbalism is influenced by both primitive Jewish notions of the heavenly garment and Hermetic lore regarding the "perfected nature" found in the magical papyri.

I would add to the discussion another text which seems to be associated with this trajectory. It is a passage from Philo's *De somniis* 1.227-232 where Philo describes the visionary experience. He reads a passage from his Greek version of Genesis 31:13 as follows: "I am the God who appeared to thee in the place of God (ἐγώ εἰμι ὁ θεὸς ὁ ὀφθείς σοι ἐν τόπῳ θεοῦ)" (1.227).²³ Philo comments on the phrase "in the place of", explaining that "to souls which are still in a body", God takes on "the likeness of angels (ἀγγέλοις εἰκαζόμενον)" (1.232).²⁴ God's proper nature, however, does not change. Rather each soul encounters his presence in "a different form (ἑτερόμορφον)" (1.232).²⁵ Furthermore, some mistakenly think that, when they view this "image (εἰκόνα)", they are seeing the archetypal original form itself (τὸ ἀρχέτυπον ἐκεῖνο εἶδος) (1.232).²⁶ Thus, those who are "unable to see the sun itself" see its "gleam" and mistake it for the sun "so some regard the image of God, his angel the Word, as his very self" (1.239). Philo says that it is not surprising that Hagar, therefore, mistakes the angel who comes to her for God (1.240).

Even though Philo does not describe these angels as "twins" of humans beings, it seems that Philo is aware of the tradition that the

---

²¹ Fossum, *Name*, 283-284.
²² On this theme, refer to L. Ginzberg, *The Legends of the Jews* 5. *Notes to Volumes I and II: From Creation to the Exodus* (Philadelphia, 1925 and reprints) 103-104 n. 93, 112-113 n. 104; W. Bousset, *Die Religion des Judentums im späthellenistischen Zeitalter*, HNT 21 (3rd ed. H Gressman; Tübingen, 1926) 318; E. Preuschen, *Die Apokryphen gnostischen Adamschriften* (Giessen, 1900) 52, and nn. 24 and 69; Str.-B. 4, 940ff., 1138.
²³ Colson and Whitaker, *Philo* 5, 416-417.
²⁴ *Ibid.*, 420-421.
²⁵ *Ibid.*, 420-421.
²⁶ *Ibid.*, 420-421.

angels are known as "images". Moreover, he argues that there exists an individualization of these angels or "images", and these can be encountered by the human. This passage is additional evidence that the notion of the angels as heavenly images was already part of Judaism prior to Jewish-Christianity.

2) *The Mythology of Separation and Return:*

a) *Adam's Lost Image:*
According to Logion 84, each person has a heavenly eternal image which came into existence before the human body.[27] Furthermore, this image is normally concealed from the person. Thus Logion 84 employs the language of religious mythology to describe the Transcendent as an external object, a divine image in heaven, which is normally sealed off from contact. This parallels Logion 83 which speaks in psychologic terms about the divine element being concealed within the person. What both Logia are saying is that there has been a separation from the divine or Transcendent.

---

[27] Interpretations of the Genesis story along these lines was not uncommon. In fact this type of interpretation is quite developed by the time of Philo. On one level, Philo interprets Genesis 1:26-27 as referring to a "heavenly" or "incorporeal" Platonic "idea" of a human being over and against the creation of the "earthly" sense-perceptible human being in Genesis 2:7. Thus he explains why the Genesis story contains two creation accounts of the human and how the "moulded" human differs from the man made in God's image. Thus he writes regarding these two types of human beings: "one is heavenly, the other earthly. Now the heavenly is made in the image of God and is completely free of corruptible and earthly substance; but the earthly was constructed from matter scattered about, which he [Moses] calls clay" (*Leg. All.* 1.31-32; cf. *Quaest. Gen.* 1.4, 2.54; *Leg. All.* 1.53-55, 1.88-89, 2.4).

Philo understands the relationship between the two creations in terms of Platonic metaphysics. Thus he describes the heavenly human who is created in God's image as "an idea or kind or seal, an object of thought, incorporeal, neither male nor female, incorruptible by nature" (*Op. mundi.* 134). In addition, the heavenly man of Genesis 1:26-27 is a copy of the Logos of God (Logos as the divine image: *Leg. All.* 3.96; *Plant.* 18; *Conf. Ling.* 97, 147; *Rev. Div. Her.* 230f.; *Fug.* 101; *Som.* 1.239, 2.45. Man in Genesis 1 as created according to it: *Leg. All.* 3.96; *Plant.* 19; *Rev. Div. Her.* 231; *Spec. Leg.* 3.207; cf. *Op. Mund.* 25).

Sometimes Philo relates in these passages that Genesis 1:26-27 refers to the creation of the *earthly* man (*Conf. ling.* 175; *Mut. nom.* 30-31) and the divine image after which he was created is identified with the Logos (*Op. mund.* 25, 69, 139; *Leg. All.* 3.96; *Quis. rer.* 230-231; *Quaest. Gen.* 2.62; cf. *Fug.* 68-71).

For a complete discussion and analysis of these passages, refer to A. J. M. Wedderburn, "Philo's 'Heavenly Man'", *NT* 15 (1973) 301-326; Kim, *Paul's Gospel*, 172 n. 2; J. Fossum, "Colossians 1.15-18a", *NTS* 35 (1989) 187-188.

This separation is alluded to in Logion 11, where Jesus says, "On the day when you were one, you became two (ϩⲙ ⲫⲟⲟⲩ ⲉⲧⲉⲧⲛ̄ⲟ ⲛ̄ⲟⲩⲁ ⲁⲧⲉⲧⲛ̄ⲉⲓⲣⲉ ⲙ̄ⲡⲥⲛⲁⲩ)".[28] According to Logion 84, this division involves being separated from one's heavenly image.

This mythology is to be associated with the Jewish tradition that the first man was created in God's image and thus had part of God's *kavod* (כבודו עמו), but this radiance was taken away from him after the Fall. In *Genesis Rabbah* 11, R. Simeon ben Judah says that the Rabbis maintained:

> Adam's glory did not abide the night with him. What is the proof? *But Adam passeth not the night in glory* (Ps. XLIX,13). The Rabbis maintain: His glory abode with him, but at the termination of the Sabbath He deprived him of his splendour and expelled him from the Garden of Eden, as it is written, *Thou changest his countenance, and sendest him away* (Job XIV,20).

Similarly in *b. Moed Katan* 15b, Bar Kappara taught apparently about Adam and Eve: "My likeness (דמות דיוקני) I had given to them, but through their sin (בעונותיהם) I changed it".[29]

This reflects the belief purported in both Jewish and Christian circles that Adam was a luminous being in the Garden before the Fall. His light was so bright that it even surpassed the brightness of the sun.[30] This understanding of Adam is rooted in speculation about Genesis 3:21 where God made Adam and Eve "garments of skin, and clothed them". According to this tradition, prior to the Fall, Adam and Eve wore garments of light which were lost as a consequence of their sin.[31] It is stated in the Babylonian Talmud, *'Aboda Zara* 8a, that the light was actually taken from Adam: "(Adam says): From the day when I sinned, the world darkened for me".

---

[28] Layton, *Nag Hammadi Codex II,2-7*, 56 and 58; Eng. trans. by Lambdin, 57 and 59.

[29] According to Abba Kohen (*Gen. R.* 23 on 4:24), the divine likeness ceased after Enoch.

[30] See L. Ginzberg, *The Legends of the Jews* 5, 97 n. 69; B. Murmelstein, "Adam, ein Beitrag zur Messiaslehre", *Wiener Zeitschrift fur die Kunde des Morgenlandes* 35 (1928) 255 n. 3; W. Staerk, *Die Erlösererwartung in den östlichen Religionen* (Stuttgart and Berlin, 1938) 11.

[31] See De Conick and Fossum, "Stripped Before God", p. 124, nn. 8 & 9. There is also a tradition that understands the verbs in Genesis 3.21 to be pluperfects, referring to the status of Adam and Eve *before* the Fall. Thus *Gen. R.* 20.12 states that the scroll of R. Meir read אור, "light", instead of עור, "skin". The Targums presuppose this wording since they read "garments of glory (יקאר)".

Adam is the Light or Lamp of the world in the Palestinian Talmud, *Sab.* 5b: "The First Man was the Light of the World, as it is written (Prov. 20.27) 'Adam's spirit (נשמה) was a lamp of God'. And Eve brought death upon him." The original significance of this passage is that Adam originates from the Light and his connection with the Light is severed through the sin of he and Eve.[32] This notion seems to be behind the Rabbinic tradition that there are six things which will be restored to man that have been lost. The lost radiance (זיו) is one of them (*Gen. R.* 12; *Tanch. Buber Bereshit* 18).

Speculations about the Genesis story clearly produced an imaginative interpretation of creation: man originally was connected with the light and his Fall caused him to be severed, at least temporarily, from these luminous beginnings. It seems that Logion 84 belongs to this milieu which held that Adam was separated from his divine radiance because of his Sin.

Logion 84, however, specifically understands this divine element to be the divine "image". There is a Samaritan tradition which taught that Adam actually lost his "image". According to the Samaritans, Adam cast off the Form of God in the Garden of Eden. Then when Moses ascended Mount Sinai, he received the image of God which Adam had lost. Thus when they speak about Moses being invested with the Light, they are referring to his endowment with Adam's lost image. So in *Memar Marqa* 5.4, we read: "He [Moses] was vested with the Form which Adam cast off in the Garden of Eden; and his face shone up to the day of his death".[33] Or, according to 6.3:

> He [Moses] drew near to the holy deep darkness where the Divine One was, and he saw the wonders of the unseen - a sight no one else could see. His image dwelt on him. How terrifying to anyone who beholds and no one is able to stand before it![34]

---

[32] See H. Odeberg, *The Fourth Gospel* (Amsterdam, 1974) 290, for his interpretation of this passage.

[33] Macdonald, *Memar Marqa*, 209.

[34] *Ibid.*, 223. This type of exegesis of Genesis 1-3 where it was argued that Adam lost the divine image seems to be early and may be already visible behind a passage in the *Wisdom of Solomon* 2:23f.: "For God created man for incorruption, and made him in the image of his own eternity, but through the devil's envy death entered the world, and those who belong to his party experience it".

This motif must represent an earlier speculation on the Genesis story since we find the tale in the *Apocalypse of Moses* that Adam and Eve were originally clothed with God's *kavod*, glory, or image. But at least Eve was separated from this glory when the garments of the glory were stripped as a consequence of her Sin. In Chapter 20, after Eve sinned, she tells us that "I knew that I was naked of the righteousness with which I had been clothed". Eve weeps, crying, "I have been estranged from my glory with which I was clothed". According to Chapter 21, Eve is distraught because the transgression brought she and Adam "down from great glory". Although it is not clear that Adam actually lost the Glory, after Adam eats of the tree, he says to Eve, "You have estranged me from the glory of God".

Speculations about this lost heavenly "image" were quite prominent in Syrian theology. In the *Hymn of the Pearl*, the analogy of the fallen soul is recorded.[35] The prince (the soul) was stripped of his "glittering robe" (his image) and was sent into Egypt (the world) where he was dressed in the Egyptian dress (the body).

It is the basic premise of the theology of the Syrian mystic Macarius that Adam "lost the very image itself (ἀπώλεσεν αὐτὴν τὴν εἰκόνα)" when he sinned in the Garden (*Hom.* 12.1; cf. 12.6, 12.8).[36] This heavenly image is the light garment or shining image of the spirit (III.19). Thus, when Adam sinned, he lost the image or the spirit (*Hom.* 12.6; cf. 20.1). This image or light garment was not only lost by Adam, but by every soul (*Hom.* 11.5-6; III.16.18). The soul, being "a beautiful likeness and image of God (καλόν ὁμοίωμα καὶ εἰκὼν θεοῦ)", was corrupted by the "passions of the dark world" through the Fall (*Hom.* 1.7).[37] The light of the soul was dressed in darkness; Macarius tells us that on the day when Adam sinned, God cried out to Adam: "After such glory, what shame you now bear! What darkness are you now!... From such light, what darkness has covered you!". Macarius interprets these words to mean that "darkness became the garment of his soul" (*Hom.* 30.7; cf. 28.4).

---

[35] Quispel, *Makarius*, esp. 40-64.

[36] H. Dörries, E. Klostermann, and M. Kroeger, *Die 50 Geistlichen Homilien des Makarios*, PTS 4 (Berlin, 1964) 107-108; Maloney, *Pseudo-Macarius*, 97.

[37] Dörries, Klosterman, and Kroeger, *Macarios*, 9; Maloney, *Pseudo-Macarius*, 41.

b) *Return to the Image:*
   (i) Reunification:

Not surprisingly, if one was separated from the divine image as the result of sin, then in order to be redeemed, one must be rejoined with the image. This is certainly the theology purported in the *Gospel of Thomas*. As we saw in Chapter Six, Section 2, during the discussion of Logion 37, salvation involves stripping the material body and renouncing it. In so doing, the adherent believed that he had returned to the prelapsarian condition of Adam.

Moreover, the refrain of "making the two into one" is known in Logion 22 and 106. According to Logion 22, a person will only enter the heavenly Kingdom when he has made the two into one, when his human image has been replaced with his heavenly light-image:

ϩⲟⲧⲁⲛ ⲉⲧⲉⲧⲛ̄ϣⲁⲣ̄ ⲡⲥⲛⲁⲩ ⲟⲩⲁ ⲁⲩⲱ ⲉⲧⲉⲧⲛ̄ϣⲁⲣ̄ ⲡⲥⲁ ⲛϩⲟⲩⲛ ⲛ̄ⲑⲉ ⲙ̄ⲡⲥⲁ ⲛⲃⲟⲗ ⲁⲩⲱ ⲡⲥⲁ ⲛⲃⲟⲗ ⲛ̄ⲑⲉ ⲙ̄ⲡⲥⲁ ⲛϩⲟⲩⲛ ⲁⲩⲱ ⲡⲥⲁ(ⲛ)ⲧⲡⲉ ⲛ̄ⲑⲉ ⲙ̄ⲡⲥⲁ ⲙ̄ⲡⲓⲧⲛ̄ ⲁⲩⲱ ϣⲓⲛⲁ ⲉⲧⲉⲧⲛⲁⲉⲓⲣⲉ ⲙ̄ⲫⲟⲟⲩⲧ ⲙⲛ̄ ⲧⲥϩⲓⲙⲉ ⲙ̄ⲡⲓⲟⲩⲁ ⲟⲩⲱⲧ ϫⲉⲕⲁⲁⲥ ⲛⲉ ⲫⲟⲟⲩⲧ ⲣ̄ ϩⲟⲟⲩⲧ ⲛ̄ⲧⲉ ⲧⲥϩⲓⲙⲉ ⲣ̄ ⲥϩⲓⲙⲉ ϩⲟⲧⲁⲛ ⲉⲧⲉⲧⲛ̄ϣⲁⲉⲓⲣⲉ ⲛ̄ϩⲛ̄ⲃⲁⲗ ⲉⲡⲙⲁ ⲛ̄ⲟⲩⲃⲁⲗ ⲁⲩⲱ ⲟⲩϭⲓϫ ⲉⲡⲙⲁ ⲛ̄ⲛⲟⲩϭⲓϫ ⲁⲩⲱ ⲟⲩⲉⲣⲏⲧⲉ ⲉⲡⲙⲁ ⲛ̄ⲟⲩⲉⲣⲏⲧⲉ ⲟⲩϩⲓⲕⲱⲛ ⲉⲡⲙⲁ ⲛ̄ⲟⲩϩⲓⲕⲱ(ⲛ) ⲧⲟⲧⲉ ⲧⲉⲧⲛⲁⲃⲱⲕ ⲉϩⲟⲩⲛ ⲉ[ⲧ]ⲙⲛ̄[ⲧⲉⲣ]ⲟ

> When you make the two one, and when you make the inside like the outside and the outside like the inside, and the above like the below, and when you make the male and the female one and the same, so that the male not be male nor the female female, and you fashion eyes in place of an eye, and a hand in place of a hand, and a foot in place of a foot, and an image in place of an image, then you will enter the Kingdom.[38]

Thus, salvation is granted only to those who have been united with their divine image, when they have made "an image in place of an image", fashioning "eyes in place of an eye, and a hand in place of a hand, and a foot in place of a foot".

According to Logion 106, "When you make the two into one, you will become sons of Man (ϩⲟⲧⲁⲛ ⲉⲧⲉⲧⲛ̄ϣⲁⲣ̄ ⲡⲥⲛⲁⲩ ⲟⲩⲁ ⲧⲉⲧⲛⲁϣⲱⲡⲉ ⲛ̄ϣⲏⲣⲱⲙⲉ)".[39] Since the title "Son of Man" was identified with God's *kavod* or Glory and was associated with angelic

---

[38] Layton, *Nag Hammadi II,2-7*, 62; Eng. trans. mine.
[39] *Ibid.*, 90; Eng. trans. mine.

traditions and the motif of the Heavenly Man,[40] it makes perfect sense in this Logion that when the separation is rectified and one reunites with one's heavenly image, then one gains angelic status, becoming a son of the Heavenly Man!

This may shed light on Paul's belief that our heavenly bodies are images of the Heavenly Man, the Christ, which must be donned at the Resurrection.[41] According to Paul in 1 Corinthians 15:35-49, there are two types of bodies: the earthly and the heavenly. In verses 40-41, Paul explains that the glory (δόξα) of the heavenly body (ἐπουρανίων) differs from that of the earthly (ἐπιγείων) just as the illumination of the sun differs from the moon and the stars. He is adamant that just as there is an earthly body (ψυχικόν), so there is a spiritual body (πνευματικόν) (v. 44). He states in verse 49 that "as we have worn the image of the earthly, we also shall wear the image of the heavenly (καθὼς ἐφορέσαμεν τὴν εἰκόνα τοῦ χοικοῦ, φορέσομεν καὶ τὴν εἰκόνα τοῦ ἐπουρανίου)". The image of the earthly corresponds to Adam while the image of the heavenly corresponds to the Heavenly Man who Paul identifies with the Christ (v. 48).

Paul, or the tradition from which he is drawing, has probably developed this theology by exegesis of Genesis 5:3 where after the Fall, Adam begot a son in his likeness (ἰδέα) and image (εἰκών). Thus from that time, the earthly bodies as images of the Fallen Adam have been reproduced. But, according to Paul, heavenly bodies as images of the Heavenly Man, the Christ, must eventually be donned at the Resurrection: "this perishable nature must put on the imperishable, and this mortal nature must put on immortality" (15:53; cf. 2 Cor 5:1-10[42]). According to Paul's theology, this

---

[40] See the excellent summary of this in Fossum, *Name*, 266ff., esp. 279 and n. 61, 337.

[41] Here Paul is refering to the creation of the first Man in Genesis 1:26-27 and the current traditions surrounding this primal man, the Anthropos. See H. Conzelmann, *1 Corinthians: A Commentary on the First Epistle to the Corinthians*, Hermeneia - A Critical and Historical Commentary on the Bible (trans. J. Leitch; bib. and refs. J. Dunkly; ed. G. MacRae; Philadelphia, 1975) 284-286; R. Reitzenstein, *Das iranische Erlösermysterium* (Bonn, 1921); W. Staerk, *Soter II: Die Erlösungserwartung in den östlichen Religionen* (Stuttgart, 1938); K. Rudolph, "Ein Grundtyp gnostischer Urmensch-Adam-Spekulation", *ZRGG* 9 (1957) 1-20; E. S. Dower, *The Secret Adam* (Oxford, 1960); J. Jervell, *Imago Dei*, FRLANT 76 (Göttingen, 1960), 96-107; H.-M. Schenke, *Der Gott "Mensch" in der Gnosis* (Göttingen, 1962); E. Brandenburger, *Adam und Christus*, WMANT 7 (Neukirchen, 1962) 68-157; Fossum, *Name*, 266-291.

[42] For a discussion of this passage, refer to De Conick and Fossum,

heavenly εἰκών must be restored and this only can happen by connection with the εἰκών of Christ. So in Romans 8:29, Paul writes: "For those whom he foreknew he also predestined to be conformed to the image (εἰκόνος) of his Son, in order that he might be the first-born of many brethern".

Also noteworthy are the Syrian traditions to this effect. In the allegory of the fallen soul in the *Hymn of the Pearl* found in the third century *Acts of Thomas*, the prince (the soul) was separated from his heavenly robe (his image) when he came into Egypt (the world) and donned the Egyptian dress (the human body). He fell asleep but was awakened by a letter from the King (God). He stripped off the "unclean dress" and left Egypt. When he returned to the Kingdom (ascended to heaven), he put on his "bright robe" which was a "mirror" of himself and which was embroidered with the image of the King (the image of God). Thus, the prince was reunited with his lost image.

This ideology is presupposed by the second century Syrian encratite leader, Tatian, who teaches that in Paradise, the soul was allied with the spirit. When it became separated from the spirit and was alone, it tended "downward towards matter". We are told that "in the beginning, the spirit was a constant companion of the soul, but the spirit forsook it because it was not willing to follow" (*Orat.* 13). In another passage, Tatian explains that the spirit was the "wings of the soul" which were "cast off through sin" and thus the soul "falls to the ground" having left behind its "heavenly companionship" (*Orat.* 20). According to Tatian, we must "seek for what we once had, but have lost", uniting the soul with the spirit and striving after "union with God". For such a person alone has been restored to "the image and likeness of God", having "advanced far beyond mere humanity - to God Himself" (*Orat.* 15).

In the Syrian father, Macarius, this theology has taken on a very developed form. Salvation involves a reunion of the soul with the lost image, the spirit. Thus Macarius states that "if anyone is naked and lacks the divine and heavenly garment which is the power of the Spirit", he is to "weep and beg the Lord" for "the spiritual garment" so that "he may be clothed" (*Hom.* 20.1). Thus:

> Everyone who is naked of that divine glory ought to be as much overcome by shame and ought to be aware of his disgrace as Adam

---

"Stripped Before God", 130-131.

was when he was naked...Let such a person, therefore, beg of Christ, who gives and adorns with glory in ineffable light (*Hom.* 20.2).

Such a person is "joined and united with the Lord" (*Great Letter* 269)[43] and must now conduct himself "according to the heavenly image" (*Great Letter* 256).[44] By so doing, the souls "become heavenly light" (*Hom.* 1.4). Thus the "old man" is discarded and a new man is donned "having new eyes in place of the old, ears replacing ears, hands for hands, feet for feet" (*Hom.* 2.2). In other words:

> All who have put off the old and earthly man and from whom Jesus has removed the clothing of the kingdom of darkness have put on the new and heavenly man, Jesus Christ, so that once again the eyes are joined to new eyes, ears to ears, head to head, to be completely pure and bearing the heavenly image (*Hom.* 2.4).

Paradoxically, this unity with the divine is described by Macarius as a state of "doubleness": once a person comes to God, he "becomes twofold (διπλοῦς)"[45] since "as you offer God any part of yourself, he himself shares with your soul similar aspects of his own being" (*Hom.* 15.22). This person is the Lord's "bride" who enters "into union with him so that he may interpenetrate it and be 'one spirit' with it" (*Hom.* 46.6). Thus Christians are "of another world, children of the heavenly Adam, a new race, children of the Holy Spirit, shining brothers of Christ, similar to their Father, the spiritual Adam" (*Hom.* 16.8).

It is noteworthy that the *Gospel of Thomas* is also aware of the tradition which we saw in Macarius that this state of unity, when the two have been made one (L. 22), can be described in terms of "doubleness". Thus Logion 11 reads: "When you come to dwell in the light, what will you do?...When you become two, what will you do?". Even this language of doubleness suggests that salvation involves a reunion with one's divine image.

(ii) *Vision:*

Undoubtedly, the "images" referred to in Logion 84 belong to the early Jewish tradition of one's divine twin, guardian angel, or image from which one was separated as the result of Adam's Sin.

---

[43] Maloney, *Pseudo-Macarius*, 269.
[44] *Ibid.*, 256.
[45] Dörries, Klostermann, and Kroeger, *Macarios*, 140.

Reunification with this heavenly image is the soteriological goal. In Logion 84, however, this reunification is described in the terms of vision since this Logion states that one must *see* one's heavenly image or double. It seems that the emphasis on gaining a vision of one's image is to be associated with the traditions of Self-vision in Hermeticism and the Greek magical papyri.

In the Hermetic tract, *The Discourse on the Eighth and Ninth* (NHC VI,6), we witness ascent followed by self-vision which brings about unity with the universal mind. There is a prayer that access be given into the eighth and ninth spheres in order to "see the form of the image that has no deficiency" (57.6-7). Then the mystagogue has his vision which he describes in the following terms:

> "For already from them the power, which is light, is coming to us. For I see! I see indescribable depths. How shall I tell you, my son?...How [shall I describe] the universe? I [am Mind and] I see another Mind, the one that [moves] the soul! I see the one that moves me from pure forgetfulness. You give me power! *I see myself* (ϯⲛⲁⲩ ⲉⲣⲟⲉⲓ)! I want to speak! Fear restrains me. I have found the beginning of the power that is above all powers, the one that has not beginning. I see a fountain bubbling with life. I have said, my son, that I am Mind. I have seen! (ⲁⲉⲓⲛⲁⲩ)...And I, Mind, understand (ⲡⲛⲟⲩⲥ ϯⲣ̄ⲛⲟⲉⲓ)" (57.29-58.22).[46]

Subsequently, the initiate attains his ascent and vision and states that "I myself see this same vision in you" (ⲁⲛⲟⲕ ϯⲛⲁⲩ ⲉⲧⲉⲉⲓⲑⲉⲱⲣⲓⲁ ⲛ̄ⲟⲩⲱⲧ ⲛ̄ϩⲣⲁⲓ ⲛ̄ϩⲏⲧⲕ̄) (59.27-28) and also describes this experiences in terms of a self-vision: "I see myself (ϯⲛⲁⲩ ⲉⲣⲟⲉⲓ)!" (60.32-61.1).[47] Self-vision in this Hermetic text brings about unity with the universal mind. Thus seeing oneself is seeing Mind and understanding one's participation in it.[48]

---

[46] P. Dirkse, J. Brashler, and D. M. Parrott, "The Discourse on the Eighth and Ninth", *Nag Hammadi Codices V,2-5 and VI with Papyrus Berolinensis 8502, 1 and 4*, NHS 11 (ed. D. M. Parrott; Leiden, 1979) 358-361.

[47] *Ibid.*, 362-363 and 364-365 respectively.

[48] Similar ideas are promoted in the Hermetic text *Poimandres*. In this tract, Hermes has a vision (*C.H.* I.4-5). Poimandres interprets for Hermes this vision: "I am the light you saw, mind, your god who existed before the watery nature that appeared out of darkness...This is what you must know: that in you which sees and hears is the word of the lord, but your mind is god the father; they are not divided from one another for their union is life...In your mind you have seen the archetypal form, the preprinciple that exists before a beginning without end". The point of this text is not to describe a Self-vision but the ideology is similar to that prescribed in the *Discourse on the Eighth and Ninth* since God is identified with the Self. Thus the

Corpus Hermeticum 13 as well contains important descriptions of Self-vision and its meaning. In this chapter, Tat has prayed that he might be taught about rebirth, wanting to know about the "way to be born again" (13.3). Hermes says that he is unable to relate anything to this end except to share a particular visionary experience when he left his human body and assumed "an immortal body" (ἀθάνατον σῶμα) (13.3). Apparently this body is his spiritual body. He is no longer "what I was before (εἰμι νῦν οὐχ ὁ πρίν). I have been born in mind" (13.3). The human body which can be experienced through the senses has disintegrated. The new Self does not have color or mass, nor can it be touched. This Self that Hermes now is cannot be seen by anyone who uses the human eyes. Thus Hermes explains: "Now you see me with your eyes, my child, but by gazing with bodily sight you do <not> understand what <I am>; I am not seen with such eyes, my child" (13.3).

Tat is frustrated and states that he feels like he is crazy because, unlike his teacher's Self-vision, he has no such vision: "I do not see myself (ἐμαυτὸν νῦν οὐχ ὁρῶ)" (13.4). Hermes then gives him more instruction regarding the need to cleanse one's Self of the twelve evil inclinations that torment the "inner person (τὸν ἐνδιάθετον ἄνθρωπον)", the person which resides in the bodily prison (13.7). These vices disappear under the influence of the ten powers of God. Once this has happened, the new spiritual birth is possible and with it divinity: "My child, you have come to know the means of rebirth. The arrival of the decad sets in order a birth of mind that expels the twelve; we have been divinized by this birth (ἐθεώθημεν τῇ γενέσει)" (13.10).

Thus Tat is finally capable of rejoicing in a Self-vision: "Father, I see the universe and I see myself in mind (τὸ πᾶν ὁρῶ καὶ ἐμαυτὸν ἐν τῷ νοί)". Hermes declares: "This, my child, is rebirth" (13.13). Moreover, this spiritual self cannot be dissolved because, unlike the sensible body, it is "immortal (ἀθάνατον)" (13.14).

Associated with these ideas about Self-vision is the theurgical practice of *lecanomancy* or bowl divination.[49] The Greek magical

---

vision of the Anthropos could be interpreted to be a vision of one's own Mind.

[49] On bowl divination, see R. Ganszyniec, "Λεκανομαντεία", *Realencyclopädie der klassischen Altertumswissenschaft* 12 (Pauly-Wissowa, 1925) 1879-89; F. Cumont, *L'Egypte des astrologues* (Bruxelles, 1937) 161; J. Capart, "Les anciens Egyptiens pratiquaient-ils déjà la lécanomancie?", *Chronique d'Egypte* 19 (1944) 263; F. Cunen, "Lampe et coupe magiques", *Symbolae Osloenses* 36 (1960) 65-71.

papyrus PGM 4.154-285 details the procedure through which one contacts the god, unites with him, and receives relevation from him. The papyrus states that "you will observe through bowl divination on whatever day or night you want, in whatever place you want, beholding the god in the water and hearing a voice from the god which speaks in verses in answer to whatever you want."[50]

Apparently, the deity manifests itself to the magician after the magician leans over the bowl and looks into the water. On the water, he sees the reflection of the deity in place of his own. This vision brings about participation in the divine nature as lines 214-221 indicate:[51]

> "I have been united with thy sacred form. I have been empowered by thy sacred name. I have received the effluence of thy goodness, Lord, God of gods, King Daimon, αθθπιομ θουτουι ταυαντι λαω απτατω". When you have done this, descend, having attained that nature, equal to God's, which is effected by this ritual union."[52]

It seems that the magician's own reflection has been identified with the deity's. Thus through this ritual the magician is divinized.

The practice of *lecanomancy* and its transformative effects filtered into Judaism as evidenced in a tale preserved in *Joseph and Aseneth* 18.[53] As Aseneth prepares herself for her wedding and is about to wash her face, she leans over the basin and regards her reflection on the water. What she sees is herself transformed. The description of her face is reminiscent of the face of an angel: "And it was like the sun and her eyes (were) like a rising morning star...".

For a comprehensive overview of Graeco-Roman revelatory divination, refer to T. Hopfner, *Griechisch-aegyptischer Offenbarungszauber* 1 and 2 (Leipzig, 1921-1924), and his article, "Mageia", *PW* (14,1) 301-393. On the mirror as a symbol in Greek and Gnostic religion, see A. Delatte, *La catoptromancie grecque et ses derives* (Paris, 1932).

[50] Lines 164-166. Trans. by H. Betz, *The Greek Magical Papyri in Translation Including the Demotic Spells* (Chicago, 1986) 40.

[51] On this, see G. Quispel, "Judaism, Judaic Christianity and Gnosis", *The New Testament and Gnosis: Essays in honour of Robert McLachlan Wilson* (eds. A. H. B. Logan and A. J. M. Wedderburn; Edinburgh, 1983) 56-57.

[52] Eng. trans. by M. Smith, *Clement of Alexandria and a Secret Gospel of Mark* (Cambridge, Mass., 1973) 221.

[53] M. Philonenko, *Joseph et Aséneth: Introduction, texte critique, traduction et notes*, SPB 13 (Leiden, 1968) 193 n. 18,7; See also R. Reitzenstein, *Historia Monachorum und Historia Lausiaca. Eine Studie zur Geschichte des Mönchtums und der frühchristlichen Begriffe Gnostiker und Pneumatiker*, FRLANT 24 (Göttingen, 1916) 247-254.

Aseneth beholds the face of a light-being with the morning star as eyes.[54] When she sees her image on the water, she sees herself transformed into her angelic counterpart.

Texts with Jewish-Christian influences are aware of the transformative effects of *lecanomancy* as well. A conversion story reported in the *Pseudo-Clementine Homilies* 13.16 reports that the woman who is chaste is "clothed with holy light". She is described as "radiant" and "into a beautiful mirror does she look, into God she gazes". Not only is she described as a light-being but when she looks at her own image, she sees God himself! She has been transformed into the deity.

We discover a similar declaration in the second century *Odes of Solomon* 13. The Ode is composed as follows:

> Behold, the Lord is our mirror.
> Open (your) eyes and see them in him.
> And learn the manner of your face,
> then announce praises to his Spirit.
> And wipe the paint from your face,
> And love his holiness and put it on.
> Then you will be unblemished at all times with him.

Looking into the mirror, one sees the Lord. This vision is described in language of transformation: seeing the image of the Lord in the mirror means that one has a new face of divinity to recognize; the old face must be wiped away and the new holy image put on; by doing so, one is purified and can now be in the presence of the Lord at all times.

Comparable ideas are discovered in the famous Syrian *Hymn of the Pearl* which is embedded in the *Acts of Thomas*. When the prince finally returns home (he ascends to the Kingdom of Heaven), he receives a garment: "When I received it, the garment seemed to me to become like a mirror to myself" (112.76) and "the image of the King of Kings was embroidered and depicted in full all over it" (112.86). Here appears the tradition that there resides with God a heavenly image of each individual. When one gains a vision of this image, one sees God himself and thus comes to a full participation in the divine nature, having gained knowledge regarding one's own divinity.

---

[54] Cf. PGM 4.3209-54 where the reflection on the water of Aphrodite is described as "light" and "shining with fire".

Interestingly, the experience of being transformed into a "Christian" is described in Pseudo-Cyprian, *De montibus sina et sion* 13[55], as seeing "Christ in ourselves as in a mirror" for "he himself instructs and admonishes us in the epistle of John his disciple to the people: thus you see me in yourselves, as one of you sees himself in water or in a mirror".

This is similar to a passage in Clement of Alexandria where the true Christian is described as adorning his soul before Christ who is his mirror; he must arrange his soul after Christ's image reflected there:

> For this is the true following of the Savior, when we seek after his sinlessness and perfection, adorning and regulating the soul before him as before a mirror and arranging it in every detail after his likeness (*Quis. Div. Salv.* 21.7).

According to Clement, the vision of the image of Christ is transformational: when one looks into Christ's mirror, one sees the true image of oneself and one's soul can transform itself accordingly, achieving sinlessness and perfection.

It is within this tradition that two passages from the Pauline letters belong: 1 Corinthians 13:12 and 2 Corinthians 3:18.[56] In the former passage, Paul uses the language of the mirror to describe the transformation which can be expected at the Eschaton, a transformation which will involve the completion of knowledge. He says:

> Βλέπομεν γὰρ ἄρτι δι' ἐσόπτρου ἐν αἰνίγματι, τότε δὲ πρόσωπον πρὸς πρόσωπον. ἄρτι γινώσκω ἐκ μέρους, τότε δὲ ἐπιγνώσομαι καθὼς καὶ ἐπεγνώσθην.
>
> For now we see in a mirror dimly, but then face to face. Now I know in part; then I shall understand fully, even as I have been fully understood.

According to Paul, one can expect when the Eschaton arrives, to

---

[55] G. Hartel, *Cyprian of Carthage. Letters and Writings*, CSEL 3 (Vienna, 1868) 117.

[56] Refer to Reitzenstein, *Historia Monachorum*, 242-255; H. Achelis, "Kaptoptromantie bei Paulus", *Theologische Festschrift für G. Nathanael Bonwetsch zu seinem 70. Geburtstage* (Leipzig, 1918) 56-63; P. Corssen, "Paulus und Porphyrios (Zur Erklärung von 2 Kor 3,18)", *ZNW* 19 (1920) 2-10; J. Behm, "Das Bildwort vom Spiegel I.Korinther 13,12", *Reinhold- Seeberg- Festschrift* 1 (ed. W. Koepp; Leipzig, 1929) 315-342; N. Hugedé, *La métaphore du miroir dans les Épitres de saint Paul aux Corinthians* (Neuchâtel and Paris, 1957); Conzelmann, *1 Corinthians*, 226-228.

come face to face with one's Self. This encounter will bear with it *gnosis* in its fullest. Unfortunately, he does not tell us the subject of this knowledge although it may very well include a new Self-understanding since he comments that he will understand fully "even as I have been fully understood".

The transformative element of Self-vision is even more prominent in 2 Corithians 3:18:

> ἡμεῖς δὲ πάντες ἀνακεκαλυμμένῳ προσώπῳ τὴν δόξαν κυρίου κατοπτριζόμενοι τὴν αὐτὴν εἰκόνα μεταμορφούμεθα ἀπὸ δόξης εἰς δόξαν καθάπερ ἀπὸ κυρίου πνεύματος.
>
> And we all, with unveiled face, beholding in a mirror the Glory of the Lord, are being changed into his likeness from one degree of Glory to another.

This passage has received an enormous amount of scholarly attention. It is my intent to focus solely on the motif in this passage that Christians who see the Glory, then become the Glory.[57] It can be argued that Paul speaks here of the face to face encounter with one's Self in a mirror by implementing the middle form of the verb κατοπτρίζω which means "to produce one's own image in a mirror" or "to behold oneself in a mirror".[58] This rendering suggests that the vision is a Self-vision comparable to those mirror visions discussed previously. When one sees oneself in a mirror, one is viewing the Lord's Glory. This vision creates change, transforming the person, degree by degree, *into* the divine Glory which he sees in the mirror.[59]

---

[57] Recently, A. F. Segal, *Paul the Convert: The Apostolate and Apostasy of Saul the Pharisee* (New Haven and London, 1990) 60, noted that "Paul's use of the language of transformation often goes unappreciated" as is the case in 2 Cor 3:18 where the Christian beholds the *kavod* as "in a mirror and are transformed into his image". On possible connections with bowl divination, see *ibid.*, 323-324 n. 94. It has been argued that the mystical beholding in 2 Cor 3:18 has been divested by Paul of its authentic mystical sense since the moment of beholding, for Paul, is primarily Christian worship. On this, see R. Bultmann, *The Second Letter to the Corinthians* (ed. E. Dinkler; trans. R. A. Harrisville, Minneapolis, 1985) 96.

[58] LSJ, "κατοπρίζω"; cf. J. Dupont, "Le chrétien, miroir de la gloire divine d'après 2 Cor. III,18", *RB* 56 (1949) 394-395; Corssen, "Paulus und Porphyrios", 2-10; Hugedé, *Metaphore du miroir*, 52-62; Bultmann, *Second Corinthians*, 90ff..

For the translation "to behold as in a mirror", refer to L. L. Belleville, *Reflections of Glory: Paul's Polemical Use of the Moses-Doxa Tradition in 2 Corinthians 3.1-18*, JSNTSup 52 (Sheffield, 1991) 279 n. 3.

For the translation "to reflect", see *ibid.*, 280-281 and n. 1 on both pages.

[59] See Reitzenstein, *Historia Monachorum*, 242-255; I. Hermann, *Kyrios und*

It is interesting that this experience is connected with conversion here rather than the Eschaton since Paul proclaims in vv. 15-16 that "whenever Moses is read a veil lies over their minds; but when a man turns to the Lord the veil is removed". Thus, the convert, with an unveiled face, can now behold that his own Glory is that of the Lord. This glory is even more splendid than the glowing face of Moses (3:7ff.; cf. Exod 34:28ff.)![60]

A passage from the *Gospel of Philip* 61.20-35 sums up the primitive theoretical basis behind Self-vision:

> It is not possible for anyone to see anything of the things that actually exist unless he becomes like them. This is not the way with man in the world: he sees the sun without being a sun; and he sees the heaven and the earth and all other things, but he is not these things. This is quite in keeping with the truth. But you saw something of that place, and you became those things. You saw the spirit, you became the spirit. You saw Christ, you became Christ. You saw [the father, you] shall become father. So [in this place] you see everything and [do] not [see] yourself, but [in that place] you do see yourself - and what you see you shall [become].

It appears that Logion 84 not only witnesses to primitive Jewish notions of one's heavenly double or guardian angel but also to the Hermetic ideas that the Self-vision is a transforming experience in which one partakes of the divine nature. Moreover, it may be that the Hermetic notion of Self-vision had filtered into Judaism and subsequently Christianity prior to the composition of Logion 84 since the Jewish text *Joseph and Aseneth*, Christian literature including Paul, and Gnosticism allude to Self-vision.

Pneuma (Munich, 1961) 55; H. Windisch, *Der zweite Korintherbrief* (Göttingen, 1924⁹) 128; C. Wagner, "Gotteserkenntnis im Spiegel und Gottesliebe in den beiden Korintherbriefen", *Bijdragen* 19 (1958) 380-381. Bultmann, *Second Corinthians*, 95, notes that "the meaning is not that we are changed into a 'likeness' of the Kyrios, but rather that we are made like his essence, thus also become δόξα...we are changed into that which we behold". Cf. Rom 8:29; Phil. 3:21. Thus, Bultmann understands the vision to be that of the "essence" not the "form".

Paul does not have to be relying exclusively on the Hellenistic concept of transformation by vision, however, since transformational visions are not uncommon in Jewish apocalyptic and mystical texts, nor is *lecanomancy* unknown to Judaism.

[60] According to W. C. van Unnik, "'With Unveiled Face', an Exegesis of 2 Corinthians iii 12-18", *NT* 6 (1963) 167, Christians are "permanently in the same situation which Moses, according to Exod. xxxiv only temporarily enjoyed" because "they now reflect the glory of God". I follow Bultmann, however, in rendering the verb "to behold oneself in a mirror" rather than "to reflect".

3) *Conclusion:*

The welding of Judaism and Hermeticism allows for a fascinating interpretation of Logion 84. When you see your corporeal bodily likeness, you are pleased. But the encounter with your heavenly Self, your image or angelic counterpart, will be a heavy burden to carry; as the text says, "How much you will have to bear". This is reminiscent of Logion 11 which describes this meeting in terms of "doubleness", asserting, "when you become two, what will you do?" The texts do not tell us *why* this experience will be so difficult. But it is imaginable that meeting one's own perfection, one's own divine double, face to face could be a traumatic experience. It is clear, however, that this encounter is a visionary experience. And, since what you behold, you become, when you behold your divine counterpart or image, you are transformed into that Glory.

PART FOUR

CONCLUSION

CHAPTER EIGHT

THE BACKGROUND AND THEOLOGY OF *THOMAS*
IN SUMMARY

1) *Thomas' Background Re-envisioned:*

I began this monograph by arguing that the evidence for the Gnostic origins of the *Gospel of Thomas* is not based on the historical reconstruction of mythology *exclusive* to Gnosticism but rather a general Hellenistic belief in the divinity of the Self and its return to its divine origin. So, it can be reasonably concluded that, because this mythology is not exclusive to Gnosticism, its presence in the *Gospel of Thomas* does not guarantee Gnostic affiliations. Further analysis yields the fact that *Thomas'* theology bears sharp differences when compared to actual Gnostic doctrine particularly in the areas of the pre-mundane Fall and theological dualism. Moreover, it was shown that at least in the case of Logion 50 where there are clear Gnostic parallels, the Gnostic authors had redacted either *Thomas'* saying or one similar to it for their own theological purposes. This suggests that *Thomas* may have impacted Gnosticism rather than vice versa.

This situation justified searching elsewhere for an explanation of *Thomas'* background, particularly in the case of those esoteric sayings which have been used in the past by scholars as evidence for *Thomas'* Gnostic affiliations. Detailed analyses of these Logia in Parts Two and Three demonstrated that they are affiliated with the esoteric tradition of early Jewish mysticism which taught pre-mortem ascent to and vision of the enthroned deity. Moreover, echoes of Hermetic and encratite teachings are heard, as well, in several of these Logia.

The complexity of this background to *Thomas* suggests that G. Quispel's source-critical analysis of *Thomas* should be reassessed. As already mentioned, Quispel posited three separate sources for *Thomas*: a Jewish-Christian, an encratite, and a Hermetic source.[1]

---

[1] See his latest summary of his position, "The *Gospel of Thomas* Revisited", *Colloque International sur les Textes de Nag Hammadi, Québec, 22-25 août 1978*, Bibliothèque Copte de Nag Hammadi 1 (B. Barq; Québec and Louvain, 1981)

He is slightly reluctant to label the Jewish-Christian source, although he prefers the *Gospel of the Nazorees*.[2] The encratite source is probably the *Gospel of the Egyptians*, while the Hermetic source is a pagan gnomology which he does not name.

In order to demonstrate *literary* dependence of one source upon another it is necessary to show parallelisms between clusters of materials in the two documents or identical wording of some length. Thus, to speak of specific texts as sources for *Thomas* is dangerous since the *Gospel of the Egyptians* and the *Gospel of the Nazorees* are fragmentary. We have no sequence of sayings in these fragmentary texts to compare with *Thomas'* sequence as we do, for instance, with Matthew and Luke who can be seen to be relying generally on Mark's sequence. We can also demonstrate that Matthew and Luke were independently editing the Q source since we find non-Markan parallel sayings in clusters and identical wording at length in non-Markan material in both gospels.

Thus, without a *cluster* of *parallel* sayings or identical wording, *Thomas'* literary dependence on the *Nazoraean* gospel can not be demonstrated with certainty. And, pointing to similarities in one saying in the *Gospel of the Egyptians* (Clem. Alex., *Strom.* 3.13.92) and in *Thomas* (L. 22 and 37), for example, is not sufficient to posit the former as a literary source for the latter.[3] In fact, if we compare and contrast the "parallel" saying in the *Gospel of the Egyptians* with that in *Thomas*, we discover that the saying as preserved by Clement of Alexandria is found in two separate Logia in *Thomas*: Logion 22 and Logion 37.

> When Salome asked when she would know the answer to her questions, the Lord said, *When you have trampled on the garment of shame, and when the two become one and the male with the female (is) neither male nor female* (*Strom.* 3.13.92).
>
> His disciples said, "When will you become revealed to us and when shall we see you?" Jesus said, "*When you disrobe without being ashamed and take up your garments and place them under your feet like little children and tread on them*, then [you will see] the Son of the Living One, and you will not be afraid" (L. 37).

239-266.

[2] Earlier in his career, Quispel argued that the Jewish-Christian source was the *Gospel of the Hebrews*; see "Some Remarks on the Gospel of Thomas", *NTS* 5 (1959) 289, and "'The Gospel of Thomas' and the 'Gospel of the Hebrews'", *NTS* 12 (1966) 371-382.

[3] Quispel, "*Thomas* Revisited", 256-257.

They said to him, "Shall we then, as children, enter the Kingdom?" Jesus said to them, "*When you make the two one,* and when you make the inside like the outside and the outside like the inside, and the above like the below, and *when you make the male and the female one and the same, so that the male not be male nor the female female,* and when you fashion eyes in place of an eye, and a hand in place of a hand, and a foot in place of a foot, and a likeness in place of a likeness, then you will enter [the Kingdom]" (L. 22).

It is, perhaps, possible that the author of the *Gospel of Thomas* split the saying in the *Gospel of the Egyptians,* then dispersed and elaborated upon it in two different areas of his text. If this is argued, then the author's reason for so doing must be determined and explained.

I suggest that it is much more plausible that *Thomas* and the *Gospel of the Egyptians* had access to a similar sayings tradition which had an encratite orientation rather than positing the *Gospel of the Egyptians* as a source for *Thomas.* This is supported by the fact that the form in which *Thomas* preserves Logion 37 and Logion 22 is more primitive than that set forth in the *Gospel of the Egyptians.* Note that the saying as is recorded in the *Gospel of the Egyptians* consists of the prostasis only. The original apodosis which may be reconstructed from Salome's question in *Strom.* 3.9.64, "then you will not die", has been removed from the saying proper and has been used to create an introductory question set forth by Salome which seems to have been, "When will I know the answer to my questions?" The author used part of the Jesus saying in order to create a dialogue out of that saying.

Logion 37 and Logion 22, however, have not experienced this division. The apodosis *and* the prostasis appear in full in both sayings. When the author of *Thomas* wanted to create a dialogue, he chose to leave the Jesus saying intact while creating an introductory question using the words in the Logia. This is seen in both Logion 37 and 22. Thus the disciples introduce Logion 37 by asking, "When will you become revealed to us and when will we see you?" In Logion 22 the disciples ask, "Shall we then, as children, enter the Kingdom?" But in both these cases, the complete Logion follows. It would seem that the author of the *Gospel of Thomas* knows of a more complete form of the Logia than the author of the *Gospel of the Egyptians.*

I present the following as a simplified diagram of this particular situation:

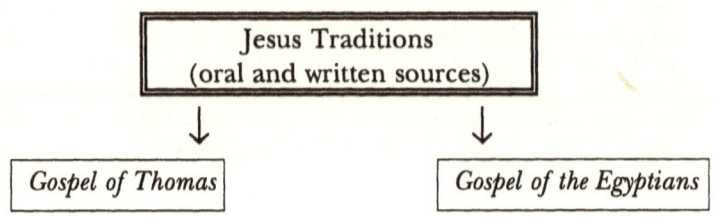

Moreover, often the Hermetic strains in *Thomas* have been informed by Judaism. Thus, for instance, we found that both Hermeticism and Jewish traditions had impacted Logion 50. As in Hermeticism, the Light is described as self-generated. And Hermetic motifs of "movement" and "rest" are present. But these concepts are welded with Jewish motifs of "children of light" and "elect of the living Father" as well as Jewish exegetical traditions involving the creation stories in Genesis. The case is similar with Logion 49, where the Hermetic concept of returning to one's origins is coupled with the Jewish notion of entering the Kingdom. Similarly, in Logion 19 the Jewish concept of Paradise and the trees is interpreted by the Hermetic motif of the five virtues and vices. We saw that this blending of Hermeticism with Judaism was quite prominent in *Thomas*' Logia in general.

The difficulty of identifying each Logion with a specific tradition is accentuated when trying to argue that *Thomas* had a Jewish-Christian source distinct from an encratite source. As my research suggests, Jewish-Christian and encratite traditions are both found in Logion 27 where Sabbath observation is connected with world abstinence. Additionally, early Jewish mystical tendencies influenced this Logion too: Sabbath observation and encratism were prerequistes for the visionary experience. Yet, according to Quispel, Logion 27 belongs to the Jewish-Christian *Gospel of the Nazorees* but not to the encratite *Gospel of the Egyptians*.[4]

It would seem rather that the encratism in *Thomas* is a tendency connected with the Jewish-Christians and with the exegetical tradition associated with the first chapters of Genesis in which these Jewish-Christians were fluent. Early Jewish mystical ascent

---

[4] Quispel, "*Thomas* Revisited", 265.

preparations are also associated with encratite practices in the *Gospel of Thomas*. Hermeticism's negative view of the body may also be connected with the encratite perspective prevalent in this gospel. Much more work needs to be done on the phenomenon of encratism and its connections with various Jewish, Christian, Greco-Roman, and Gnostic movements in the ancient world.

This investigation suggests that the exact distribution of the Logia in *Thomas* among different sources may be impossible. It is probable, however, as Quispel argues, that *Thomas* had access to more than one source, since this gospel contains doublets (L. 101 and 55; 106 and 48; 5 and 6; cf. 113 and 51).[5] Two of these doublets, Logia 101 and 55, and Logia 106 and 48, are especially interesting to the present discussion. Logion 101 is seen to have an encratite emphasis when compared to its twin Logion 55 since it proclaims a negative view of human procreation:[6]

> Whoever does not hate his father and his mother as I do cannot become a disciple to me. And whoever does not love his father and his mother as I do cannot become a [disciple] to me. For my mother [gave me falsehood], but [my] true [mother] gave me life (L. 101).

> Whoever does not hate his father and his mother cannot become a disciple to me. And whoever does not hate his brother and sisters and take up his cross in my way will not be worthy of me (L. 55).

The same is true of Logion 106 and its double, Logion 48, where Logion 106 stresses the encratite notion of the two becoming one:[7]

> When you make the two one, you will become the sons of man, and when you say, "Mountain, move away", it will move away (L. 106).

> If two make peace with each other in one house, they will say to the mountain, "Move away", and it will move away (L. 48).

Because of the encratite orientation of these doublet sayings, it may be argued that at least one of the sources for *Thomas*' sayings was more encratite than the other(s).

It seems that, beyond the fact that *Thomas* had access to more than one source, the most we can determine are the *traditions*, be

---

[5] Quispel, "Some Remarks", 286-289; idem, "*Thomas* Revisited", 224.
[6] Quispel, "*Thomas* Revisited", 257; idem, "Some Remarks", 287-288; idem, "Encratism", 78-79.
[7] Quispel, "Some Remarks", 287-288.

they in oral or written form, behind *Thomas'* sources. These traditions include a type of Hermeticism similar to that found in *Poimandres* or Zosimus, a Hermeticism which has been informed by Judaism. Additionally, encratism and early Jewish mysticism impacted some of *Thomas'* Logia.

2) *Thomas' Mystical Soteriology:*

The combination of these traditions, which were major currents in the ancient Christian world, makes for a fascinating ideology in the *Gospel of Thomas*. *Thomas* presents a mystical soteriological model where it is necessary for each individual to seek his own salvation by first preparing himself properly for his vision quest. This preparation is intended to purify the individual and consists of taking on an encratite lifestyle.

Theologically, encratism is the avenue by which the Thomasites believed that they had literally overcome the sin of the first man. By maintaining celibacy and rejecting marriage in favor of singlehood, they felt that they were "fasting from the world". They had become the blessed "little children" innocent of sex who were able to reenter Paradise. They were the purified ones who had returned to Paradise and the sinless state of the androgynous prelapsarian Man. They were now like the angels who "stand" before God's Throne.

Once the person has been purified, he works to ascend into the heavenly realms, successfully making his way past the terrifying angels who guard the sacred sphere. The method of ascent included the memorization and repetition of correct information about the aspirant's origin and identity when he was confronted by these angels.

The mystic's ultimate goal, however, is to see God. Because the *visio Dei* functions as the transformative experience which serves to immortalize the individual, the Thomasites have preserved a saying of Jesus in which he commands them to be mystics: to seek to see God or his hypostasis in their lifetimes. Without this experience, they could only expect death. Thus, for the Thomasites, salvation hinges on the *visio Dei*.

The mystical encounter with the divinity is also described by the *Gospel of Thomas* as a vision and reunion with one's heavenly image, the image which they probably believed had been lost when Adam sinned. The vision of the heavenly double was actually a vision of God which transformed the person into the divinity upon whom he had gazed.

This experience was associated with Self-knowledge: when one had gained the knowledge of one's divine Self and the nothingness of the body and the material world, one was transposed from mortality to immortality. One's true origin was from the "Light" which manifested itself through the forms of the angels into humans. These humans were the elect of the Father and eventually would return to him. Their sign or verification of their origin and ultimate destiny was their knowledge that even though they participate in the "movement" of the created order, they also share in the blessed state of the immobility or "rest" of God.

Thus, when they ascended, this knowledge insured them safe passage into the divine realm. Moreover, as they ascended, they stripped themselves of the material body and its vices. Once in Paradise, they would put on the new body of the five virtues; they would encounter their heavenly image and fashion "eyes in place of an eye, and a hand in place of a hand, and a foot in place of a foot, and an image in place of an image". In so doing, they were admitted to the citizenship of the Kingdom and life everlasting.

BIBLIOGRAPHY

Achelis, H, "Kaptoptromantie bei Paulus", *Theologische Festschrift für G. Nathanael Bonwetsch zu seinem 70. Geburtstage* (Leipzig, 1918) 56-63.
Adam, A., "Grundbegriffe des Mönchtums in sprachlicher Sicht", *ZKG* 65 (1953/54) 209-39.
Alberry, C. R. C., *A Manichaean Psalm-Book Part II. Manichaean Manuscripts in the Chester Beatty Collection 2* (Stuttgart, 1938).
Alexander, P. S., "The Historical Setting of the Hebrew Book of Enoch," *JJS* 28 (1977) 156-180.
——, "3 (Hebrew Apocalypse of) Enoch", *OTP* 1 (1983) 223-315.
Amidon, P. R., *The Panarion of St. Epiphanius, Bishop of Salamis. Selected Passages* (New York and Oxford, 1990).
Anderson, F. I., "2 (Slavonic Apocalypse of) Enoch", *OTP* 1 (1983) 91-221.
Anderson, G., "Celibacy or Consummation in the Garden? Reflections on Early Jewish and Christian Interpretations of the Garden of Eden", *HTR* 82 (1989) 129-130.
Arnold-Döben, V., *Die Bildersprache des Manichäismus*, Arbeitsmaterialien zur Religionsgeschichte 3 (Köln, 1978).
Attridge, H., "Appendix: The Greek Fragments", *Nag Hammadi Codex II,2-7 together with XII,2 Brit. Lib. Or. 4926 (1), and P. Oxy. 1, 654, 655* 1: *Gospel According to Thomas, Gospel According to Philip, Hypostasis of the Archons, and Indexes*, NHS 20 (Leiden, 1989) 96-128.
Aune, D. E., "The Apocalypse of John and Graeco-Roman Revelatory Magic", *NTS* 33 (1987) 481-501.
Baarda, T., "Thomas and Tatian", *Early Transmission of the Words of Jesus: Thomas, Tatian and the Text of the New Testament* (eds. J. Helderman and S. J. Noorda; Amsterdam, 1983) 37-49.
——, "'If you do not Sabbatize the Sabbath...'. The Sabbath as God or World in Gnostic Understanding (Ev. Thom., Log. 27)", *Knowledge of God in the Graeco-Roman World*, EPRO (eds. R. van den Brock, T. Baarda, and J. Mansfeld; Leiden, 1988) 178-201.
Babbitt, F. C., *Plutarch's Moralia* 2, LCL 222 (Cambridge, Mass., 1928 and reprints).
Bacher, W., *Die Agada der palästinensischen Amoräer* 1 (Strassburg, 1892).
Baker, A., "Pseudo-Macarius and the Gospel of Thomas", *VC* 18 (1964) 215-225.
——, "'Fasting to the World'", *JBL* 84 (1965) 291-294.
——, "The 'Gospel of Thomas' and the Syriac 'Liber Graduum'", *NTS* 12 (1965/66) 49-55.
Baynes, C. A., *A Coptic Gnostic Treatise contained in the Codex Brucianus [Bruce MS. 96. Bod. Lib. Oxford]. A Translation from the Coptic: Transcript and Commentary* (Cambridge, 1933).
Bauer, J., "Das Thomas-Evangelium in der neuesten Forschung", *Geheime Worte Jesu: Das Thomas-Evangelium* (eds. R. Grant and D. Freedman; Frankfurt, 1960) 182-205.
——, "The Synoptic Tradition in the Gospel of Thomas", *SE* 3, TU 88 (Berlin, 1964) 314-317.
Beck, E., "Ein Beitrag zur Terminologie des ältesten syrischen Mönchtums", *Antonius Magnus Eremita*, Studia Anselmiana 38 (Rome, 1956) 254-267.
Beckwith, R. T., "The Prehistory and the Relationship of the Pharisees, Sadducees, and Essenes: A Tentative Reconstruction", *RevQ* 11 (1982) 3-46.

Behm, J., "Das Bildwort vom Spiegel I.Korinther 13,12", *Reinhold- Seeberg-Festschrift* 1 (ed. W. Koepp; Leipzig, 1929) 315-342.
Belleville, L. L., *Reflections of Glory: Paul's Polemical Use of the Moses-Doxa Tradition in 2 Corinthians 3.1-18*, JSNTSup 52 (Sheffield, 1991).
Berthelot, M., *Collection des Anciens Alchimistes Grecs* 3 (Paris, 1888).
Betz, H. D., "The Delphic Maxim ΓΝΩΘΙ ΣΑΥΤΟΝ in Hermetic Interpretation", *HTR* 63 (1970) 465-484.
——, "The Delphic Maxim 'Know Yourself' in the Greek Magical Papyri", *HR* 21 (1981) 157-158.
——, *The Greek Magical Papyri in Translation Including the Demotic Spells* (Chicago, 1986).
Bianchi, U., *Le Origini dello Gnosticismo. Colloquio di Messina 13-18 Aprile 1966. Testi e Discussioni*, Studies in the History of Religions, *NumenSup* 12 (Leiden, 1967).
——, "A propos de quelques discussions récentes sur la terminologie, la définition et la méthode de l'étude du gnosticisme", *Proceedings of the International Colloquium on Gnosticism*, KVHAH, Filol.-filos. ser. 17 (Stockholm, 1977) 16-26.
——, "The Religio-Historical Relevance of Lk 20:34-36", *Studies in Gnosticism and Hellenistic Religions, presented to Gilles Quispel on the Occasion of his 65th Birthday*, EPRO 91 (eds. R. van den Broek and M. J. Vermaseren; Leiden, 1981) 31-37.
Bietenhard, H. "ὄνομα, etc.", *TDNT* 5 (1967) 268-269.
Black, M., *The Scrolls and Christian Origins*, BJS 48 (Chico, 1961).
——, "The Tradition of Hasidaean-Essene Asceticism: Its Origins and Influence", *Aspects du Judéo-Christianisme* (Paris, 1965) 19-33.
Blanco, A. G., "Hermeticism. A Bibliographical Approach", *ANRW* 2.17.4 (New York, 1984) 2253-2257.
Blenkinsopp, J., *Prophecy and Canon: A Contribution to the Study of Jewish Origins* (Notre Dame, 1977).
Blonde, G., "Encratisme", *Dictionnaire de Spiritualité* 4 (eds. M. Viller, F. Cavallera, and J. De Guibert; Paris, 1960) 628-642.
Blumenthal, D. R., *Understanding Jewish Mysticism: A Source Reader: The Merkabah Tradition and the Zoharic Tradition* 1 (New York, 1978).
Böhlig, A., and Wisse, F., *The Gospel of the Egyptians*, NHS 4 (Leiden, 1975).
Bolgiani, F., "La tradizione eresiologica sull'encratismo, II. La confutazione di Clemente di Alessandria", *AAST* 96 (1961-1962) 537-664.
Bonsirven, J., *Le Judaisme Palestinien* 2 (Paris, 1935).
Borgen, P., *Bread From Heaven*, NTSup 10 (Leiden, 1965).
——, "God's Agent in the Fourth Gospel", *Religions in Antiquity, Essays in Memory of Erwin Ramsdell Goodenough*, Studies in the History of Religions 14 (ed. J. Neusner; Leiden, 1968) 148.
——, "Some Jewish exegetical traditions as background for Son of Man sayings in John's Gospel (John 3:13-14 and context)", *ETL* (1977) 243-58.
——, "Philo of Alexandria. A Critical and synthetical survey of research since World War II", *ANRW* 2.21.1 (Berlin, 1984) 98-154.
Bousset, W., "Die Himmelsreise der Seele", *ARW* 4 (1901) 136-169.
——, "Eine judische Gebetssammlung im siebenten Buch der Apostolischen Konstitutionen," *Wilhelm Bousset, Religionsgeschichtliche Studien*, NTSup 50 (ed. A. F. Verheule; Leiden, 1979) 231-286.
——, *Die Religion des Judentums im späthellenistischen Zeitalter*, HNT 21 (3rd ed. H. Gressman; Tübingen, 1926).
Boyance, P., "Les deux démons personnels dans L'Antiquité Grecque et Latine", *RP* 59 (1935) 189-202.
Brandenburger, E., *Adam und Christus*, WMANT 7 (Neukirchen, 1962) 68-157.

Brandt, W., *Mandäische Schriften* (Göttingen, 1893).
Bréhier, E., *Les idées philosophiques et religieuses de Philon d'Alexandrie* (Paris, 1908).
Breslin, J., *A Greek Prayer* (Malibu, n.d.).
Broek, R. van den, and Quispel, G., *Corpus Hermeticum* (Amsterdam, 1991).
Brown, Pa., "The Sabbath and the Week in Thomas 27", *NT* 34 (1992) 193.
Brown, Pe., *The Body and Society: Men, Women, and Sexual Renunciation in Early Christianity*, Lectures on the History of Religions 13 (New York, 1988).
Buckley, J. J., "An Interpretation of Logion 114 in *The Gospel of Thomas*", *NT* 27 (1985) 245-272.
Budge, E. A. Wallis, *The Book of the Dead: The Papyrus of Ani, Scribe and Treasurer of the Temples of Egypt, About B.C. 1450* 1 and 2 (New York and London, 1913).
Bultmann, R., "Zur Geschichte der Lichtsymbolik im Altertum", *Exegetica. Aufsätze zur Erforschung des Neuen Testaments* (ed. E. Dinkler; Tübingen, 1967) 323-355.
——, *The Gospel of John. A Commentary* (trans. G. R. Beasley-Murray, R. W. N. Hoare, and J. K. Riches; Philadelphia, 1971).
——, *The Second Letter to the Corinthians* (ed. E. Dinkler; trans. R. A. Harrisville; Minneapolis, 1985).
Capart, J., "Les anciens Egyptiens pratiquaient-ils déjà la lécanomancie?", *Chronique d'Egypte* 19 (1944) 263 plus photos on face page.
Casey, R. P., *The Excerpta ex Theodoto of Clement of Alexandria*, SD 1 (London, 1934).
Cerfaux, L., and Garitte, G., "Les paraboles du Royaume dans L'Évangile de Thomas", *Muséon* 70 (1957) 307-327.
Chadwick, H., "St. Paul and Philo of Alexandria", *BJRL* 48 (1966) 286-307.
Charles, R. H., *The Apocrypha and Pseudepigrapha of the Old Testament* 2 (Oxford, 1913 and reprints).
Charlesworth, J. H., *The Old Testament Pseudepigrapha* 1 and 2 (New York, 1983 and 1985).
——, "History of the Rechabites", *OTP* 2 (1985) 443-461.
Chavannes, É., and Pelliot, P., *Un traité manichéen retrouvé en Chine* (Paris, 1912).
Chernus, I., "Visions of God in Merkabah Mysticism", *JSJ* 13 (1982) 123-146.
Cohen, J. D., *From the Maccabees to the Mishnah* (Philadelphia, 1987).
Cohen, M. S., *The Shi'ur Qomah: Texts and Recensions*, Texte und Studien zum Antiken Judentum 9 (Tübingen, 1985).
Collins, J. J., *The Apocalyptic Vision of the Book of Daniel*, HSM 16 (Missoula, 1977).
Colpe, C., "Die 'Himmelsreise der Seele' ausserhalb und innerhalb der Gnosis," *Le Origini dello Gnosticismo, Colloquio di Messian 13-18 Aprile 1966*, Studies in the History of Religions, *NumenSup* 12 (ed. U. Bianchi; Leiden, 1967) 429-447.
——, "Daena, Lichtjungfrau, zweite Gestalt: Verbindungen und Unterschiede zwischen zarathustrischer und manichäischer Selbst-Anschauung", *Studies in Gnosticism and Hellenistic Religions, presented to Gilles Quispel on the Occasion of his 65th Birthday*, EPRO 91 (eds. R. van den Broek and M. J. Vermaseren; Leiden, 1981) 58-77.
Colson, F. H., and Whitaker, G. H., *Philo* 1, LCL 226 (Cambridge, Mass., 1929 and reprints); *Philo* 2, LCL 227 (Cambridge, Mass., 1927 and reprints); *Philo* 3, LCL 247 (Cambridge, Mass., 1930 and reprints); *Philo* 5, LCL 275 (Cambridge, Mass., 1934 and reprints); *Philo* 9, LCL 363 (Cambridge, Mass., 1941 and reprints).
Connolly, R. H., "Aphraates and Monasticism", *JTS* 6 (1905) 522ff.

Conzelmann, H., "φῶς, etc.", *TDNT* 9 (1974) 310-358.
———, *1 Corinthians: A Commentary on the First Epistle to the Corinthians*, Hermeneia - A Critical and Historical Commentary on the Bible (trans. J. Leitch; bib. and refs. J. Dunkly; ed. G. MacRae; Philadelphia, 1975).
Copenhaver, B. P., *Hermetica: The Greek Corpus Hermeticum and the Latin Asclepius in a New English Translation, With Notes and Introduction* (Cambridge, 1992).
Coppens, J., "Le célibat essénien", *Qumran, sa piété, sa théologie et son milieu* (ed. M. Delcor; Paris, 1978) 297-303.
Corbin, H., "Le Récit d'Initiation et l'Hermetisme en Iran", *Eranos* 17 (1949/50) 158-187.
———, *Avicenne et le Récit Visionnaire* 1 (Paris 1954).
Cornélis, E., "Quelques éléments pour une comparison entre l'Évangile de Thomas et la notice d'Hippolyte sur les Naassènes", *VC* 15 (1961) 83-104.
Corssen, P., "Paulus und Porphyrios (Zur Erklärung von 2 Kor 3,18)", *ZNW* 19 (1920) 2-10.
Cowley, A. E., *The Samaritan Liturgy* (Oxford, 1909).
Culianu, I. P., "L'"Ascension de l'âme' dans les mystères et hors des mystères," *La Soteriologia dei culti orientali nell'Impero romano* (eds. U. Bianchi and M. J. Vermaseren; Leiden, 1982) 276-302.
———, *Psychanodia I: A Survey of the Evidence Concerning the Ascension of the Soul and Its Relevance* (Leiden 1983).
———, *Expériences de l'Extase* (Paris, 1984).
———, *The Tree of Gnosis: Gnostic Mythology from Early Christianity to Modern Nihilism* (Eng. trans. H. S. Wiesner and I. Coulianu; San Francisco, 1992).
Cumont, F., *Recherches sur le Manichéisme* 1: *La Cosmogonie manichéenne* (Brussels, 1908).
———, *L'Egypte des astrologues* (Bruxelles, 1937).
———, *Lux Perpetua* (Paris, 1949).
Cunen, F., "Lampe et coupe magiques", *SO* 36 (1960) 65-71.
Davies, P., "Hasidim in the Maccabean Period", *JJS* 28 (1977) 127-140.
Davies, S. L., *The Gospel of Thomas and Christian Wisdom* (New York, 1983).
Dean-Otting, M., *Heavenly Journeys: A Study of the Motif in Hellenistic Jewish Literature* (Frankfurt, 1984).
De Conick, A. D., "Fasting From the World: Encratite Soteriology in the Gospel of Thomas", *The Notion of "Religion" in Comparative Research. Selected Proceedings of the XVIth IAHR Congress, Rome, 3rd-8th September, 1990* (ed. Ugo Bianchi; Rome, 1994) 425-440.
———, "The *Dialogue of the Savior* and the Mystical Sayings of Jesus", *VC* 49 (1995).
———, "'Blessed are those who have not seen' (John 20:29): Johannine Polemic Against Ascent and Vision Mysticism" (forthcoming).
De Conick, A. D., and Fossum, J., "Stripped Before God: A New Interpretation of Logion 37 in the Gospel of Thomas", *VC* 45 (1991) 123-150.
Delatte, A., *La catoptromancie grecque et ses derives* (Paris, 1932).
Dieterich, A., *Eine Mithrasliturgie* (Berlin, 1923).
Dillon, J., *The Middle Platonists*, CLL (London, 1973).
Dirkse, P. A., and Brashler, J., "The Prayer of Thanksgiving", *Nag Hammadi Codices V, 2-5 and VI with Papyrus Berolinensis 8502, 1 and 4*, NHS 11 (ed. D. Parrott; Leiden, 1979) 375-387.
Dirkse, P. A., Brashler, J., and Parrot, D. M., "The Discourse on the Eighth and Ninth", *Nag Hammadi Codices V, 2-5 and VI with Papyrus Berolinensis 8502, 1 and 4*, NHS 11 (ed. D. Parrott; Leiden, 1979) 358-375.
Dirkse, P. A., and Parrott, D. M., "Asclepius 21-29", *Nag Hammadi Codices V, 2-5 and VI with Papyrus Berolinensis 8502, 1 and 4*, NHS 11 (ed. D. Parrott; Leiden, 1979) 395-451.

Dodd, C. H., *The Bible and the Greeks* (London, 1935).
——, *The Interpretation of the Fourth Gospel* (Cambridge, 1968).
Dodds, E. R., "The Astral Body in Neoplatonism" *Proclus. The Elements of Theology* (Oxford, 1933) 313-321.
Doresse, J., *L'Évangile selon Thomas. <<Les Paroles Secrètes de Jésus>>* (Plon and Rocher, 1957, and revised and augmented second ed. 1988).
——, *The Secret Books of the Egyptian Gnostics* (Rochester, Vermont, 1958 and 1986 reprint).
Dörries, H., Klostermann, E., and Kroeger, M., *Die 50 Geistlichen Homilien des Makarios*, PTS 4 (Berlin, 1964).
Dower, E. S., *The Secret Adam* (Oxford, 1960).
Drijvers, H. J. W., "Quq and the Quqites", *Numen* 14 (1967) 104-129.
——, "Bardaisan of Edessa and the Hermetica", *Jaarbericht van het Vooraziatisch-Egyptisch Genootschap ex Oriente Lux* 21 (Leiden, 1969/70) 190-210.
——, "Edessa und das jüdische Christentum", *VC* 24 (1970) 4-33.
——, "Facts and Problems in Early Syriac-Speaking Christianity", *The Second Century* 2 (1982) 157-175.
Duchesne-Guillemin, J., *The Hymns of Zarathustra. Being a Translation of the Gathas together with Introduction and Commentary* (London, 1952).
Dupont, J., "Le chrétien, miroir de la gloire divine d'après 2 Cor. III,18", *RB* 56 (1949) 392-411.
Dupont-Sommer, A., "Adam. 'Père du Monde' dans la Sagesse de Solomon (10,1.2)", *RHR* 119 (1939) 182ff.
Ehlers, B., "Kann das Thomasevangelium aus Edessa stammen? Ein Beitrag zur Frühgeschichte des Christentum in Edessa", *NT* 12 (1970) 284-317.
Emmel, S., *Nag Hammadi Codex III,5. The Dialogue of the Savior*, NHS 26 (Leiden, 1984).
Fallon, F. T., and Cameron, R., "The Gospel of Thomas: A Forschungsbericht and Analysis", *ANRW* 2.25.6 (New York, 1988) 4213-4224.
Feldman, L. H., "Scholarship on Philo and Josephus (1937-59)", *Classical World* 54 (1960/61) 281-91, and 55 (1961/62) 36-39.
Festugière, A.-J., *Hermès Trismégiste* 3. *Fragments extraits de Stobée. I-XXII* (Paris, 1954).
Fieger, M., *Das Thomasevangelium: Einleitung, Kommentar, und Systematik* (Münster, 1991).
Finkelstein, L., *MGWJ* 76 (1932) 529-530.
Fitzmyer, J. A., "The Oxyrhynchus Logoi and the Coptic Gospel of Thomas", *Essays on the Semitic Background of the New Testament* (London, 1971) 355-433.
Fossum, J., "Jewish-Christian Christology and Jewish Mysticism", *VC* 37 (1983) 260-287.
——, *The Name of God and the Angel of the Lord*, WUNT 36 (Tübingen, 1985).
——, "Gen. 1,26 and 2,7 in Judaism, Samaritanism, and Gnosticism", *JSJ* 16 (1985) 202-239.
——, "Kyrios Jesus and the Angel of the Lord in Jude 5-7", *NTS* 33 (1987) 226-243.
——, "The Magharians: A Pre-Christian Jewish Sect and Its Significance for the Study of Gnosticism and Christianity", *Henoch* 9 (1987) 303-344.
——, "Colossians 1.15-18a in the Light of Jewish Mysticism and Gnosticism", *NTS* 35 (1989) 183-201.
——, "Sects and Movements", *The Samaritans* (ed. A. D. Crown; Tübingen, 1989) 368-377.
——, "Glory כבוד δόξα", *Dictionary of Deities and Demons in the Bible* (eds. K. van der Toorn *et.al.*; Leiden, 1995).
——, "John 1.51, Targumic Tradition, and Jewish Mysticism" (forthcoming).

Fowden, G., *The Egyptian Hermes: A Historical Approach to the Pagan Mind* (Cambridge, 1986).
Fraade, S. D., "Ascetical Aspects of Ancient Judaism", *Jewish Spirituality from the Bible through the Middle Ages* 13 (ed. A. Green; New York, 1986) 253-288.
Francis, F. O., "Humility and Angelic Worship in Col 2:18", *ST* 16 (1962) 109-134.
Frend, W. H. C., "The Gospel of Thomas: Is Rehabilitation Possible?", *JTS* 18 (1967) 13-26.
Friedmann, M., *Pesikta Rabbati* 1 (Vienna 1880, second ed. Tel Aviv, 1963) and trans. Braude (New Haven and London, 1968).
Gall, A. von, *Basileia tou theou* (Heidelberg, 1926).
Ganszyniec, R., "Λεκανομαντεία", *PW* 12 (1925) 1879-89.
Gaster, M., "Das Shiur Komah", *Studies and Texts in Folklore, Magic, Medieval Romance, Hebrew Apocrypha and Samaritan Archaeology* 2 (New York, 1971) 1343-1348.
Gärtner, B., *The Theology of the Gospel according to Thomas* (trans. E. Sharpe; New York, 1961).
Ginzberg, L., *The Legends of the Jews* 5. *Notes to Volumes I and II: From Creation to the Exodus* (Philadelphia, 1925 and reprints).
——, *The Legends of the Jews* 6. *Notes to Volumes III and IV: From Moses in the Wilderness to Esther* (Philadelphia, 1928 and reprints).
Goodenough, E. R., *By Light, By Light* (New Haven, 1935).
——, *The Politics of Philo Judaeus* (New Haven, 1938).
——, *An Introduction to Philo Judaeus* (New Haven, 1940).
——, *Jewish Symbols in the Greco-Roman Period* 1-13 (New York, 1953-68).
——, "Philo Judaeus", *IDB* 3 (New York, 1962) 796-99.
Goodhart, H. L., and Goodenough, E. R., "A Bibliography of Philo", *The Politics of Philo Judaeus* (ed. E. R. Goodenough; New Haven, 1938) 130-321.
Grant, R. M., "Notes on the Gospel of Thomas," *VC* 13 (1959) 170-180.
——, "The Mystery of Marriage in the Gospel of Philip", *VC* 15 (1961) 129-140.
Grant, R. M., and Freedman, D. N., *The Secret Sayings of Jesus* (New York, 1960).
Grenfell, B., and Hunt, A., *ΛΟΓΙΑ ΙΗΣΟΥ: Sayings of Our Lord from an Early Greek Papyrus* (London, 1897).
Gribomont, J., "Le monachisme au sein de l'Église en Syrie et en Cappadoce", *Studia Monastica* 7 (1965) 2-24.
Griffith, F. L., and Thompson, H., *The Leyden Papyrus: An Egyptian Magical Book* (London, 1904; New York, 1974).
Grobel, K., "How Gnostic is the Gospel of Thomas?", *NTS* 8 (1962) 367-373.
Gruenwald, I., "New Passages from *Hekhalot* Literature", *Tarbiz* 38 (1969) 354-372, and *Tarbiz* 39 (1970) 216-217.
——, "*Re'uyot Yehezkiel*", *Temirim* 1 (1972) 101-139.
——, "Knowledge and Vision: Towards a Clarification of Two 'Gnostic' Concepts in the Light of Their Alleged Origins", *Israel Oriental Studies* 3 (1973) 63-107.
——, "Jewish Esoteric Literature in the Time of the Mishnah and Talmud", *Immanuel* 4 (1974) 37-46.
——, "Aspects of the Jewish-Gnostic Controversy", *The Rediscovery of Gnosticism: Proceedings of the International Conference on Gnosticism at Yale, New Haven, Connecticut, March 28-31, 1978* 2 (ed. B. Layton; Leiden, 1980-1981) 713-723.
——, *Apocalyptic and Merkavah Mysticism*, AGJU 14 (Leiden, 1980).
——, "The Problems of Anti-Gnostic Polemic in Rabbinic Literature", *Studies in Gnosticism and Hellenistic Religions* (eds. R. van den Broek and M. J. Vermaseren; Leiden, 1981) 171-189.

———, "Jewish Merkabah Mysticisim and Gnosticism", *Studies in Jewish Mysticism* (eds. J. Dan and F. Talmage; Cambridge, Mass., 1982) 47-55.
———, "Jewish Apocalypticism in the Rabbinic Period", *The Encyclopedia of Religion* 1 (ed. M. Eliade; New York, 1987) 336-342.
———, *From Apocalypticism to Gnosticism, Studies in Apocalypticism, Merkavah Mysticism, and Gnosticism* (New York and Paris, 1988).
Guillaumont, A., "Νηστεύειν τόν κόσμον (P. Oxy. 1, verso, I,5-6)", *BIFAO* 61 (1962) 15-23.
———, "À propos du célibat des Esséniens", *Hommages à André Dupont-Sommer* (Paris, 1971) 395-404.
———, "Monachisme et éthique judéo-chrétienne", in *Judéo-Christianisme: Recherches historiques et théologiques offertes en hommage au Cardinal Jean Danielou*, RSR (Paris, 1972) 199-218.
———, "Situation et signification du Liber Graduum dans la spiritualité Syriaque", *OrChrA* (1974) 311-322.
———, "Liber Graduum", in *Dictionnaire de Spiritualité* 9, 749-754.
Guillaumont, A., Puech, H.-Ch., Quispel, G., Till, W., and Yassah 'Abd al Masih, *The Gospel According to Thomas* (San Francisco, 1959).
Gummere, R. M., *Seneca, Ad Lucilium Epistulae Morales* 2, LCL (New York, 1917).
Guthrie, W., *Orpheus and Greek Religion: A Study of the Orphic Movement* (New York, 1966).
Haenchen, E., *Die Botschaft des Thomas-Evangeliums*, Theologische Bibliothek Töpelmann 6 (Berlin, 1961).
Halperin, D. J., *The Merkabah in Rabbinic Literature* (New Haven, 1980).
———, *The Faces of the Chariot: Early Jewish Responses to Ezekiel's Vision* (Tübingen, 1988).
———, "Ascension or Invasion: Implications of the Heavenly Journey in Ancient Judaism," *Religion* 18 (1988) 47-67.
Harl, M., "A propos des *Logia* de Jésus: le sens du mot *monachos*", *REG* 73 (1960) 464-474.
Harrington, D. J., "Pseudo-Philo", *OTP* 2 (1985) 297-377.
Harrington, D. J., and Cazeaux, J., *Pseudo-Philon: Les Antiquités Bibliques* 1, SC 229 (Paris, 1976).
Hartel, G., *Cyprian of Carthage. Letters and Writings*, CSEL 3 (Vienna, 1868).
Helderman, J., *Die Anapausis im Evangelium Veritatis*, NHS 18 (Leiden, 1984).
Hengel, M., *Judaism and Hellenism* 1 (Philadelphia, 1974).
Henning, W. B., *Sogdica*, James G. Forlong Fund 21 (London, 1940).
Hermann, I., *Kyrios und Pneuma* (Munich, 1961).
Higger, M., *Massekhtot Derekh Erez* (1935).
Higgins, A. J. B., "Non-Gnostic Sayings in the Gospel of Thomas", *NT* 4 (1960) 292-306.
Hilgert, E., *Studia Philonica* 1 (1972) 57-71, 2 (1973) 55-73, 3 (1974/75) 117-125, 4 (1976/77) 79-85, 5 (1978) 113-120, 6 (1979/80) 197-200.
Himmelfarb, M., "Heavenly Ascent and the Relationship of the Apocalypses and the *Hekhalot* Literature", *HUCA* 59 (1988) 73-100.
———, *Ascent to Heaven in Jewish and Christian Apocalypses* (Oxford, 1993).
Hopfner, T., *Griechisch-aegyptischer Offenbarungszauber* 1-2 (Leipzig, 1921 and 1924).
———, "Mageia", *PW* (14,1) 301-393.
Horsley, R. A., "Spiritual Marriage with Sophia", *VC* 33 (1979) 30-54.
Horst, P. W. van der, "Observations on a Pauline Expression", *NTS* 19 (1973) 181-187.
Hübner, H., "Zölibat in Qumran?", *NTS* 17 (1971) 153-67.
Hugedé, N., *La métaphore du miroir dans les Épitres de saint Paul aux Corinthians* (Neuchâtel and Paris, 1957).

Jacobs, L., *Jewish Mystical Testimonies* (New York, 1976).
James, M. R., *The Biblical Antiquities of Philo*, in *Translations of Early Documents 1: Palestinian Jewish Texts* (London, 1917).
Janowitz, N. *The Poetics of Ascent: Theories of Language in a Rabbinic Ascent Text* (New York, 1989).
Jansen, H. L., "Die Frage nach Tendenz und Verfasserschaft im Poimandres", *Proceedings of the International Colloquium on Gnosticism, Stockholm, August 20-25, 1973*, KVHAH, Filol.-filos. ser., 17 (eds. G. Widengren and D. Hellholm; Stockholm, 1977) 157ff.
Jastrow, M., *A Dictionary of the Targumim, the Talmud, Babli and Yerushalmi, and the Midrashic Literature* 1 (New York, 1950).
Jellinek, A., *Bet ha-Midrasch* 6 (Jerusalem, second edition, 1938).
Jervell, J., *Imago Dei*, FRLANT 76 (Göttingen, 1960).
Jung, C. G., *Psychology and Alchemy*, The Collected Works of C. G. Jung 12 (trans. R. F. C. Hull; London, 1968).
Kaplan, A., *Meditation and Kabbalah* (York Beach, Maine, 1982).
Kasser, R., *L'Évangile selon Thomas: Présentation et commentaire theologique*, Bibliotèque Théologique (Neuchâtel, 1961).
Kee, H., "'Becoming a Child' in the Gospel of Thomas," *JBL* 82 (1963) 307-314.
Kim, S., *The Origins of Paul's Gospel*, WUNT 4 (Tübingen, 1981).
Kim, Y. O., "The Gospel of Thomas and the Historical Jesus", *The Northeast Asia Journal of Theology* 2 (1969) 17-30.
King, K., "Kingdom in the Gospel of Thomas", *Forum* 3 (1987) 48-97.
Klijn, A. F. J., "A Survey of the Researches into the Western Text of the Gospels and Acts (1949-1959)", *NT* 3 (1959) 1-27.
———, "Das Thomasevangelium und das altsyrische Christentum", *VC* 15 (1961) 146-159.
———, "The 'Single One' in the Gospel of Thomas," *JBL* 81 (1962) 271-278.
———, *The Acts of Thomas. Introduction-Text-Commentary*, NTSup 5 (Leiden, 1962).
———, *A Survey of the Researches into the Western Text of the Gospels and Acts: Part Two* (Leiden, 1969).
———, "Christianity in Edessa and the Gospel of Thomas", *NT* 14 (1972) 70-77.
Klijn, A. F. J., and Reinink, G. J., *Patristic Evidence for the Jewish-Christian Sects*, NTSup 36 (Leiden, 1973).
Kloppenborg, J. S., Meyer, M. W., Patterson, S. J., Steinhauser, M. G., *Q Thomas Reader* (Sonoma, 1990).
Kmosko, M., *Liber Graduum*, Patrologia Syriaca 1,3 (Paris, 1926).
Knibb, M. A., "Martyrdom and Ascension of Isaiah", *OTP* 2 (1985) 143-176.
Koester, H., "GNOMAI DIAPHOROI: The Origin and Nature of Diversification in the History of Early Christianity", *Trajectories through Early Christianity* (eds. J. M. Robinson and H. Koester; Philadelphia, 1971) 114-157 = *HTR* 58 (1965) 279-318.
———, "One Jesus and Four Primitive Gospels", *Trajectories through Early Christianity* (eds. J. Robinson and H. Koester; Philadelphia, 1971) 158-204.
———, "Introduction to the Gospel of Thomas", *The Other Bible: Ancient Alternative Scriptures* (ed. W. Barnstone; San Francisco, 1984) 299-300.
———, *Ancient Christian Gospels* (Philadelphia, 1990).
Koester, H., Pagels, E., "Introduction", *Nag Hammadi Codex III,5. The Dialogue of the Savior*, NHS 26 (ed. S. Emmel; Leiden, 1984) 1-17.
Kohler, K., "Merkabah", *The Jewish Encyclopedia* 8 (ed. I. Singer; New York, 1904) 500.
Krauss, S., *Griechische und lateinische Lehnwörter im Talmud, Midrash und Targum* 2 (Berlin, 1899).

Kretschmar, G., "Ein Beitrag zur Frage nach dem Ursprung frühchristlicher Askese", *ZThK* 61 (1964) 27-67.
Kroll, J., *Die Lehren des Hermes Trismegistos*, Beiträge zur Geschichte der Philosophie und Theologie des Mittelalters 12.2.4 (Münster, 1914).
Kropp, A. M., *Ausgewählte koptische Zaubertexte* 1 (Bruxelles, 1930).
Lampe, G. W. H., *The Seal of the Spirit* (London, 1951).
Lasch, R., "Das Pfeifen und Schnalzen und seine Beziehung zu Dämonenglauben und Zauberei", *ARW* 18 (1915) 589-593.
Layton, B., *The Gnostic Scriptures* (New York, 1987).
——, *Nag Hammadi Codex II,2-7 together with XII,2 Brit. Lib. Or. 4926 (1), and P. Oxy. 1,654, 655* 1: *Gospel According to Thomas, Gospel According to Philip, Hypostasis of the Archons, and Indexes*, NHS 20 (ed. B. Layton; Leiden, 1989).
Leisegang, H., *Der Heilige Geist* 1.1 (Berlin, 1919).
——, "La Connaissance de Dieu au Miroir de l'âme et de la nature", *RHPR* 17 (1937) 145-171.
——, "Philon", *PW* 20,1 (Stuttgart, 1941) cols. 1-50.
Lelyveld, M., *Les Logia de la Vie dans L'Évangile selon Thomas*, NHS 34 (Leiden, 1987).
Levenson, J. D., *Sinai and Zion: An Entry into the Jewish Bible* (San Francisco, 1985).
Lewy, H., *Sobria Ebrietas*, BZNW 9 (Giessen, 1929).
Lichtenberger, H., *Studien zum Menschenbild in Texten der Qumrangemeinde*, SUNT 15 (Göttingen, 1980).
Lidzbarski, M., *Das Johannesbuch der Mandäer* (Berlin, 1915).
——, *Mandäische Liturgien*, Abhandlungen der Königlichen Gesellschaft der Wissenschaften zu Göttingen 17 (Berlin, 1920).
Lieb, M., *The Visionary Mode: Biblical Prophecy, Hermeneutics, and Cultural Change* (London, 1991).
Lieberman, S., "How Much Greek in Jewish Palestine?", *Biblical and Other Studies* (ed. Alexander Altmann; Cambridge, Mass., 1963) 123-141.
Lipsius, R. A., and Bonnet, M., *Acta Apostolorum Apocrypha* 1 (Leipzig, 1891).
Lowy, S., "Some Aspects of Normative and Sectarian Interpretation of Scriptures", *ALUOS* 6 (Leiden, 1969) 112ff.
MacDonald, D. R., *There is No Male and Female: The Fate of a Dominical Saying in Paul and Gnosticism*, HDR 20 (Philadelphia, 1987).
Macdonald, J., *Memar Marqah. The Teaching of Marqah* 2, BZAW 83 (Berlin, 1963).
MacRae, G., "Nag Hammadi and the New Testament", *Gnosis: Festschrift für Hans Jonas* (Göttingen, 1978) 144-157.
Mahé, J.-P., "Le Sens des symboles sexuels dans quelques textes Hermétiques et gnostiques", *Les Textes de Nag Hammadi: Colloque du Centre d'Histoire des Religions, Strasbourg, 23-25 Octobre 1974*, NHS 7 (ed. J.-E. Ménard; Leiden, 1975) 123-145.
——, "Les définitions d'Hermès Trismégiste à Asclépius", *RSR* 50 (1976) 193-214.
——, *Hermès en Haute-Égypte* 1: *Les Textes Hermétiques de Nag Hammadi et Leurs Parallèles Grecs et Latins*, BCNH 3 (Québec, 1978).
——, *Hermès en Haute-Égypte* 2: *Le Fragment du Discours Parfait et les Définitions Hermétiques Arméniennes*, BCNH 7 (Québec, 1982).
——, "Fragments Hermétiques dans les Papyri Vindobonenses Graecae 29456 r^0 et 29828 r^0", *Mémorial André-Jean Festugière* (eds. E. Lucchesi and H. D. Saggrey; Genève, 1984) 51-64.
——, "La Voie d'Immortalité á la lumière des *Hermetica* de Nag Hammadi et de Découvertes plus Récentes", *VC* 45 (1991) 347-375.
Maier, J., "Das Gefährdungsmotiv bei der Himmelsreise in der jüdischen apokalyptik und 'Gnosis'," *Kairos* 5 (1963) 18-40.

Maloney, G. A., *Pseudo-Macarius. The Fifty Spiritual Homilies and the Great Letter*, The Classics of Western Spirituality (New Jersey, 1992).
Marcus, R., *Philo Supplement 1*, LCL 380 (Cambridge, Mass., 1953 and reprints).
Marx, A., "Les racines du célibat essénien", *RQ* 7 (1970) 323-42.
Mead, G. R. S., "The Spirit Body: An Excursion into Alexandrian Psycho-Physiology", *The Quest* (1910) 472-488.
——, *The Doctrine of the Subtle Body in Western Tradition* (London 1919).
Meeks, W. A., *The Prophet-King*, NTSup 14 (Leiden, 1967).
——, "Moses as God and King", *Religions and Antiquity*, Studies in the History of Religions, *NumenSup* 14 (ed. J. Neusner; Leiden, 1968) 354ff.
——, "The Image of the Androgyne: Some Uses of a Symbol in Earliest Christianity", *HR* 13 (1974) 165-208.
Ménard, J., *L'Évangile selon Thomas*, NHS 5 (Leiden, 1975).
Merrill, E., *Qumran and Predestination: A Theological Study of the Thanksgiving Hymns*, STDJ 8 (Leiden, 1975).
Meyer, M., "Making Mary Male: The Categories 'Male' and 'Female' in the Gospel of Thomas", *NTS* 31 (1985) 554-570.
——, *The Ancient Mysteries. A Sourcebook: Sacred Texts of the Mystery Religions of the Ancient Mediterranean World* (San Francisco, 1987).
——, *The Gospel of Thomas: The Hidden Sayings of Jesus* (San Francisco, 1992).
Meyer, M., and Smith, R., *Ancient Christian Magic: Coptic Texts of Ritual Power* (San Francisco, 1994).
Meyer, R., *Hellenistisches in der rabbinischen Anthrolopogie*, BWANT 74 (Stuttgart, 1937).
Milik, J. T., *Ten Years of Discovery in the Wilderness of Judea*, SBT 26 (London, 1959).
Mirecki, P. A., "Coptic Manichaean Psalm 278 and Gospel of Thomas 37", *Manichaica Selecta. Studies presented to Professor Julien Ries on the occasion of his seventieth birthday*, Manichaean Studies 1 (eds. A. van Tongerloo and S. Giversen; Lovanii, 1991).
Mole, M., "Le Pont Cinvat et l'Initiation dans le Mazdeisme", *RHR* 157 (1960) 155-185.
Morard, F.-E., "Monachos Moine, Historie du terme grec jusqu'au 4e siècle", *Freiburger Zeitschrift für Philosophie und Theologie* (1973) 332-411.
——, "Encore quelques réflexions sur monachos", *VC* 34 (1980) 395-401.
Morray-Jones, C., *Merkabah Mysticism and Talmudic Tradition* (Ph.D. Dissertation, University of Cambridge, 1988).
——, "Hekhalot Literature and Talmudic Tradition: Alexander's Three Test Cases", *JSJ* 22 (1991) 1-39.
——, "Transformational Mysticism in the Apocalyptic-Merkabah Tradition", *JJS* 48 (1992) 1-31.
——, "Paradise Revisited (2 Cor. 12.1-12): The Jewish Mystical Background of Paul's Apostolate", "Part 1: The Jewish Sources", *HTR* 86:2 (1993) 177-217, and "Part 2: Paul's Heavenly Ascent and its Significance", *HTR* 86:3 (1993) 265-292.
——, "The Body of the Glory: *Shi'ur Qomah* and Transformational Mysticism in the Epistle to the Ephesians" (forthcoming).
Moulton, J. H., "'It is his angel'", *JTS* 3 (1902) 514-527.
Murdock, W. R., and MacRae, G. W., "The Apocalypse of Paul", *Nag Hammadi Codices V,2-5 and VI with Papyrus Berolinensis 8502, 1 and 4*, NHS 11 (ed. D. M. Parrott; Leiden, 1979) 47-63.
Murmelstein, B., "Adam ein Beitrag zur Messiaslehre", *WZKM* 35 (1928) 51ff.
Murray, G., "Critical Appendix on the Orphic Tablets", *Prolegomena to the Study of Greek Religion* (ed. J. Harrison; New York, 1959 3rd ed.) 659-673.

Murray, R., *Symbols of the Church and Kingdom: A Study in Early Syriac Tradition* (Cambridge, 1975).
——, "The Exhortation to Candidates for Ascetical Vows at Baptism in the Ancient Syriac Church", *NTS* 21 (1974/75) 60-70.
Mussies, G., "Catalogues of Sins and Virtues Personified (NHC II,5)", *Studies in Gnosticism and Hellenistic Religions presented to Gilles Quispel on the Occasion of his 65th Birthday*, EPRO 91 (eds. R. van den Broek and M. J. Vermaseren; Leiden, 1981) 315-335.
Nagel, P., *Die Motivierung der Askese in der alten Kirche und der Ursprung des Mönchtums*, TU 95 (Berlin, 1966).
Nazzano, A. V., *Recenti Studi Filoniani (1963-70)* (Napoli, 1973).
Neusner, J., *Studying Classical Judaism: A Primer, Judaisms* (Louisville, 1991).
Newsom, C., *Songs of the Sabbath Sacrifice* (Atlanta, 1985).
——, "Merkavah Exegesis in the Qumran Sabbath Shirot", *JSJ* 38 (1987) 11-30.
Nock, A. D., "Greek Magical Papyri", *Essays on Religion and the Ancient World* 1 (ed. Z. Stewart; Cambridge, Mass., 1972) 187ff.
Nock, A. D., and Festugière, A.-J., *Hermès Trismégiste* 1. *Corpus Hermeticum. Traités I-XII* (Paris, 1945); *Hermès Trismégiste* 2. *Traités XIII-XVIII. Asclépius* (Paris, 1945); *Hermès Trismégiste* 4. *Fragments extraits de Stobée. XXIII-XXIX. Fragments divers* (Paris, 1945).
Norden, E., *Agnostos Theos: Untersuchungen zur Formengeschichte Religiöser Rede* (Berlin, 1913).
Odeberg, H., *The Hebrew Book of Enoch or Third Enoch* (2nd ed. with a new prolegomenon by J. C. Greenfield; New York, 1973).
——, *The Fourth Gospel* (Amsterdam, 1974).
E. Pagels, *The Johannine Gospel in Gnostic Exegesis* (Nashville, 1973).
——, *The Gnostic Paul: Gnostic Exegesis of the Pauline Letters* (Philadelphia, 1975).
——, "Adam and Eve, Christ and the Church: A Survey of Second Century Controversies concerning Marriage", *The New Testament and Gnosis: Essays in Honour of Robert McL. Wilson* (eds. A. H. B. Logan and A. J. M. Wedderburn; Edinburgh, 1983) 146-175.
Pascher, J., Ἡ βασιλικὴ Ὁδός, *der Königsweg zu Wiedergeburt und Vergöttung bei Philon von Alexandrien* (Paderborn, 1931).
Pasquier, A., "L'eschatologie dans l'Évangile selon Marie: étude des notions de nature et d'image", *Colloque International sur les Textes de Nag Hammadi, Québec, 22-25 août 1978*, BCNH 1 (ed. B. Barc; Québec-Louvain, 1981) 390-404.
——, *L'Évangile selon Marie*, BCNH 10 (Quebec 1983).
Parrott, D. M., "The Scribal Note", *Nag Hammadi Codices V, 2-5 and VI with Papyrus Berolinensis 8502, 1 and 4*, NHS 11 (ed. D. Parrott; Leiden, 1979) 389-393.
——, *Nag Hammadi Codices III,3-4 and V,1 with Papyrus Berolinensis 8502,3 and Oxyrhynchus Papyrus 1081, Eugnostos and the Sophia of Jesus Christ*, NHS 27 (Leiden, 1991).
Patterson, S., *The Gospel of Thomas and Jesus* (Sonoma, 1993).
Pearson, B. A., "Jewish Elements in *Corpus Hermeticum* I (*Poimandres*)", *Studies in Gnosticism and Hellenistic Religions presented to Gilles Quispel on the Occasion of his 65th Birthday*, EPRO 91 (Leiden, 1981) 336-348.
Peterson, E., "Die Befreiung Adam aus der ἀνάγκη", *Frühkirche, Judentum, und Gnosis* (Freiburg, 1959) 107-128.
——, "Einige Beobachtungen zu den Anfängen der christlichen Askese", *Frühkirche, Judentum, und Gnosis* (Freiburg, 1959) 209-220.
——, "Einige Bemerkungen zum Hamburger Papyrusfragment der 'Acta Pauli'", *Frühkirche, Judentum, und Gnosis* (Freiburg, 1959) 183-208.

——, "Die 'Taufe' in Acherusischen See", *Frühkirche, Judentum, und Gnosis* (Freiburg, 1959) 310-332.
Pétrement, S., *A Separate God: The Christian Origins of Gnosticism* (trans. C. Harrison; New York, 1990).
Philonenka, M., "Essénisme et Gnose chez le Pseudo-Philon: Le symbolisme de la lumière dans le *Liber Antiquitatum Biblicarum*", *Le Origini dello Gnosticismo. Colloquio di Messina 13-18 Aprile 1966*, Studies in the History of Religions, *NumenSup* 12 (ed. U. Bianchi; Leiden, 1967) 401-410.
——, *Joseph et Aséneth: Introduction, texte critique, traduction et notes*, SPB 13 (Leiden, 1968).
Polotsky, H. J., and Böhling, A., *Kephalaia* 1. *Manichaische Handschriften der Staatlichen Museen Berlin, Bd. 1* (Stuttgart, 1940).
Preisendanz, K., *Papyri Graecae Magicae. Die Griechischen Zauberpapyri* 1-3 (new ed. A Henrichs; Stuttgart, 1973-74).
Preuschen, E., *Die Apokryphen gnostischen Adamschriften* (Giessen, 1900).
Procksch, O., "Die Berufungsvision Hesekiels", *Beiträge zur alttestamentlichen Wissenschaft. Karl Budde Festschrift*, BZAW 34 (Giessen, 1920) 141ff.
Puech, H.-Ch., "Un logion de Jésus sur bandelette funérarie", *RHR* 147 (1955) 126-129.
——, Une collection des paroles de Jésus récemment retrouvée: L'Évangile selon Thomas", *CRAIBL* (1957) 146-166.
——, "Une collection des paroles de Jésus récemment découverte en Égypte: L'Évangile selon Thomas", *RHR* 153 (1958) 129-133.
——, "Explication de *l'Évangile selon Thomas* et recherches sur les Paroles de Jésus qui y sont réunies", *Annuaire du Collège de France* 58 (1958) 233-239; 59 (1959) 255-264; 60 (1960) 181; 61 (1961) 175-181.
——, "Doctrines ésotériques et thèmes gnostiques dans l'Évangile selon Thomas'", *Annuaire du Collège de France* 62 (1962) 199-213; 63 (1963) 199-213; 64 (1964) 209-217; 65 (1965) 247-256; 66 (1966) 259-262; 67 (1967) 253-260; 68 (1968) 285-297; 69 (1969) 269-283.
——, "The Gospel of Thomas", *New Testament Apocrypha* 1 (eds. E. Hennecke and W. Schneemelcher; Eng. trans. R. McL. Wilson; Philadelphia, 1963) 278-307.
——, *En quête de la Gnose* 2 (Paris, 1978).
Quasten, J., *Patrology* 1 (Westminster, 1950).
Quispel, G., "The Gospel of Thomas and the New Testament", *VC* 11 (1957) 189-207.
——, "Das Hebräerevangelium im gnostischen Evangelium nach Maria", *VC* 11 (1957) 139-144.
——, L'Évangile selon Thomas et les Clémentines", *VC* 12 (1958) 181-196.
——, "Some Remarks on the Gospel of Thomas", *NTS* 12 (1958/59) 276-290.
——, "L'Évangile selon Thomas et le Diatessaron", *VC* 13 (1959) 87-117.
——, "L'Évangile selon Thomas le 'texte occidental' du Nouveau Testament", *VC* 14 (1960) 204-215.
——, "The 'Gospel of Thomas' and the 'Gospel of the Hebrews'", *NTS* 12 (1966) 371-382.
——, *Makarius, das Thomasevangelium, und das Lied von der Perle*, NTSup 15 (Leiden, 1967).
——, "Makarius und das Lied von der Perle", *Le Origini dello Gnosticismo, Colloquio di Messina 13-18 Aprile 1966*, Studies in the History of Religions, *NumenSup* 12 (ed. U. Bianchi; Leiden, 1967) 625-644.
——, "Gnosticism and the New Testament", *Gnostic Studies* 1, Nederlands Historisch-Archaeologisch Instituut te Istanbul 34,1 (Leiden, 1974) 196-212.
——, "Das Ewige Ebenbild des Menschen. Zur Begegnung mit dem selbst in

der Gnosis", in *Gnostic Studies* 1, Nederlands Historisch-Archaeologisch Instituut te Istanbul 34,1 (Leiden, 1974) 140-157.
——, "Gnosis and the New Sayings of Jesus", *Gnostic Studies* 2, Nederlands Historisch-Archaeologisch Instituut te Istanbul 34,2 (Leiden, 1975) 180-209.
——, "L'Evangile selon Thomas et Les Origines de l'Ascese Chretienne", *Gnostic Studies* 2, Nederlands Historisch-Archaeologisch Instituut te Istanbul 34,2 (Leiden, 1975) 98-112.
——, "The Syrian Thomas and the Syrian Macarius", in *Gnostic Studies* 2, Nederlands Historisch-Archaeologisch Instituut te Istanbul 34,2 (Leiden, 1975) 113-121.
——, "Genius and Spirit", *Essays on the Nag Hammadi Texts in Honour of Pahor Labib*, NHS 6 (ed. M. Krause; Leiden, 1975) 155-169.
——, *Tatian and the Gospel of Thomas* (Leiden, 1975).
——, "Ezekiel 1:26 in Jewish Mysticism and Gnosis", *VC* 34 (1980) 1-13.
——, "The *Gospel of Thomas* Revisited", *Colloque International sur les Textes de Nag Hammadi. Québec, 22-25 août 1978*, BCNH 1 (ed. B. Barc; Québec, 1981) 218-266.
——, "Judaism, Judaic Christianity and Gnosis", *The New Testament and Gnosis: Essays in honour of Robert McLachlan Wilson* (eds. A. H. B. Logan and A. J. M. Wedderburn; Edinburgh, 1983) 46-68.
——, "The Study of Encratism: A Historical Survey", *La Tradizione dell'Enkrateia, Atti del Colloquio Internazionale - Milano 20-23 Aprile 1982* (ed. U. Bianchi; Rome, 1985) 35-81.
——, "Review of M. Williams, *The Immovable Race*", *VC* 40 (1986) 411-412.
——, "Hermeticism and the New Testament, especially Paul", *Religion: Gnostizismus und Verwandtes*, ANRW 2.22 (ed. W. Haase; forthcoming).
Rabbinowitz, J., *Midrash Rabbah* 7 (London and New York, 1939, reprint 1983).
Rahmani II, I. E., *Testamentum Domini nostri Jesu Christi* (Moguntiae, 1899).
Reitzenstein, R., *Poimandres* (Leipzig, 1906).
——, *Historia Monachorum und Historia Lausiaca. Eine Studie zur Geschichte des Mönchtums und der frühchristlichen Begriffe Gnostiker und Pneumatiker*, FRLANT 24 (Göttingen, 1916).
——, *Das iranische Erlösungsmysterium* (Bonn, 1921).
——, *Hellenistic Mystery-Religions: Their Basic Ideas and Significance*, Pittsburgh Theological Monograph Series 15 (trans. J. E. Steely; Pittsburgh, 1978).
——, "Griechische Lehren", *Studien zum antiken Synkretismus aus Iran und Griechenland*, Studien der Bibliothek Warburg 7 (Leipzig, 1926 and 1965 reprint).
Rengstorf, K. H., "Urchristliches Kerygma und 'gnostische' Interpretation in einigen Sprüchen des Thomasevangeliums", *Le Origini dello Gosticismo. Colloquio di Messina 13-18 Aprile 1966. Testi e Discussioni*, Studies in the History of Religions, NumenSup 12 (ed. U. Bianchi; Leiden, 1967) 565-566.
Richardson, C., "The Gospel of Thomas: Gnostic or Encratite?", *The Heritage of the Early Church: Essays in Honor of G. V. Florovsky*, OrChrA 195 (eds. D. Neiman and M. Schatkin; Rome, 1973) 65-76.
Roques, R., "'L'Évangile selon Thomas': son édition critique et son identification", *RHR* 157 (1960) 187-218.
——, "Gnosticisme et Christianisme: L'Évangile selon Thomas", *Irénikon* 33 (1960) 29-40.
Rordorf, W., *Sunday. The History of the Day of Rest and Worship in the Earliest Centuries of the Christian Church* (trans. A. A. K. Graham; London, 1968).
Rousseau, A., and Doutreleau, L., *Irénée de Lyon, Contre les Hérésies* II, SC 264 (Paris, 1979).

Rowland, C., "The Visions of God in Apocalyptic Literature", *JSJ* 10 (1979) 137-154.
——, *The Open Heaven: A Study of Apocalyptic in Judaism and Early Christianity* (New York, 1982).
——, "John 1.51, Jewish Apocalyptic and Targumic Tradition", *NTS* 30 (1984) 498-507.
Rowley, H. H., *The Biblical Doctrine of Election* (London, 1950).
Rubinkiewicz, R., "Apocalypse of Abraham", *OTP* 1 (1983) 681-705.
Rudolph, K., "Ein Grundtyp gnostischer Urmensch-Adam-Spekulation", *ZRGG* 9 (1957) 1-20.
——, *Die Mandäer* 2, FRLANT 75 (Göttingen, 1960/61).
——, *Gnosis und Gnostizismus*, WF 262 (Darmstadt, 1975).
——, "Der Mandäismus in der neuen Gnosisforschung", *Gnosis* (eds. B. Aland et al.; Göttingen, 1978) 244-277.
——, *Gnosis* (trans. R. McL. Wilson; San Francisco, 1983).
——, "'Gnosis' and 'Gnosticism' - Problems of their Definition and Their Relation to the Writings of the New Testament", *The New Testament and Gnosis: Essays in honor of Robert McLachlan Wilson* (eds. A. H. B. Logan and A. J. M. Wedderburn; Edinburgh, 1983) 21-37.
Runia, D. T., *Philo of Alexandria: An Annotated Bibliography, 1937-1986* (Leiden, 1992).
Safrai, S., *The Jewish People in the First Century: Historical Geography, Political History, Social, Cultural, and Religious Life and Institutions* 2 (eds. S. Safrai and M. Stern; Philadelphia, 1976).
——, "The Pharisees and the Hasidim", *Sidic* 10 (1977) 12-16.
——, "The Pious (*Hasidim*) and the Men of Deeds", *Zion* 50 (1985) 133-154.
Sanders, J. T., *Schismatics, Sectarians, Dissidents, Deviants: The First One Hundred Years of Jewish-Christian Relations* (Valley Forge, 1993).
Sandmel, S., *Philo's Place in Judaism: A Study of Conceptions of Abraham in Jewish Literature* (New York, 1956, aug. ed. 1971).
——, *Philo of Alexandria: An Introduction* (New York, 1979).
Säve-Söderbergh, T., "Gnostic and Canonical Gospel Traditions (with special reference to the Gospel of Thomas)", *Le Origini dello Gnosticismo, Colloquio di Messina, 13-18 Aprile, 1966. Testi e Discussioni*, Studies in the History of Religions, *NumenSup* 12 (ed. U. Bianchi; Leiden, 1967) 552-562.
Schäfer, P., *Rivalität zwischen Engeln und Menschen* (Berlin 1975).
——, *Synopse zur Hekhalot-Literatur*, Texte und Studien zum Antiken Judentum 2 (Tübingen, 1981).
——, "Tradition and Redaction in Hekhalot Literature, *JSJ* 14 (1983).
——, "Merkavah Mysticism and Rabbinic Judaism", *JAOS* 104 (1984) 537-554.
——, "The Aim and Purpose of Early Jewish Mysticism", *Hekhalot-Studien*, Texte und Studien zum Antiken Judentum 19 (Tübingen, 1988) 277-295.
Schenke, H.-M., *Der Gott "Mensch" in der Gnosis* (Göttingen, 1962).
——, "The Function and Background of the Beloved Disciple in the Gospel of John," *Nag Hammadi, Gnosticism, and Early Christianity* (eds. C. W. Hedrick and R. Hodgson, Jr.; Peabody, 1986) 111-125.
Schechter, S., מסכת אבות דרבי נתן בשתי נוסחאות, Versions A and B (Vienna, 1887; reprinted New York, 1945).
Schiffman, L. H., "The Recall of Rabbi Nehuniah ben Ha-Qanah from Ecstasy in the *Hekhalot Rabbati*", *Association for Jewish Studies Review* 1 (1976) 269-281.
——, "Merkavah Speculation at Qumran", *Mystics, Philosophers and Politicians* (eds. J. Reinharz and D. Swetschinski; Durham, North Carolina, 1982) 15-47.
——, *Sectarian Law in the Dead Sea Scrolls: Courts, Testimony, and the Penal Code*, BJS 33 (Chico, 1983).

——, *From Text to Tradition: A History of the Second Temple and Rabbinic Judaism* (Hoboken, New Jersey, 1991).
Schoedel, W. R., "Naassene Themes in the Coptic Gospel of Thomas", *VC* 14 (1960) 225-234.
——, "(First) Apocalypse of James", *Nag Hammadi Codices V, 2-5 and VI with Papyrus Berolinensis 8502, 1 and 4*, NHS 11 (ed. D. Parrott; Leiden, 1979) 65-109.
Scholem, G., "Über eine Formel in den Koptisch-gnostischen Schriften und ihren jüdischen Ursprung", *ZNW* 30 (1931) 170-176.
——, *Major Trends in Jewish Mysticism* (New York, 1941).
——, *Jewish Gnosticism, Merkavah Mysticism and Talmudic Tradition* (New York, 1960).
——, *Kabbalah* (Jerusalem and New York, 1974).
——, *Origins of the Kabbalah* (Princeton, 1987).
——, *On the Mystical Shape of the Godhead: Basic Concepts in the Kabbalah* (foreword J. Dan; trans. J. Neugroschel; ed. and revised according to 1976 Hebrew ed. J. Chipman; New York, 1991).
Scholer, D. M., *The Works of Philo. New Updated Edition* (trans. C. D. Yonge; Peabody, Mass., 1993).
Schrage, W., *Das Verhältnis des Thomas-Evangeliums zur synoptischen Tradition und zu den koptischen Evangelienübersetzungen: Zugleich ein Beitrag zur gnostischen Synoptikerdeutung*, BZNW 29 (Berlin, 1964).
Schultz, J. P., "Angelic Opposition to the Ascension of Moses and the Revelation of the Law", *JQR* 61 (1971) 282-307.
Scott, W., *Hermetica 1. Introduction, Texts, and Translation* (Oxford, 1924; reprinted London, 1968).
——, *Hermetica 2. Notes on the Corpus Hermeticum* (Oxford, 1925; reprinted London, 1968).
——, *Hermetica 3. Notes on the Latin Asclepius and the Hermetic Excerpts of Stobaeus* (Oxford, 1926; reprinted London, 1968).
——, *Hermetica 4. Testimonia* (intro., addenda, and indices A. S. Ferguson; Oxford, 1936; reprinted London, 1968).
Segal, A. F., "Heavenly Ascent in Hellenistic Judaism, Early Christianity, and their Environment," *ANRW* 2.23.2, (1980) 1333-1394.
——, "Hellenistic Magic: Some Questions of Definition", *Studies in Gnosticism and Hellenistic Religions, presented to Gilles Quispel on the Occasion of his 65th Birthday*, EPRO 91 (eds. R. van den Broek and M. J. Vermaseren; Leiden, 1981) 349-375.
——, *Paul the Convert: The Apostolate and Apostasy of Saul the Pharisee* (New Haven and London, 1990).
Segal, J. B., "Pagan Syriac Monuments in the Vilayet of Urfa", *AS* 3 (1953) 97-119.
——, "The Sabian Mysteries. The planet cult of ancient Harran", *Vanished Civilizations* (ed. E. Bacon; London, 1963) 201-220.
——, "Some Syriac Inscriptions of the 2nd and 3rd century A.D.", *BSOAS* 14 (1954) 97-120.
——, *Edessa 'The Blessed City'* (Oxford, 1970).
Sjöberg, E., "בן אדם und בר אנש im Hebräischen und Aramäischen", *Acta Orientalia* 21 (1950-1951) 57-65 and 91-107.
Smith, J. Z., "The Garments of Shame," *HR* 5 (1966) 217-238.
Smith, M., "Observations on Hekhalot Rabbati" *Biblical and Other Studies* (ed. Alexander Altmann; Cambridge, Mass., 1963) 142-160.
——, "Goodenough's 'Jewish Symbols' in retrospect", *JBL* 86 (1967) 53-68.
——, "On the Shape of God and the Humanity of Gentiles", *Religions in Antiquity. Essays in Memory of Erwin Ramsdell Goodenough* (ed. J. Neusner;

Leiden, 1968) 315-326.
——, Book review of "The Origins of Gnosticism", *JBL* 89 (1970) 82-84.
——, *Clement of Alexandria and a Secret Gospel of Mark* (Cambridge, Mass., 1973).
——, "Ascent to the Heavens and the Beginning of Christianity", *Eranos* 50 (1981) 403-429.
——, "The History of the term *Gnostikos*", *The Rediscovery of Gnosticism: Proceedings of the International Conference on Gnosticism at Yale, New Haven, Conn., March 28-31, 1978* 2, SHR 41,2 (ed. B. Layton; Leiden, 1981) 796-807.
——, "Helios in Palestine", *Eretz Israel* 16 (1982) 199-214.
——, "Two Ascended to Heaven - Jesus and the Author of 4Q491", *Jesus and the Dea Sea Scrolls* (ed. J. H. Charlesworth; New York, 1992) 290-301.
Smyth, K., "Gnosticism in 'The Gospel according to Thomas'", *HeyJ* 1 (1960) 189-198.
Staerk, W., *Die Erlösererwartung in den östlichen Religionen* (Stuttgart and Berlin, 1938).
Stählin, O., *Clemens Alexandrinus, Werke II*, Die griechischen christlichen Schriftstellen der ersten drei Jahrhunderte 15 (new ed. by L. Früchtel; Berlin, 1962).
Stanley, T., *The Chaldaean Oracles as Set Down By Julianus* (New Jersey, n.d.).
Steck, O. H., "Die Aufnahme von Genesis 1 in Jubiläen 2 und Esra 6," *JSJ* 8 (1977) 154-182.
Strack, H. L. and Billerbeck, P., *Kommentar zum Neuen Testament aus Talmud und Midrasch* 1-4 (Munich, 1922-1928).
Stroumsa, G., "Form(s) of God: Some Notes on Metatron and Christ", *HTR* 76 (1985) 269-288.
Strugnell, J., "The Angelic Liturgy", *VTSup* 7 (Leiden, 1960) 318-345.
Tabor, J. D., *Things Unutterable: Paul's Ascent to Paradise in its Greco-Roman, Judaic, and Early Christian Contexts*, Studies in Judaism (New York, 1986).
Theissen, G., "Itinerant Radicalism: The Tradition of Jesus Sayings from the Perspective of the Sociology of Literature, *Radical Religion* 2 (trans A. Wire; 1976) 84-93.
——, *The Sociology of Early Palestinian Christianity* (trans. J. Bowden; Philadelphia, 1978).
——, *The Social Setting of Pauline Christianity* (trans. J. Schütz; Philadelphia, 1982).
——, *Studien zur Soziologie des Urchristentums*, WUNT 19 (Tübingen, 1983).
Thiering, B., "The Biblical Source of Qumran Asceticism", *JBL* 93 (1974) 429-444.
Till, W. C., "Die Berliner gnostische Handschrift", *Europäischer Wissenschafts-Dienst* 4 (1944) 19-21.
——, *Die gnostischen Schriften des Koptischen Papyrus Berolinensis 8502*, TU 60 (Berlin, 1955; second ed., H. M. Schenke; Berlin, 1972).
Till W. C., and Carratelli, G. P., "Εὐαγγέλιον κατα Μαρίαμ", *La parola de passato* 1 (1946) 260-265.
Trigg, J. W., "The Angel of Great Counsel: Christ and the Angelic Hierarchy in Origen's Theology", *JTS* 42 (1991) 35-51.
Turner, H., and Montefiore, H., *Thomas and the Evangelists*, SBT 35 (London, 1962).
Turner, J. D., *The Book of Thomas the Contender from Codex II of the Cairo Gnostic Library from Nag Hammadi (CG II, 7): The Coptic Text with Translation, Introduction, and Commentary*, SBL Dissertation Series 23 (Missoula, 1975).
Unnik, W. C. van, "'With Unveiled Face', an Exegesis of 2 Corinthians iii 12-18", *NT* 6 (1963) 153-169.
Vaillant, A., *Le livre des secrets d'Hénoch: Texte slave et traduction française*, TIES 4 (Paris, 1952; reprint 1976).

Vermes, G., *The Dead Sea Scrolls. Qumran in Perspective* (Philadelphia, revised ed. 1977).
Vielhauer, P., "ΑΝΑΠΑΥΣΙΣ Zum gnostischen Hintergrund des Thomasevangeliums", *Apophoreta. Festschrift für Ernst Haenchen*, BZNW 30 (ed. W. Eltester; Berlin, 1964) 281-299.
Vööbus, A., *Celibacy, A Requirement for Admission to Baptism in the Early Syrian Church*, Papers of the Estonian Theological Society in Exile 1 (Stockholm, 1951).
——, *History of Asceticism in the Syrian Orient. A Contribution to the History and Culture in the Near East: Early Monasticism in Mesopotamia and Syria* 2, CSCO 197,17 (Louvain, 1960).
Vriezen, T. C., *Die Erwählung Israels nach dem Alten Testament*, ATANT 24 (Zurich, 1953).
——, *An Outline of Old Testament Theology* (Newton, Mass., 1958).
Wagner, C., "Gotteserkenntnis im Spiegel und Gottesliebe in den beiden Korintherbriefen", *Bijdragen* 19 (1958) 380ff.
Waszink, J. H., *Quinti Septimi Florentis Tertulliani. De Anima. Edited with Introduction and Commentary* (Amsterdam, 1947).
Wedderburn, A. J. M., "Philo's 'Heavenly Man'", *NT* 15 (1973) 301-326.
Weinfeld, M., "Sabbath, Temple and the Enthronement of the Lord", *Mélanges bibliques et orientaux en l'honneur de M. Henri Cazelles*, AOAT 212 (eds. A. Caquot and M. Delcor; Neukirchen-Vluyn, 1981) 501-512.
Wertheimer, S. A., *Batei-Midrašot* 1-2 (Jerusalem 1950-1953).
Widengren, G., *The Ascension of the Apostle and the Heavenly Book*, Uppsala University Årsskrift 7 (Uppsala, 1950).
——, "Der iranische Hintergrund der Gnosis", *ZRGG* 2 (1952) 103-104.
——, *Religionens värld* (2nd ed., Stockholm, 1953).
——, *The Gnostic Attitude* (trans. B. A. Pearson; Santa Barbara, 1973).
Williams, M., *The Immovable Race: A Gnostic Designation and the Theme of Stability in Late Antiquity*, NHS 29 (Leiden, 1985).
Wilson, R. McL., "The New Testament in the Gnostic Gospel of Mary", *NTS* 3 (1956/57) 236-243.
——, "The Early History of the Exegesis of Gen. 1.26", *TU* 63 (1957).
——, "The Coptic 'Gospel of Thomas'", *NTS* 5 (1958/1959) 273-276.
——, "'Thomas' and the Growth of the Gospels", *HTR* 53 (1960) 231-250.
——, *Studies in the Gospel of Thomas* (London, 1960).
——, *The Gospel of Philip: Translated from the Coptic text, with an introduction and commentary* (London, 1962).
Wilson, R. McL., and MacRae, G. W., "The Gospel according to Mary", *Nag Hammadi Codices V, 2-5 and VI with Papyrus Berolinensis 8502, 1 and 4* , NHS 11 (ed. D. Parrott; Leiden, 1979) 453-471.
Windisch, H., *Der zweite Korintherbrief* (Göttingen, 1924 and reprints).
Winston, D., "Was Philo a Mystic?", *Studies in Jewish Mysticism, Proceedings of Regional Conferences Held at the University of California, Los Angeles and McGill University in April, 1978* (eds. J. Dan and F. Talmage; Cambridge, Mass., 1982) 15-39.
Wolfson, H. A., *Philo* 1 (Cambridge, Mass., 1947).
Zandee, J., "'The Teachings of Silvanus' (NHC VII, 4) and Jewish Christianity", *Studies in Gnosticism and Hellenistic Religions, Presented to Gilles Quispel on the Occasion of his 65th Birthday*, EPRO 91 (eds. R. van den Broek and M. J. Vermaseren; Leiden; 1981) 498-584.

AUTHOR INDEX

Achelis, H., 169 n. 56.
Adam, A., 5 n. 12.
Alberry, C. R. C., 82 n. 58.
Alexander, P. S., 59 n. 47
Amidon, P. R., 131 n. 24.
Anderson, G., 132 and n.26.
Arnold-Döben, V., 82 n. 58.
Attridge, H., 26 n.84; 126 n.2.
Aune, D. E., 38 n.40.

Baarda, T., 6 n.13; 128 and ns.12-15; 129.
Babbitt, F. C., 151 ns. 5 and 6.
Bacher, W., 152 n.7.
Baker, A., 6 ns. 17 and 18; 127 and n.8.
Baynes, C. A., 93 n. 87.
Bauer, J., 12 n. 45.
Beck, E., 5 n. 12.
Beckwith, R. T., 132 n.27.
Behm, J., 169 n.56.
Belleville, L. L., 170 n.58.
Berthelot, M., 116 n.50.
Betz, H. D., 9 n.31; 33 n.15; 37 n.39; 38 n.40; 58 ns. 42-44; 119 n.63; 120 and n. 66; 167 n.50.
Bianchi, U., 7 n.20; 15 n.50; 92 n.85.
Bietenhard, H., 113 n.41.
Black, M., 132 n.27; 138 n.40.
Blanco, A. G., 9 n.30.
Blenkinsopp, J., 132 n.26.
Blonde, G., 3 n.3.
Blumenthal, D. R., 29 n.1.
Bolgiani, F., 4 n.4.
Borgen, P., 34 n.20; 35 n.27; 36 n.30; 37 and ns. 34 and 36.
Bousset, W., 29 n.2; 33 n.16; 123 ns. 69 and 70; 156 n.22.
Boyance, P., 150 n.4.
Brandenburger, E., 162 n.41.
Brandt, W., 87 n.67.
Bréhier, E., 35 and n.22.
Breslin, J., 51 ns. 26 and 27.
Broek, R. van den, xii.
Broek, R. van den, and Quispel, G., 9 n.30.
Brown, Pa., 129 n.17.
Brown, Pe., 3 n.3.
Buckley, J. J., 19 and n.65.

Budge, E. A. Wallis, 50 ns. 19-22.
Bultmann, R., 73; 74 and n.27; 109 n.33; 170 ns.57 and 58; 171 ns.59 and 60.

Cameron, R., xi.
Capart, J., 166 n.49.
Casey, R. P., 24 n.79; 48 n.14.
Cerfaux, L., and Garitte, G., 12 and n.43.
Chadwick, H., 36 and n.32.
Charles, R. H., 67 n.10; 104 n.16.
Charlesworth, J. H., 58 n.45; 76 n.35; 77 n.41; 139 n.42.
Chavannes, É., and Pelliot, P., 82 n.58.
Chernus, I., 107 n.25.
Cohen, J. D., 32 n.9.
Cohen, M. S., 102 n.11.
Collins, J. J., 132 n.27.
Colpe, C., 151 n.4.
Colson, F. H., and Whitaker, G. H., 32 ns. 10-11; 46 n.8; 66 ns. 5-9; 104 ns. 17-19; 137 n.37; 156 ns.23-26.
Connolly, R. H., 5 n.12.
Conzelmann, H., 65 n.3; 162 n.41; 169 n.56.
Copenhaver, B. P., 8 n.30.
Coppens, J., 34 n.19.
Corbin, H., 154 n.15.
Cornélis, E., 12 n.42.
Corssen, P., 169 n.56; 170 n.58.
Cowley, A. E., 90 n.80.
Culianu, I. P., 29 n.2; 81 n.56; 82 ns. 57-58.
Cumont, F., 81 n.54.
Cunen, F., 166 n.49.

Davies, P., 132 n.27.
Davies, S. L., 14 n.49.
Dean-Otting, M., 29 n.2.
De Conick, A. D., 7 n.22; 72 ns. 24-25.
De Conick, A. D., and Fossum, J., 7 n.22; 18 n.58; 19 n.68; 117 n.54; 144 and ns. 54 and 56; 145 ns. 57 and 58; 146 n.62; 158 n. 31; 162 n. 41.

AUTHOR INDEX

Delatte, A., 167 n.49.
Dieterich, A., 58 n.41; 155 n.18.
Dillon, J., 150 n.4.
Dirkse, P. A., and Brashler, J., 9 n.30.
Dirkse, P. A., Brashler, J., and Parrot, D. M., 9 n.30; 165 ns. 46-47.
Dirkse, P. A., and Parrott, D. M., 9 n.30.
Dodd, C. H., 113 n.42.
Dodds, E. R., 155 n.18.
Doresse, J., 80 n.50.
Dörries, H., Klostermann, E., and Kroeger, M., 160 ns. 36 and 37; 164 n. 45.
Dower, E. S., 162 n. 41.
Drijvers, H. J. W., 6 n.13; 10 and n.36; 11.
Duchesne-Guillemin, J., 48 n.14.
Dupont, J., 170 n.58.
Dupont-Sommer, A., 23 n. 76.

Ehlers, B., 5 n.12.

Fallon, F. T., and Cameron, R., 6 n. 13; 44; 45 n.4; 64 and n.2.
Feldman, L. H., 34 n. 20.
Festugière, A.-J., 9 n.30. Fieger, M., 13 n.45.
Finkelstein, L., 133 and n.29.
Fitzmyer, J. A., 123 n.67; 127 n.7; 144 n.53.
Fossum, J., xi; 16 n.54; 22 ns. 73 and 74; 25 ns. 82 and 83; 31 n. 8; 66 n.10; 69 n.18; 90 ns. 78, 79, and 81; 101 n.6; 102 n.9; 103 n.13; 105 n.21; 113 n.43; 115 n.49; 116 ns. 52 and 53; 130 n. 19; 134 n.31; 153 ns. 9 and 10; 156 n.21; 157 n.27; 162 ns. 40 and 41.
Fowden, G., 8 n.30.
Fraade, S. D., 5 n.12.
Francis, F. O., 4 n.5; 135 n.33.
Frend, W. H. C., 14 n.49.
Friedmann, M., 106 n.23.

Gall, A. von, 151 n.4.
Ganszyniec, R., 166 n.49.
Gaster, M., 69 and n.20.
Gärtner, B., 12 and n. 43; 93 n.86; 113 n.40; 149 n.3.
Ginzberg, L., 56 n.33; 156 n.22; 158 n.30.

Goodenough, E. R., 35 and ns. 23-26; 36 n.30; 65 n.4.
Goodhart, H. L., and Goodenough, E. R., 34 n.20.
Grant, R. M., 21 n.70.
Grant, R. M., and Freedman, D. N., 12 and n.42; 80 n.50; 93 ns. 86-87; 113 n.40.
Grenfell, B., and Hunt, A., 4 and n.7; 126 ns.4 and 5; 127; 129 n.16.
Gribomont, J., 5 n.12.
Griffith, F. L., and Thompson, H., 38 n.40.
Grobel, K., 14 n.49.
Gruenwald, I., 30 and n.4; 57 ns. 35, 37, and 38; 102 n.10; 111 n.36; 125 n.72; 142 n.50.
Guillaumont, A., 5 n.12; 6 n.17; 34 n.19; 101 n.6; 127 n.8.
Guillamont, A., H.-Ch. Puech, G. Quispel, W. Till, and Yassah `Abd al Masih, 101 n.6.
Gummere, R. M., 45 n.7.
Guthrie, W., 51 and ns.23-25.

Haenchen, E., 12 and n.44; 13; 93 ns. 86 and 87.
Halperin, D. J., 30 n.5; 56 n.32.
Harl, M., 4 and n.11; 136 n.36.
Harrington, D. J., 76 n.35.
Harrington, D. J., and Cazeaux, J., 77 ns.40 and 44. Hartel, G., 169 n.55.
Helderman, J., 93 n.86.
Hengel, M., 132 n.27.
Henning, W. B., 82 n.58.
Hermann, I., 170 n.59.
Higger, M., 47 n.9.
Higgins, A. J. B., 14 n.49.
Hilgert, E., 34 n.20.
Himmelfarb, M., 29 n.2.
Hopfner, T., 167 n.49.
Horsley, R. A., 33 ns. 12 and 13.
Horst, P. W. van der, 82 n. 59.
Hübner, H., 34 n.19.
Hugedé, N., 169 n.56.

James, M. R., 76 n.35.
Janowitz, N., 29 n.1.
Jansen, H. L., 38 n.41.
Jastrow, M., 152 n.7.
Jellinek, A., 153 n.10.
Jervell, J., 162 n.41.
Jung, C. G., 116 n.50.

Kaplan, A., 29 n.1.
Kasser, R., 93 ns.86 and 87.
Kee, H., 146 n.61.
Kim, S., 157 n.27.
Kim, Y. O., 14 n.49.
King, K., 14 n.49.
Klijn, A. F. J., xii; 4 n.8; 6 n.13; 48 n.16; 89 n.74; 146 n.61.
Klijn, A. F. J., and Reinink, G. J., 103 n.12; 116 n.51.
Kloppenborg, J. S., Meyer, M. W., Patterson, S. J., Steinhauser, M. G., 149 n.3.
Kmosko, M., 6 n.17; 127 n.9.
Knibb, M. A., 60 n.48.
Koester, H., xii; 5 n.12; 6 n.13; 13 and ns.47 and 48.
Koester, H., Pagels, E., 72 n.23.
Kohler, K., 36 and n.31.
Krauss, S., 152 n.7.
Kretschmar, G., 5 n.12.
Kroll, J., 37 n.39.
Kropp, A. M., 37 n.34.

Lampe, G. W. H., 110 n.34.
Lasch, R., 58 n.41.
Layton, B., 14 n.49; 16 n.53; 17 n.56; 18 n.61; 20 ns.71 and 72; 43 n.1; 53 n.29; 80 n.49; 89 ns. 72, 73, and 75; 91 n.83; 100 n.2; 101 ns.4, 6; 108 n.30; 109 n.31; 112 n.38; 115 ns.46-48; 117 ns.55 and 56; 118 ns. 57 and 58; 119 ns. 60 and 61; 123 n.68; 126 ns. 2 and 3; 127 n. 11; 144 n.53; 148 n.1; 158 n.28; 161 ns.38 and 39.
Leisegang, H., 35 and n.21.
Lelyveld, M., xi; 49 and n.18.
Levenson, J. D., 132 n.26.
Lewy, H., 109 n.32; 111 n.37.
Lichtenberger, H., 75 n.31.
Lidzbarski, M., 87 n.66; 88 ns.68-70.
Lieb, M., 107 n.27.
Lieberman, S., 47 and ns. 10 and 12; 78 n. 47.
Lipsius, R. A., and Bonnet, M., 127 n.10.
Lowy, S., 133 n.30.

MacDonald, D. R., 18 n.58.
Macdonald, J., 110 n.35; 159 ns.33 and 34.
MacRae, G., 12 n.45.
Mahé, J. -P., 8 and n.26; 9 n.30; 10 and ns.32-35; 67; 68 n.11; 119 n.62.
Maier, J., 59 n.46.
Maloney, G. A., 124 n.71; 164 ns.43 and 44.
Marcus, R., 70; 78 ns.45 and 46.
Marx, A., 34 n.19.
Mead, G. R. S., 155 n.18.
Meeks, W. A., 18 n.58; 37 and n.37.
Ménard, J., 12 n.45; 80 n.50; 93 n.86; 149 n.3.
Merrill, E., 76 n.34.
Meyer, M., 18 n.58; 19 and n.67; 51 n.26; 64 and n.1; 101 n.6; 136 n.36.
Milik, J. T., 132 n.27.
Mirecki, P. A., xi; 144 n.56.
Mole, M., 151 n.4.
Morard, F.-E., 4; 5 n.11; 136 n.36.
Morray-Jones, C., 30 and n.6; 31 and ns.7 and 8; 105 n.22; 107 n.27; 114 n.44; 130 and n.20; 146 n.63.
Moulton, J. H., 151 n.4.
Murdock, W. R., and MacRae, G. W., 44 n.3; 61 n.51.
Murmelstein, B., 158 n.30.
Murray, G., 51 ns. 26 and 27.
Murray, R., 5 n.12.
Mussies, G., 81 n.53.

Nagel, P., 5 n.12.
Nazzano, A. V., 34 n.20.
Newsom, C., 34 n.17.
Nock, A. D., and Festugière, A.-J., 8-9 ns. 30 and 31.
Norden, E., 45 ns. 5 and 6.

Odeberg, H., 29 n.1; 159 n.32.

Pagels, E., 20 n.70.
Pascher, J., 35 and n.20.
Pasquier, A., 60 n.50.
Parrott, D. M., 9 n.30; 68 ns.12-17.
Patterson, S., 7 n.21; 15 and n.52; 89 n.76; 93 n.86; 112 n.39; 136 ns. 35-37.
Pearson, B. A., 39 n.41.
Peterson, E., 23 and n.76; 132 n.25; 155 and ns.19 and 20; 155 ns. 18 and 20.
Pétrement, S., 24 n.80; 25 and n.81.
Philonenka, M., 76 n.36; 167 n.53.
Polotsky, H. J., and Böhling, A., 82 n.58.
Preisendanz, K., 38 n.40.

Puech, H.-Ch., 3 and ns. 1, 4, and 6; 5 n.12; 6 n.15; 13 and n.46; 27 n. 85; 101 n.6; 113 n.40; 148; 149 n.2.

Quasten, J., 54 n.30.
Quispel, G., xi; 3 and ns.2 and 3; 4 and ns.9 and 10; 5 n.12; 6 ns.13-18; 7 and ns.19, 20, and 23; 8 and ns.24-25, 27-30; 15 and n.52; 19 n.62; 22 n.73; 28; 39 and n.41; 60 n.50; 67 n.10; 89 n.77; 101 ns. 5 and 6; 131 and ns.23 and 25; 150 and n.4; 151; 153 n.11; 154; 160 n.35; 167 n.51; 175 and n.1; 178 n.4; 179 ns.7-9.

Rahmani II, I. E., 154 n.12.
Reitzenstein, R., 37 n.39; 81 and ns. 53 and 55; 155 n.18; 162 n.41; 167 n.53; 169 n.56; 170 n.59; 176 ns. 2 and 3.
Rengstorf, K. H., 19 and n.63.
Richardson, C., 4 n.8.
Roques, R., 12 n.45.
Rordorf, W., 131 n.22; 134 n.32.
Rousseau, A., and Doutreleau, L., 54 n.30.
Rowland, C., 31 n.8; 65 n.3; 76 n.35; 77 n.38; 99 n.1; 153 n.9.
Rowley, H. H., 86 n.63.
Rubinkiewicz, R., 56 n.34.
Rudolph, K., 15 n.50; 24 n.80; 57 n.39; 87 n.65; 110 n.34.
Runia, D.T., 34 n.20.

Safrai, S., 133 ns. 27 and 28.
Sanders, J. T., 32 n.9.
Sandmel, S., 35-36 n.27.
Säve-Söderbergh, T., 12 n.45.
Schäfer, P., 28 n.1; 57 n.35; 103 n.14; 141 ns.45-47.
Schenke, H.-M., 113 n.40; 162 n.41.
Schechter, S., 47 n.11; 79 n.48.
Schiffman, L. H., 34 ns. 17 and 19; 142 n.50.
Schoedel, W. R., 52 n.28.
Scholem, G., 30 n.3; 36; 57 n.39; 62 n.52; 103 ns. 14 and 15; 105 n.20; 107 n.26; 130 n.21; 142 and n.50; 143 n.51; 154 and ns.14 and 15; 155 and ns.16 and 17; 156.
Scholer, D. M., 34 n.20.
Schrage, W., 12 n.45.
Schultz, J. P., 57 n.36.
Scott, W., 9 n.30; 116 n.50.

Segal, A. F., 29 n.2; 31 n.8; 36 n.33; 37 n.38; 170 n.57.
Segal, J. B., 11 ns.37-39.
Sjöberg, E., 69 n.18.
Smith, J. Z., 144 ns. 55 and 56.
Smith, M., 14 n. 49; 15 n.50; 28 n.1; 33 n.14; 34 and n.18; 37 and n.34; 38 and n.40; 57 n.38; 58 n.40; 76 n.33; 139 n.42; 142 n.50; 167 n.52.
Smyth, K., 12 and n.42.
Staerk, W., 158 n.30; 162 n.41.
Stählin, O., 145 n.59.
Stanley, T., 74 n.28.
Steck, O. H., 65 n.3.
Stroumsa, G., 70 n.20.
Strugnell, J., 34 n.17.

Tabor, J. D., 29 n.2.
Theissen, G., 7 n.21; 89 n.77.
Thiering, B., 138 n.41.
Till, W. C., 101 n.6.
Till W. C., and Carratelli, G. P., 60 n.50.
Trigg, J. W., 154 n.13.
Turner, H., and Montefiore, H., 12 n.45.
Turner, J. D., 6 n.16; 11 n.40.

Unnik, W. C. van, 171 n.60.

Vermes, G., 87 n.64
Vielhauer, P., 12 n.45; 19 and n.64; 93 ns.86 and 87.
Vööbus, A., 132 n.25.
Vriezen, T. C., 86 n.63.

Wagner, C., 171 n.59.
Waszink, J. H., 17 n.57.
Wedderburn, A. J. M., 157 n.27.
Weinfeld, M., 132 n.26.
Wertheimer, S. A., 57 n.36; 106 ns. 23 and 24.
Widengren, G., 29 n.2; 48 n.14.
Williams, M., 80 and ns. 50-52; 91 n.84.
Wilson, R. McL., 11 n.41; 12 n.45; 20 n.69; 60 n.50.
Wilson, R. McL., and MacRae, G. W., 60 n. 50.
Windisch, H., 171 n.59.
Winston, D., 36 n.28.
Wolfson, H. A., 36 n.27.

Zandee, J., 22 n.74; 48 n.15; 81 n.53.

LOGION INDEX

3) 8; 89.
3b) 39; 117-119; 122-124; 148.
4) 7; 26.
5) 103.
6b) 103.
7) 8.
11) 7; 15; 17; 158; 164; 172.
12) 129.
13) 39; 105; 111-112; 114.
14) 7.
15) 15; 39; 97; 99.
16) 7; 89-90.
18) 15; 80; 91.
19) 91; 178.
19b) 80; 83; 85-86; 91.
21) 145 n.60.
22) 7; 17-20; 145 n. 60; 161; 164; 176-177.
23) 7; 89.
24) 71; 115-116; 148.
25) 15.
26) 15.
27) 7; 39; 97; 126 and n.1; 127-129; 131; 134-135; 143 and n. 52; 178.
27b) 129.
28) 7.
29) 115-117; 148.
31) 15.
32) 15.
33) 7.
34) 15.
35) 15.
36) 7.
37) 7; 18; 97; 117; 124; 126; 143; 144 and ns.54 and 56; 146; 147 n.64; 161; 176-177.
40) 15.
42) 7.
45) 15.
46) 7.
47) 15.
48) 179.
49) 7; 15; 44; 53; 89; 135-136; 178.
50) 15; 23; 39; 41; 43; 44 and n.2; 45; 48 n.14; 49-50; 52-55; 57-71; 73; 77 n.39; 79; 88; 93 and n.87; 95; 99-100; 124; 135-136; 178.
51) 7; 95; 179.
54) 7; 15; 143 n.52.
55) 7; 179.
56) 7-8; 39; 117; 148.
59) 39; 97; 123-124.
60) 7; 15.
61) 23.
63) 7.
64) 7.
67) 8 and n.28; 15; 39; 118; 148.
67b) 117.
68) 15.
69) 15.
70a) 117; 148.
72) 23.
77) 21; 114.
78) 7.
80) 7-8; 39; 117; 148.
82) 39; 105; 108-109; 114.
83) 15; 39; 97; 99-101; 103; 105; 109; 115-116; 148-149.
84) 15; 39; 97; 148; 150; 157-159; 164-165; 171-172.
85) 16-17; 115; 117.
86) 7; 15.
87) 8.
88) 15.
92) 15.
94) 15.
95) 7.
97) 7.
101) 7; 15; 179.
103) 15.
104) 7.
106) 161-162; 179.
108) 39; 105; 109; 114.
110) 7; 127.
111) 118-119; 148.
111b) 8 and n.29; 39.
112) 8.
113) 179.
114) 7; 18-20.

NAME AND SUBJECT INDEX

`Aboda Zara, 158.
Aboth, 46.
Aboth de-R. Nathan, 47; 78-79.
Abraham, 56; 59; 102; 130; 137; 153 n.9; *Apocalypse of*, 30; 56; 59; 137; *Testament of*, 56; 59.
Achamoth, Echamoth, 20; 52; 54.
Acts, 111 n.37; 153.
Adam, 7; 16-18; 20-21; 24-25; 56; 59; 77; 85-86; 92; 102; 115-117; 125; 135; 144-146 and n.61; 147; 149; 155; 157; 158 and n.31; 159-164; 181.
Adam and Eve, Life of, 56.
Adoil, 66 and n.10.
Adul Barakat, 154 n.15.
Akiba, Rabbi, 29, 57; 103.
Ananias, 136.
Androgyny, 149. See also Man, androgynous prelapsarian; Male, becoming, and recombining with female.
Angel(s), 23-25; 28; 33; 51; 56-59; 61; 63-64; 68-70; 75 and n. 29; 87-88; 90-93; 95-96; 99-100; 103; 105; 107; 109; 112; 135 n.33; 138-139; 141; 146; 149-151; 152 and n.7; 153-154 and ns. 9 and 13; 156-157; 161-162; 164; 167-168; 172; 180-181; fallen, 77 n.38; hostility of, 56 and n. 52; 57-58; 63. See also Standing, Ones.
Anthropos, 16; 70 and n.21; 116; 162 n.41; 166 n.48. See also *Phōs*.
Aphrodite, 168 n.54.
Apocalypticism, Jewish, 29-32; 38; 55; 59; 86; 146. See
also Eschaton, End and Eschatology, apocalyptic.
Apostolic Constitutions, 131.
`Aqabiah ben Mahalaleel, Rabbi, 46.
Archon, 44; 55; 82.
Ascetic, asceticism, 3 n.3; 5 n.12; 9-10; 127-128; 131; 135 n.33; 136-139; 141-143.
Ascend, ascension, ascent, 10; 28-29; 31-34; 37 and n.38; 38-39; 43-44; 50; 52; 54-55; 57; 61; 64; 71-72; 73;

80-86; 90-91; 95; 99; 105; 108-111; 114; 121; 125; 130; 133-134; 135 n.33; 136-137; 140-144; 146-147; 165; 175; 178; 180-181. See also Heavenly journeys.
Asclepius, 12; 79; 94-95.
Astrology, 85.

Baba Batra, 102.
Bachelor, 4; 136. See also *Iḥidaja*, and *Monachos*.
Banaah, Rabbi, 102.
Baptism, 144 and n.56.
Bar Kappara, 158.
Bardaisan, 11.
Baruch, 56; 59; *2 Baruch*, 65; 75 n.29; 137; *3 Baruch*, 56.
Ben `Azai, Rabbi, 46.
Blasphemy, 112.
Body, of God, 102 115-117; 125-126; cf. 162; 166; human, 115-117; 119-123; 125; 139-140; 143-146; 148; 156-157; 161-163; 172; 181.
Book of the Dead, 50.
Born of woman, 56 and n.33; 100.
Bridal Chamber, 5; 21.
Bride, 150, 164.
Bridegroom, 48, 150.

Celibacy, celibate, 5; 32-34; 89, 92; 96; 132; 134-135; 138; 140; 143; 146; 180. See also Ascetic, asceticism, and Encratism, encratite.
Cerinthus, 26 n.83.
Chaldaean Oracles, 74.
Child, children, 43; 123; 135; 144; 145-146 and ns.60 and 61; 164; 176-178; 180.
Chronicles, First, 130; Second, 129.
Codex Brucianus, 93 n.87.
Colossians, 82-83; 135 n.33.
Clement of Alexandria, 3; 6; 7; 117; 127; 134; 169; 176; *Stromata*, 6-7; 18; 117; 127; 134; 145-146; 176. See also *Egyptians, Gospel of*.
Corinthians, First, 111 n.37; 162; 169-170; Second, 169-171.
Corpse, 119-120; 122.

NAME AND SUBJECT INDEX

Corpus Hermeticum, 8; 9 and n.30; 10 and n. 32; 11; 22; 67; 71; 79; 81-82; 93-94; 107-108; 119-120; 166.
Cyril of Jerusalem, 26.

Daena, 151 n.4.
Daimon, 150-151 and n.4.
Danger, of divine encounter, 107; 114; 126; 136; 147. See also Angel(s), hostility of.
Daniel, 136.
Definitions of Hermes Trismegistos to Asklepios, 8; 10; 119.
Deification, 45-46; 72; 81; 108 and n.28; 113; 120; 125. See also Immortality, immortalize, immortalization, and Transformation.
Demiurge, 16-17; 21-22 and n.75; 23-25; 128.
Derekh Eres Rabba, 46-47.
Deuteronomy, 86, 90.
Deuteronomy Rabba, 152 and n.7.
Dialogue of the Savior, 72; 124.
Diatessaron, 6 and n.13.
Diet, 7; 136-138; 141.
Discourse on the Eighth and Ninth, 10; 12; 143; 147; 165-166 and n.48.
Double, doubleness, 164-165; 172; 181.
Doublets, 179.
Drink, Drinking, 99; 105; 109-115; 125.

Ebionites, 8; 116; 130-131.
Edessa, 5 and n.12; 10; 11.
Egyptians, Gospel of, Clem. Alex. *Strom.*, 18; 145; 176-178.
Eikon, 148; 152 and n.7; 153 and ns. 9 and 11. See also Image.
Elect, 43; 53; 73; 76; 79; 86-89; 91-92; 95-96; 110; 123; 135; 178; 181.
Eliezer ben Hyrkanos, Rabbi, 29.
Elkesai, Elkesaites, 8; 17; 102-103; 116; 130.
Elohim, 69 n.19.
Elysius, 151.
Empedocles, 150 n.4.
Encratism, Encratite, 3; 4; 5; 6 and n.17; 7; 18; 28; 32; 89; 91-92; 96; 117; 127-129; 130 and n.25; 134-135; 143-144; 145 and n.60; 147; 175; 177; 179-180.
Enoch, 31; 56; 59, 106; *1 Enoch*, 30;

56; 74-75; 100; 104; 59; 109-110; 146; *2 Enoch*, 56; 59; 66; 90; 100; 102; 105 n.22; *3 Enoch*, 22 n.75; 56; 59-60; 100; 106-107.
Epiphanius, 54-55; 103.
Eschatology, 96; 134; 143 n.52; apocalyptic, 13; 134; realized, 13; 134. See also Apocalypticism, Jewish and Eschaton.
Eschaton, End, 74; 76; 149; 169; 171. See also Apocalypticism, Jewish, and Eschatology.
Essenes, 33.
Eugnostos the Blessed, 68; 115-116.
Eusebius, 131.
Euthynous, 151.
Eve, 18; 20; 144-145; 149; 158 and n.31; 159-160.
Excerpts of Stobaei, 22; 71; 79; 108 n.28.
Excerpts of Theodotus, 47; 48 n.14; 149-150.
Exegesis of the Soul, 11.
Exodus, 101; 104; 112-113; 120-121.
Exodus Rabba, 69.
Ezekiel, 28-31; 101-102; 107 n.27.
Ezra, 136; *4 Ezra*, 65; 110-111; 136.

Fall, 17; 20; 24; 85-86; 117; 145-146; 158 and n.31; 159-160; 162; 175.
Fast, fasting, 3; 28; 32; 34; 126-129; 135-137; 180.
Fate, 45-46; 116.
Female, 151 n.4. See also Male, recombining with female.
Fire, 47; 56-57; 79; 99; 101-103; 105 and n.22; 106 and n.23; 107 and n.27; 108 and n.29; 109-114; 125-126.
Five, compartments of the worlds of Light and Darkness, 81-82; plantary spheres, 81-82; trees, 80-82; 83-84; virtues and vices, 82-83; 178.
Form, 69-70; 102; 116; 155-156; 159; 181.
Fravashi, 151 n.4.

Garment, 81, 83; 105 n.22; 107; 111; 117; 120; 144-146; 155-156; 158 and n.31; 160; 163; 168; 176.
Genesis, 19; 22; 65; 69; 84; 95; 130; 132; 144-146; 152; 153 n.9; 156; 157 n.27; 158; 159 and n.34; 160; 162 and n.41; 178.

NAME AND SUBJECT INDEX 207

Genesis Rabba, 69; 78; 130; 152; 158 and n.31.
Genius, 150-151 and n.4.
Ghayat al-hakim, 155.
Gibbôr hayil, 138.
Glory, 17; 29; 31; 47; 57; 99; 101-102; 104; 105 and n.20; 114 n.44; 126; 139; 142; 158 n.31; 160-163; 170-172; 175; Hidden, 103; Great, 16; 104; 116.
Gnostic, Gnosticism, 5 n.12; 11-15; 24-27; 32; 38; 44; 47; 49; 54-55; 63-64; 124-125; 128-129; 148-149; 171; 179; Proto-, 25 n.83.
Gnosis, 14-15; 24; 170.
Greek Magical Papyri, 23; 33; 38 n.40; 155; 165-167; 168 n.54. See also *Mithras Liturgy*.

Habakkuk, 136.
Hagigah, b., 56.
Hania ben Hanina, Rabbi, 152.
Harran, 10-11.
Hasîdim, 132-133 and n.27.
Heavenly journeys, 30; 38; 64. See also Ascend, ascension, ascent.
Hebrews, Epistle to, 134; *Gospel of*, 8 n.25; 176 n.2.
Heimarmene, 116.
Hekhalot, 28-30; 33; 38; 55; 58; 63; 114 n.44; 141-142. See also Mysticism, Hekhalot.
Hekhalot Rabbati, 57; 62; 107; 141-142; 153 n.9.
Hekhalot Zutrati, 103; 114 n.44; 143 n.52. Helios, 22-23; 38; 76.
Heracleonites, 54.
Hermetic, Hermeticism, 8 and 8-9 n.30; 9-10; 14; 22-23; 28; 37 and n.39; 38-39; 46-47; 49; 57; 67-68; 70-71; 79; 80-81; 83; 85; 91; 93 and n.87; 95-96; 108-109; 119 and n.63; 120; 122-123; 128; 154; 156; 165 and n.48; 171-172; 178-180.
Hermas, 154.
Hermes, 10; 35; 81; 107; 155; 165 n.48; 166.
Hippolytus, 26; 103; 110.
Horace, 150 n.4.
Hymn of the Pearl, 160; 163; 168.

Iaoel, 59.
Iḥidaja, 4. See also Bachelor, and *Monachos*.
Image, 39; 43; 65; 68; 70 and n.21; 77; 95; 100-102; 109; 115; 125; 135; 140; 148-172 and ns. 4, 7, 9, 34; 180-181.
Immovable God, 93.
Immobility, 80; 94-95.
Immortality, immortalize, immortalization, 10; 33; 72; 83-86; 90; 107-108; 120-121; 124; 162; 166; 180-181.
Immutability, 90 n.78.
Imperishablity, 91-92; 162.
Irenaeus, 54-55; 145.
Ishmael, Rabbi, 29; 59; 103; 142; 153.
Isaac, 56; 59; *Testament of*, 56; 153 n.9.
Isaiah, 56; 59; 60 n.49; 114 n.44; 134; 136; *Ascension of*, 56; 60; 90; 105 n.22; 136-137.
Isis, 35.

Jacob, 140-141; 153 n.9.
James, 51-53; 129-131; *Apocryphon of*, 71; *First Apocalypse of*, 51-55; 62-63.
Jeremiah, 139.
Jewish-Christian, Jewish-Christianity, 7-8; 16; 17; 28; 48 n.15; 116; 128-131; 153-154; 157; 168; 175-176; 178.
Job, Testament of, 135 n.33.
Joel, 136.
John, First Epistle of, 143 n.52; 147 n.64; Gospel of, 72-73; 109-110 n.33; 113 and n.42.
Josab, 136.
Joshua ben Levi, Rabbi, 151-153.
Joseph and Aseneth, 167-168; 171.
Josephus, 33.
Jubilees, 132, 134.
Judah ben Barzilla al-Bargeloni, 104-105 n.20.
Judaism, Hellenistic, 35; Rabbinic, 30-31; 35; 38; 46-47; 69; 141; 159; Second Temple, 32; 38. See also Mysticism, Jewish.
Julius Cassianus, 117; 145.
Justin, the Gnostic, *Book of Baruch*, 26 n.83; 110.
Justin, Martyr, 17; 115.

Kabbalah, Kabbalism, 154; 156.
Kavod, 29; 99; 101-103; 105-106; 113; 125; 158; 160-161; 170 n.57; Hidden, 105; 115; 125.

Kingdom, 5; 13; 18; 39; 44; 53; 61; 73; 79; 89; 108 and n.29; 109; 122-123; 125-126; 128-129; 132; 134-136; 161; 163-164; 168; 178; 181; of Darkness, 82.
Knowledge, 24; 27; 38; 45-46; 48; 51; 54; 85; 92; 96; 110; 114; 168;-169; 170. See also Self-knowledge.

Laodicea, Council of, 131.
Law, 34; 110; 130; 138; 141; 143; 147. See also Torah.
Lecanomancy, 166-171 and n.59.
Legend of the Ten Martyrs, 153.
Levi, 56; 59; *Testament of*, 56; 83 n.60.
Leviticus, 129.
Leviticus Rabba, 78.
Liber Graduum, 6 and n.17; 127.
Light, 9; 13; 21; 22 and ns. 74-75; 23-24; 35; 39; 43; 47; 64-68; 70 and n.21; 71-79; 81; 88-89; 95; 99; 100-101; 103; 105-106; 108-109; 111; 114-118; 125-126; 135; 149; 158 and n. 31; 159-161; 164; 165 and n.48; 168 and n.54; 178; 181; contrast with Darkness, 73-76 and n.32; 160; embodied, 115-117; 125; sons of, 23; 73-74; 75 and n.31; 76-79; 87-88; 92; 96.
Life, 9-10; 45; 71; 74; 91; 125; sons of, 87.
Likeness, 101-102; 148-149; 158; 162.
Living Father, Living One, Living God, 43; 53-54; 58; 88; 118; 123-124; 176; 178; son(s) of, 89; 118; 123-124; 135; 144.
Logos, 37 n.39; 66; 106; 140; 157.
Luke, Gospel of, 108 n.29; 176.
Lysis, 151.

Ma`aseh Merkavah, 141.
Macarius, 6 and n.18; 124; 160; 163; *Homilies*, 6; 124; 163-164.
Male, becoming, 18-20; 149-150; recombining with female, 7; 18-21; 145; 149-150; 161; 176-177.
Man, androgynous prelapsarian, 7; 18 n.58; 20; 180; earthly, 157 n.27; 164; heavenly, 157 n.27; 162; 164; son of, 161-162.
Mandean, Mandeism, 72; 87-88; 92; 111 n.36.
Mandean literature, 93; *Book of John*, 72; *Ginza*, 72; *Mandean Liturgy*, 72.

Manichaean, Manichaeanism, 26-27; 81-82; 151 n.4; 154.
Marcosians, 54.
Marcus, 69-70.
Mark, Gospel of, 49-50; 129 n.17; 176.
Marriage, 21; 92; 137; 180.
Martyrdom, 52; 55.
Mary, *Gospel of*, 60-61; Magdalene, 60.
Matthew, 112; Gospel of, 143 n.52; 153-154; 176.
Megillah, 100.
Memar Marqa, 90; 110; 159.
Merkavah, 28-29; 30-32; 36-37; 99; 141-142. See also Mysticism, Jewish.
Merkavah Shelemah, 141.
Messina, 14-15.
Metatron, 22 n.75; 59; 153.
Micah, 136.
Michael, 59.
Midrash Gedullah Mosheh, 106.
Midrash Qoheleth, 152-153.
Midrash Ruth, 130.
Midrash Tehillim, 152 and n.7.
Mind, 80; 94-95; 106; 120-121; 165 and n.48; 166.
Mithras Liturgy, 33; 38; 58; 63; 155. See also *Greek Magical Papyri*.
Moed Katan, 158.
Monachos, 4; 89; 136 and n.36. See also Bachelor and *Iḥidaja*.
Moses, 31; 35; 56-57; 90 n.81; 91; 100-101; 104; 106; 110; 120-121; 130; 140-141; 152-153; 157 n.27; 159; 171 and n.60; *Apocalypse of*, 56; 160; *Assumption of*, 56.
Movement, 43; 93 and n. 87; 94-96; 135; 178; 181.
Mysterium conjunctionis, 154.
Mystery cults, religions, 35; 73-74.
Mysticism, Jewish, 28; 31-32; 36-39; 44; 59; 63-64; 69; 93; 99; 101; 114 n.44; 124-125; 128-130; 135 n.33; 137; 139; 143; 146-147; 175; 178; 180. See also Hekhalot and Merkavah.

Naassenes, 12; 26-27; 93 n.87.
Nag Hammadi, 11.
Nathan, Rabbi, 141.
Name, of God, 16; 69-70; 112-113 and ns. 40 and 42; 114 and n.44; 142. See also *Shem hammephorash*.

NAME AND SUBJECT INDEX 209

Nazoraean, 8; 130.
Nazorean, 72.
Nazorees, Gospel of, 8; 176; 178.
Nebo, 10.
Nehunyah ben Ha-Qanah, Rabbi, 29; 142.
Noah, 139-140.
Niddah, b., 133.
Not born of woman, 100.
Nous, 120. See also Mind.
Numbers Rabba, 69.

Origen, 154 and n.13.
Origin, 9; 39; 47-48; 53; 55; 58; 61; 64-66; 78; 80; 88; 95; 181.
Orpheus, 35.
Orphic, 14, 62; grave plates, 51.
Osiris, 50-51.

Papyrus Oxyrhynchos Fragment 1, 4; 126-127.
Paradise, 80; 83-86; 91-92; 111; 134-135; 146-147; 154; 163; 178; 180.
Passwords, 33; 57-58; 93.
Paul, 36; 61-62; 88; 111 n.37; 162-163; 169-171; *Apocalypse of*, 61-63.
Paul and Thecla, Acts of, 127.
Pentecost, 111 n.37.
Perfected nature, perfected body, 154 and n.15; 155-156.
Pesikta Rabbati, 105-106.
Peter, 112; 153.
Phanael, 59.
Philip, 54; *Gospel of*, 20-21; 149-150; 171.
Philo of Alexandria, 20; 25; 32; 34-36; 37 and n.38; 46; 65-66; 70 n.21; 77-78; 84 and n.62; 85; 94 n.88; 104; 106; 111; 120-127; 137; 139-141; 146; 156; 157 n.27.
Phōs, 17; 21; 22 and ns. 74-75; 23; 116.
Physiologus, 84.
Pindar, 150 n.4.
Pistis Sophia, 44 n.2; 154.
Place, 70-73; 77-79.
Plato, Platonism, 14; 25; 37; 150 n.4; 157 n.27.
Pleroma, 20; 24; 44; 125; 150.
Plotinus, 150 n.4.
Plutarch, 150-151.
Poimandres, 11; 82; 165; 166 n.48; 180. See also *Corpus Hermeticum*.
Poverty, of body, 115; 117; 138.

Power, 17; 105; 115; Great, 16 and n.54; 17; 115-116; Hidden, 17; 102-103.
Prayer of Thanksgiving, 12.
Predestination, 88.
Pre-Fall state, 135; 140; 145; 146 and n.61. See also Prelapsarian state, Primordial state, and Man, androgynous prelapsarian.
Prelapsarian state, 18; 20; 92; 161. See also Pre-Fall state, Primordial state, and Man, androgynous prelapsarian.
Primordial state, 48; 145-146; 149. See also Pre-Fall state, Prelapsarian state, and Man, androgynous prelapsarian.
Prophet, like Moses, 17; True, 116.
Psalms, 151-152.
Pseudo-Clementina, 104; 116; 143 n.52.
Pseudo-Cyprian, 169.
Pseudo-Philo, 76-77.
Purify, purification, purity, 28; 34; 51; 126; 135-136; 138-140; 142; 143 and n.52; 147 n.64; 180.
Pythagorean, 151.

Quelle, 13; 176.
Qumran, Qumranite, 33-34; 38; 75 and n.31; 76; 87; 92; 105; 111 n.36; 138-139.

Raguel, 59.
Raguila, 59.
Raphael, 59.
Rebirth, 81; 83; 166.
Rechabites, History of, 58.
Repose, 13; 43; 77; 135. See also Rest.
Rest, 55; 93 and ns.86-87; 94-96; 178; 181. See also Repose.
Resurrection, 92; 95; 134; 162.
Reunification, 161-165. See also Male, recombining with female.
Revelation, 124.
Romans, 163.

Sabbath, 126; 128; 129 and n.17; 130-135; 143; 158; 178.
Sakta, 133-134.
Salma, 154.
Salvation, 7; 19; 24; 39; 117; 123-124; 161; 164; 180. See also Soteriology.

NAME AND SUBJECT INDEX

Samaritanism, 16 n.54; 90; 110; 159; *Liturgy*, 90 n.81. See also *Memar Marqa*.
Samoila, 59.
Satornilos, 25 n.83; 70 n.21.
Scribal Note, 12.
Seal, 57-58.
Sefer Raziel, 103.
Self, divine, 83; 118-119; 121-123; 125; 148-149; 151 n.4; 154; 166; 172; 175; 181.
Self-control, 84; 137. See also Encratism, encratite.
Self-generation, 65; 67; 95; 100; 178.
Self-knowledge, 9; 11; 21 n.71; 39; 45; 48; 117-123; 148; 181.
Self-vision, 165-172 and n.48. See also Vision, visionary experience, and *Visio Dei*.
Seneca, 45-46.
Sentences of Sextus, 12.
Servius, 150-151 n.4.
Seven, cosmic levels, 82; fountains, 110; vices, 82.
Shabbat, b., 57; y., 159.
Shamelessness, 145.
Shem hammephorash, 113 and n.42.
Shiur Komah, 22 n.75; 69; 102-103.
Silvanus, Teachings of, 11-12; 17; 22 n.74; 48; 115.
Sign, 43; 50; 53-54; 57-58; 62; 93; 95; 181.
Simeon ben Ele`azar, Rabbi, 78-79.
Simeon ben Judah, 158.
Simon Magus, 17.
Simonian, Simonianism, 16 n.54; 25 n.83; 90.
Sin, 7; 24; 77-78; 86; 92; 117; 125; 144-145; 147; 158-161; 164.
Single One, 89. See also Bachelor, *Monachos, Iḥidaja*, Solitary.
Socrates, *H.E.*, 131.
Solitary, 53; 79; 89. See also Bachelor, *Monachos, Iḥidaja*, Single One.
Solomon, 152-153; 168; *Odes of*, 6; 83-84; 88; 92-93; 110 n.33; 111 and n.36; *Wisdom of*, 159 n.34.
Sophia, 16; 20-21; 22 n.75; 35; 137.
Soteriology, 39; 80; 144; 146-147; 165; 180. See also Salvation.
Standing, 89-92; encratites, 89-92; 96; Ones, 90; 180.
Stoic, Stoicism, 37.

Stoning, 112-113.
Suhrawardi of Aleppo, 154 n.15.
Symmachians, in Marius Victorinus, 116.
Syzygy, 154.

Tatian, 163.
Teacher of Righteousness, 76.
Temple, 34; 132.
Testamentum Domini, 154.
Theophilius of Antioch, 145.
Therapeutae, 32; 34; 38; 137-138.
Thomas, *Acts of*, 6 and n.15; 17; 48; 114; 116; 163; *Book of the Contender*, 6 and n. 16, 11-12.
Throne, Throne-chariot, 34; 59; 90; 99; 101-102; 105; 142-143; 152-153 and n.9; 154; 180; -room, 99-100. See also Merkavah.
Tongues of fire, 111 n.37.
Torah, 139; 141; 143.
Transformation, 38 n.40; 39; 74; 77; 81; 90; 99; 105 and n.22; 106-107; 108 and n.28; 109-115; 125-126; 130; 138; 146-147; 167-169; 170 and n.57; 171 and n.59; 180-181.
Trampling, 144-145 and n.58.
Tree(s), five, 80; 85; 91-92; 178; of Life, 84; of Paradise, 85; vision of, 84.
Trimegistos, 68.
Truth, Gospel of, 47.
Tsaddik, 130.
Twelve, garments, 81; vices, 81; zodiac divisions, 81-82.
Twin, twinship, 154; 156; 164.

Unbegotten, 67-68.
Unmoving, trees, 80; 91.
Unmoved Mover, 94-95.

Valentinus, 21 n.71; 69.
Valentinian, Valentinianism, 12; 20-21; 23-24; 27; 47; 149-150; 151 n.4.
Vices, 81-84; 85 and n.62; 86; 178; 181.
Virgin, virginity, 32-33; 131; 135 n.33; 137; 139.
Virtues, 81-84; 85 and n.62; 86; 178.
Visio Dei, 39; 114; 126; 147; 180.
Vision, visionary experience, 28-34; 37 and n.38; 38 and n.40; 39; 61; 72-73; 76-77; 84; 94; 99; 102 n.10;

104-105; 107-108; 110-111; 120-121; 123-125; 129; 135-142; 143 and n.52; 144; 146; 147 and n.64; 148; 151; 156; 164-172 and n.59; 175-176; 178; 180-181; ecstatic versus eschatological, 123-125 and n.69.

Wealth, Great, 16; 115-116; 125.

Yahweh, 113 and n.42. See also Name, of God.
Yehuda, Rabbi, 78.
Yohanan, Rabbi, 78.
Yotser Bereshith, 22 n.75.

Zadok, sons of, 87.
Zosimos, the Rechabite 58-59; the Hermetic, 116; 180.

SUPPLEMENTS TO VIGILIAE CHRISTIANAE

1. TERTULLIANUS. *De idololatria.* Critical Text, Translation and Commentary by J.H. WASZINK and J.C.M. VAN WINDEN. Partly based on a Manuscript left behind by P.G. VAN DER NAT. 1987. ISBN 90 04 08105 4
2. SPRINGER, C.P.E. *The Gospel as Epic in Late Antiquity.* The *Paschale Carmen* of Sedulius. 1988. ISBN 90 04 08691 9
3. HOEK, A. VAN DEN. *Clement of Alexandria and His Use of Philo in the* Stromateis. An Early Christian Reshaping of a Jewish Model. 1988. ISBN 90 04 08756 7
4. NEYMEYR, U. *Die christlichen Lehrer im zweiten Jahrhundert.* Ihre Lehrtätigkeit, ihr Selbstverständnis und ihre Geschichte. 1989. ISBN 90 04 08773 7
5. HELLEMO, G. *Adventus Domini.* Eschatological Thought in 4th-century Apses and Catecheses. 1989. ISBN 90 04 08836 9
6. RUFIN VON AQUILEIA. *De ieiunio* I, II. Zwei Predigten über das Fasten nach Basileios von Kaisareia. Ausgabe mit Einleitung, Übersetzung und Anmerkungen von H. MARTI. 1989. ISBN 90 04 08897 0
7. ROUWHORST, G.A.M. *Les hymnes pascales d'Éphrem de Nisibe.* Analyse théologique et recherche sur l'évolution de la fête pascale chrétienne à Nisibe et à Édesse et dans quelques Églises voisines au quatrième siècle. 2 vols: I. Étude; II. Textes. 1989. ISBN 90 04 08839 3
8. RADICE, R. and D.T. RUNIA. *Philo of Alexandria.* An Annotated Bibliography 1937–1986. In Collaboration with R.A. BITTER, N.G. COHEN, M. MACH, A.P. RUNIA, D. SATRAN and D.R. SCHWARTZ. 1988. repr. 1992. ISBN 90 04 08986 1
9. GORDON, B. *The Economic Problem in Biblical and Patristic Thought.* 1989. ISBN 90 04 09048 7
10. PROSPER OF AQUITAINE. *De Providentia Dei.* Text, Translation and Commentary by M. MARCOVICH. 1989. ISBN 90 04 09090 8
11. JEFFORD, C.N. *The Sayings of Jesus in the Teaching of the Twelve Apostles.* 1989. ISBN 90 04 09127 0
12. DROBNER, H.R. and KLOCK, CH. *Studien zur Gregor von Nyssa und der christlichen Spätantike.* 1990. ISBN 90 04 09222 6
13. NORRIS, F.W. *Faith Gives Fullness to Reasoning.* The Five Theological Orations of Gregory Nazianzen. Introduction and Commentary by F.W. NORRIS and Translation by LIONEL WICKHAM and FREDERICK WILLIAMS. 1990. ISBN 90 04 09253 6
14. OORT, J. VAN. *Jerusalem and Babylon.* A Study into Augustine's *City of God* and the Sources of his Doctrine of the Two Cities. 1991. ISBN 90 04 09323 0
15. LARDET, P. *L'Apologie de Jérôme contre Rufin.* Un Commentaire. 1993. ISBN 90 04 09457 1
16. RISCH, F.X. *Pseudo-Basilius: Adversus Eunomium IV-V.* Einleitung, Übersetzung und Kommentar. 1992. ISBN 90 04 09558 6
17. KLIJN, A.F.J. *Jewish-Christian Gospel Tradition.* 1992. ISBN 90 04 09453 9
18. ELANSKAYA, A.I. *The Literary Coptic Manuscripts in the A.S. Pushkin State Fine Arts Museum in Moscow.* ISBN 90 04 09528 4
19. WICKHAM, L.R. and BAMMEL, C.P. (eds.). *Christian Faith and Greek Philosophy in Late Antiquity.* Essays in Tribute to George Christopher Stead. 1993. ISBN 90 04 09605 1
20. ASTERIUS VON KAPPADOKIEN. *Die theologischen Fragmente.* Einleitung, kritischer Text, Übersetzung und Kommentar von Markus Vinzent. 1993. ISBN 90 04 09841 0

HENNINGS, R. *Der Briefwechsel zwischen Augustinus und Hieronymus und ihr Streit um den Kanon des Alten Testaments und die Auslegung von Gal. 2,11-14.* 1994. ISBN 90 04 09840 2

BOEFT, J. DEN & HILHORST, A. (eds.). *Early Christian Poetry.* A Collection of Essays. 1993. ISBN 90 04 09939 5

McGUCKIN, J.A. *St. Cyril of Alexandria: The Christological Controversy.* Its History, Theology, and Texts. 1994. ISBN 90 04 09990 5

REYNOLDS, Ph.L. *Marriage in the Western Church.* The Christianization of Marriage during the Patristic and Early Medieval Periods. 1994. ISBN 90 04 10022 9

PETERSEN, W.L. *Tatian's Diatessaron.* Its Creation, Dissemination, Significance, and History in Scholarship. 1994. ISBN 90 04 09469 5

GRÜNBECK, E. *Christologische Schriftargumentation und Bildersprache.* Zum Konflikt zwischen Metapherninterpretation und dogmatischen Schriftbeweistraditionen in der patristischen Auslegung des 44. (45.) Psalms. 1994. ISBN 90 04 10021 0

HAYKIN, M.A.G. *The Spirit of God.* The Exegesis of 1 and 2 Corinthians in the Pneumatomachian Controversy of the Fourth Century. 1994. ISBN 90 04 09947 6

BENJAMINS, H.S. *Eingeordnete Freiheit.* Freiheit und Vorsehung bei Origenes. 1994. ISBN 90 04 10117 9

SMULDERS s.j., P. (tr. & comm.). *Hilary of Poitiers' Preface to his* Opus historicum. 1995. ISBN 90 04 10191 8

KEES, R.J. *Die Lehre von der* Oikonomia *Gottes in der* Oratio catechetica *Gregors von Nyssa.* 1995. ISBN 90 04 10200 0

BRENT, A. *Hippolytus and the Roman Church in the Third Century.* Communities in Tension before the Emergence of a Monarch-Bishop. 1995. ISBN 90 04 10245 0

RUNIA, D.T. *Philo and the Church Fathers.* A Collection of Papers. 1995. ISBN 90 04 10355 4

DE CONICK, A.D. *Seek to See Him.* Ascent and Vision Mysticism in the Gospel of Thomas. 1996. ISBN 90 04 10401 1

CLEMENS ALEXANDRINUS. *Protrepticus.* Edidit M. MARCOVICH. 1995. ISBN 90 04 10449 6

www.ingramcontent.com/pod-product-compliance
Lightning Source LLC
Chambersburg PA
CBHW030342240426
43661CB00052B/1721